BEYOND THE TEXT:
FRANCISCAN ART
AND THE CONSTRUCTION
OF RELIGION

Edited by Xavier Seubert
and Oleg Bychkov

FRANCISCAN
INSTITUTE
PUBLICATIONS

© 2013 Franciscan Institute Publications
Saint Bonaventure University
Saint Bonaventure, New York 14778
www.franciscanpublications.com

International Standard Book Number
ISBN: 978-1-57659-340-0

Library of Congress Cataloging-in-Publication Data

Beyond the text : Franciscan art and the construction of religion / edited by Xavier Seubert
and Oleg Bychkov. – First [edition].
   pages cm
   Includes index.
   ISBN 978-1-57659-340-0 (hard cover) – ISBN 978-1-57659-359-2 (ebook) 1. Franciscan art. 2. Christianity
   and art. I. Seubert, Xavier J., 1944- editor of compilation. II. Bychkov, Oleg V., 1966 - editor of compilation.
   N7854.B49 2012
   246 – dc23
      2012042493

Project management: Jim Bindas, Books & Projects, LLC
Text design and producton: Mike Tincher, T DESIGN, Minneapolis, MN
Cover design by Jill M. Smith

Cover illustration: *Jesus Christ Gives the Rule to Francis of Assisi.* 15th century illuminated manuscript of Angelo Clareno's *A History of the Seven Tribulations of the Order of Brothers Minor.* Ms. Vitt. Em. 1167 in the Bibliotheca Nazionale Centrale, Rome.

Franciscan Institute Publications
email: fip@sbu.edu
Toll-free: 1-855-810-2065
Fax: 716-375-2113

Artificibus saeculi tertii quartique decimi
notis ignotisque qui corpus coloratum formatumque
spiritui Franciscano perhibuerunt

To the artists of the thirteenth and fourteenth centuries,
both the well known and the unknown, who created bodies of color
and form for the Franciscan spirit

CONTENTS

PREFACE

lthough art has been an aspect of Franciscan history at least since the building of the great San Francesco Basilica in Assisi in the thirteenth century, the importance of art in formulating and interpreting the early Franciscan movement has not always been given due emphasis. Francis of Assisi is arguably one of the most beloved saints of Roman Catholic history, but it was not until the mandate of the Second Vatican Council to all religious orders and congregations to go back to their roots and rediscover their charisms, that the foundational documents of the Franciscan movement were translated and collated into a format for wide distribution and consumption.[1] Both before the Council and to the present day textual criticism of the foundational Franciscan documents and of the philosophical and theological texts of the Franciscan intellectual tradition has been conducted at the Franciscan research institutes at Grottaferrata in Italy and St.

Bonaventure University in New York. Textual evidence, however, is very often the exclusive or privileged tool for understanding the Franciscan past.

The art accompanying the Franciscan movement has not always been received with the same seriousness; it is often seen as decorative and inspirational, but not as providing something essential for the interpretation of Franciscanism. Art, however, frequently reveals what is not or cannot be articulated in words. Artistic formulations can give expression to intuitions and sensitivities that cannot yet or cannot fully be verbalized.[2] Although in recent decades significant Franciscan art historical works have been produced,[3] the field has not yet received the audience it deserves in the illumination of the Franciscan essence. The present volume is a small attempt in this direction.

From art historical, social, textual, theological and philosophical perspectives, the essays in this volume probe the art and visual culture of the early Franciscan movement to reveal insights and nu-

---

[1]   We think here especially of the landmark compendium edited by Marion A. Habig and produced by the Franciscan Herald Press in 1972: *St. Francis of Assisi: Writings and Early Biographies. English Omnibus of the Sources for the Life of St. Francis.*

[2]   A recent example of this is the excellent study by Julian Gardner: *Giotto and His Publics: Three Paradigms of Patronage* (Cambridge, MA: Harvard University Press, 2011).

[3]   See, for instance: John V. Fleming, *From Bonaventure to Bellini: An Essay in Franciscan Exegesis* (Princeton: Princeton University Press, 1982); Rona Goffen, *Spirituality in Conflict: Saint Francis and Giotto's Bardi Chapel* (University Park: The Pennsylvania State University Press, 1988); Anne Derbes, *Picturing the Passion in Late Medieval Italy: Narrative Painting, Franciscan Ideologies and the Levant* (Cambridge: Cambridge University Press, 1996); Rosalind Brooke, *The Image of St. Francis: Responses to Sainthood in the Thirteenth Century* (Cambridge: Cambridge University Press, 2006).

ances of the life and power of this revolutionary phase of the Catholic religion. The "construction of religion" in the title refers to epoch-making changes in the religious life of the thirteenth century which were introduced by the mendicant friars. Art was a major trajectory within this undertaking. In order to point up the essential connection of art to the broader project, the essays go beyond a purely aesthetic analysis in demonstrating the multi-dimensional dynamics of Franciscan art and architecture. The interdisciplinary interpretations which are performed here will hopefully indicate the importance of this field of investigation to Franciscan studies, just as all the advances in the textual criticism of Franciscan sources have been invaluable in understanding Franciscan art and architecture.

Although the essays in this volume cover a wide array of artistic media, from architecture to painting to manuscript illumination, the images and themes that echo through the essays serve as unifying threads among them. Thus the image of the "Man of Sorrows" in the Franciscan context echoes through several essays, and so does the image of the crib at Greccio. Various artistic media naturally unite groups of essays: thus three essays are dedicated to manuscript illuminations and two to architecture, providing a contrast and similarities between the use of images in Franciscan and Dominican contexts. Two essays attempt to ground certain features of Franciscan art in deeper theological contexts. Another unifying idea is the contextual nature of artistic images, the use of which is determined by the local contexts of religious communities, both theologically and geographically. Perhaps, the strongest and most innovative message that unites most essays is about the role of art in a religious and theological context. First of all, it is not only the "high" art produced by first-rate masters that deserves the attention of art historians. Secondly, recent trends in theological aesthetics indicate that art, in a religious and theological context, such as the Franciscan tradition, does not function as an object of "disinterested contemplation." It functions liturgically, memorially, meditatively, and politically in expressing certain traits of a specific religious community and through which the community creatively and visually constructs and reconstructs its history.[4]

The editors and other contributors to the volume wish to thank Franciscan Institute Publications and especially Jim Knapp, Executive Director of Franciscan Institute Publications, and Sr. Margaret Carney, OSF, President of St. Bonaventure University, for allowing us to initiate what we hope will be an enduring collaboration between Franciscan art history and Franciscan studies. Special gratitude goes to Judith Johnston, a true Brother Jacoba to many Franciscan friars and whose generosity made this volume possible. The initial impetus for this volume was provided during a conference on Franciscan art in Denver, May 2008, sponsored by the Franciscan Friars of Holy Name Province and the May Bonfils Stanton Memorial Fund in Denver. To them also we owe an enduring debt of gratitude.

Xavier Seubert
Oleg Bychkov

---

[4] See essays by N. Wolterstorff and A. Garcia-Rivera in O. Bychkov and J. Fodor, eds., *Theological Aesthetics After von Balthasar* (Aldershot: Ashgate, 2008).

LIST OF CONTRIBUTORS

William Barcham has specialized in Venetian art and culture. His articles and books study the 17th and 18th centuries in particular, and he wrote a biography of Federico Cornaro, Gianlorenzo Bernini's patron for the Cornaro Chapel in Rome. He was a Fellow at the American Academy in Rome in 1998-1999.

Oleg Bychkov, is a Professor of Theology at St. Bonaventure University. He holds a Ph.D. from the Center for Medieval Studies, University of Toronto (1999). His areas of expertise are classical languages, medieval philosophy and theology, and contemporary aesthetics. He has authored and co-edited several books and published essays and encyclopedia entries on ancient, medieval and contemporary aesthetics. Bychkov has written and translated extensively on the work of John Duns Scotus.

William Cook is the Distinguished Teaching Professor of History (Emeritus) at the State University of New York-Geneseo where he has taught for over 30 years. Dr. Cook has an M.A. and Ph.D. in Medieval History from Cornell University and an undergraduate degree from Wabash College (IN). Cook has received numerous teaching awards including the CASE Professor of the Year for the state of New York. He has authored several books about the medieval world and Francis of Assisi.

Theresa Flanigan is an Associate Professor at the College of Saint Rose who specializes in Italian late Medieval and Renaissance art and architectural history. She has published on the Ponte Vecchio in Florence and the development of the Florentine Oltrarno. Her current research explores relationships between Renaissance art and Renaissance notions of vision, intellectual comprehension, and affective devotion. Presently, she is writing a book on vision, design, and devotion at the Church of San Marco, Florence.

David Flood, O.F.M., is a member of the Eastern Canadian Franciscan Province. He studied Franciscan history with Kajetan Esser and helped him with his edition of the Early Franciscan writings. Flood's education includes a B.A., Université Laval, an M.A., Université de Montréal and a Ph. D. in history and philosophy, University of Cologne. Flood is an internationally known medieval scholar who has published several books on Peter of John Olivi. He is presently a scholar in residence at The Franciscan Institute, St. Bonaventure, NY.

Holly Flora is Associate Professor of Art History at Tulane University. Her research explores the intersections of narrative, imagination, and gender in the art of medieval Italy. She is the author of *The Devout Belief of the Imagination: the Paris Meditationes Vitae Christi and Female Franciscan Spirituality in Trecento Italy* (Turnhout: Brepols, 2009).

Cristina Cruz González is an art historian at Oklahoma State University. She received her doctorate from the University of Chicago in 2009 and is now finishing a book on Franciscan image theory in the New World. She has published several articles and has been the recipient of numerous awards, including a Getty Research Fellowship.

David Haack, O.F.M., earned the doctoral degree in Art History from Syracuse University in 1999. His dissertation is entitled *Content and Controversy in choir and convent images of St. Francis of Assisi, 1300-1450*. Dr. Haack is currently an associate professor of art history and studio art at St. Bonaventure University (1998 - present); and the Franciscan Institute Graduate School (2000 - present). As a studio oil painter, Dr. Haack creates contemporary images of Franciscan life inspired by the original documents of the Franciscan Order and the life of St. Francis of Assisi.

Trinita Kennedy is Curator at the Frist Center for the Visual Arts. She specializes in Italian art and architecture during the period 1200 to 1550. She is now organizing a major exhibition entitled Sanctity Pictured: The Art of the Dominican and Franciscan Orders in Renaissance Italy, which will open in October 2014.

Irving Lavin is one of America's most distinguished art historians. A graduate of Harvard University, he has written extensively on the history of art from late antiquity to modern times. His interests have focused primarily on the correlation between form and meaning in the visual arts. His numerous books on Italian painting, sculpture, and architecture of the Renaissance and Baroque periods include *Bernini and the Crossing of St. Peter's* (1968); *Bernini and the Unity of the Visual Arts* (1980); *Past-Present: Essays on Historicism in Art from Donatello to Picasso* (1993); *Santa Maria del Fiore: Il Duomo di Firenze e la Vergine Incinta* (1999); and *Caravaggio e La Tour: La Luce Occulta di Dio* (2000).

Marilyn Aronberg Lavin's art historical work is in Italian Renaissance art, with emphasis on Piero della Francesca; (see website: http://projects.ias.edu/pierotruecross). Her prize winning books are: *PDF: The Flagellation (1972, 1990); The Place of Narrative: Mural Decoration in Italian Churches, 413-1600* (1994); and *Seventeenth-Century Barberini Documents and Inventories of Art* (Charles Rufus Morey Award for Distinguished Scholarship, 1977). She has taught at Yale, Princeton, and the Università di Roma, La Sapienza. In 1991 she created the first Listserv for art history that now has ca.1000 members from 22 countries (caah@.princeton.edu).

Robert Lentz, O.F.M., is a Franciscan friar who has painted Byzantine icons for forty years. As a young man, he studied iconography in the atelier of a Greek Orthodox monastery in Boston. Although he has many large icons in churches, he is best known for his smaller icons that challenge preconceptions about holiness. For thirty years his work has been reproduced for popular distribution throughout the world.

Beth Mulvaney is a Professor of Art History and Head of the Art Department at Meredith College in Raleigh, North Carolina. In addition to her scholarship on the Assisi San Francesco frescoes, she also is working on nuns' patronage at Santa Maria dei Miracoli in Venice and the Franciscan convent once adjoined to the church.

Lynn Ransom is the Project Manager for the Schoenberg Database of Manuscripts at the University of Pennsylvania. In addition to her work on Franciscan iconography, she has published on the career of the American Librarian, theologian, and manuscript scholar Ernest Cushing Richardson (1860-1939).

Xavier John Seubert, O.F.M., is the Thomas Plassmann Distinguished Professor of Art and Theology Emeritus at St. Bonaventure University in Allegany, NY and the Professor of Liturgy and Sacramental Theology at Christ the King Seminary in Buffalo, NY. He has published widely in sacramentality and the religious dimensions of art and is presently working on a book on the sacramentality of art. He is a frequent lecturer at The Cloisters of The Metropolitan Museum of Art in New York City.

INTRODUCTION: THE EARLY ITALIAN REPRESENTATIONS OF FRANCIS OF ASSISI

William Cook

volume such as this one is important because it brings together scholars and artists who study early images of Francis as well as following trajectories of those early stages into the twenty first century. Fortunately, we are not only scholars or artists because all of us study and celebrate and are moved by images of Cimabue and Giotto while also being inspired by new images of Francis. I find myself seeking out images of Francis anywhere I can find them. I like the Marvel Comic version of the life of Francis,[1] for example. And recently, an Australian writer brought me into contact with the work of a rather quirky Australian artist of the life of Francis, Arthur Boyd. I in fact happily wrote an epilogue for a book about that art.[2] I discovered in a garden in Nairobi a lovely statue of an African Francis, and I also am moved by He Qi's beautiful Asian Francis with a flute and three birds in a bamboo forest.

In this essay, I will limit myself to genuine early images of Francis.[3] When I write or talk about specific works of art from the thirteenth and fourteenth centuries, I do so with the slightly muted confidence of one who has studied surviving works for the last 35 years. However, when I write and speak more generally about patterns and developments, I recognize the quicksand in which I stand. The important cataloguer of early Italian painting, Edward Garrison, suggested late in his life that perhaps as little as one percent of thirteenth century panel paintings survive, and the survival rate is probably not much better for frescoes. In my catalogue of early images of Francis, which contains works before 1320, there are 206 entries. If Garrison is right, there may have been 20,000 images. Even if he is off by a factor of 10, we would still have had more than 2000 images in Italy created within a century of the saint's death.

So, how do we know which surviving works are typical of what was produced? Which ones represent for us a hundred similar ones that have now been lost? Which ones were unique? Given problems of provenance and dating for so many early works, we also have to speculate with a great deal of caution about which works derive from which. Whenever I look at the Stigmatization in the cycle

---

1   *Francis: Brother of the Universe* (Marvel Comics, 1980).
2   W.R. Cook, "Epilogue," in *Arthur Boyd & Saint Francis of Assisi* (Macmillan Art Publishers, 2004).
3   W.R. Cook, *Images of St. Francis of Assisi in Painting, Stone and Glass from the Earliest Images to ca. 1320 in Italy. A Catalogue* (Florence/Perth: L.S. Olschki/University of Western Australia, 1999); further abbreviated as *Images*.

of Francis' life in the Upper Basilica in Assisi,[4] I assume its originality since it differs in significant ways from earlier surviving Stigmatizations that can be dated. Yet, is there a lost prototype? Will we, without lucky discoveries, never know the answer to that question?

However, I will work with what we have rather than what once was or what might have been. But it is important to remember that all conclusions are based on assumptions about surviving works that might prove incorrect if we could go back to examine all that was created during that extraordinarily fertile first century of Franciscan art. I want to address two important matters. First, I will propose in a hardly original manner that the art of the Franciscan Order plays a vital role in the development of style in Italy at least in part due to the life and spiritual practices of Francis himself. Then I want to examine the forms that early Franciscan art takes, suggesting that each of them was an innovation designed to present the life and spiritual genius of Francis and the work of the Order he founded.

About 125 years ago, the German Heinrich Thode published an important book, *Franz von Assisi und die Anfänge der Kunst der Renaissance in Italien*[5] (*Francis of Assisi and the Beginnings of the Art of the Renaissance in Italy*), which exists in French and Italian translations but which has never been rendered into English. Of course, Thode had fewer known works to examine, and we now know that many of them were misdated and misattributed. However, his observations and his basic argument, implicit in the book's title, are still worthy of consideration.

Certainly it is inarguable that many of the important early images of Francis are landmarks in the history of painting. Whether we examine form or content, the art of and for the Franciscan Order is central to any study of late medieval and early Renaissance painting. With regard to form, we have the saint's dossal that we can trace to Bonaventura Berlinghieri's signed and dated panel of 1235 in Pescia.[6] Undoubtedly, the now destroyed cross by Giunta Pisano for the Basilica in Assisi that Brother Elias commissioned in 1236 is an important prototype for later medieval crucifixes.

In the next generation of paintings, especially the fresco cycle in the Upper Basilica of Assisi[7] and the cycle by Giotto in the Bardi Chapel in Santa Croce in Florence,[8] there are innovations that are universally recognized. We also have hints of the groundbreaking work of Ambrogio Lorenzetti for the Franciscan Order at San Francesco in Siena from surviving fragments and written descriptions. Since one of the important elements of both the Florentine and Sienese images is the artists' use of classical models, we sense that what we are looking at is the beginning of Renaissance style. As Millard Meiss pointed out more than a half century ago, the road to the Renaissance had its detours. Still, in the early fifteenth century, artists consciously return to important innovations of the first half of the fourteenth century.

Scholars ponder why around 1300 and a bit after, painters began to look more carefully at survivals from classical antiquity and also to develop a style that is more natural, whether it is the weighty figures of Giotto or the squirming baby Jesus of Ambrogio Lorenzetti's Presentation in the Temple for the Siena Cathedral, now in the Uffizi Gallery in Florence. I want to suggest two key reasons and that they can be associated with two individuals, one pagan and one Christian, one

[4] *Images* Plate 25s, p. 55.
[5] Berlin: G. Grote, 1904.
[6] *Images* Plate 141, p. 165; cf. W.R. Cook, ed., *The Art of the Franciscan Order in Italy* (Leiden: Brill, 2005) [further abbreviated as AFOI, Ahlquist & Cook], Plate 1.
[7] *Images* Plate 25, pp. 50-51, 54-58.
[8] *Images* Plate 68, p. 98; AFOI, Ahlquist & Cook Plate 6.

ancient and one recent, one who was of the highest intellect and one a man who preached to birds and rescued worms: Aristotle and Francis of Assisi.

The rediscovery in the West and translation into Latin of virtually the entire corpus of Aristotle that we know today is of course a central story in the history of European thought. By a bit after 1300, Dante can refer to Aristotle simply as "the philosopher" and also as "the master sage of those who know."

Let me focus on one foundational principle of Aristotelian thought: all knowledge begins with sense perception. There are enormous ramifications to the acceptance of this principle. If it is so, it follows that we must carefully record what our senses perceive in order to gain knowledge. It is not coincidental that it is in the Ile de France, at the center of which is the University of Paris, that we find the development of a highly individuated and realistic sculptural style in the thirteenth century. The north and south porches of Chartres and the facades of Amiens and Rheims cathedrals reveal a significantly different way of seeing than the tympanum of Sainte Foi in Conques and the capitals at Autun and Vézelay, made less than a century earlier. The smiling angel of the Annunciation and the classically inspired adjacent Visitation at Rheims introduce us to a new realism and individuation. Countless examples of specific species of plants found in gothic decoration are another example of the startling newness of this art.

Given the influence of Aristotle on western theologians in the thirteenth century, it is quite possible that his philosophical realism had an impact on the development of Gothic art. On the other hand, the importance of Francis for the development of a more realistic and individualized art in Italy is barely recognized, despite Thode's claim a century and a quarter ago. Let me preface my comments by pointing out more generally why art was such an important tool of the Franciscan Order, while it played a much smaller role in the development of the Dominicans.

We should remember that one of the most important and profound experiences of the young Francis occurred while he was praying before a crucifix in the crumbling church of San Damiano near Assisi. At that time, according to Celano's *Second Life of St. Francis*, "the wounds of the sacred passion were impressed deep in his heart, though not yet on his flesh...." In fact, the Three Companions stated this more clearly:

> this [impression of the wounds on his heart] was brilliantly shown afterwards in the *renewal* of those wounds that were miraculously impressed on and most clearly revealed in his body. (emphasis mine)[9]

Keeping in mind the key role a painting played in Francis' spiritual development, let us return to the argument for Francis as a key figure in understanding the development of Renaissance style.

One of the most important elements of Francis' spirituality was his love of all God's creatures and his belief that, since all creatures have the same 'parent,' God, they are indeed all brothers and sisters. Of course, that brother- and sisterhood is most famously expressed in the Canticle of the Creatures. If we regard trees and rocks and birds as our brothers and sisters, does that not at least suggest that we look at them carefully and recall them with some accuracy?

Both Celano and Bonaventure tell us, in language that is no doubt foreign to Francis' way of speaking, that in beautiful things Francis saw Beauty itself and that he made of all creation a

---

[9]   *The Founder,* vol. 2 of *Francis of Assisi. Early Documents,* eds. R.J. Armstrong, J.A. Wayne Hellmann, and W.J. Short (New York/ London/Manila: New City Press, 2000), 76.

ladder by which he was able to climb up and embrace God. Or, to use another of Bonaventure's metaphors, creatures were footprints; by following them, Francis was able to find God.

A few years ago, I was camping on the Crow Reservation in Montana with a member of the tribe named Benny. While I was doing some task, I noticed Benny examining what I thought was just a bit of dirt near a stream. He got up and announced that about twenty minutes ago, an elk had been drinking from that stream. He came to that conclusion by a careful examination of its footprints. If we are going to 'track' God, would that not require a careful and accurate examination of God's footprints?

Let's turn to the well known story of Francis orchestrating the Christmas crib at Greccio in 1223. He decided to recreate the birth of Jesus at Christmas for the people of Greccio. Within limits, he did so with great accuracy. He brought to the place of worship an ox and ass, not a horse and a pig or just any old available farm animals, but species that, as legend has it, were present at the birth of the Messiah. He also had a manger with straw. Getting the details right was important if people were going to be able to imagine Bethlehem in Greccio. If they were to experience the incarnation and not merely commemorate it, then carefully recreating the scenario from Bethlehem at Greccio was vital. Ewert Cousins has wonderfully described what Francis was trying to offer to those present at Greccio as the mysticism of the historical event.[10]

In addition to the brotherhood of creatures and the mysticism of the historical event, let us add another element to our understanding of Francis as an important source for the development of new styles of art during the Renaissance. Here is how Bonaventure in the *Legenda Maior* describes Francis' descent from LaVerna after his reception of the stigmata:

> ...Francis came down from the mountain, bearing with him the likeness of the Crucified depicted not on tablets of stone or on panels of wood carved by hand, but engraved on parts of his flesh by the finger of the living God (XIII,5).

Thus, it is obvious that perceiving directly the wounds on Francis' body is the best possible way of understanding and sharing what he experienced. Viewing a panel showing Francis with the wounds of Christ is less efficacious than seeing Francis as he descended from the mountain. Francis is living while a panel of wood is inanimate.

However, let me reflect on another passage from the *Legenda Maior* to understand the importance of panel paintings of Francis for those who could not see him in the flesh. When Francis is asked if he approves of friars engaged in study, he replies:

> I am indeed pleased [that my brothers study] as long as, after the example of Christ, of whom we read that he prayed more than he read, they do not neglect zeal for prayer (XI,1).

Of course, this is Bonaventure's language, not Francis'. However, let us consider the implications of this statement for Franciscan art. To imitate Christ, we must pray more than we read because that is what Christ did. However, we are not able to observe directly Christ in prayer. To know that he prayed more than he read, we must read that he did so.

---

[10]   Ewert Cousins, "Francis of Assisi: Christian Mysticism at the Crossroads," in Steven T. Katz, ed., *Mysticism and Religious Traditions* (Oxford: Oxford University Press, 1983), 163-91.

So, how do we know that Francis uniquely bore Christ's wounds in his body, that his flesh was transformed by the finger of the living God? Of course, we can read about it. However, we also can see it because of Francis' stigmatized image on a painted panel of wood. So, we are able to experience Francis through an image on wood the way that Francis experienced Christ on the cross through an image on wood at San Damiano.[11]

Let me turn to a discussion of the sorts of images that were created to represent Francis and events from his life plus his posthumous miracles; for one can make the argument, as I suggested at the beginning, that the major forms of these images were created in order to propagate the cult and Order of Francis of Assisi.[12]

When we think of that image of Christ crucified before which Francis prayed at San Damiano (now located in Santa Chiara in Assisi), it does not present a suffering Christ but rather a triumphant one. The earliest painted cross of this type is dated 1138 and is located in Sarzana in Liguria. It is fair to say that based on such early images of the crucifixion, Christ is represented as the conqueror of death rather than a suffering servant.

On the other hand, Francis' devotion to the Crucified Christ is clear, and it is because his conformity to Christ Crucified that he received the stigmata at LaVerna. In some real way, at LaVerna Francis became what he so passionately loved. Now, we know that in Byzantium, well before and during the time of Francis, there was some tradition of representing a suffering Christ. There are also a few crosses in Italy of this type that scholars have dated more or less to the time of Francis, although it is difficult to be confident of any

precise dates. If they are prior to Francis' life, then of course they owe nothing to Francis' devotion to the cross. There is no particular reason that a Byzantine form of the crucifixion should not have been known and recreated in Italy, especially after the establishment of the Latin Kingdom in Constantinople in 1204. After all, there is clearly a significant cross-fertilization between Byzantine and Italian forms of art as a result of the Fourth Crusade.

As Anne Derbes shows in her excellent book *Picturing the Passion*,[13] the Franciscans did a lot of focused borrowing of images from Byzantium and northern Europe when creating the Order's art. To her, the most important question is why the Franciscans chose certain images while ignoring others.

With the development of large painted crosses, the answer appears to be clear. Francis' own devotion to the Crucified Christ called for a different sort of cross than the *Christus Triumphans* that was dominant in central Italy at that time (the San Damiano cross, relatively new when Francis prayed before it in 1206, is a good example of this form). In 1236, Brother Elias, Minister General at the time, commissioned a wooden cross for the Basilica in Assisi. We should remember that despite Elias' later downfall, he was an intimate friend and confidant of Francis, one who knew the saint and his spiritual journey. According to early sources, it was Elias who announced at the time of Francis' death the discovery of the stigmata on the saint's body.

Giunta Pisano's cross for the Basilica showed the suffering Christ, *Christus Patiens*. The Assisi cross of 1236 is something of a prototype for countless crosses large and small for the next hundred years. Unfortunately, Giunta's cross was destroyed in the 18th century, but we have a 17th-century

---

[11] Cf. *Images* Plate 68, p. 98.

[12] Cf. T. Johnson, "Lost in Sacred Space: Textual Hermeneutics, Liturgical Worship, and Celano's Legenda *ad Usum Chori*," *Franciscan Studies* 59 (2001): 109-31.

[13] A. Derbes, *Picturing the Passion in Late Medieval Italy: Narrative Painting, Franciscan Ideologies, and the Levant* (Cambrige: Cambridge University Press, 1996).

'copy' of it. We also have later crosses of this type by Giunta himself, for example at San Domenico in Bologna as well as in the museum of the Portiuncula in Assisi. More importantly, of course, we have so many crosses whose iconographic lineage can be traced back to Giunta.

The cross in Assisi contained a small image of Elias at its base. In a cross from the 1260s in Santa Chiara in Assisi, we have not only its patron, Abbess Benedicta and St Clare but also a larger image of Francis embracing the feet of Christ.[14] This may be the earliest of many crosses containing small images of Francis. Some are close to the Santa Chiara cross while a larger group shows a tiny Francis beside the feet of Christ (well known examples are in Perugia and Montefalco).[15] There are also several processional crosses that contain a bust of Francis beneath the crucifixion. All of these are more or less dramatic expressions of the experiential nature of Francis' encounter with Christ.

Although these crosses with Francis unsurprisingly have a Franciscan provenance, the new form of crucifixion, the *Christus Patiens*, almost completely replaced the older *Christus Triumphans* rather quickly in Italy. A cross painted in the late thirteenth century of the old type needs to be explained; for example, scholars have suggested that such a *Christus Triumphans* cross in Spoleto is consciously archaic, perhaps replacing a beloved and miracle-producing image that had been damaged or destroyed.

To show a triumphant Christ on the cross is not in a literal sense historical. Certainly nothing in the gospels suggests anything other than that Christ suffered an agonizing death. However, the new image of the suffering Christ represents, although not necessarily in literal detail, an attempt to recreate for viewers what it was like on that day.

Of course, these images are not meant to be historical representations in the modern sense. But, analogous to the Christmas crib in Greccio, it became important to get some details right, to make crucifixions recognizable so that viewers could really imagine themselves there as, in a different scale, Francis himself is often present in these images.

The year before Giunta's commission in Assisi, Bonaventura Berlinghieri of Lucca painted, signed, and dated a gabled panel (often referred to as the Pescia dossal, as it is still in the church of San Francesco in Pescia, Italy)[16] with a large central image of Francis and three narrative sections on each side depicting stories from Francis' life and posthumous miracles, the source for which was Thomas of Celano's *First Life of St. Francis*. As far as we know, the Pescia panel is the earliest painting of this type in Italy. Thus we can infer that the new form was created to present the life and miracles of this new saint. For the remainder of the thirteenth century and into the beginning of the fourteenth, this type of image was created not only to present Francis of Assisi but for other saints both old (Mary Magdalen, now in the Accademia Gallery in Florence) and new (Margaret of Cortona, now in the Museo Diocesano in Cortona, and Clare at Santa Chiara in Assisi).

Scholars have suggested two possible origins for this new form, although they are not mutually exclusive. Unsurprisingly, one is a form originating in the Byzantine Empire. There survive small rectangular icons from the monastery of St. Catherine on Mount Sinai with a similar juxtaposition of image and narratives. It is clear that Berlinghieri was aware of certain decorative motifs found in Byzantine painting, so it is not a great stretch to imagine that he has used and modified this form by multiplying the size and placing a gable on the top.

---

[14] *Images* Plate 28, p. 64.
[15] *Images* Plate 102, p. 130.
[16] *Images* Plate 141, p. 165.

We need to recall that after the Fourth Lateran Council in 1215, which many scholars believe that Francis attended and whose decrees were important guidelines for Francis and his Order, decreed that priests should consecrate the bread and wine facing east, i.e. standing in front of the altar. Thus, many paintings that were altar frontals became obsolete since they could not be viewed during the consecration. A surviving altar frontal in the Pinacoteca in Siena is evidence that priests saying mass also inadvertently damaged these paintings by kicking them. Hence, there was great need for new forms of art to decorate altars, ones that could sit on the back of the altar and thus provide a background for the faithful as the priest consecrated the bread and wine. If Berlinghieri's dossal in Pescia is in fact the earliest painting in this new form, it might in part be a response to a new need for churches generally as well as a new way to tell of a new saint.

The other possible source for the dossal is the *Christus Triumphans* type of cross. These images usually contain narrative sections on the apron, stories that lead up to the crucifixion and stories that follow it. Hence, the argument goes, it is appropriate for images of Francis, that most Christ-like of men and one like Christ bearing wounds in his hands, feet, and side in the central images of the panel, to be in the form that is a visual analogue of Christ's passion as represented on large crosses. Whether such crosses are a direct source for the dossal, we probably will never know. However, I think we can be confident that viewers saw a connection between the dossal and traditional representations of the crucifixion. After all, both central figures have the same wounds!

One interesting aspect of the dossals of Francis is that at one and the same time we see a timeless image of the saint while simultaneously we see the stories of his life that led to his salvation plus the help Francis provides from heaven for those on earth in need. Hence, the viewers move between time and eternity as they look at and pray before such an image. And, they not only see a way of life that leads to salvation but also see Francis in heaven still serving humanity through intercession, the results of which are present to them. In somewhat variant forms, there are seven surviving dossals featuring Francis that date back to the thirteenth century. All but the latest, the one in Siena,[17] contain posthumous miracles; and three of them (Pisa, Assisi, and the Vatican) contain only posthumous miracles.

The dossal also invites the viewer to read Francis' life in a non-linear way. There is usually a roughly chronological organization of the events in Francis' life reading either clockwise from the lower left corner (Siena dossal) or counter clockwise beginning in the upper left (Bardi dossal in Florence).[18] However, there are many exceptions to a chronological presentation. For example, the story of Christmas at Greccio follows the Stigmatization in the Siena dossal; three preaching stories from different periods of Francis' life are together in lower left side of the Bardi panel. Posthumous miracles always follow the narrative of Francis' life and are not mixed with events of that narrative.

There are often visual clues that encourage viewers to connect stories that are not presented consecutively. For example, in the Siena dossal, Francis kneels in two stories—the vision at San Damiano and the Stigmatization. There is a bishop present in the first scene on the panel (Francis stripping before the bishop) and the last one (death of Francis), although Bonaventure is explicit that Bishop Guido was not in Assisi at the time of Francis' death. Since these are the first and last stories of the cycle and are opposite one another, they

---

[17] *Images* Plate 180, p. 209.
[18] AFOI, Ahlquist & Cook, Plate 6.

provide an institutional frame for the story. Francis' life starts with a bishop embracing him, and his soul goes to heaven with his bishop present as he is conducted to new life.

The third form of Franciscan panel painting is the simple full-length image of Francis holding a book and displaying tiny stigmata. We often assume that this is an age-old form of representing a saint, but the evidence suggests that it too is a new form created to present Francis. The creator is almost certainly Margarito d'Arezzo, and it may be another borrowing from the tradition of Byzantine icons. There are seven surviving images of Francis by Margarito, the earliest of which is in the Pinacoteca in Arezzo.[19] If the survival rate for this sort of painting is as low as Garrison believed, there were once hundreds of these panels in Franciscan churches.

Scholars are not sure how these images were used in churches. They were certainly not altarpieces. Some speculate that they may have hung at entrances of Franciscan churches; others suggest they may have hung on columns. The images, which probably were first created in the 1230s, must have been for the small Franciscan churches that had sprung up in Italy, virtually all of which were replaced by larger edifices later in the thirteenth or in the fourteenth century.

The fact that large new churches were being built within a few decades of when Margarito painted these panels may help to explain why the form did not continue. These panels, typically a bit more than a meter in height, would have been almost invisible in churches such as Santa Croce in Florence or San Francesco in Siena. Furthermore, there were more complex images, in particular dossals, that probably led to the demise of the sort of painting that Margarito created. And before the end of the thirteenth century, the new template for

representing Francis was the fresco cycle in the Upper Basilica in Assisi.[20] The role of frescoes in telling of Francis on a much grander scale probably also led to fewer commissions of large crosses and the gradual demise of the dossal.

Despite the fact that these new forms of art to a great extent did not last more than a century, they were enormously successful in telling the story of Francis and in preaching the gospel as Francis and his followers understood it. Panels like those of Margarito presented a simple, gospel-following, approachable man. They emphasized Francis' simplicity. In them, Francis had no nimbus. Even the stigmata were not emphasized.

The dossals allowed people to learn the pattern of Francis' life. They no doubt also helped to explain who the friars were and what their ministries focused on. Of course, that is in part because the friars chose stories to be depicted that linked Francis to their work in the present. One example would be the story of Francis driving demons out of Arezzo, a story that, according to Bonaventure, was about Francis making peace between factions in the city. By the time that story came to be depicted, friars were indeed negotiating peace between and within Italian city-states with some regularity. The dossals, since all but one that survives have posthumous miracles, presented Francis as a saint to be invoked and suggested Assisi as a place of pilgrimage. The focus on certain types of miracles in the dossals (the same miracle stories were repeated in these paintings) even could suggest some of Francis' 'specialties' as an intercessor.

The images with Francis at the feet of the suffering Jesus,[21] himself bearing Christ's wounds, introduced Francis as one who had direct experience of Christ and also suggested that it was possible to be mystically present at the crucifixion even more

---

[19]   *Images* Plate 6, p. 30.
[20]   *Images* Plate 25, pp. 50-51.
[21]   *Images* Plates 5, 21, 28, 60, 80, 88, 135, 136, 137, 169, 178, 180, 184, 186, 190, 191; pp. 29, 48, 64, 92, 111, 118, 160-62, 198, 207, 210, 214, 216, 219-20.

than 1200 years after the historical event. Along with re-enactments of the Christmas crib at Greccio in Franciscan churches, these crosses furthered the new sort of mysticism that Ewert Cousins called the mysticism of the historical event.[22]

Again, what largely replaced these different forms of representation of Francis on wood were fresco cycles. With the exception of the frescoed image of Francis in Subiaco,[23] which has been dated between the 1220s and the 1240s, there are essentially no surviving frescoes from the period that saw the creation of dossals, *Christus Patiens* crosses, and panels by Margarito. One reason, no doubt, is the small size of the earliest Franciscan churches. However, with the building and decoration of the Basilica in Assisi and the subsequent construction of numerous large Franciscan churches, everything changed. There was a fresco cycle of Francis' life in the Lower Basilica[24] painted at virtually the same time Bonaventure completed his *Legenda Maior*. And less than 30 years later came the twenty eight stories of the life and miracles of Francis in the Upper Basilica,[25] which largely defined both the content and style of countless cycles of Francis' life, beginning with the one in San Francesco in Rieti[26] probably painted within a decade of its prototype. Within a couple of decades came the cycle in the Aracoeli in Rome of Pietro Cavallini[27] and the magnificent frescoes of Giotto in the Bardi Chapel of Santa Croce in Florence. Even as we move into the fifteenth century, the most important representations of Francis are in fresco, Benozzo Gozzoli's in Montefalco and Domenico Ghirlandaio's in Santa Trinita in Florence perhaps being the best known of them.

Of course, there were many non-narrative images of Francis that were created in the fourteenth and fifteenth centuries. Overwhelmingly, they were parts of large altarpieces. We do not know where the polyptych originated, but there are early Franciscan examples such as that of Guido da Siena from Colle Valdelsa. Whatever the origin, we have at least parts of many such altarpieces including Ugolino di Nerio's for Santa Croce in Florence. Sometimes the saints were full length while in other panels they are busts. Sometimes casual observers assume that there continued to be single 'portraits' of Francis because they hang in many museums. However, they are almost always pieces from dismembered polyptychs.

One of the interesting elements of these images in polyptychs is that with the creation and prevalence of predellas, it became possible to combine the non-narrative image and usually one story from Francis' life. One example is the altar in the chapel of the sacristy of Santa Croce in Florence, where Giovanni da Maiano's image of Francis 'stands on' a representation on a much smaller scale of the Stigmatization. In the two-sided altarpiece of Taddeo di Bartolo for San Francesco in Perugia, the predellas collectively contained twelve stories from Francis' life, seven of which have survived in Hannover and 's-Heerenberg. This combination of two originally different formats for presenting Francis is interesting and effective.

There are several reasons to look carefully at these polyptychs, although I sometimes get the sense that even some scholars think that most of them look alike. The images of Francis contain almost countless variations. Sometimes Francis has a book, occasionally open with a legible text. These passages are not always the same and may come

---

22 E. Cousins, "Francis of Assisi...," loc. cit.
23 *Images* Plates 192, 193, pp. 221-22.
24 *Images* Plate 11, p. 34.
25 *Images* Plate 25, pp. 50-51.
26 *Images* Plate 151, p. 180.
27 *Images* Plates 157, 159, 160, pp. 187-88, 190.

from scripture or the Rule. Francis sometimes has a cross. The stigmata, especially the side wound, are not always represented in the same way. At the end of the thirteenth century there appears a version of Francis without a beard, and there is scholarly controversy in which I have engaged about the significance of the image of Francis without a beard. In some images Francis wears sandals, an oddity given the Rule; this is especially true in paintings originating in the Venetian sphere of influence. Paying attention to some of these differences helps us to analyze individual paintings and may also collectively tell us about how Francis and his legacy were perceived somewhat differently in different places and eras.

Another interesting way to look at the polyptychs containing Francis is to see what saints accompany Francis, especially which ones he is adjacent to and juxtaposed with. My research conducted a few years ago for a series of lectures concluded that in Florentine images, Francis was often in the company of other founders of orders—Benedict, Augustine, even Dominic. However, in Siena, he was significantly more often in the company of martyrs, ascetics, and contemplatives. This may suggest different emphases in these two neighboring city-states. It would hardly be the only thing that Florence and Siena disagreed on! Another interesting way of studying these images, if we know the provenance of an altarpiece, is to see how different the collection and arrangement of saints is in houses of friars and Clares compared to churches of other orders or cathedrals.

I have focused on public images of the saint, although we know of many private images, especially in manuscripts, where illuminations depict stories never found in the monumental public art I have been discussing.

Here I have focused on images of Francis in Italy. However, there should be more thorough and systematic study of images of Francis in the rest of Catholic Europe. Among the earliest images of Francis are two Limoges enamels in Paris. We find Francis entering the kingdom of heaven in the Last Judgment of the central tympanum of the façade of Amiens Cathedral. A surviving window in the Barfusskirche in Erfurt is also quite an early, although limited, narrative cycle of the saint's life. It is possible that one of the Limoges enamels is the earliest depiction of the Stigmatization, and it is likely that the depiction of the side wound through a tear in Francis' habit originated north of the Alps and was brought to Italy by window makers for the Upper Basilica in Assisi.

It is clear from what I have presented that the creation not just of new images but of new forms of images to present Francis of Assisi to the public in the thirteenth century was a broad and carefully orchestrated program. The Friars Minor set out with an elaborate program of images to win the hearts and minds of people. This is particularly notable when we see how rarely the Dominicans presented their founder visually. And the Franciscan use of art to propagate the cult of their founder was also in stark contrast with the other mendicant orders, the Augustinians and Carmelites. Looking at the mendicant churches and noting the families who were their patrons, the contrast between the Franciscans and other new orders cannot be attributed to difference in patronage.

Let me close with a series of exhortations for those who study Franciscan art, especially the earliest art of the Order. I offer the first three especially to scholars, who are my co-workers.

1. We need to make our study of the art of the Franciscan Order quite broad. Of course, we must try to understand provenance, make attributions, and study style. And it is important to examine fragments of altarpieces and see if we cannot, using modern technology and good old fashioned measuring and other such techniques, put at least some of them back together. Yet we cannot stop there. We need to ask broader questions about the purpose and meaning of the art. We must try to understand its role in the vocation and ministry of the friars. These sorts of tasks cannot be carried out well if those studying them do not have a broad knowledge that today we would call interdisciplinary. Essays in the present volume admirably attend to the need for an interdisciplinary focus.

2. We should address audiences beyond scholars in our own disciplines and subdisciplines. We academics know the temptation and the comfort of only talking to ourselves. We need to show our findings to people in a wide range of disciplines and specialties. There are too many people who study religion generally and the Franciscans in particular who still think of the art largely as illustration of texts and to some extent as tangential to the most important inquiries into the Order's history and purpose. We need to speak to those folks so that they are encouraged to have a much needed intellectual conversion.

3. To return to my first point, we need to show scholars of the late Middle Ages and the Renaissance that there is an important causal link between the representation of the life of Francis and the development of Renaissance style and indeed the Renaissance itself. This is perhaps a bit easier case to make in light of many new studies of Christianity in the Renaissance. Still, there are scholars who take for granted that the fact that so many 'advances' in art were made in the creation of art for the Franciscan Order is largely a coincidence or a matter of patronage.

The last two exhortations are offered to an audience that includes art historians but are also important to friars who do not study their tradition systematically and to artists.

4. We should present the early art of the Franciscan Order to those who will create the next generation of Franciscan art. We should suggest and provide examples how the art of an earlier time was an inspiration to and model for artists of subsequent generations without at all limiting changes that make new art speak to the concerns and conditions of the present. I think of how Ghirlandaio in the 1480s in Santa Trinita quoted Giotto's frescoes from across town in Santa Croce but also created a quite different presentation of Francis for the Sassetti family than Giotto had done for the Bardi family a century and a half earlier. And much earlier, the painter of the cross in Santa Chiara took the bold step of adding Francis at the base of his cross rather than only placing the patron, as Giunta Pisano had done a quarter of a century earlier. And what about the painters of the frescoes in San Francesco in Pienza in the late fourteenth century who added stories, for example Francis and the Wolf of Gubbio, a story not found in the official vita which had been virtually the only source for visual images since its publication more than a century earlier?

5. I want to remind everyone the original purpose of the art: to encourage people to love and follow the example of Francis, to support and follow his followers, and to seek Francis' help. When we are studying sacred art, it is important to remember that as much as it is important to study the economics and politics of these works, we should not ignore their intent. If we do, then we fail to understand perhaps the most essential element of what we are studying.

For those of us who study this art and share a faith with Francis, we should remember the success of the art. We should ask what power to teach and to move it may still have for people in the 21st century as it does for many of us. If the art was for spiritual growth, moral improvement and theological engagement, can we ignore that reality or assume it worked, but no longer works? And if it does not work for all, is that not a reason to instruct and encourage artists who will make those works of art, by no means only paintings, that help to shape the lives of contemporary Christians?

6. I want to end with a brief description of a recent experience I had teaching many of the paintings I have mentioned here to friars and sisters in Nairobi. First, they were taken by the beauty of the images and, unlike some folks in Europe and North America, they were not put off by the lack of realism and the repetitions of certain conventions. The art we study is closer to traditional art in non-Western cultures than it is to the modern West. I urged the Franciscans I addressed to find inspiration and even some models in these works but then to take the spirit rather than the letter and create their own Franciscan images for Kenyans. They will use different symbols and choose different stories. They will create something quite new to convey the truth of something quite old. That is exactly what the artists of thirteenth-century Italy who were decorating Franciscan churches were doing with the Christian story when they presented it through the new lens of one of the most creative Christians ever, Francis of Assisi.

THE JOY OF ST. FRANCIS:
BELLINI'S PANEL IN THE FRICK COLLECTION**

Marilyn Aronberg Lavin

he Painting: 1

(Fig. 1) In a moment of rapture, St. Francis steps back, weight on his right foot and arms extended low at his sides. With his hands turned forward, he shows tiny red marks of the stigmata on each palm; the protruding left foot once also bore the mark of piercing.[1] Facing toward the left, he raises his eyes heavenward and opens his mouth; he is unshaven, bareheaded, and has no halo. He wears the Franciscan hooded habit gathered at the waist with twisted rope tied in three knots symbolizing the main virtues to which the Friars Minor are devoted: obedience, chastity and poverty. A folded sheet with traces of color is tucked in the belt under his arm. Although the subject of the painting has been called a "stigmatization," the habit is immaculate, with no sign of the chest wound, the fifth of the usual stigmata marks. The setting is a broad landscape that develops spatially from right to left into an ever deepening vista. In fact, besides the animals that are present—a wild ass, two birds, and a distant flock of sheep—the two major protagonists are the saint and his natural surroundings. The figure is charismatic and the landscape—its impressive size, the warm green and earthy colors, the palpability of the light, and the intimate perfection of its many details—make the painting one of the most

---

**   Most of the citings of Franciscan sources were made possible by the use of a CD-Rom of the relatively recent English edition R. J. Armstrong, J. A. Wayne Hellmann, and W. J. Short, eds., *Francis of Assisi: Early Documents*, 3 vols. [vol.1 - The Saint; vol. 2 - The Founder; vol. 3 - The Prophet] (Hyde Park, N.Y.: New City Press, 1999-2001), with electronic search apparatus, made available to me by the editors. This edition has clarified the chronology and authenticity of thirteenth- and early fourteenth-century Franciscan literature. For their generosity I am exceedingly grateful to the editors and to Dr. Daniel Michaels for technical guidance and moral support. In most cases I have referred only to the earliest version of each citation, with references to *Early Documents*, volume, name of the source, date, and page in the volume, although the electronic search mechanism makes it possible to follow the later iterations and their variants.

Since this article was first published (*Artibus et Historiae* 55 (2007): 1-16), the painting has undergone (March-April, 2010) a deep scientific analysis under the direction of Charlotte Hale, the Metropolitan Museum of Art Paintings Conservator. Her study revealed a number of important new facts about Bellini's painting process and the original condition of the work. Hale presented a public lecture on her findings on June 8, 2011 at the Frick Collection which is available on line:
http://www.artbabble.org/video/frick/charlotte-hale-bellinis-st-francis-desert-new-discoveries. Accessed October 25, 2012. A scholarly publication will follow. The new information, where pertinent, will be noted as we go along.

[1]   One of the new observations made by Hale 2011; the mark, originally a small dot of opaque red pigment covered with a transparent daub of red lake, is now invisible to the naked eye having been worn away in early cleanings.

Fig 1.

compelling—and innovative—works of art of the Italian Early Renaissance.

The painting entered the Henry Clay Frick collection in New York in 1915 with the title *St. Francis in the Desert*, and the date of about 1480; some scholars now believe it could be slightly earlier.[2] I assume it was painted between 1475 and 1480. The title comes from the first reference to the work that has come down to us, found in the remarkable list of art objects seen by the Venetian connoisseur Marcantonio Michiel (1486?-1552) in the various collections he visited in 1520s. Michiel describes Bellini's painting as follows:

> In casa de M. Taddeo Contarino.
> La tavola del San Francesco nel deserto a oglio fu opera de Zuan Bellino, cominciata da lui a M. Zuan Michiel e ha un paese propinquo finito e ricercato mirabilmente.[3]

The passage has been interpreted in various ways, including that the painting was begun for Michiel but finished for someone else; also that it was almost, but not quite finished. The use of word "paese" stimulated the idea that interest in landscape as such was growing and that the figure of St. Francis might be incidental to the subject. The consensus, now, is that the painting was commissioned by Michiel, that the landscape was highly finished and that the figure of St. Francis is the focal point of all that surrounds it.[4] Michiel underscores this point with his description that still serves as a title: "San Francesco nel *deserto*," or St. Francis in the desert, taking *deserto* as it is used in Italian to mean any deserted wilderness or countryside. Understanding the title as merely descriptive, however, is deceptive. For, whether consciously or not, it provides the key to the painting's meaning by signaling its most unusual aspect. No such image, either narrative or devotional, had precedence in the Franciscan repertory.[5] Several authors have tried to identify the panel as a rather unusual scene of the Stigmatization by associating the burst of celestial rays at the upper left and the unnaturally bending tree (see Fig. 16) with the burning rays that brought to Francis the nail and lance wounds of Christ's passion.[6] But

---

[2] C. Ryskamp, et al., *Art in the Frick Collection: Paintings, Sculpture, Decorative Arts* (New York: Harry N. Abrams, 1996), 47. See M. Meiss, *Giovanni Bellini's St. Francis in the Frick Collection* (Princeton: Princeton University Press, 1964); and R. Goffen' *Giovanni Bellini* (New Haven: Yale University Press, 1989), 107-11. The medium is oil on poplar panel, 124.46 cm x 141.92 cm; slightly shaved at the top. The lack of any tempera in the medium and the minimal loss of surface at the top are other of Hale's 2011 discoveries.

[3] "The panel of St. Francis in the desert painted in oil is the work of Giovanni Bellini, begun by him for Mr. Giovanni Michiel and has a landscape nearby finished and thought-out admirably." The manuscript found and published as "anonymous" by Jacopo Morelli [1745-1819], *Notizia d'opere di disegno*; 2nd ed, ed. G. Frizzoni (Bologna: N. Zanichelli, 1884); the author was identified by Th. Frimmel in *Il Anonimo; Notizia d'opere del disegno / Marco Antonio Michiel* (Vienna, 1896); reprinted and introduced by C. De Benedictis (Florence: Edifir, 2000), in the series *Le voci del museo. Collana di museologia e museografia*. The text was translated into English as *Il Anonimo: notes on pictures and works of art in Italy made by an anonymous writer in the sixteenth century*, trans. P. Mussi, ed. G. C. Williamson (London: G. Bell and Sons, 1903). The painting was later taken to England by Buchanaan; passed through the collections of Muray, Dingwall (# 187), Holloway, Driver, and finally was bought by Henry Clay Frick, No. 3, Cat. 1935; see F. Heinemann, *Giovanni Bellini e I Belliniani*, 2 vols. (Venice: Neri Pozza, 1962), 1, 65, no. 218.

[4] See Meiss 1964, 20-22. A. R. Turner, *The Vision of Landscape in Renaissance Italy* (Princeton: Princeton University Press, 1966), 59-65, discusses the qualities of the landscape at length. J. M. Fletcher, "The Provenance of Bellini's Frick 'St. Francis'", *Burlington Magazine* 114 (1972): 206-214, proposes that the translation of *paese* could be town or village (of which there is one in the background) as well as landscape.

[5] As Meiss 1964, 20 and 52, pointed out, the iconography of St. Jerome meditating in the desert was common theme by the mid-15th century but was never before Bellini applied to St. Francis.

[6] Although the angle of the rays emanating from the clouds makes it unlikely there was ever anything above them, the suggestion that originally there was a seraph in the upper left before the cutting of the panel has been made more than once. Hale (2011) ruled out this possibility in her discovery that the loss of wood at the top of the panel is no more than a few centimeters. In 1660, Marco Boschini (*La Carta del Navegar Pittoresco*, ed. A. Pallucchini [Venice: Istituto per la collaborazione culturali, 1966]), described a scene of the *Stigmatization* by Bellini which included a seraphic crucifix. The painting could not have been the Frick panel, however, since the author meticulously describes the burning rays joining the extremities of Christ to those of Francis.

this identification leaves unaccounted several salient facts: 1) Francis is depicted with only three of the canonical five wounds;[7] 2) He is shown standing, a position very rare in stigmatization scenes.[8] 3) there are few such scenes from which Francis's companion Brother Leo is absent; and 4) while many stigmatizations are set in rocky surroundings, there are none in which the landscape is so prominent and so conspicuously filled with specific details of nature.

The prominence of the landscape, moreover, sets the stage for an astonishing number of innovations that differentiate Giovanni Bellini from the long and distinguished tradition from whence his style evolved. Giovanni and his older brother Gentile studied and worked with their father Jacopo Bellini (ca. 1400-1471), frequently collaborating with him on commissioned works. After Jacopo's death and at that of his wife Anna, the older son inherited Jacopo's artistic remains which included the two now famous bound books of drawings, one on vellum preserved in Paris, and the other on paper in the British Museum. There has been frequent discussion of how the young men made use of these drawings, in some cases, bringing them to completion, and even using them as the basis for their own independent creations.[9] It seems not to have been observed, nevertheless, that an aspect of Giovanni's *St. Francis* composition depends rather explicitly on one of Jacopo's drawings that represents a true *Stigmatization of St. Francis*. This drawing is on two vellum sheets that fit together perfectly, as is often the case in the Paris Notebook (Fig. 2; the reproduction here shows the two halves juxtaposed).[10] The stigmatization proper is on right sheet with St. Francis in the usual kneeling position, but, typical of Jacopo's quirky variations on tradition, shown from the back facing into the pictorial space. He gazes upward to the right where the seraphic crucifix appears in the sky. The rays from Christ's wounds are directed to the five appropriate points on Francis's body but, although the hatchings in the surrounding areas are reserved, the hands have not been inked in. Brother Leo, his mouth open in concentration, sits on the ground in the lower left, reading a book, possibly a breviary. A deer, the hind quarters of an ass(?), the façade of the La Verna chapel on the right, and a rocky mount on the left, are included in the setting for the figure. None of these details is particularly pertinent for Giovanni's composition. But the left half of the drawing is extraordinarily relevant. With the other part of the rocky mount now on the right, the view opens leftward onto a deep landscape. Among the details are a reclining deer, a winding stream with bridges, and a remarkable rabbit hunt directed by a young man who commands the hounds to chase a running hare. Farther on there is a walled town and more hills in the background. The amazing thing is that there is also a creature (Fig. 3, a long-nosed rodent?), burrowed into the hill with only its head protruding. This motif, as we shall see, dramatically predicts the same arrangement for a rabbit in Giovanni's painting. Besides

7   The three are the two hands and the left foot, the right foot being hidden under the habit. Their miniscule size and subtle technical treatment indicate that the marks were never particularly emphasized.

8   The earliest accounts of Francis's experience describe it occurring while he was at prayer: *Francis of Assisi: Early Documents*, vol. 2, Bonaventure of Bagnoregio, *Major Life of St. Francis* (1260-63), 632, says: "On a certain morning about the feast of the Exaltation of the Cross [September 14], while Francis was praying on the mountainside, he saw a Seraph having six wings, fiery as well as brilliant, descend from the grandeur of heaven." Meiss (1964), 51 points out the longevity of the traditional kneeling position. See also C. Frugoni, *Francesco e l'invenzione delle stimmate: una storia per parole e immagini fino a Bonaventura e Giotto* (Turin: G. Einaudi, 1993), pls. 1, 3-5, 10-11, 13-14, 18, for thirteenth-century manuscript variations in the forms of the scene.

9   See B. Degenhart and A. Schmitt, *Jacopo Bellini, the Louvre Album of Drawings*, trans. F. Mecklenburg (New York: George Braziller, 1984). C. Eisler, *The Genius of Jacopo Bellini: the Complete Paintings and Drawing* (New York: Harry N. Abrams, 1989).

10   Degenhart (1984), 18, pl. 80-81, as folios 64v-65 [old numbers 71v-72], Louvre Inv. R. E. 1533; and Eisler (1989), 392-93, pls. 255-56, identified as lead point gone over with ink on vellum; said to be in Jacopo's "late style," i.e. 1460s.

the animal-in-the-hole, the concept of a vast, spreading landscape as a setting for St. Francis in an unconventional pose would seem to lie behind the son's version. Having digested the inspiration of Jacopo's inventive composition, moreover, Giovanni then develops his father's somewhat additive approach into a more sophisticated naturalism, and infuses it with suave and remarkably rich meaning.

The revelation of much of this meaning is owing to John V. Fleming whose 1982 study of the painting sets forth the elements of Franciscan theology, typology, and symbolism that lie behind Bellini's invention.[11] A major part of his analysis makes clear how Francis and his devotional practices were profoundly correlated to the anchorite tradition, with repeated and lengthy retreats into the solitude of the woods and mountains, including Monte La Verna where the stigmatization occurred. As Fleming says, Francis embraced the withdrawal from ordinary social life to give praise to God and combat the enemies of salvation.[12] In this light, the nomenclature "San Francesco nel Deserto" could be seen not only as apt but also as essential to what the image is meant to convey.

Yet, as useful as Fleming's work will always remain, there are fundamental art historical observations and questions that have not previously been broached. First and foremost is the question: Bellini alluded to the *Stigmatization* theme with small but blood-red nail wounds, but why is what would be an equally bloody chest wound omitted? In many stigmatization scenes otherworldly rays of light generate Francis's wounds. Flashing celestial rays here descend from the sky at the upper left but why are they directed not at St. Francis but, as I will purport, at a bending tree? Then there is the unusual underlying reciprocity between the figure of St. Francis and the landscape, in both a physical

and an iconographical sense. It is not that Bellini portrayed St. Francis in a landscape, but, as I hope to show, that he has depicted the saint as a physical entity whose spiritual force gives shape to the natural forms that surround him.

On another level, it has not been asked what contemporary Franciscan activity, particularly in the Veneto, might have entered into the motivation of the commission? What in the patron's and/or Bellini's immediate experience might have called forth this representation at this time? Whatever the content, furthermore, what function was the panel supposed to fulfill? Was it to serve a practical purpose, such as an altarpiece, or, in spite of its extraordinarily large size, does it represent a rare but growing genre of private devotional image? Some of these questions I cannot answer. But some I would like to address from a previously untried starting point: In the lagoons of Venice there is an island called "San Francesco del Deserto," and on that island there was a great deal of religious activity around the same time as the painting. Although the setting of the painting is obviously not literally an island, I will suggest that the spiritual desert defined by this island played a role in Bellini's compelling creation.

St. Francis and the Island

The island of San Francesco del Deserto is some five kilometers northeast across the lagoon from the city of Venice, quite near the tip of Isola Sant' Erasmo, in the diocese of Torcello (Fig. 4). Lush and green, today it is anything but a desert in the commonly accepted sense of the term. But true to its name, it remains an isolated place for quiet meditation and spiritual renewal. The island has been inhabited since the Middle Byzantine period, and by the early thirteenth century was

[11]   J. V. Fleming, *From Bonaventure to Bellini. An Essay in Franciscan Exegesis* (Princeton: Princeton University Press, 1982); and idem, *An Introduction to the Franciscan Literature of the Middle Ages* (Chicago: Franciscan Herald Press, 1977).
[12]   Fleming (1982), "The Desert, Moses, Elijah," 32-74.

Fig 2.

Fig 3.

Fig 4.

privately owned by a rich Venetian merchant named Iacopo Michiel. The name of the island at that time was Isola delle Due Vigne.[13] Like many of the islands in the lagoon, this one is rich in myths. But unlike the other, larger islands, all the stories here concern a visit of St. Francis of Assisi. It is said that on his way back from the Orient, Francis and a companion (Fra Illuminato), after being caught in a storm, took refuge on the island and stayed for some time; the visit is said to have occurred in 1220. While on the island, the saint built for himself a tiny dwelling of wood and rushes and a small chapel in which to pray.[14] During this time he and his companion often meditated out in the open where the birds were plentiful and constantly singing. They sang so much and so loudly, in fact, that the friars found it difficult to concentrate and bid the birds to be silent until they finished saying the hours of the Divine Office. A miracle followed in which the birds obeyed St. Francis's wishes and remained still until he released them. The locale and the miracle are considered verified by a passage in the official Life of St. Francis by the great Franciscan saint and theologian, Bonaventure of Bagnoregio (1221-d. 1274):

"Another time when he was walking with a brother through the marshes of Venice (*alio tempore...per paludes Venetiarum cum quodam fratre*) ... he came upon a large flock of birds singing among the reeds..." and so on.[15]

Other miracles St. Francis is said to have performed on the island concern a particular tree. Again Francis is described as on his way home from the Orient, this time passing first through Albania. There he took for himself the branch of a pine tree to use as a walking stick and thence proceeded northward. The story continues: "Before leaving the island, Francis planted his staff in the ground where it miraculously germinated, becoming a pine tree that grew to an extraordinary height, as one still sees it flourishing.... Today because of its outstanding height it is supported by scaffolding. And eating its fruit or soaking its bark in water and drinking the elixir with devotion, the sick are healed."[16] The huge tree, which was in the friars' cloister, when it could no longer withstand the elements, was taken down and the remains brought in to a chapel on the side of the convent church where the stump is still seen

---

[13]   The chief modern historian of the island is Francesco Ferrari, O.F.M., *Il francescanesimo nel Veneto dalle origini ai reperti di S. Francesco del deserto : appunti per una storia della provincia veneta dei frati minori* (Bologna: Documentaziones scientifica editrice, 1990), see especially 559ff.; also idem, *S. Francesco del Deserto* (Bologna: Documentaziones scientifica editrice, 1992), which is an abbreviated version of the previous citation, including only the chapters that deal directly with island. Henceforth I will refer only to the later edition. As Ferrari points out, Michiel is a very old and by now very common name in Venice; the early history of the aristocratic family included at least one Doge, namely Vitale Michiel II, in the second half of the twelfth century.

[14]   This account mirrors that of Francis taking up his abode at the Porziuncola (Santa Maria degli Angeli) and building his little dwelling with his own hands; Mario Sensi, *Il Perdono di Assisi* (Santa Maria degli Angeli: Edizioni Porziuncola, 2002), 267-326.

[15]   "When he saw them, he said to his companion: 'Our Sister Birds are praising their Creator, so we should go in among them and chant the Lord's praises and the canonical hours.' When they had entered among them, the birds did not move from the place; and on account of the noise the birds were making, they could not hear each other saying the hours. The saint turned to the birds and said: 'Sister Birds, stop singing until we have done our duty of praising God!' At once they were silent and remained in silence as long as it took the brothers to say the hours at length and to finish their praises. Then the holy man of God gave them permission to sing again. When the man of God gave them permission they immediately resumed singing in their usual way." Bonaventure, *Major Life*, vol. 2, chap. 8, ¶ 9, 592. This miracle, repeated by Bonaventure in his Sermon III on St. Francis, *Doctoris seraphici S. Bonaventurae...Opera omnia*, 10 vols. (Collegii a S. Bonaventura: Quaracchi, 1882-1902), vol. 9, 583, and is of course often compared to those that occurred in Bevagna and Alviano. It also appears in the chapter on St. Francis in the Golden Legend; Jacobus de Voragine, *The Golden Legend: Readings on the Saints*, trans. W. G. Ryan, 2 vols. (Princeton: Princeton University Press, 1993), 2: 227.

[16]   "Prima di quì partirsi piantò in Terra il suo bastone, che germogliando miracolosamente, divenne un'alberto di Pino, e crebbe poi ad una straordinaria grandezza, come tuttavia si vede sempre fruttidero, che per la sua smisurata altezza è hoggidì sostenuto da più pontelli, ed i suoi frutti mangiatai, ò posta della sua cortecciа nell'acqua, e bevuta da gl'Infermi con divotione si risanano"; Vincenzo Maria Coronelli, *Isolario, descrittione di tutte l'isole*, vol. 2, *Dell'Atlante Veneto* (Venice: the author, 1696), "Isola di S. Francesco del Deserto," 35, col. 1.

today. The present-day friars who guide visitors around the island repeat this tale, making sure to explain that it is "only a legend." It is important to recognize, however, that any story connecting St. Francis to a tree (or to wood) implicitly refers to one of the basic metaphors of Franciscan theology: the *Arbor Vitae* or Tree of Life which produced the wood of Christ's cross, and the cross of Christ was the emblematic object to which Francis directed most of his religious zeal.[17] Thus the legend of the walking stick sprouting into a beautiful tree is really about Francis bringing true religion to the island and assuring salvation for the people who come there to pray.[18] Legend or not, it is clear from various reports of the masses of worshippers who came to the island that the tree's miraculous qualities were long believed in and sought after.[19]

Taken literally, the legend presents something of a problem. In the Rule of St. Francis it is specifically stated that the friars, unless they were very old and infirm, were forbidden to wear shoes or carry a walking stick.[20] Therefore, one must assume it was believed that, after his momentous voyage to the east, Francis was so weary and ill that he found the need for physical support.

Iacopo Michiel (d. 1233) the island's owner, late in life became an avid follower of St. Francis. He and his wife Maria Gradenigo assumed marital abstinence and followed the Rule as closely as they could. Just before he died, Michiel presented the island as a gift to the Franciscan order and supported the transformation of the little buildings St. Francis had left into a church and small convent (Fig. 5).[21]

---

[17] References to St. Francis's dedication to the cross and its wood are ubiquitous in the literature. A poem quoted in apposition to the description of Fra Silvestro's vision of a golden cross coming from the mouth of St. Francis, reported by Thomas of Celano in his "Remembrance of the Desire of a Soul, or The Second Life" (*Vita Secunda*, 1245-47), *Francis of Assisi: Early Documents*, vol. 2, 320, will suffice here:

> Is it surprising/ that Francis appeared crucified/ when he was always so much with the cross? /Is it any wonder /that the wondrous cross, /taking root inside him, /and sprouting in such good soil/ should bear remarkable flowers, leaves, and fruit?/ Nothing of a different kind/ could come to be produced by such soil, which that wonderful cross from the beginning claimed/ entirely for itself.

The great fresco (now detached) *Tree of Life* from the refectory of Santa Croce in Florence, painted by Taddeo Gaddi ca. 1360 is a visual representation of this theological concept. See A. Ladis, *Taddeo Gaddi: Critical Reappraisal and Catalogue Raisonné* (Columbia, MO./London: University of Missouri Press, 1982), 171-82, no. 23, color plate p. 7.

[18] The story of the blossoming rod has its source in the Old Testament, when Aaron is chosen by the Lord as his High Priest: Book of Numbers, chap. 17: 3-10: "6. And Moses spoke to the children of Israel: and all the princes gave him rods one for every tribe: and there were twelve rods besides the rod of Aaron. 7 And when Moses had laid them up before the Lord in the tabernacle of the testimony: 8 He returned on the following day, and found that the rod of Aaron for the house of Levi, was budded: and that the buds swelling it had bloomed blossoms, which spreading the leaves, were formed into almonds." As we shall soon see, the Francis was associated with Aaron typologically as a priestly leader.

[19] Prof. Louise Bourdua (Warwick University, UK), told me about the presence of the real tree on the Island of San Francesco del Deserto, information for which I shall always be deeply grateful. The 1475 *dogale* of Pietro Mocenigo and the 1477 bull of Pope Sixtus IV mention the high attendance at the island. All of the official documents, *dogali* and bulls, I will now refer to are reproduced in Latin in Ferrari (1992), 176-82. I provide English translations of the documents in my 2007 publication, 249-52.

[20] "It was the third year of his conversion when he began to repair this church. At this time he wore a kind of hermit's dress, with a leather girdle about his waist; he carried a staff in his hands and wore shoes on his feet. One day the gospel was being read in that church about how the Lord sent out his disciples to preach. The holy man of God, who was attending there, in order to understand better the words of the gospel, humbly begged the priest after celebrating the solemnities of the Mass to explain the gospel to him. The priest explained it all to him thoroughly line by line. When he heard that Christ's disciples should not possess gold or silver or money, or carry on their journey a wallet or a sack, nor bread nor a staff, nor to have shoes nor two tunics, but that they should preach the kingdom of God and penance, the holy man, Francis, immediately exulted in the spirit of God. "This is what I want," he said, "this is what I seek, this is what I desire with all my heart." The holy father, overflowing with joy, hastened to implement the words of salvation, and did not delay before he devoutly began to put into effect what he heard. Immediately, he took off the shoes from his feet, put down the staff from his hands, and, satisfied with one tunic, exchanged his leather belt for a cord. After this, he made for himself a tunic showing the image of the cross, so that in it he would drive off every fantasy of the demon." *Francis of Assisi: Early Documents*, vol. 3, "The Life of Saint Francis by Thomas of Celano" (*Vita Prima*, 1229), 201-02. Francis himself mentioned the prohibition of the walking stick in the second version of his Rule: *Francis of Assisi: Early Documents*, vol. 1, "*The Earlier Rule*" (1209/10-1221), 73. See below, further to this discussion.

[21] All these transactions are documented in Iacopo's testament, 4 March 1233; see Ferrari (1992), 157-166, for documentation of Iacopo Michiel's life, and p. 175 for the legal document of Michiel's donation.

The history of the island during the next two hundred years is based on chronicle accounts by Doge Andrea Dandolo, Doge Francesco Foscari, Marino Sanudo, F. Gonzaga, Francesco Sansovino, and Luke Wadding, which are gathered together in the publications of Father Ferrari.[22] In these years during which Conventual Franciscans lived in the convent in relative peace, the actual name used to designate the locale went through a number of changes. It is referred to as: S. Franciscus de Maiorbio (or de Maçorbo); S. Franciscus de Burano (or de Buriano de Mari); S. Franciscus in Insula (or de Insula, or de Ysolella); and S. Franciscus de Vinea (or S. Franciscus de Contrata [or de Contratis, or Contratarum, or de la Contrade]). The title S. Franciscus de Vinea persisted into the fifteenth century; it is this name that appears in the 1401 testament of the noble matron, Frangola Giustinian [wife of Francesco], who left a legacy of twenty gold ducats to be used to restore the convent and to receive her tomb monument just inside the church portal.[23] Some time later, the island experienced an infestation of malaria and the Conventual community transferred into the city of Venice, to the convent of San Marco della Vigna, the name of which then became San Francesco della Vigna.[24] By the mid 1440s, malaria had rendered the island uninhabitable.[25] It is probable that the title *San Francesco del Deserto*, said to be "di origine popolare" arose during this period when the island was completely abandoned.[26]

The Island and the Osservanza

After a period of desolation and after the epidemic subsided, concern for the island was rekindled in a most spectacular way. All during the years of the island's degradation a new movement was germinating within the Franciscan order. This was the return to the strict rule of St. Francis preached by St. Bernardine of Siena (1380-1444), and codified as the *Riformazioni di frate Bernardino*. By the time Bernardine died and was canonized (1450), his followers, called the Observants or Osservanti, had grown in number almost with the same intensity as the order itself had spread in the early thirteenth century. Four times Bernardine came to Venice and moved the populace with his charismatic sermons, causing a dramatic mass conversion to the Osservanza, including that of the Conventual Franciscan community at San Francesco della Vigna and the church of San Giobbe.[27] Following his death, Bernardine's preaching campaign was carried on by the newly elected Vicar General of the order and equally magnetic speaker, John Capistran (1386–1456). Making heresy and anti-Turkish

---

[22]　Ferrari (1992), 187-97.

[23]　The tomb was dismantled and its parts used for various structural members during the nineteenth-century rebuilding. See Anton-Maria da Vicenza [Padre Lettore, Cronologo della Rif. Prov. Veneta], *Memorie storiche del convento e della chiesa di San Francesco del Deserto, nelle lagune di Venezia, pubblicate nell'occasione che la religiosa famiglia dei minori reformati vi rientra ad abitare* (Venice: Tip. G. Merlo, 1865), 39-41, quoting Luke Wadding. See also Ferrari (1992), 70.

[24]　Ferrari (1992), 62-67, documents these name changes.

[25]　Here is Anton-Maria da Vicenza's description, loc.cit.: "incuria e negligenza, ridotti a tanta desolazione e squallore, che i fabbricati già minaccianti rovina, e la chiesa trovavasi affatto spoglia d'ogni ornamento e di quanto era necessario del divin culto; e che anzi dal non celebrarvisi I divini Uffizi, quell luogo era divenuto quasi profane…."

[26]　Cf. Ferrari (1992), 62.

[27]　Bernardine was in Venice in 1405, 1422, 1429, and a year before he died, in 1443. He was associated with the island in the chronicle of Sansovino (1663), who claimed that he traveled to the island and performed a miracle by cleansing the water in one of the courtyard wells. Ferrari (1992), p. 71, n.3. believes the journey was probably to another island in the lagoon. See P. Bargellini, *San Bernardino da Siena* (Brescia: Morcelliana, 1934); G. P. Thureau-Dangin, *The Life of S. Bernardino of Siena*, annot. G. F. Hill (Boston/London: P.L. Warner, 1911); J. Moorman, *The History of the Franciscan Order* (Oxford: Clarendon Press, 1968), 457-66. In 1470, St. Bernardine was declared patron of Venice; see S. Tramontin, "Il 'Kalendarium' veneziano," in *Culto dei santi a Venezia*, ed. S. Tramontin, 2 vols. (Venice: Edizioni Studium Cattolico Veneziano, 1965), 2:299, with an altar dedicated to him in S. Marco.

propaganda his major themes, Capistran became known as a great theologian, an expert in canon law, and, surprisingly, as a skillful soldier.[28] During his trips to Venice he was apprised of the situation on the Island of San Francesco, and no doubt recognized the opportunity to expand Observant influence in the region. His fame brought him access to Doge Francesco Foscari (in office 1423-1457), with whom he must have discussed the island's miserable state. In response, Francesco Foscari issued a formal proclamation (*dogale*). Although a rebuilding campaign on the island had probably started two years earlier, Foscari lifted a previous proscription and conceded to the *frati minori dell'osservanza* permission to beg and collect alms throughout the territory of the Republic. He states that the purpose of such begging was to restore the divine worship and continuous prayer following the rule of the Osservanza, and to amplify the church and monastery of S. Francesco del Deserto.[29] Capistran continued his petition back in Rome, voicing his concern for the convent directly to the pope, Nicholas V (1447-1455), who granted possession of the island specifically to the Observant Franciscans, but did so only verbally. An Observant friar, Nicolò Erizzo, member of an aristocratic Venetian family, was appointed to oversee the work, and a number of friars from San Francesco della Vigna moved out to the island to carry it out. The restoration took nine years to complete. The most important changes made to the buildings in this campaign were 1) the construction of the apse; 2) the addition of a chapel dedicated to St. Bernardine off the left side of the nave and 3) the refurnishing of the adjacent Byzantine chapel now dedicated to the Virgin. A small, walled area between the latter and the main apse was retained to designate the space of St. Francis's original tiny dwelling/chapel.[30]

In celebration of the completion of the campaign, Pope Pius II issued a bull, *Ad perpetuam rei memoriam*, dated 9 September 1460, granting the Observant friars permanent and now juridical possession of the island. He emphasizes this point using language that, even if it is rhetorical and conventional, seems surprisingly strong. He states that the monastery had reached a "point of devastation and calamity through the carelessness and negligence of its overseers [the Conventuals]," and that the buildings had "suffered miserable collapse," and were "despoiled and deprived of their ornaments and liturgical instruments." He further reports that in its inability of offer Divine Worship, the place had become "almost profane and open to illicit dealings." [31] The piety of the Observant friars, he promises, would counteract these evils, and he remarks that their rule included saying the Divine Office night and day, a devotion that seems to have been specific to this faction of the order at this time.[32] Ostensibly, the bull responds to a petition of three noble Venetian citizens and Observant devotees, Ludovico Lando, Francesco Lipomanno

---

28 Under Pope Calixtus III in 1456 John Capistran was put in charge of a military campaign against a Muslim army operating in the Balkans, and he played an active role in the defense of Belgrade on the River Danube. He died in an epidemic that swept through the army almost immediately after the battle. He was canonized in 1690. See P. Petrecca, *San Giovanni da Capestrano* (Florence: Atheneum, 1992).

29 The proclamation is dated 26 June 1453.

30 Many other changes were made during the following centuries including raising the floor level (there are now grates in the floor to allow views of the level of the earlier building), and the addition of a Mary chapel that forms a second apse, parallel to the main sanctuary. This architectural history is studied by Ferrari (1992), chap. 11, and Appendix, 201-219, including ground plans of the various stages of the buildings and courtyards as they were revealed during formal excavations carried out in the 1960s.

31 There is an inscription on the façade of the entrance to the monastery listing the prohibitions on the island of illicit things, such a swearing, dancing, and game playing.

32 The practice was continued by the Cappuchins; cf. Servus Gieben, "La cultura materiale dei cappuccini nel primo secolo (1525-1619)," in *Collectanea Franciscana* 69 (1999): 145-173, esp. 166-73, and *idem*, "La vita quotidiana nei conventi," in *I Cappuccini in Emilia-Romagna. Storia di una presenza*, eds. G. Pozzi and P. Prodi (Bologna: EDB, 2002), 198-215, esp. 198-99.

and Tomaso Mocenigo, who ask for permission to finance the project. The pope agrees and since the project will "bring about the increase of divine worship, the propagation of religion, and the consolation of persons devoted to us and to the Apostolic See," he grants the petitioners permission. In recognizing Fra Nicolò Erizzo as the project manager he notes that while Pope Nicholas V had given permission for the project, no written documents had been obtained. Pius therefore continues, again using surprisingly strong words, by clarifying the line of authority over the Osservanti in order to quell anyone from trying to reinstate the Conventuals. Such a move, he says, would cause "devotion of the faithful (to) cease," and "scandals between two factions (to) arise." He ends by threatening that if the Conventuals try to interfere, even if his commands are contrary to tradition, it would bring down the wrath of "omnipotent God and the Holy Apostles Peter and Paul."

Two months later, Pius issued a second bull directed to the ruling authorities of the order in the Veneto (Provincia di San Antonio da Padova), the Vicar General and Provincial Vicar, telling them he had written to the "guardiani " of two Observant churches in Venice, San Francesco della Vigna and San Giobbe, confirming that he had made the Osservanti sole possessors of the island, and repeating that he had done so because the Conventuals had "ruined, despoiled, and deserted the place." He enjoins the overseers to carry out his orders, not withstanding "certain others (doing) the contrary."[33]

Six years later, the monastery was in full function and frequently visited by the faithful. The then reigning pope, Paul II (1464 to 1471), states in his bull of 8 July 1466, that in seeking "to enhance the spiritual rewards for visitors to the church," which he calls S. Francisci de Contrata, he was establishing an indulgence for the remission of seven years and seven quadragenas to those who come to the island on the Feast of the Stigmata, September 17, from First Vespers to Second Vespers.[34] He then changes the name of the church (but not the island) to *S. Francisci de Stigmatibus*, or St. Francis of the Stigmata, a rather unusual dedication at this time.[35]

In 1474 Pietro Mocenigo, a relative of one of the supporters of the restoration campaign, was appointed doge, and a year later, on 2 June 1475, he noted that the island sanctuary "has come to such a point of devotion and celebrity" that it should "be developed from a good state to a better one and be increased in its devotion." He therefore renews the beneficent concession of his predecessor Francesco Foscari, reconfirming the "begging privileges to the friars of S. Francesco del Deserto," and further relieving them of all taxes.[36]

Papal generosity to the island then continued when Pope Sixtus IV (1471-1483), himself a Franciscan friar, emitted a bull on 13 December 1477 defining reasons it was preferable to worship in a church dedicated to St. Francis. This was especially true because of the saint's eternal blessedness which

---

[33] The exchanging of houses was a wide-spread issue in the order during most of the fifteenth century; see Moorman (1968), 489-90. The difficulties between Conventuals and Observants came to a head in the early sixteenth century and the Observants were recognized officially as the dominant faction of the order in 1517 under Pope Leo X. See ibid., 479-500, 569-85; R. Goffen, *Piety and Patronage in Renaissance Venice: Bellini, Titian, and the Franciscans* (New Haven: Yale University Press, 1986), 80-82, provides a succinct précis of the situation.

[34] The Feast of the Stigmata was established for Franciscans in the fourteenth century under either Benedict XI (1303-04) or Benedict XII (1334-42). It was expanded for the universal church under Paul V 1615, at the insistence of Cardinal Bellarmino, and later made a double. See the *Enciclopedia Cattolica*, 12 vols.(Città del Vaticano: Ente per l'Enciclopedia cattolica e per il Libro cattolico, 1949-1954), vol. 11: col 1344. The *quadragenas* or "forty blows but one" (hence 7 times 39) was a common form of punishment suffered by St. Paul who mentions it in 2 Cor 11:25. In the Middle Ages it seems to have come to mean forty days of penance.

[35] Aside from the chapel dedicated to the Stigmata in Santa Maria degli Angeli in La Verna itself, where the miracle took place, I have not found a single church with this dedication that dates before the mid-16th century.

[36] In the same year the Senate of Venice declared the Feast of St. Francis (October 4) was to be marked with a public celebration; Tramontin (1965), 2:316.

had allowed a lowly novice like Sixtus himself to rise to the "height of the highest apostleship." Thus he wishes the church dedicated to the "Saint of the Stigmata, also known as del Deserto", to bring increased refreshment to the Venetian people who "gladly flock there in copious numbers," having it do so by heightening the indulgence for visiting the island. All individuals of either sex who came to the island on the Feast day would now receive indulgence for one quarter of all their sins, provided they have no previous remissions for the same sins.[37]

The monastery became the focal point for Observant order when in 1480 it offered hospitality to all the friars who participated in the Provincial Chapter. During this meeting, another famous Observant preacher, Fra Bernardine of Feltre, was elected as "definitore" of the order.[38] It is quite possible, furthermore, that all the commotion in relation to the island and the amplified presence of the Osservanza helped to bring about the 1485 publication of Ubertino da Casale's controversial book *Arbor vitae crucifixae* (Venice: Andrea da Bonetis), virtually suppressed for more than a century but deeply influential on the thought and preaching of St. Bernardine of Siena.[39]

One last significant development occurred at San Francesco del Deserto during this period. Ludovico Lando, one of the original patrons of the rehabilitation campaign, expected the chapel dedicated to St. Bernardine for which he had provided funds, to be his own and his family's mortuary chapel. When he died (the precise date is unknown) his intension was recorded on his tomb.

The ownership of the chapel then went to Alvise Lando, apparently Ludovico's son, who mentions it in his own will. Stated there is the fact that Alvise leaves the chapel to his son-in-law, his universal heir whom he designates as a *nobile*, by the name of Pietro Bembo. This Bembo, who was certainly not the famous humanist/cardinal (1470-1547), decided not to be buried on the island and in 1485 renounced all claim to the chapel and gave it to the resident friars.[40]

The conclusion from this historical account is that during the span of years in which it is most likely that Giovanni Bellini painted his *St. Francis in the Desert*, the revitalization of the convent island and the devolvement of its supervision to the Observant Franciscans was under the direct patronage of the Vatican, several Venetian doges, and for the spiritual benefit of Venetian citizens. Any major Venetian artistic commission concerned with Franciscan matters could hardly fail to take this state of affairs into consideration.

The Island, the Osservanza and the Painting

I hasten to say that no evidence has come to light connecting Bellini's commission directly to the island. There is, however, much internal visual evidence that seems to bring them together. First it should be said that there are enough elements drawn from the iconography of the stigmatization to reference the recent rededication of the church on the island. But by the same token, the features I have noted as missing

---

[37]   Under the watch of Sixtus IV on April 4, 1482, Bonaventure of Bagnoregio was finally canonized. Fleming (1982), 161-62 discusses the view that Bonaventure's canonization could be relevant to the manufacture of Bellini's painting. His argument is weakened by the general consensus that the painting predated this event. See further to this point below in the text.

[38]   This Bernardine (1439-1494, real name Martino Tomitani) became the great promulgator of the Mons Pietatis, the Church-run banks created to quell the success of Jewish pawnbrokers.

[39]   Again Fleming (1982), 161-62, mentions this event as a possible factor in the motivation of the commission, whereas I am suggesting that the stimulus worked the other way around.

[40]   After the transfer, the chapel, which was later rededicated to the Resurrection and then to St. Antonio, was used for monastic burials. See Ferrari (1992), 79-81.

from the traditional subject matter are sufficient to show that, while alluding to it, Bellini has not represented the moment of the miracle.[41] At the same time, along with allusions to the major miracle he also refers to many other sacred experiences in the life of St. Francis, all with the same level of emphatic reserve. Evidently, therefore, his mission was of a larger scope than to represent any one episode or occasion. In fact, I believe that Bellini has encapsulated multiple pious incidents in the saint's life into one composition for the purpose of presenting a kind of summa of Francis's mystical beliefs and aspirations.

Fundamental to recognizing the visual cues within the painting's glorious naturalism is what Fleming calls Franciscan "Biblicism," and Bonaventure's "theology of history," that is, the spiritual bond between Francis and the Old Testament patriarchs and prophets, as well as between Francis and Christ. The most pervasive of the Old Testament parallels, or types as they are called, is with Moses (and to some extent Aaron), as described throughout the biographies of Thomas of Celano and Bonaventure of Bagnoregio. The parallels are definitive: Francis on Mount La Verna followed Moses on Mount Horeb in experiencing direct contact with God; Francis shared with Moses (along with Aaron), the role of law-giver, the Rule of the order paralleling the Tablets of the Commandments. As Moses led his people through the desert to the Promised Land, so Francis provided his followers with the way to salvation.[42]

This last Mosaic allusion begins the journey into the pictorial space at the extreme right of the composition moving leftward in sharp perspective. Entrance is through a little hut, the object closest to the picture plane (Fig. 6). Built against the outside face of a rock cave, the room is covered by leaves and vines supported by wooden staves. Fleming posits that this rudimentary shelter recalls the sukkah Moses ordered to be built by the Israelites to celebrate their survival in the desert.[43] The workmanship of this flimsy construction is painted in amazing detail. Bellini has meticulously differentiated the wood of all four rough hewn staves; three are trees, one is a vine. The mixed materials are reminiscent of Jacob of Voragine's descriptions of Christ's cross in the *Golden Legend*, where it is said to have been made of four types of wood.[44] The inner chamber in the rock is partitioned by a gate made of carefully woven sprouting reeds. With the carpentry lectern and a 'misericordia' seat Bellini displays Francis's scrupulous craftsmanship.[45] With beautifully planed and doweled planks, he provided tools for his penance: on the slanted front of the lectern is a closed book bound in red leather.[46] Quite possibly, the book is a breviary in reference to Francis's re-editing of the Divine Office, the prayers said in private at various hours, into a convenient single volume friars could carry with them as they moved about.[47] Hanging on a branch above the book is a rope-driven bell to sound the hours of the Divine Office. On the upper

---

[41]   Hale (2011) shows that the panel was shaved no more than a few centimeters at the top, and concludes that there never was any space that could have accommodated the representation of a seraph, proving the subject of the painting is not a *Stigmatization*.

[42]   Fleming (1982), *passim*. Among the myriad references in Bonaventure's writings, see his Sermon 10, "On the Feast of the Transferal of the Body of St. Francis from San Giorgio in Assisi to the Basilica of San Francesco" (1267), *Francis of Assisi: Early Documents*, vol. 2, 737-46, esp. 742, 745.

[43]   Fleming (1982), 75-98. This occasion is remembered in the Feast of *Sukkot* or *Tabernacles* (Leviticus 23:42). Down to the present day, the Sukkah is required to have a penetrable roof through which one can see the stars. I point out that the shack could also recall Francis's Porziuncola shack in the Spoletine valley; see above.

[44]   Namely, palm, cedar, cypress, and olive. Jacob attributes this information to Gregory of Tours; Voragine (1993), 1: 278. The vine that bends to provide the roof has often been said to symbolize the Eucharist.

[45]   Hale (2011) found that Bellini corrected his own underdrawings here, adjusting the perspective, and adding the shelf, cross and skull over other previously designed details.

[46]   According to Hale (2011), the red hue of the book was originally somewhat brighter.

[47]   E. J. Quigley, *The Divine Office: a Study of the Roman Breviary* (Dublin: M.H. Gill, 1920), Chapter 2. This modified Roman Breviary was adopted officially under Nicholas III (1277-1280).

Fig 5.

Fig 7.

Fig 9.

Fig 10.

Fig 6.

Fig 8.

shelf of the lecture is a human skull. The death's head is placed like the skull of Adam frequently seen at the foot of the cross in *Crucifixion* scenes, designating Calvary, the tomb of the original sinner replaced by Christ through his sacrifice. The cross itself is devotional, without a corpus, and with a very long thin stem that reaches to the ground; at the crossbar hangs a crown of thorns, the painful instrument that mocked Christ as "king of the Jews," before his crucifixion. These symbols of the passion characterize the deepest aspect of Francis's devotion, as he strove to emulate his beloved savior. Moreover there is tangible evidence that Francis was aware of the symbolic juxtaposition of cross and skull. He used it himself in his drawing of a Tau-shaped cross with skull on the parchment known as the chartula (Fig. 7) preserved at the Sacro Convento in Assisi.[48] All these attributes and their functions call to mind the dwelling/chapel Francis himself is said to have built after his arrival on the island in the Venetian lagoon.

Within this sacral hut, a bent-handled walking stick and a pair of clogs (*zoccoli*) lie on the ground near the base of the lectern. As previously mentioned, according to the Rule of the St. Francis, these particular physical aids are strictly forbidden for use by any but the most infirm friars; their presence here surely alludes to this regulation. Late in life Francis was plagued by many painful illnesses and is said to have suffered from them more and more each day as his life came to a close. Because of his weakness he is frequently described as being in need of these very supports. In the painting,

however, he seems rejuvenated, almost robust, which in turn might explain their disuse here. The discarded zoccoli, in fact, are not only another reference to Moses, they also emphasize Francis's bare feet, an element that will be mentioned again below. At the same time, the cane brings to mind the legend of the auspicious walking stick that Francis brought with him to the island and planted in the ground as he left. This reference too will be discussed further on, in relation to the bending tree on the opposite side of the composition.

Just outside the hut is a little garden, raised up by four courses of worked stones (Fig. 8). The artist's vast knowledge of botany evinced here was surely nurtured in his father's shop, where isolated plant and animal studies abound. Giovanni's representation of plants as growing organisms might be thought of as highly evolved versions of what Otto Pächt called "plant portraits," that is, scientific specimens aesthetically conceived in their natural settings.[49] But having achieved this technique, he proceeded to go beyond naturalism. The plants in this plot, and elsewhere in the painting, are so realistically rendered that Meiss, long ago, was able to identify most of them.[50] What Meiss did not say is that they are all those that would be found together in a convent garden, grown for use in cooking but more importantly for making medicine. The stalky leaves in the right corner are orris, or *iris germanica*, the root of which makes tea used for its diuretic, emetic, and cathartic properties and to treat bronchitis, colds, coughs, diarrhea and dropsy. It is still used to strengthen gums and

[48]   Fleming, moreover, refers to this same autograph document to explain the apparent absence from the scene of Brother Leo: he identifies the object tucked in Francis's rope belt as the folded parchment *chartula* on which, besides the sign of the cross, Francis wrote the Laud, *Tu es sanctus Dominus Deus*. He wrote this Laud for Brother Leo when they were in the wilderness together and Leo was having a difficult time concentrating on his prayers. In this way, Bellini rendered Leo present, at least in spirit; Fleming (1982), 99-112, figs. 24 and 25. According to Hale (2011) there are a few marks in color on the object folded into Francis's cord belt, but nothing legible.
[49]   See Otto Pächt's essential article on this subject: "Early Italian Nature Stories and the Early Calendar Landscape," *Journal of the Warburg and Courtauld Institutes* 13, no. 1/2 (1950): 13-47. This article includes a description of the history of medical manuals, listing plants and the remedies they provided, starting in antiquity and coming to a climax in the early fifteenth century (25-37).
[50]   Meiss (1964), 15f.

freshen the breath.[51] The tall, straight plant, fleshy green leaves below and paired yellow blooms above, is mullein, or *verbascum thapsus*, sometimes called "Jacob's staff."[52] The leaf is used for respiratory disorders, warts, earaches, intestinal cramps, and painful, inflamed skin injuries. Remembering Francis's illnesses, these plants are all things he himself would have put to medicinal use.[53] They are also things that Francis loved, which he spoke about and often stopped to admire.[54] Behind the mullein plant is a bush of green juniper, found commonly throughout Europe, furnishing food, fuel, and wood for shelter and utensils. Fleming points out that the juniper alludes to the prophet Elijah, a typological forerunner of Francis, who lay beneath a juniper bush in the desert and was refreshed with cakes and water brought by an angel (I Kings 19).[55]

As the parapet wall curves around toward the left, there begins a grouping of naturalistic details, aligned in an upward-moving vertical column, all of which are formed by Franciscan concepts (Fig. 9). Under the folds of Francis's right sleeve is the rabbit mentioned earlier, peeking out of an improbably small opening in the stones. As we have seen, Jacopo Bellini provided his son with an intriguing prototype for the motif, but not the species (Fig. 3). Giovanni follows his father's lead but clearly identifies the animal as a rabbit, or hare (*Lepus*). As explained by Fleming, the rabbit, symbolically speaking, is Moses, and as such is the forerunner of Francis. The idea stems from a passage in Exodus in which God speaks to Moses:

> And when my glory shall pass, I will set thee in a hole of the rock, and protect thee with my right-hand till I pass: And I will take away my hand, and thou shalt see my back parts: but my face thou canst not see. (Ex. 33: 22-23)

Commenting on this passage St. Jerome remarks: "The rocks are the refuge for rabbits… Whence it is said of Moses at the time when he fled Egypt and was the little rabbit of the Lord." [56] This remark produced a long tradition which includes at least one ingenious representation of Moses himself in the "hole of the rock" (Fig. 10); the fourteenth-century illumination shows Moses crouching, partially in a hole with his head protruding, observing God from behind.[57] Bellini continues this tradition, presenting the mild, voiceless creature as a reference to Moses in his conversation with the Lord, and predicting the colloquy in which Francis is engaged.

The underlying point of the typological parallel with Moses is to prove how Christianity superseded Judaism and to show Francis's role in the supersession. The people Moses led out of bondage understood the power of God without recognizing the Messiah. The result was that their religion withered and dried. Bellini expressed this

---

51 Orris root can also be used for colic and liver congestion. Oil made from the root is still used in cosmetics and perfumes. It was used to treat bad breath and to treat water retention. It is no longer used internally, although it is still a common ingredient in talcum powders.

52 Also called Flannel leaf, Grandmother's flannel, or Bunny's Ears. The information concerning the medicinal use of the plants mentioned here is discussed by M. Grieve, *A Modern Herbal*, 2 vols. (London: J. Cape, 1931).

53 See below for further remarks on the illnesses of St. Francis.

54 See *Francis of Assisi: Early Documents*, vol. 3, Celano, "First Life," chap. XXVIII, ¶81, 251.

55 Fleming associates the health-giving water jug nearby on the ground with the same reference. But it could as easily refer to the Virgin Mary, chief patron of Francis and his constant spiritual companion, one of whose epithets is the "Spiritual vessel (Pray for us)," from the Litany of Loreto (or the Litany of the Blessed Virgin).

56 Fleming (1982), 60, where St. Jerome's passage is given: *lepusculus Domini*.

57 François Avril, *Manuscript Painting at the Court of France, the Fourteenth century (1310-1380)*, trans. Bruce Benderson (New York: George Braziller, 1978), no. XX, 36-37, 114, pl. 38. The manuscript contains the Pentateuch, the Historical Books, the Hagiographa, and the Prophets, each represented on fol. 1 in separate, tiny scenes. The books that are included in our Fig. 10 represent the Pentateuch.

concept in the dried and hacked off stump of a fig tree, backed by thorny brier, at the end of the parapet. The stump betokens the decay of the once flourishing religion of the Jews.[58] The Christian replacement takes the form of an even more impressive emblem of the supersession in a second ligneous image, directly above the rabbit. Here is one of Bellini's most inspired representations, and surely the most prodigious of all Fleming's recognitions. From another stump there springs a thin, almost spindly young sprout, affixed to the old dried plant with a grafting knot (Fig. 11).[59] This small knot holds a young olive branch (the scion of Christianity to the old stalk, the broken staddle of the Jews [Romans 11:23-26]).[60] The flourishing sapling is contrasted to the utterly dry tree just beyond the sanctuary area, and is parallel to the upright figure of Francis. Through his inventive composition, and the guidance of Franciscan sources, Bellini is thus generating a theological landscape that embraces Francis, literally and figuratively.

The embrace continues. Meiss noted that the rock cliff behind Francis reflects the shape of the saint's body (Fig.11). He found the source of this motif in a passage appended to the *Little Flowers of St. Francis*. The story describes how, while on a mountain top, Francis was tempted by the devil and tried to escape by turning toward the solid rock wall. Suddenly the rock "opened and received his body within it; and, as if he had placed his hands and face in liquid wax; the form of the hands and face of St. Francis remained impressed upon the stone; and thus, with the help of God, he escaped out of the hands of the devil."[61] Bellini enlarged the account by representing the declivity in the rock in the shape not only of the upper body but also Francis's two outstretched arms, confirming and emphasizing the cruciform shape. But he did not stop here.

As we have noted, the saint's protruding left foot is bare. The obvious allusion is to the rule against wearing shoes and to the strict adherence to this rule revived and promulgated by the Observant movement. Bellini insists upon the importance of this regulation by forming the rocky habitat into the shape of Francis's bare foot: the hill behind the saint seems to ooze downward in a lava-like flow, forming the same motif as the bare foot with all the toes included (Fig. 12).[62] This emulation even incorporates the shape of the hem of Francis's habit in the sun-dried brush that covers the surface. The general outline of this 'petrapod' is repeated further down the slope in a larger, less organized but still recognizable reflection of the original form. The rule of the discalced friars thus is likewise the rule of the rocks.

The general shape of the limestone cliffs rising behind the mesa has been specifically correlated with the cliffs at La Verna, where Francis often retired to find the much sought after solitude for his meditation and penance, and where he is said to have received the marks of the Stigmata two years before his death.[63]

---

[58]　Fleming (1982), 150-52.

[59]　Hale (2011) found a similar tiny knot represented in the cord of the bell in Francis's study, which she interprets as a naturalistic detail to make the cord easier to pull.

[60]　See Fleming (1982), 152, for Bonaventure's discussion of this metaphor on the basis of Augustine, who discusses Paul's agronomy.

[61]　The locale became a pilgrimage site, as the rest of the account proclaims. Meiss (1964), 24, refers to *Fioretti: Considerazioni sulle Sacre Sante Stimmate*, ed. F. Casolini (Milan: Mondadori, 1926), 232. The English translation he gives is from the Everyman's Library edition (New York: Dutton, 1951), 148. See now: *Francis of Assisi: Early Documents*, vol. 3, 566-658, where the appended passage is not included.

[62]　These areas contrast in color with the more prismatic white hills and cliffs, as though they consisted of slightly difference materials, as congealed lava would contrast with sedimentary limestone. Hale (2011) notes that their bluish-green color results from the addition of azurite pigment. See below for Bellini's use of lapis blue.

[63]　Meiss (1964), 22.

Fig 11.

Fig 12.

Fig 13.

Fig 14.

Fig 15.

The rest of the landscape, however, resembles little of the Tuscan countryside. The flat fields below the hillside open on to a view of a walled town with its castle dominating from above. The town is approached by an arch-supported bridge over a substantial river flowing toward the right.[64] After one bend, the river is dammed by a rocky sluice channeling the level of the water to drop and flow toward the sea (Fig. 15). We note here that the radiance descending from the upper left corner of the painting, naturalistically causes shadows that fall to the right (i.e. behind Francis) at an angle that implies the sun's rays are emanating from the south at mid-morning. Thus the river flowing toward the right heads eastward. In the northeast of Italy that would be toward the Adriatic sea. What Bellini has done is to transport an allusion to the sacred locale of La Verna, north and eastward, bringing its pertinence and efficacy to the land of the Veneto.[65]

The nearby water in the Venetian "desert" has attracted two avian creatures, hardly the song birds that greeted Francis on the island and interrupted his prayers. They are, nonetheless, water birds that dwell in the marsh lands, as the story describes. Again Bellini has abstracted from the narrative and added to the meaning. Both birds, carefully rendered, are members of the heron family, one large, one small. In the lower left foreground a shy bittern (*Ixobrychus minutus*) sits on the branch of a dry tree (Fig. 14).[66] This type of bird spends most of the time picking its way quietly through the densest marshes, looking for frogs and other small semi-aquatic creatures. Bellini shows the bittern raising its beak in a characteristic pose to drink from a stream that spews from a clay spout protruding unnaturally from a ridge in the hill. "Water springing from the rock" has been associated with the miracle Francis performed for the thirsty man, and further, as another parallel with Moses when he struck water from the rock of Horeb.[67]

In spite of the beauty Bellini gives it, the bittern is one of the unworthy birds named by Isaiah [34: 11] as inhabiting the remains of Zion after the day of God's vengeance against its wickedness. The bird thus represents the Christian Zion for which Francis entered the desert of penance where he is said ceaselessly to mourn and pray. It may have been a penitential gesture that led Bellini to place his own signature on the same dry tree that holds the little bird. Penance is further symbolized by the other marsh bird, the tall grey heron standing out in the open on the ledge in the middle distance (Fig. 15).[68] As told by Hugh of St. Victor, the heron shuns carrion "as the righteous in the corrupt world," living the hermitic life and offering penance for the souls of the elect.[69] The heron shares it color and its meaning with the nearby donkey standing in attendance with its ear up in a listening position (see Fig. 13). This *asinello* has been called the *onager*, or wild ass, identified by Joachim of Fiore as the "spiritual man of the third status."[70] Most pertinent

---

[64]   Hale (2011) found changes from the underdrawing in the shape of the bridge.

[65]   Turner (1966), 59-65, proposes that the setting is Venetian rather than Tuscan.

[66]   Pächt (1950) again describes the visual traditions that led to the closely observed representation of birds. The identification of the bittern is owing to Meiss (1964), 65-67, a consummate birdwatcher, who observes that while represented in a very realistic manner, it lacks the usual creamy streak in wing area. Keith Christiansen (2011) identifies this bird as a kingfisher (many geni, one of which is *Halcyon* [from the Greek myth of Alcyone] noted as very colorful, often characteristically blue).

[67]   Francis's miracle of drawing water from the rock is found in Bonaventure of Bagnoregio, "The Minor Legend of Saint Francis" (1260-1263), chap. 5, Third Lesson, in *Francis of Assisi: Early Documents*, vol. 2, 705; the Mosaic story is Exodus 17:6.

[68]   Meiss said it is "apparently *Ardea cinerea*, but lacking its crest"; see next note.

[69]   Migne, Pat. lat., vol. 177, col. 47; see E. P. Evans, *Animal Symbolism in Ecclesiastical Architecture* (London: W. Heinemann, 1896), 148, cited by Meiss (1964), note 67.

[70]   Other suggestions are that it is the donkey ridden several times by Francis when he was ill and frail, and most particularly the one from which he dismounted to supply miraculously the water for his thirsty attendant. See above note. 67.

are Fleming's citation of St. Bonaventure's sermonizing on the animal, and associating it with two principal Franciscan disciplines: penance and poverty in the hermitic life.[71]

The final element on the plateau with Francis is the misshapen tree (Fig. 16), probably the most extraordinary component of the picture. The trunk in its lower part is tall and straight, but as it separates into two branches, it bends backwards in an unnatural curve. The thick cluster of leaves sprouting at the top, curve back in the opposite direction. It is as though the tree has been knocked back and is contracting in the middle as if responding to a direct blow. The contortion responds to the series of glowing rays of golden light that emanate from a hidden source beyond the upper left corner of the painting, usually associated with the rays that burned the stigmata into the Francis's flesh. I deny this association, and I do so primarily because the rays (if one follows their trajectory carefully) are not directed at the figure of the saint but at the tree and at its peculiar gyrations (Fig. 16).[72] And further, where the rays strike, the dark green leaves are bleached to a much lighter, almost beige color.[73]

There are a series of allusions in this image:
1) The mere existence of a tall, miraculously performing tree brings to mind the story of the life-giving tree that sprouted from Francis's walking stick as he was about to leave the island in the lagoon.[74] Again, Bellini has taken his start from a traditional story and expanded it for a new purpose.

2) He transforms the tree of the story from a lowly pine into a laurel, *laurus nobilis*, the leaves of which symbolize glory everlasting. In antiquity laurel was used for the wreaths rewarding superior athletes, statesmen, philosophers and poets. One of the reasons it was chosen for this honor was its ability to burn without being consumed. With this shift, the scorched but not consumed leaves of the tree evoke the first contact between Moses and God in which "the Lord (whose face he does not see) appeared to him in flames of fire out of the midst of a (laurel) bush; and he saw that the bush was on fire and was not burnt."

3) This was the very moment God told Moses: "Come not nigh hither, put off the shoes from thy feet: for the place whereon thou standest is holy ground." (Exodus 3:5).[75] Hence the abandoned *zoccoli* outside Francis's hut.

4) Most important is the following account of one of Francis's visions; it is found in Thomas of Celano's "First Life." The vision took place just after the third version of Francis's Rule was approved by Pope Innocent III (April 16, 1209):

For when he had gone to sleep one night, he seemed to be walking down a road, and

---

[71] Epiphany sermon and the fifth Annunciation sermon on poverty (*Opera* IX, 153 and 676). On the ass and hermitic life, see Gregorio Penco, "Il Simbolismo animalesco nella letteratura monastica," *Studia monastica* 6 (1964): 19-20, cited by Fleming. The ass can also signify humility, as when the pope himself rides a mule instead of a horse; Jörg Traeger, *Der reitende Papst. Ein Beitr. z. Ikonographie d. Papsttums* (Munich: Schnell & Steiner, 1970). See Fleming (1982), 37-41 for the many other identifications of the ass.

[72] See further to this discussion below. Meiss (1964), 25, claims that in reaction to this startling phenomenon, the shepherd tending his flock in the background leans on his staff in open-mouthed amazement. He refers to the account in the *Considerazioni*, where shepherds who saw the light of the stigmatization are described.

[73] Hale (2011) reports that, by turning his brush over, Bellini built up the amount of oil paint used to color the beams of light, thereby creating shadows that emphasize the forms. She further observes that originally the tree was even more curved than it is now, and that more and darker leaves were added, covering parts of the hills and sky. It seems to me that Bellini made this change to bring out the paleness of the lower leaves.

[74] Coronelli (1696), loc.cit.

[75] Fleming (1982), 51-57.

Fig 16.

Fig 18.

Fig 20.

Fig 17.

Fig 19.

alongside it stood a tree of great height. That tree was lovely and strong, thick and exceedingly high. It came about that when he approached the tree and stood under it and marveled at its beauty and height, the holy man himself rose to so great a height that he touched the top of the tree. Taking it into his hand, he easily bent it to the ground. It really happened this way, when the Lord Innocent, a very high and lofty tree in the world, bent himself so kindly to (Francis's) wish and request. [76]

Thus Bellini's tree not only recalls the island's miraculous pine; not only recalls Moses's and therefore Francis's colloquy with God; not only shows the place of Francis's retirement to the sacred ground, but, through the vision's papal approval and reference to the rule, also declared the religious importance of the Franciscan order and of Francis as its leader, and identifies the Observant reform and its contemporary possession of the island as juridically valid. Bellini thus freighted the arboreal image with meanings that continue and expand his notion of Francis as the spiritual force that gives shape to his surroundings.

As the creator of these naturalistically rendered typologies, St. Francis stands in the foreground (Fig. 11), his pose is reemphasized as all but unprecedented in Franciscan imagery. Previously, when Francis was shown standing

alone, as in many thirteenth-century altarpieces, his arms are bent at the elbow, either with both hands turned forward to show the nail holes or in one hand carrying a book. One of the earliest such images is Bonaventura Berlinghieri's altarpiece (Fig. 17). There is surely a reference to such hallowed images here, albeit vastly softened and humanized. Where he is kneeling, his arms are bent and hands held at his sides up above his waist, as in Jacopo Bellini's drawing (Fig. 2). [77] The pose with arms spread out and low, palms turned forward, might be related to one of the standard positions of prayer promulgated by the Dominican order (Fig. 18), where the worshipper is kneeling. [78] A Franciscan example with the arms in this pose, earlier than Bellini, is in the scene of the Stigmatization, by Michele Giambono (d. 1462, Fig. 19), but again with a kneeling figure. [79]

I suggest the precedent for Bellini's standing figure is, surprisingly enough, not in the visual tradition, but in the writings of Bonaventure (and the many sources that follow him). There, Bonaventure describes Francis as: "The holy man [who] was accustomed to fulfill the canonical hours with no less reverence than devotion. Although he was suffering from diseases of the eyes, stomach, spleen, and liver, he nevertheless did not want to lean against a wall or partition while he was chanting the psalms. He always fulfilled the hours *standing up straight and without a hood* without letting his

---

[76]   Celano, "First Life," chap. XIII, ¶33, in *Francis of Assisi: Early Documents*, vol. 1, 212–13.

[77]   Attempts have been made (e. g. Fleming [1982], 81) to relate Bellini's pose to figures of Christ in scenes of the Transfiguration. However, in most such scenes, including the one by Bellini himself, Christ's arms are also bent at the elbow and held above the waist professing his divine state, not, as here, extended downward and outward. Much more closely associated with the Transfiguration gesture is another form of upright figures of St. Francis with both arms held up. This type appeared in later thirteenth-early fourteenth-century scenes of Francis's post-mortem appearance at Arles, such as in the narrative cycle in the Upper Church of San Francesco in Assisi, repeated by Giotto in his fresco cycle in the Bardi Chapel (Florence, Santa Croce).

[78]   William Hood, *Fra Angelico at San Marco* (New Haven/London: Yale University Press, 1993), pl. 194, Cell 21, 6th mode.

[79]   Formerly (?) in the collection of Count Vittorio Cini. Land (1980), 29–51, quite rightly relates the pose in Giambono's panel and others to the theme of the Man of Sorrows. See also T. Franco, *Michele Giambono e il monumento a Cortesia da Serego in Santa Anastasia a Verona* (Padua: Poligrafo, 1998), 105, 134, fig. 77. I thank Dr. Franco Novello of the Fondazione Giorgio Cini, Istituto de Storia dell'Arte, for providing me with this information and the archival photograph reproduced here.

eyes wander about and without dropping the syllables" (my emphasis).[80]

The illnesses and physical decay Francis suffered at the end of his life, mentioned by Bonaventure, are legendary. Yet, as we have observed, in the painting he looks almost vigorous. It is Francis himself who explains his miraculous revitalization and its image in the painting. He says it came to him through the power of divine grace. As the sick and dying saint was being carried back to the Porziuncola, he tells his followers the good news:

> (God) has revealed to me that in a few days, that is, in this illness, that (my) end would come. And in this revelation God assured me of the remission of all my sins and the blessedness of paradise. Until that revelation I wept over my death and my sins. But after that revelation was made to me, I am filled with such joy that I cannot weep anymore; I am living in joy all the time. That is why I sing and I will keep singing to God Who has given me the gifts of grace and assured me of the gifts of the glory of paradise.[81]

In the painting, the hirsute Francis raises his eyes directly up. He does not gaze toward the rays of light that descend on the tree—although it is not by coincidence that both references to contact with God are directed upward—but fixedly to the heavens above him.[82] Bellini has portrayed him in the midst of his vision, as he himself describes, communing directly with God (Fig. 20). Hearing that he has been forgiven all his sins, he steps back, looks up, and opens his mouth "to sing and keep singing."[83] Inside his little chapel, he had said the Divine Office; he had contemplated Christ's sacrifice under the crown of thorns and on the cross. In the gruesome death's-head he had seen more than the skull of Adam, the first sinner and the first to be redeemed. He had wept over his sins and seen his own death. Stepping out onto the hallowed ground, he casts down his no longer needed walking stick; he removes his profane shoes. And in the midst of a landscape formed by his beliefs, Francis extends his arms not only in the ancient orant position of prayer, but also opening his heart joyfully to receive the assurance of God's grace.

I have now concluded my discussion of all the details that are represented in the painting. But perhaps even more important is the one

---

80   Bonaventure, *Major Life*, chap. 10, ¶6, in *Francis of Assisi: Early Documents*, vol. 2, 609; emphasis mine.

81   *The Deeds of Blessed Francis and his Companions by Ugolino Boniscambi of Montegiorgio (1328-1337)*, chap.18 [The Death of Saint Francis is Revealed to Lady Jacoba of Settesoli and Eternal Salvation is Revealed to Blessed Francis], in *Francis of Assisi: Early Documents*, vol. 3, 472. The "*Deeds*" and its Italian translation, "*The Little Flowers*" (see above note 61), according to the editors of *Francis of Assisi: Early Documents*, vol. 3, 429, "may well be the written response to Jerome of Ascoli's [later Nicholas IV] request in 1276 for information concerning the saint and his first followers. Subsequently, *The Little Flowers* became a first and perhaps major source of information concerning Francis of Assisi."

    There are many instances in Bonaventure's official account of Francis's life in which he knows ahead of time the day of his death, and several friars who witnessed his death claimed they saw his soul go "straight to heaven"; e.g. *Major Life*, in *Francis of Assisi: Early Documents*, vol. 1, 641, 644; *Minor Life*, Lesson 5, ibid., 716. The many "joys" of St. Francis, even as he suffered from his severe illnesses, are certified in the General Introduction to Volume Two of *Francis of Assisi: Early Documents* (p. 11; referring to the texts compiled in Volume One). An electronic search of the word "joy" in the three volumes results in 766 hits.

82   Hale (2011) shows that Bellini used lapis lazuli, the most expensive of all painting materials, for the bright blue sky.

83   As to what he is singing, many scholars have proposed various canticles written by Francis—'Cantico di frate sol,' in the *Laudes Creaturarum*, or the "Canticle of Created Things." Goffen (1986), 114 and idem (1989), 109-10, suggests an intercessory prayer quoted by Thomas of Celano. Francis sang throughout his life and sang mostly for joy. At the end, the sources say that as he died, he had begun to sing a psalm of David, number 141 (140), "I have cried to thee, O Lord, hear me: harken to my voice, when I cry to thee…", part of the annual Rubrics at Vespers and sung on November 2 at the Commemoration of the Faithful Departed.

major element that is not represented: the much-to-be-expected wound on the right side of Francis's chest, the fifth and often the bloodiest of the five marks of the stigmata.[84] As far as I know, in a painting of St. Francis, Bellini's omission is unique. Our attention is called to this lacuna by the broad expanse, in pristine condition, of Francis's breast and its almost central position in the composition. This extraordinary anomaly derives, I believe, from the fact that, as we have just seen, Francis was miraculously informed of the day of his death and assured of his acceptance in heaven while being carried back to his tiny dwelling place, the Porziuncola. Like Christ, he had the marks of the nails on his extremities, and like Christ, who lived briefly on the cross before he "gave up the ghost" (John 19: 30), in the midst of his final illness, Francis had time to glory triumphantly in his forgiveness.[85] With ingenious delicacy, by not representing the side wound, Bellini reminds the viewer that the chest wound was delivered after Christ had died (John 19:34). And although Francis did all he could to follow the footsteps of his savior (and become the *Alter Christus*) the subject of the painting is not the death of Francis, but his life. Like the living Christ who was a true man on the cross until the moment he said: "Father, into thy hands I commend my spirit" (Luke 23, 46), Bellini shows St. Francis in all his earthly manifestations—*il poverello*, law giver, leader of his people, mother of his order, and joyful penitent conversant with God.[86] He shows him without a halo, and thus although forgiven, Francis is not yet a saint. While the partial marks of the stigmata show the means of his mission, just as important are all the things that surround him—the sanctuary, the plants, the animals, the flowering land, the peaceful city, the light—everything Francis loved and called his sisters and brothers. The things that Bellini painted, in effect, the whole landscape, are the "other face of God." When Moses was told he could not see the face of God, but could only see God's "back parts" (*posteriora mea*), this earthy paradise is what he was told to look at from his place in the hole of the rock, after God's glory had passed by.[87] As the Observant Franciscans created a new paradise on the island in the Venetian marshes, so St. Francis flourishes here not <u>in</u> deserto, but <u>del</u> Deserto,

---

84   Hale (2011) makes no mention of over-painting or restoration of this area. Flora Lewis, "The Wound in Christ's side and the Instruments of the Passion: Gendered Experience and Response," in *Women and the Book: Assessing the Visual Evidence*, eds. Lesley Smith and Jane H.M. Taylor (London/Toronto: The British Library and University of Toronto Press, 1996), 204-29, provides a detailed bibliography on the subject of the chest wound.

85   There is a long history of representations of Christ on the cross without the side wound that begins in the Early Christian period and re-emerges in the early 12th century with a type of Christ Triumphant that became known as the *Volto Santo*. In the latter, exposed hands and feet show nail holes but the rest of the body is covered by an unsullied gown; see Gertrude Schiller, "The Passion of Jesus Christ," in *Iconography of Christian Art*, 2 vols., trans. Janet Seligman (Greenwich, Ct.: New York Graphic Society ITD, 1972), 2, 93, 144-45.

86   Bellini's achievement seems to reflect some examples of the painted crosses of the late 12th and 13th centuries in Tuscany, where Christ's head is upright, eyes open and, in a few cases, without the chest wound; Evelyn Sandberg-Vavala, *La Croce Dipinto Italiana e l'Iconografia della Passione* (Verona: Casa Editrice Apollo, 1929), *passim*, and Schiller, as in the previous note. A reprise of the concept then ensued beginning in the 16th century, following Michelangelo's important drawing for Vittoria Collona (1538-40), where the living Christ crucified raises his head to look upward with eyes wide open; Reiner Haussherr, *Michelangelos Kruzifixus für Vittoria Colonna: Bemerkungen zu Ikonographie und theologischer Deutung* (Opladen: Westdeutscher Verlag, 1971). The prototype engendered a wide-spread proliferation of instances of the *Cristo vivente* throughout Europe, more and more frequently with no chest wound in his glorified body. This phenomenon has been elaborately studied by Francesco Negri Arnoldi, "Origine e diffusione del Crocifisso barocco con l'immage del Cristo vivente," *Storia dell' arte* 20 (1974): 57-80. Oddly enough, none of these authors has made a point of the temporal implications of Christ being shown before or after the centurion's lance has delivered its blow.

87   See Fleming (1982), 59f., for his discussion of these lines. One wonders if Jacopo Bellini, in his Stigmatization drawing (Fig. 2) did not already have this passage in mind when he turned St. Francis with his back to the picture plane and set the scene in a broad expanse of nature.

not *in* the desert, but *of* the desert, the penitential substance of the desert, from where he leads the souls of the faithful into the paradise of grace.

———•———

Postlude: The Painting: 2

In relating the presumed date of the painting with the renewal campaign on the island, two historical names came to light: Alvise Lando (son of Ludovico who was buried in the convent church), and Pietro Bembo (son-in-law of Alvise). Who these men were and what, if any, connections they had with Bellini's patron, Zuan Michiel, or with the artist himself, remain in the realm of speculation. According to Litta's publication, there was an Alvise Lando who at one point (1463) was Podestà of Torcello, and it may have been he who inherited the chapel in the convent church. As for Alvise's son-in-law, Pietro Bembo, three documented possibilities can be suggested: one Pietro Bembo, the son of Francesco, was a senator in Bergamo (1480); another, the son of Giacomo Bembo, was a soldier who died in 1495; and the last was *bailo*, Venetian dialect for ambassador, to Turkey and Syria.[88] Whoever this Pietro Bembo was, as we have seen, in 1485 he decided not to be buried on the island. Whether either of these men were interested in painting is not possible to ascertain and, as has been mentioned, name

of Zuan Michiel appears in no document that would relate him to the island. Yet, it hardly seems fortuitous that the family name of this man and the name of the original owner of the island are one and the same: Michiel.[89] Much more important is the fact that the painting directly reflects the new Observant presence on the island in so many ways it encourages the conjecture that all these men, Lando, Bembo, and Michiel, were members of an Observant Franciscan lay order or confraternity that used the island from time to time as a devotional retreat, going there to meditate and pray, to receive the indulgence, and to celebrate the Feast of the Stigmatization.

Taking into account the considerable size of the panel (124.46 cm x 141.92 cm), it is not inconceivable that the patron looked forward, at one point or another, to mounting it as an altarpiece that would recall the island refuge as part of his devotional life.[90] But even had this been the case, he must have reconsidered. The fact that in the sixteenth century the painting was listed in a private collection makes it unlikely that it ever was displayed in an ecclesiastical setting.

There is the further issue of the profuse and intimate knowledge of Franciscan theology manifest in the composition. The task of scanning the literature in the 1470s would have been quite difficult although not impossible for the laymen as well as for Bellini owing

---

[88]   Re: Alvise Lando, cf. P. Litta, *Famiglie celebri di Italia*, 16 vols. (Milan: Presso Paolo Emilio Giusti, 1883ff.), vol. 5, unpaginated; also mentioned as Governor of Trau (Dalmatia) in 1473. E. A. Cicogna, *Delle Inscrizioni Veneziane*, 7 vols. in 6 (Bologna, 1842 [reprint: Bologna: Fonni, 1969]), vol. 5, 481-90, calls the son of Francesco Bembo "Capitano, Cavaliere e Senatore"; and the son of Giacomo "sopracomito di galera sotto Gallipoli" who died in the siege the Venetian Armada made on Monopoli. For Pietro Bembo, *bailo*, the highest ranking representative of Venice to Constantinople, in the second half of the fifteenth century, see *Dizionario biografico degli italiani* (Rome: Istituto della Enciclopedia italiana, 1960-) vol. 8, 125, where the source is given as M. Sanudo, *Diarii…*, vol. 111.

[89]   Fletcher (1972), 209, suggests that the commissioner might have been Zuan Iacopo Michiel, a statesman mentioned by Sanudo as a member of the Council of Ten from 1497 to the end of his life (1513). While this man may have been from the next generation, I point out that the second name, Iacopo, was also the same as that of the original owner of the island. Goffen (1989), 306, note 140, reports that having found many persons with the name of Zuan Michiel in Venice during this period, she searched wills and other documents, but found no evidence of the commission.

[90]   Fletcher (1972), 209, refers to such cases in Venice, where the altarpieces originally displayed in private dwellings were willed to the future funeral chapels of the owner.

to the lack of published versions then in circulation. For members of the order, however, the information was anything but recondite. Stories of St. Francis's life, his sayings, his theology, and his devotional practices were the subject of meditation and discussion of every day of every member of the order at every convent. If the commissioner were a contributing member of an Observant Franciscan foundation, fruitful discussions between the *frati*, the donor and the artist would have figured in the realization of the image. Certainly the sympathetic and informed inventiveness Bellini

showed for the subject is the characteristic that elicited, much later in his career, the comments about his inimitable and obstinate will to "vagare" through traditional subjects. The passage is from [the real] Pietro Bembo's letter to Isabella d' Este dated 1506.[91] It has been quoted more than once in relation to the Frick painting, usually with the suggestion that Bellini's intention was directed toward idiosyncrasy. Yet, what is truly outstanding about the Frick panel is Bellini's knowledgeable, respectful, and original way of adhering to strict orthodoxy.

---

[91] "...il quale ha piacere che molto signati termini non si diano al suo stile, uso come dice di sempre vagare a sua voglia nelle pitture, che quanto è in lui possano soddisfare a chi le mira." First published in G. Gaye, *Carteggio inedito d'artisti dei secoli XIV, XV, XVI*, 3 vols. (Florence: Presso G. Molini, 1840), 2:73.

OCULAR CHASTITY: OPTICAL THEORY, ARCHITECTURAL BARRIERS, AND THE GAZE IN THE RENAISSANCE CHURCH OF SAN MARCO IN FLORENCE *

Theresa Flanigan

Introduction

Today, upon entering the Florentine Church of San Marco, the present-day visitor is permitted an unobstructed view of the nave from the church's main entrance to the high altar (as in Fig. 1). Such an expansive view, however, was not possible for the mid fifteenth-century visitor, whose gaze would have been controlled by two no longer extant architectural partitions called *tramezzi* (Fig. 2). These circa 16.5-foot tall walls were erected in 1438-39 as part of the pre-existing church's renovation for its new Observant Dominican occupants, a project financed by the Medici family and attributed to one of the period's most significant architects Michelozzo di Bartolomeo. San Marco's *tramezzi* functioned to limit visual access between the nave, transept, and choir-presbytery by framing and focusing the laity's view of the high altar and by preventing the friars from viewing or being viewed by female congregants located in the lower nave, the farthest space from the friars' choir. In this essay, I will contextualize the desire for ocular control within the church by relating it to the early Renaissance understanding of the physiological and epistemological natures of the visual process, which also informed contemporary theological discourse about the dangers of the gaze and the rise of new optics-based art theory.

The Dominican Renovation of San Marco, 1438-9

Construction of the church of San Marco was begun in 1299 for a congregation of Sylvestrine monks on a piazza a few blocks north of the Florence Cathedral, between the current via Cavour (formerly via Larga) and via Ricasoli.[1] In 1436, an order of Observant Dominican friars from San Domenico in Fiesole aided by Pope Eugenius IV acquired the formerly Sylvestrine church and its adjacent monastic complex. This transfer of San Marco's ownership necessitated a renovation of the church interior that took place between 1438 and 1439, was sponsored by Cosimo and Lorenzo

---

* A version of this paper was first presented at the annual conference of the Renaissance Society of America in 2009. The drawings were produced for me by Ann Cosgrove and generously funded by a 2010 College of Saint Rose Scholars and Artists Grant.

[1] For San Marco's early building history, see: Hans Teubner, "San Marco in Florenz: Umbauten vor 1500. Ein Beitrag zum Werk des Michelozzo," *Mitteilungen des Kunsthistorischen Institutes in Florenz* 23 (1979): 242-3; Franco Carboni and Mario Salmi, "La Chiesa di S. Marco e il Chiostro di S. Domenico," in *La Chiesa e il Convento di San Marco a Firenze* (Florence: Giunti, 1989), vol. I, 259-61; and Magnolia Scudieri, "Michelozzo a San Marco e il convent preesistente," in *Michelozzo: Sculttore e architetto*, ed. Gabriele Morolli (Florence: Associazione Dimore Storiche Italiane, 1998), 107-8.

Fig 1. San Marco, Florence. Present day view of the church interior. (photo: Elissa Ebersold, published by permission).

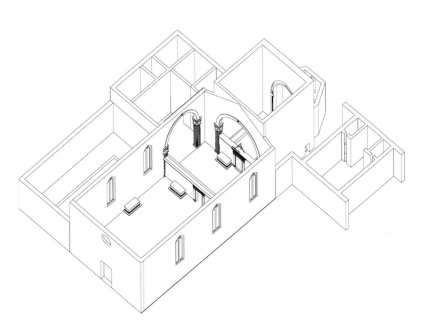

Fig 2. San Marco, Florence. Axonometric reconstruction of the church following the renovations of 1438-9 (reconstruction: author; drawing: Ann Cosgrove).

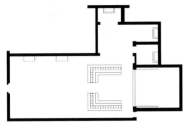

Fig 3. San Marco, Florence. Plan of the church before renovations of 1438-9 (reconstruction: author; drawing: Ann Cosgrove).

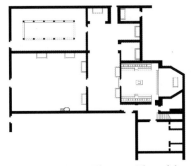

Fig 4. San Marco, Florence. Plan of the church after the renovations of 1438-9 (reconstruction: author; drawing: Ann Cosgrove).

de'Medici, and is attributed to the architect Michelozzo di Bartolomeo (also known as Michelozzo Michelozzi).[2]

According to the *Annals of the Convent of San Marco of Florence* (written in the 1450s), in 1438-1439, repairs were made to the pre-existing church and San Marco's interior was enlarged with the addition of a polygonal apse to house a new high altar, for which the Medici commissioned Fra Angelico to paint a new high altarpiece to be the church's visual focus (see Fig. 6). In addition, the Sylvestrine's U-shaped choir was removed from the nave and a new Dominican choir was built within the square-shaped space of the former *cappella maggiore* (Fig. 3; Fig. 4). The following passage from the *Annals* records the church's new layout:

> ...the choir that used to be in the middle of the church was removed, it [the new choir] was arranged transversely, that is, along the length of the arm of the church, for [use by] the laymen, and the rest of the body of the church is for the use of women. And in this manner the triple distinction is evident. First, is the choir or oratory of the friars, which is enclosed, so that the laity is separate; second is the choir of the laity in the second part of the church; third is the lower church, that is said to be for women, here were erected four altars and here were made seats for hearing the confessions of women (see Fig. 4).[3]

These three spaces are similarly designated in a biography of San Marco's late fifteenth-century prior Fra Girolomo Savonarola (d.1498) that describes an Epiphany celebration within the church in which the friars "sang matins and did three stations, one in the lower part of the church, the women's part, one in the choir for the laymen, and the third in the choir for the friars."[4] These texts indicate that the tripartite division of San Marco

---

[2]   This commission is described in the *Annalia Conventus S. Marci de Florentia*, ms. 1505 in Bibl. Laurenziana, Cod. S. Marco 370, fol. 5r-7r, also published in Raoul Morçay, "La cronaca del convento fiorentino di San Marco," *Archivio storico italiano* 51 (1913): 1-29; and in Teubner, "San Marco in Florenz," 244-51 and 263, doc. IX. The earliest source to attribute this project to Michelozzo is the second edition (1568) of Giorgio Vasari, *Le vite de' piu eccelenti pittori scultori ed architettori*, trans. Gaetano Milanesi, vol. 2., 439-41 (Florence: G. C. Sanzoni, 1906).

[3]   I am in the process of publishing separately a full explanation of my reconstruction of San Marco's 1439 appearance, which differs slightly from previous reconstructions. The quoted text comes from the *Annalia Conventus S. Marci de Florentia*, ms. 1505 in Bibl. Laurenziana, Cod. S. Marco 370, fol. 5r-7r. The full passage as published by Teubner ("San Marco in Florenz," 264, doc. XII) reads: "Eodem similiter tempore reparata est ex parte interiori tota ecclesia et reornata a praefatis fratribus Cosima et Laurentio, et tectum similiter in duabus trabibus seu cavallettis; et chorus qui erat in medio ecclesiae reductum [sic] fuit per eius transversum, id est per longum bracchium ecclesiae, pro viris laicis, et reliquum corpus ecclesiae pro uso mulierum. Et sic triplex distinctio apparuit. Prima est chorus seu oratorium fratrum, reclausum, tanquam a laicis separatum; secunda est chorus laicorum in secunda parte ecclesiae; tertia est ecclesia inferior, quae dicitur mulierum, ubi fuerunt erecta quattuor altaria et ubi facta fuerunt sedilia pro audientia confitentium mulierum."

[4]   *La Vita del beato Ieronimo Savonarola, scritta da un Anonimo del secolo XVI e già attribuita a fra Pacifico Burlamacchi* (1498), as published in Richard Trexler, *Public Life in Renaissance Florence* (Binghamton, New York: Academic Press, 1980), 189-90.

[5]   San Marco's *tramezzi* are recorded in the following documents: *Annalia Conventus S. Marci*, ms. 370 (1437-1439), fol. 5r-7r, published in Teubner, "San Marco in Florenz," 264, doc. XII; *Annalia Conventus S. Marci*, ms. 370, fol. 29r-29v (1517), published in Teubner, "San Marco in Florenz," 265, doc. XIV; *Annalia Conventus S. Marci*, ms. 370, fol. 39r-v (1564), published in Teubner, "San Marco in Florenz," 267, doc. XVIII, 1; *Annalia Conventus S. Marci*, ms. 370, fol. 76r-v (May, 1563), published in Teubner, "San Marco in Florenz," 268, doc. XX; and P. Serafino Loddi, *Notizie de Soggetti, e cose piu memorabilia del convento di S. Marco di Firenze dell'Ordine de Predicatori*, ms. 1736 in Santa Sabina, Rome, 19th century copy in the Archive of San Marco, fol. 121, published in Teubner, "San Marco in Florenz," 267, doc. XVIII, 2. The choir wall appears in two drawings: a plan of San Marco by Giorgio Vasari the younger, Uffizi, Florence, A 4861, dated between 1564 and 1578; and an Anonymous "Pianta del Coro Vecchio di San Marcho (1679)," Biblioteca Laurenziana, *Ricordanze di S. Marco*, no. 906 (*Libro di Ricordanze D*, 1637-1780), 70-2. The text that accompanies this plan reads: "Ricordo come fino nel 1679 il Convento fece la soffitta della chiesa... Fece anco 2 pilastri di pietra nel'ingresso del coro, con 2 colonne di pietra, col suo arco, levando i 2 altari che vi stavano di S. Giacinto e di S. Marco." The text that accompanies this plan reads: "Stando il coro in questa maniera, furono levati i 2 altari da piede, segnati F, e messe le colonne nel luogo h, e restò aperto tutto il coro da piedi."

segregated the religious from the laity and the laity according to gender.

Further archival evidence reveals that the sub-division of San Marco's interior was achieved with the erection of two dividing walls, called *tramezzi*,[5] each measuring approximately 5 meters (circa 16.5 feet)[6] with a single opening at the center,[7] recalling the rood screen in the fresco of the *Miracle of the Crib* from San Francesco in Assisi (c. 1290-1300) (Fig. 5). The singular openings in each of San Marco's *tramezzi* would have aligned down the central axis of the nave to permit the only view from the transept and nave of the body of Christ, which was temporarily present in the Eucharist and permanently visible in the high altarpiece by Fra

Angelico, whose main panel depicts the *Enthroned Virgin and Child Surrounded by Angels and Saints Mark, Dominic, John the Evangelist, Francis, Lawrence, Peter Martyr, Cosmas and Damian* (completed circa 1441, now in the Museo di San Marco, Florence) (Fig. 6).[8] This view was almost certainly enframed by the two classicizing door-frames, each consisting of two Corinthian pilasters supporting an entablature with a quincunx frieze of Medicean heraldic balls (*palle*), that are currently housed in the church's apse (Fig. 7).[9] From the nave, the view of Christ's body was literally framed by each wall's central opening whose classicizing architectural surround resembles the altarpiece's presumed frame (now lost) and the painted

---

[6]   The choir screen must have stood approximately 5 meters tall (circa 16.4 feet) to accommodate the circa 3.5 meter (over 11 feet) height of the altarpieces painted by Fra Bartolomeo in circa 1515 in order to flank the choir entrance, the altars that stood beneath them, and likely a crowning cornice. These altarpieces are *St. Mark the Evangelist* (Palatine Gallery, Florence), which measures 3.4 meters (circa 11 feet), and a lost *St. Sebastian with an Angel* (known through a copy in San Francesco, Fiesole) that was replaced in 1594 by the circa 3.4 meter (c.11 feet) tall *Virgin Appearing to St. Hyacinth* (Pinacoteca, Lucca) painted by Jacopo Ligozzi. Giorgio Vasari (Le vite..., vol. 4, 188) records *St. Mark* and *St. Sebastian* at San Marco and mentions that *St. Mark* hung on the choir wall. This placement is also indicated by the Anonimo Gaddiano of c. 1540 (*Il Codice Dell' Anonimo Gaddiano ... Nella Biblioteca Nazionale di Firenze*, ed. Cornel von Fabriczy [Florence, 1893], 85). For further discussion of these altarpieces and their placement see Janet Cox-Rearick, "Fra Bartolomeo's St. Mark Evangelist and St. Sebastian with an Angel," *Mitteilungen des Kunsthistorischen Instituts in Florenz* 18 (1974): 329-54 (esp. pp. 341-2); and Eadem, "Fra Bartolommeo: St. Sebastian with an Angel," in *The Collection of Francis I: Royal Treasures* (New York: Harry N. Abrams, 1996), 168-70. According to Vasari, the two paintings were unframed. Instead, the figures were surrounded by illusionistic painted niches and the altarpieces were, according to Cox-Rearick, "set slightly into the surface of the wall." There is no evidence for altars or altarpieces on the choir screen prior to the sixteenth century.

[7]   A document of 1470 locates the tomb of the Brunelleschi family "between the door at the front of the church [presumably the main entrance] and the first gate [of the nave *tramezzo*], approximately under the pulpit, where one preaches" (*La sepoltura de'suoi passati [dei Brunelleschi] e in Santo Marco tra la porta dinanzi di chiesa e 'l primo canciello, circa sotto 'l pergamo, dove si predica*). This document is published in Teubner, "San Marco in Florenz," 262, doc. VI. Teubner mislocates this gate within the doorway of the choir screen, which would have been neither the first opening from the church entrance, nor located near the pulpit, the current version of which stands in approximately its original location. The Renaissance location of the pulpit is recorded in the *Annalia Conventus S. Marci*, ms. 370, fol. 39r-v (1564), published in Teubner, "Il San Marco in Florenz," 267, doc. XVIII.

[8]   *The San Marco Altarpiece's* main panel originally stood above a predella containing scenes from the *Lives of Saints Cosmas and Damian* (the Medici family's patron saints) flanking a central predella panel depicting the *Lamentation Over the Dead Christ*. In the lower third of the altarpiece's main panel, just above the *Lamentation* panel, is a miniature scene depicting the *Crucifixion* painted in front of a gold ground. The altarpiece's frame also contained standing figures of saints and *beati*. Most of these pieces have been separated from the main panel and now reside in various collections. See the most recent reconstructions of the full altarpiece in Cristina Acidini Luchinat and Magnolia Scudieri, eds., *L'Angelico ritrovato: studi e ricerche per la Pala di San Marco* (Livorno: Sillabe, 2008).

[9]   Both doorframes can be dated to the early fifteenth century based on their stylistic relationship to the impost blocks of the remaining fifteenth-century pilasters in San Marco's choir and apse and to other works attributed to Michelozzo and sponsored by the Medici, such as the doorway to the novitiate corridor in Santa Croce (c. 1440-45) and the frieze decoration on the corbels of the Medici-sponsored Franciscan church of Bosco ai Frati that was renovated by Michelozzo in the 1420s. These two fifteenth-century doorframes certainly could not have originated in their present location in the apse because door openings do not appear at this location in the plan by Vasari the younger (after 1564) or in the 1678 plan of the choir and apse. Moreover, doors located in this position as part of the Michelozzian renovation would have opened directly from the apse to the outdoors (an unlikely situation) as the apse was not surrounded by conventual structures until 1506. It is much more likely that these two doorframes were commissioned as part of the 1438 renovation of San Marco; and the very visible central axis of the nave of the church is the most appropriate place for such ornate and expensive doorframes to have been originally located. Giuseppe Marchini ("Il San Marco di Michelozzo," *Palladio* 6 (1942): 105-8) is the first scholar to date one of these doorframes to the Michelozzian renovation of the church, claiming that it likely framed the central opening in the choir screen.

Fig 5. St. Francis and the Miracle of the Crib at Greccio, Lower Church, San Francesco, Assisi, c. 1290-1300.
(photo: Art Resource, published by permission)

Fig 6. Fra Angelico, San Marco Altarpiece, completed circa 1441.
(photo: Art Resource, published by permission)

Fig 7. Doorframe with Medici palle, San Marco, Florence (photo: author).

Fig 8. San Marco, Florence. Reconstructed view from just inside the main entrance of the lower church towards the high altar
(reconstruction: author; drawing: Ann Cosgrove).

architecture of the throne at the altarpiece's center that enframes the Virgin and Child. This triple framing with repeating elements (including Medici *palle*) formed a perspectival unity between the masonry architecture, wooden framing, and painted altarpiece, which was certainly meant to be seen and understood in this visual context (Fig. 8).[10]

The Observant Dominican Order's move from San Domenico in Fiesole to the more centrally located church of San Marco in downtown Florence resulted in a distinct set of spatio-visual problems for the church's renovating architect. A greater presence of a lay congregation had to be accommodated during mass, all of whom would require visual access to the high altar, while at the same time monastic segregation (especially of novices) from the laity had to be maintained.[11] During mass, therefore, the church's architecture had to direct and focus the laity's view towards the high altar and its altarpiece, while also obscuring their view of the friars in their choir. The church's

architecture thus had to both accommodate and control the gaze. The solution at San Marco differed in both its economy and visual control from other Florentine examples, such as at Santa Maria Novella, Santa Croce, Santissima Annunziata, and Santa Maria del Carmine, where a freestanding u-shaped choir was combined with a vaulted bridge-like *tramezzo* (often referred to as a *ponte*).[12] Instead, Michelozzo's solution for the friar's choir positioned the friars along the side walls of an enclosed choir facing each other rather than out towards the nave, recalling typical U-shaped choir arrangements, such as San Marco's previous Sylvestrine choir and the freestanding choir arrangements that stood at this time in other Florentine churches. However, the solution at San Marco differed from these other Florentine examples in that the friars' choir was spatially distinct from the nave (rather than a space-within-a-space), two *tramezzi* were used instead of one to divide the church interior, and, more significantly, the *tramezzi* at San Marco were

---

[10]   For discussions of earlier complexes where there is a conscious integration of architecture, painting, and viewpoint, see John White, *Birth and Rebirth of Pictorial Space* (Cambridge, Mass.: Harvard University Press, 1987), 126-30; Martin Kemp, *The Science of Art: Optical Themes in Western Art from Brunelleschi to Seurat* (New Haven and London: Yale University Press, 1990), 9 (on the Bardi Chapel in Santa Croce); Samuel Y. Edgerton, *Heritage of Giotto's Geometry: Art and Science on the Eve of the Scientific Revolution* (Ithaca: Cornell University Press, 1991), 47-87 (on the modillion borders at San Francesco, Assisi) and Marvin Trachtenberg, *Dominion of the Eye: Urbanism, Art, and Power in Early Modern Florence* (Cambridge: Cambridge University Press, 1997), 165-84 (on the architecture and decoration of Santa Croce). As I have argued elsewhere, the difference at San Marco is the stricter adherence of the design to Euclidian geometry as found in Alberti's treatise *On Painting* (i.e., the complete integration of the visual pyramid and the one-point perspectival system).

[11]   Following the Fourth Lateran Council of 1215, receipt of communion by the laity was obligatory at least once a year, typically at Easter and only after confession, penance, and absolution of the communicant's sins. Sight of the consecrated and raised Host was considered sacramentally effective (replacing taste), making visual access to the high altar necessary. See Biernoff, *Sight and Embodiment in the Middle Ages* (New York: Palgrave Macmillan, 2002), ch. 6, especially 140-3. However, in his *Opera a ben vivere...* (c. 1450), San Marco's Fra Antonino Pierozzi recommends to Dianora Tournabuoni that she fast and confess at least once a month and that she receive communion once a week *if it does not make her too conspicuous* (thus this degree of frequency was optional, not mandatory). See the commentary on this treatise in "S. Antonino of Florence," *The Church Quarterly Review* 46 (1898): 437-9.

[12]   For these other Florentine *tramezzi* see: Marcia B. Hall, "The Tramezzo in the Italian Renaissance, Revisited," in *Thresholds of the Sacred: Architectural, Art Historical, Liturgical and Theological Perspectives on Rood Screens East and West*, ed. Sharon E.J. Gerstel (Cambridge, Harvard University Press, 2006), 215-32; Eadem, "The *Ponte* in Santa Maria Novella: The Problem of the Rood Screen in Italy," *Journal of the Warburg and Courtauld Institutes* 37 (1974): 157-73; Eadem, "The *Tramezzo* in Santa Croce, Florence, Reconstructed," *Art Bulletin* 56 (1974): 325-41; Eadem, *Renovation and Counter-Reformation: Vasari and Duke Cosimo in Sta. Maria Novella and Sta. Croce*, 1565-1577 (Oxford: Oxford University Press, 1979); Eadem, "The Operation of Vasari's Workshop and the Designs for S. Maria Novella and S. Croce," *The Burlington Magazine* 112 (1970): 797-99. Reconstructions of the *tramezzi* at the Santissima Annunziata and Santa Maria del Carmine can be found in Mario Fabbri, Elvira Garbero Zorzi, and Anna Maria Petrioli Tofani, *Il luogo teatrale a Firenze* (Milan: Electa, 1975); and in Nerida Newbigin, *Feste d'Oltrarno: Plays in Churches in Fifteenth Century Florence*, 2 vols. (Florence: L.S. Olschki, 1996). The church of Ognissanti also contained a *tramezzo*, but not of the bridge type. For reconstructions, see Irene Hueck, "Le opere di Giotto per la chiesa di Ognissanti," in *La Madonna d'Ognissanti di Giotto restaurata* (Florence : Centro Di, 1992), 37-50. Similar dividing structures existed in medieval and renaissance churches in England, where such a divider is called a choir, chancel, or rood screen (depending on location and function), in France where it is called a *jubé*, and in Germany where it is called a *lettner*. For examples outside of Italy see Hall, "The Tramezzo in Santa Croce," 166-70.

more solid than these Florentine *ponti*, allowing only a single axis of visual access to the high altar from the transept and nave. San Marco's *tramezzi*, therefore, both served to limit and focus one's view. The atypical use of two wall-style *tramezzi* at San Marco created a double barrier between the friars and the church's female congregants, who would have been too far away to have been able to peer directly into the choir as in the fresco from Assisi (see Fig. 5). In addition, the *tramezzi* limited the view into the body of the church by the friars, who would have been seated against the side walls of the choir. The positioning of the friars combined with the double barrier between friars' choir and "lower church" would have made the viewing of the female congregation by the friars virtually impossible.

San Marco's Dominicans had to be particularly careful about visually engaging with the female laity. *The Constitution of the Order of Friars Preachers* declares "It is a grave fault.... If anyone going to a place where women are present '*fixes his eye*,' at least does so habitually, or if he speaks alone with a woman about anything other than confession or honest matters" (italics mine).[13] This restriction was complicated by the fact that church may have been one of the few public spaces in fifteenth-century Florence where upper class women could be seen. Evidence from the period suggests that some women used this opportunity as a chance for self-display,

thereby actively encouraging the gaze.[14] This situation is commented upon in a sermon of alphabetized vices by San Marco's Fra Antonino Pierozzi, who stated, "The twenty-second letter is Y, which means, that which is an image of idols (*Ymago idolorum*), for thus she paints and embellishes herself as an idol, going into the church of God thus decorated with precious gold and stones, like a prostitute."[15] Here women are equated with idols, turning desirous viewing of them into idolatry, a violation of the second commandment. Echoing Fra Antonino, San Marco's later prior Fra Girolamo Savonarola similarly compared women to idols:

> Look at the habits of Florence, at how Florentine women marry off their daughters. They show them around and dress them up as if they were nymphs, and first, they take them to Santa Liperata [the Duomo]. These are your idols and you have placed them in my temple.[16]

These statements suggest anxiety on the part of San Marco's Dominicans that women could become objects of unchaste visual desire (idolatry) if the eye was left vulnerable to gaze upon them within the church.[17] At San Marco, one method for

---

[13] *Constitution of the Order of Friars Preachers*, 17. 42. See the translation of the Dominican Constitution in William Hood, *Fra Angelico at S. Marco* (New Haven: Yale University Press, 1993), 294.

[14] For scholarship regarding women in church during the Renaissance see: Margaret Aston, "Segregation in Church," in *Women in the Church*, eds. W.J. Shields and Diana Wood (Oxford: Blackwell, 1990), 237-94; Adrian Randolph, "Regarding Women in Sacred Space," in *Picturing Women in Renaissance and Baroque Italy*, eds. Geraldine A. Johnson and Sara F. Matthews Grieco (Cambridge: Cambridge University Press, 1997), 17-41; and Robert Gaston, "Sacred Place and Liturgical Space: Florence's Renaissance Churches," in *Renaissance Florence: A Social History*, eds. Roger J. Crum and John T. Paoletti (Cambridge, Mass.: Cambridge University Press, 2006), 331-52. For women in Renaissance society in general see: Judith C. Brown and Robert C. Davis, *Gender and Society in Renaissance Italy* (London and New York: Longman, 1998); and Natalie Tomas, '*A Positive Novelty': Women and Public Life in Renaissance Florence* (Monash: Monash Publications in History, 1992).

[15] As quoted by Adrian Randolph, "Regarding Women in Sacred Space," 35.

[16] Savonarola, Sermon XVIII (5 March 1496), as quoted in *Renaissance Art Reconsidered: An Anthology of Primary Sources*, eds. Carol M. Richardson, Kim W. Woods, and Michael W. Franklin (Oxford: Blackwell Publishing, 2007), 312-13.

[17] Men were not the only ones who gazed at women in church. In a letter to her son, Alessandra Strozzi records going to church to view (and judge) a possible wife for him (as quoted in Randolph, "Regarding Women in Sacred Space," 35-36): Going Sunday morning to the Ave Maria in Santa Reparata [Santa Maria del Fiore] for the first Mass, as I had done a few mornings of the feast in order to see that girl of the Adimari...I found her of the Tanagli...she seemed to me to have a beautiful body, and well-made; she is big, like Caterina [Alessandra's daughter], or larger; good flesh, but not of that white type: but she is of good being; she has a long face and not very delicate features, but not those of the rustic sort: and it seemed to me, that she was not affected in her gait and appearance.

guarding against such sinful gazing was to architecturally control visibility within the church. The arrangement of San Marco's renovated interior and the design and placement of its *tramezzi* functioned to virtually eliminate the possibility of direct visual contact between the friars and female laity during mass (sermons were separate from the mass during this period and are thus beyond the scope of this essay).[18]

The attention to visibility within the church by San Marco's Dominican Observants may be linked with the order's particular visual culture. According to Dallas Denery, by the late thirteenth century Dominicans had become so concerned with visibility that they "constructed a notion of the self as self-presentation, as the continuous object of an audience gaze, these observations, adjustments and adaptations were everything."[19] Denery argues that the expanding public role of Dominican friars as instructors, preachers, and confessors in the late medieval period resulted in a shift towards an ocularcentrism in which members of the order became increasingly visually self aware. His evidence includes Dominican instructional treatises and manuals on preaching and confession that consider a friar's external appearance a reflection of the friar's internal moral state and his increased role as an exemplar to others through his appearance and behavior. It was, therefore, imperative that he avoid sin or any semblance of immoral conduct. The Dominican friar was instructed to be constantly conscious of his appearance to others (lay audience, monastic brothers, and all-seeing God) and to

himself. As the constant object of the gaze, the friar was instructed to always take into consideration his behavior and regulate it accordingly. This meant control of his gaze and his private and public presence, both within and beyond the confines of the church and monastery. In the remainder of this essay, I will contextualize this desire for ocular control apparent at San Marco by relating it to the early Renaissance understanding of the visual process, which also informed contemporary theological discourse and artistic theory.

The Visual Paradox

seeing [...] most of all the senses, makes
us know – Aristotle, *Metaphysics*, 980a
Thou hast wounded my heart, my sister, my
spouse, with a glance of the eyes.
– Song of Songs 4.9

During the late medieval and early Renaissance periods, vision had both positive and negative connotations, as sight was linked with both spiritual enlightenment and corporeal desire. Sight's primacy as an epistemological power was most influentially proclaimed by Aristotle, who stated:

All men by nature desire to know. An indication of this is the delight we take in our senses; for even apart from their usefulness they are loved for themselves; and above all others the sense of sight. For not only with a view to action, but even when we are

---

[18]   The arguments presented in this essay are part of a larger project I am working on that examines the relationship between Dominican visuality and the various functions (including mass, preaching, and confession) of the Church of San Marco and its high altarpiece. Other solutions may have been employed during sermons. Temporary curtains appear in a seventeenth-century fresco in the first cloister of San Marco depicting Fra Antonino Pierozzi preaching in San Marco and in a late fifteenth-century woodcut showing Fra Girolamo Savonarola preaching in the Florentine Cathedral. Similar curtains may have been used to segregate the laity during sermons in San Marco, when the laity of both genders would have been present together in the lower church where the pulpit was located. The lower church was, therefore, not always just for women as suggested by the descriptions of the space cited at the beginning of this essay that must be interpreted as referring to the spatial location of the congregation during mass, which was the church's primary function.

[19]   Dallas Denery, "*Pondere Statera Meditationis*: Self as Self-Presentation in Early Dominican Religious Life," in *Seeing and Being Seen in the Later Medieval World: Optics, Theology and Religious Life* (Cambridge: Cambridge University Press, 2005), 19-38.

not going to do anything, we prefer seeing (one might say) to everything else. The reason is that this, most of all the senses, makes us know and brings to light many differences between things.[20]

Since Antiquity, the eyes were considered to provide the brain (linked, since the time of Galen, with the soul) with the most varied and useful data for the intellectual processing of objects in the visible world.[21] Vision was also exalted by the Early Christian thinker St. Augustine, who claimed that there were two types of vision – corporeal vision (seeing with the "eyes of the body") and spiritual vision (seeing with the "eyes of the mind"). For St. Augustine, physical vision was the noblest of the senses because it was considered most analogous to spiritual vision; he stated: "Let us therefore use in particular the testimony of the eyes, because this sense far excels the rest, and although it is a different kind of vision, is closest to spiritual vision."[22] Following St. Augustine, vision came to rank at the top of the Christian hierarchy of the senses as the sensory faculty that best enables us to understand God the creator through our visual observation of the natural world.[23] By the thirteenth century, knowledge of optics and the related properties of light were essential to the study of theology and all branches of natural philosophy, including, but not limited to, human perception.[24]

In addition to being the noblest epistemological sense, vision was also considered the most dangerous sense because of its relationship with baser carnal sensuality. The Bible contains several passages that associate vision with the sins of desire, temptation (as in the stories of the Genesis Temptation, David and Bathsheba, and Suzanna and the Elders), and even adultery. St. Matthew claims that merely gazing upon a woman could violate the seventh commandment: "But I tell you that anyone who looks at a woman lustfully has already committed adultery with her in his heart."[25] In addition, the *Bible's* "Song of Songs" characterizes the female gaze as having the power to wound: "Thou hast wounded my heart, my sister, my spouse, with a *glance of the eyes*" (italics mine),[26] a trope (the penetrating or wounding

[20] Aristotle, *Metaphysics*, 980a, as translated in *The Basic Works of Aristotle*, ed. Richard McKeon (New York: The Modern Library, 2001), 689.

[21] For summaries of the history of optics before Descartes see David Lindberg, *Theories of Vision from Al-Kindi to Kepler* (Chicago and London: University of Chicago Press, 1976) and Martin Jay, *Downcast Eyes: The Denigration of Vision in Twentieth-Century French Thought* (Berkeley: University of California Press, 1993), 21-82. Useful overviews of late medieval (perspectivist) optics are also provided by: A. Mark Smith, "Getting the Big Picture in Perspectivist Optics," *Isis* 72, no. 4 (1981): 568-89; Suzannah Biernoff, *Sight and Embodiment in the Middle Ages* (New York: Palgrave Macmillan, 2002), 63-110; Katherine H. Tachau, "Seeing as Action in the Thirteenth and Fourteenth Centuries," in *The Mind's Eye: Art and Theological Argument in the Middle Ages*, eds. Jeffrey F. Hamburger and Anne-Marie Bouché (Princeton: Princeton University Press, 2006), 336-59; and Nader El-Bizri,"Classical Optics and the Perspectival Traditions Leading to the Renaissance," in *Renaissance Theories of Vision*, eds. John Shannon Hendrix and Charles H. Carman (Farnham, England and Burlington, Vt.: Ashgate, 2010), 11-30. For vision's epistemological nature see: Katherine H. Tachau, *Vision and Certitude in the Age of Ockham: Optics, Epistemology, and the Foundations of Semantics 1250-1345* (Leiden and New York: E. J. Brill, 1988); Michael Camille, "Before the Gaze: The Internal Senses and Late Medieval Practices of Seeing," in *Visuality Before and Beyond the Renaissance: Seeing as Others Saw*, ed. Robert S. Nelson (Cambridge: Cambridge University Press, 2000), ed. 197-223; David Summers, *The Judgment of Sense: Renaissance Naturalism and the Rise of Aesthetics* (Cambridge: Cambridge University Press, 1990); and Stuart Clark, *Vanities of the Eye: Vision in Early Modern European Culture* (Oxford: Oxford University Press, 2009), 1-45.

[22] Augustine, *On the Trinity*, 11.1.1. For Augustine on vision see Margaret Miles, "Vision: The Eye of the Body and the Eye of the Mind in Saint Augustine's '*De trinitate*' and '*Confessions*'," *The Journal of Religion* 63, no. 2 (1983): 125-42.

[23] For the broadest discussion of vision as the "noblest of the senses" see Jay, *Downcast Eyes*, 21-82. See also Summers, *The Judgment of Sense*, 32-9.

[24] Tachau, "Seeing as Action in the Thirteenth and Fourteenth Centuries," 349.

[25] Gospel of St. Matthew, 5:28. This is discussed in Biernoff, *Sight and Embodiment*, 46.

[26] Song of Songs, 4:9.

gaze) that is also commonly found in medieval amorous and popular literature.[27] In these examples, man's downfall often results from gazing upon the female body or from being the object of the female gaze.

The dangers of the female gaze were also recounted in sermons. The very popular preaching manual *The Moral Treatise on the Eye*, written sometime between the 1260s and 1280s by the Franciscan scholar and preacher Peter of Limoges (Pierre Lacepierre de Limoges, d.1306), employs the most up-to-date optical theory to explicate various ways that sight could lead to sin.[28] His seventh chapter entitled, "How Eyes of Women Have Much Unchasteness by which Many are Wounded," cites the *exemplum* of a young hermit who spies women for the first time and confides to his abbot that upon viewing these women he became overcome with desire for them. The abbot follows with a lesson to the other monks in which he states, "how dangerous to the mind is the sight of women. For this innocent boy who had not seen a woman before and who grew up in the sight of hermits alone, is now overcome with lust."[29] Peter also claims that being object of the female gaze could be even more dangerous than gazing upon a woman. He states: "No one without being out of his mind would look at a basilisk whose sight kills; therefore no one should look at a woman whose sight destroys and kills."[30]

Moreover, he characterizes the female gaze as "poisonous" and explains its workings as an emissive process:

It seems probable that similar kinds of poisonous rays (*radii venenosi*) are given off when a woman looks at a man lustfully, for then a libidinous vapor arises from the heart of the woman up to her eyes henceforth the vapor infects her visual rays, which so infected as they are emitted, come to the eyes of men and infect them, whence the infection enters the heart of man.[31]

Peter thus describes the female gaze as able to "infect" the hearts of men, which he goes on to compare with the way rabies infects the minds and hearts of dogs.[32] If just looking upon a woman could "infect" men's hearts and bring upon sinful desires of the flesh, especially in cloistered males (as in Peter's example of the hermit), then vision in monastic churches, such as San Marco, had to be controlled in order to maintain ocular chastity.

Notions of the infectious female gaze may derive from ancient superstitions surrounding the 'evil eye's' ability to harm its victim and from Aristotle's claim that menstrual blood contained evil humors that could be emitted from the eyes of women to infect objects in their trajectory.[33] Peter's explanation of female vision reflects a

27   See, for example, Barbara Newman, "Love's Arrows: Christ as Cupid in Late Medieval Art and Devotion," in *The Mind's Eye: Art and Theological Argument in the Middle Ages*, eds. Jeffrey F. Hamburger and Anne-Marie Bouché (Princeton: Princeton University Press, 2006), 263-86.
28   For analyses of Peter of Limoges' *Moral Treatise on the Eye* see: David L. Clark, "Optics for Preachers: The *De oculo morali* by Peter of Limoges," *Michigan Academician* 9, no. 3 (1977): 329-43; Biernoff, *Sight and Embodiment*, 51-2; Dallas Denery, *Seeing and Being Seen in the Later Medieval World: Optics, Theology and Religious Life* (Cambridge: Cambridge University Press, 2005), ch. 3; and Richard C. Newhauser, "Peter of Limoges, Optics, and the *Science of the Senses*," *Senses & Society* 5, no. 1 (2010): 28-44.
29   Peter of Limoges, *De oculo morali*, 8.A.vii., as quoted by David L. Clark, "Optics for Preachers," 342.
30   Ibid.
31   Ibid. Also quoted in Biernoff, *Sight and Embodiment*, 51-2.
32   Peter of Limoges, *De oculo morali*, 8.A. vii, as quoted by David L. Clark, "Optics for Preachers," 342.
33   Biernoff, *Sight and Embodiment*, 52. Aristotle, *De insomniis* 3, 459b23-460a23. This claim is repeated in Peter of Limoges, *The Moral Treatise on the Eye*, trans. Richard Newhauser (Toronto: Pontifical Institute of Mediaeval Studies, 2012), 100.

revival of extramissionist ideas about the eye as an active agent, able to affect visual objects with its rays. Such anxiety about viewing women and being the object of their gaze reveals the perceived power of women in the late middle ages as both active agents and passive receptors of vision. Recently this has led the medievalist Suzannah Biernoff to question the universality of the twentieth-century model of the "gaze," which is seen as primarily masculine and unidirectional between an active (masculine) viewer and passive (feminine) subject.[34]

Ultimately such anxiety over the female gaze and female bodily functions derived from a relative ignorance about the female body that was rooted in a deeply patriarchal society. Madeline Caviness has suggested a link between the denigration and denial of the female gaze in the medieval period to a desire to maintain male hegemony by permitting only men the right to stare, historically considered an aggressive, dominant, and therefore masculine behavior that would have been perceived as threatening when performed by the typically "weaker" sex.[35] The gaze, especially the female gaze, was thus considered to have the power to penetrate, infect, and even morally or mortally destroy its object of desire, making vision potentially dangerous and the eye a vulnerable orifice in need of protection and control.

Renaissance Visual Theory

The early Renaissance theological interpretation of the gaze was based on late medieval perspectivist optical theory. The establishment in the medieval period of the university system and the scholastic revival of Aristotelian thought greatly influenced the development of Western European optics. The most significant of these late medieval optical theorists, called perspectivists (*perspectiva* is Latin for optics), was the Franciscan scholar Roger Bacon (d. 1292), who synthesized ancient Greek and medieval Arabic optical theories (especially that of Ibn al-Haytham, called Alhacen in the West) with Aristotelian and Christian thought to develop a hybrid theory of vision. Bacon's theory, via his own treatises and those of his followers John Pecham (d. 1292) and Erazmus Ciolek Witelo (d. between 1280 and 1314), remained the dominant optical theory throughout the late Medieval and Renaissance periods.[36] In early fifteenth century Florence, Baconian optics continued to be lectured on and debated at the University of Florence, most notably by Blasius of Parma (d. 1416) and Paolo Toscanelli (d. 1482).[37] By the mid 1430s, copies of optical treatises by Alhacen, Bacon, and Witelo were available in Florence and apparently accessible to the artist Lorenzo Ghiberti (a known

---

[34] Biernoff, *Sight and Embodiment*, 57-59

[35] Madeline Caviness, *Visualizing Women in the Middle Ages: Sight, Spectacle, and Scopic Economy* (Philadelphia: University of Pennsylvania Press, 2001), 19-20.

[36] Bacon's perspectivist theory was the main optical theory in Europe until the discoveries of Kepler and Descartes in the seventeenth century. For Roger Bacon's optical theory and its influence see the sources cited above in note 21 and David C. Lindberg, "Lines of Influence in Thirteenth-Century Optics: Bacon, Witelo, and Pecham," *Speculum* 46, no. 1 (1971): 66-83.

[37] For an overview of early Renaissance optics see Lindberg, *Theories of Vision*, 147-54. For analyses of the influence of perspectivist optics on the art of early Renaissance Florence, see: John White, *Birth and Rebirth of Pictorial Space*, 126-30; Alessandro Parronchi, "Le 'misure dell'occhio' secondo Ghiberti," as reprinted in *Studi su la Dolce Prospettiva* (Milan: A. Martello, 1964), 331-48; Samuel Edgerton, *The Renaissance Rediscovery of Linear Perspective* (New York: Harper and Row, 1975); Kemp, *The Science of Art*, 21-26; Edgerton, *The Heritage of Giotto's Geometry*, ch. 3; Jack M. Greenstein, "On Alberti's 'Sign': Vision and Composition in Quattrocento Painting," *Art Bulletin* 79, no. 4 (1997): 669-98; David Summers, *Vision, Reflection, and Desire in Western Painting* (Chapel Hill: University of North Carolina Press, 2007), 43-77; Samuel Edgerton, *The Mirror, the Window, and the Telescope: How Renaissance Perspective Changed Our Vision of the Universe* (Ithaca and London: Cornell University Press, 2009); and the essays contained in *Renaissance Theories of Vision*, eds. John Shannon Hendrix and H. Charles Carman (Farnham, England and Burlington, VT: Ashgate, 2010).

collaborator with both Michelozzo and Fra Angelico),[38] who cites these sources in his unfinished artistic treatise called *The Commentaries* that contains a substantial chapter on optics.[39] Some of these manuscripts may have been borrowed from San Marco's benefactor Cosimo de'Medici, who is believed to have possessed copies of Bacon's *Perspectiva* and *De multiplicatione specierum* which were subsequently donated to the San Marco Library.[40] In addition, perspectivist optics would have been known to Florence's mendicant preachers and scholars of the Franciscan and Dominican orders, such as Fra Antonino Pierozzi (later made Archbishop of Florence, died in 1459, and was canonized as St. Antoninus), who was one of San Marco's founders and the convent's second prior,[41] and whose magisterial *Summa theologica* (written in the 1450s) contains passages on light and vision that reveal a knowledge of Baconian optics.[42]

Bacon's optical theory was primarily intromissionist in that all objects radiate species (sensible forms, also called 'images,' 'likenesses,' or 'similitudes') in the form of Euclidian visual cones or pyramids from every point on their surface, which impress themselves onto the surrounding medium (usually air) and propagate themselves infinitely, according to a process he derived from an earlier medieval optical theorist Robert Grosseteste (d. 1253) called the "multiplication of species."[43] Visible objects were thus able to constantly impress

---

[38]   Ghiberti likely shared ideas with Michelozzo, his business partner from 1417 to 1423, and with Fra Angelico, with whom he collaborated on the Linaiuoli Tabernacle. Both artists may have been exposed to the same sources that were circulating in Ghiberti's workshop, which according to Samuel Edgerton (*Heritage of Giotto's Geometry*, 98), was a place where early fifteenth-century artists gathered to discuss ideas. Ulrich Middeldorf has also suggested that Fra Angelico was influenced by Ghiberti's sculpture, an influence that may have gone both ways as Andrew Butterfield has noted similarities in composition between Ghiberti's relief panels for the Gates of Paradise of the Florentine Baptistery and contemporary paintings by Fra Angelico. Ulrich Middeldorf, "L'Angelico e la scultura," *Rinascimento* 6:2 (1955): 179-94, and Andrew Butterfield, "Art and Innovation in Ghiberti's Gates of Paradise," in *The Gates of Paradise: Lorenzo Ghiberti's Renaissance Masterpiece*, ed. Gary Radke (New Haven and London: Yale University Press, 2007), 31. For Michelozzo's business partnerships with Ghiberti and Donatello see Harriet McNeal Caplow, "La bottega di Michelozzo," in *Michelozzo scultore e architetto*, 1396-1472, ed. Gabriele Morolli (Florence: Associazione Dimore Storiche Italiane, 1998), 231-6.

[39]   Lorenzo Ghiberti, *I Commentari*, ed. Ottavio Morisani (Naples: Riccardo Riccardi Editore, 1947), 48-215. Ghiberti's discussion of optics in his *Third Commentary* appears to be mostly based on Witelo's *Perspectiva* (1270-78) and on an Italian translation of Alhacen's *Kitāb al-manāzir*, specifically MS. Vat. 4595. For Ghiberti's optical sources see: "Lorenzo Ghiberti Lists the Sources for Perspective," in *Renaissance Art Reconsidered: An Anthology of Primary Sources*, eds. Carol M. Richardson, Kim W. Woods, and Michael W. Frankin (Malden: Blackwell Publishing, 2007), 41-2; Graziela F. Vescovini, "Contributo per la storia della fortuna di Alhazen in Italia: Il volgarizzamento del MS. Vat. 4595 e il *Commentario terzo* del Ghiberti," *Rinascimento* 5 (1965): 1749; Lindberg, *Theories of Vision*, 152-4; and Richard Krautheimer and Trude Hess-Krautheimer, *Lorenzo Ghiberti* (Princeton: Princeton University Press, 1956), 306-14. For analysis of the relationship between optical theory and Ghiberti's art see: Alessandro Parronchi, "Le 'misure dell'occhio' secondo Ghiberti," 331-48;   White, *The Birth and Rebirth of Pictorial Space*, 126-30; Edgerton, *Renaissance Rediscovery*, 73 and 77; Edgerton, *Heritage of Giotto's Geometry*, 97-98; and Kemp, *The Science of Art*, 25-6.

[40]   Edgerton, *Heritage of Giotto's Geometry*, 97. Two copies of Bacon's *Perspectiva* and one copy of *De multiplicatione specierum* can still be found in the Laurentian Library (which inherited much of San Marco's collection) and two fourteenth-century copies of Bacon's *Perspectiva* are in the Biblioteca Riccardiana. See also Berthold A. Ulman and Philip A. Stadter, *The Public Library of Renaissance Florence: Niccolò Niccoli, Cosimo de'Medici and the Library of San Marco* (Padua: Antenore, 1972).

[41]   For Antoninus' role as founder, patron, and prior of San Marco, see: Raoul Morçay, *Saint Antonin, fondateur du Convent de Saint-Marc, Archivéque de Florence 1389-1425* (Tour-Paris, 1914); and Tito Centi, "S. Antonino Pierozzi (Fondatore di S. Marco)," in *La chiesa e il convento di San Marco* (Florence: Cassa di Risparmio di Firenze, 1989), vol. 2, 61-78.

[42]   Specifically, Fra Antonino Pierozzi's *Summa Theologica* (transcribed in the 1450s and completed c. 1477) contains a chapter on optics entitled "On the Twelve Properties of the Divine Grace and their Similarity to Material Light" that expands upon the theories of Grosseteste, Bacon, and Pecham, especially in his discussion of how the "light of grace" (his interpretation of species) "pervades the universe according to optical principles." St. Antoninus, "De duodecim proprietatibus divinae gratiae et similitudine lucis materialis," *Summa Theologica*, book IV, titulus VIII, caput I, cols. 461-468. This is noted in Edgerton, *Renaissance Rediscovery*, 75 and Edgerton, *Heritage of Giotto's Geometry*, 103-4. See also Edgerton, *The Mirror, the Window, and the Telescope*, 30-38.

[43]   Both Grosseteste and Bacon wrote treatises entitled *De multiplicatione specierum* (*On the Multiplication of Species*). For a comparison of the theories of Grosseteste and Bacon see Lindberg, *Theories of Vision*, 94-103 (Grosseteste) and 107-21 (Bacon); and Tachau, "Seeing as Action and Passion in the Thirteenth and Fourteenth Centuries," 338-52. The term *species* was also used by St. Augustine. See, for example, his treatise *On the Trinity*, 11.9.16.

their species upon all other bodies in the paths of their visual pyramids, with or without being seen by the eye. In addition to seeing vision as an intromissive process, Bacon also took over the ancient Greek atomist, and subsequently Platonic, view that for vision to take place the eye must exude its own species out toward other objects in the visible world (a form of extramission). According to Bacon, in order for an object to be seen, species produced by the soul and emitted from the eye had to combine with or "ennoble" the species radiated from the visible object.[44] Attention of the eye was, therefore, necessary for sight to take place. This extramissionist aspect of Bacon's theory is morally significant because it allows for the possibility of human agency, and therefore individual responsibility, in the visual process. Specifically, it provided the soul with the ability to extend itself beyond the limits of the body by empowering the free will to choose and connect with its objects of visual desire.[45] Bacon's theory accommodates Augustine's belief that the viewer's soul *both* initiates vision and "absorbs into itself" the form of its object.[46] Thus, Bacon was able to synthesize the extramissionist theories of Aristotle and earlier Greek thinkers with that of Alhacen, and with St. Augustine's discourse on the empowered soul, making sight and its visual objects *both* active and passive.[47]

Vision as Affection

Bacon also claimed that the eye, as an impressionable medium in itself, receives an object's visual species and that this species continue to propagate through the eye's anatomy, the optic nerve, the internal senses within the brain, and the rest of the visio-perceptual continuum until the object's likeness or 'phantasm' fully impressed upon the soul, where it had the potential to activate desire and affect the viewer's bodily response. This impression of form (without matter) results in a transformation or 'movement' (*alloiosis*) of the impressionable object (in this case the soul) that Aristotle and others have compared to the imprint one creates when making a wax seal.[48] Following Aristotle, the soul is assimilated with its visual object to become "potentially like what the perceived object is actually."[49] Visual objects were, therefore, considered active agents able to impress upon and alter the viewer's soul. Through this transformative process (called 'movement' or 'affection') the beholder actually takes on the "likeness" of her/his visual object. In other words, the viewer becomes like the viewed and the visual object becomes a part of the viewer, forever stored in the soul's memory for use in future cognition.

The soul's internal transformation was also thought to animate physical response by directing the will to move the body. This bodily movement registers externally as an action, gesture, and/or emotion. Thus, the movement of the viewer's soul (called affection) became externally apparent as the animated viewer became a reflection of her/his visible object – literally "we are what we see." In an extreme example, St. Augustine (who also believed in the soul's movement) claimed that images viewed by a pregnant woman could impress themselves onto the fetus and thereby affect the appearance of the

---

44   For Roger Bacon's optical theory see sources cited above in note 21.

45   Roger Bacon, *Opus maius*, 1.7.2: "an animate thing produces species that partake some measure of the power of the soul." This follows Augustine, *On the Trinity*, 11.2.2 and 11.2.5. See Miles, "Vision," 125-42.

46   For Augustine's theory see Miles, "Vision," 128.

47   On the dual nature of perspectivist vision see Tachau, "Seeing as Action and Passion in the Thirteenth and Fourteenth Centuries," 336-59.

48   This analogy can be found in Aristotle, *On the Soul*, 2.12.412b6-9 (translation from *The Basic Works of Aristotle*, 580): "By a 'sense' is meant what has the power of receiving into itself sensible forms of things without matter. This must be conceived of as taking place in the way in which a piece of wax takes on the impress of a signet-ring without the iron or gold...." Others who have made similar analogies include Plato (*Theatetus*), Augustine (*On the Trinity*, 11.2.3), and St. Thomas Aquinas (*Summa theologica*). See Camille, "Before the Gaze," 208-9; and Clark, *Vanities of the Eye*, 15.

49   Aristotle, *On the Soul*, 2.4.418a.

newborn child.[50] Similarly, in his *Ten Books on Architecture* (written c. 1452), the most renowned author of early Renaissance artistic theory, Leon Battista Alberti, seems to echo Augustine when he claims that

> whenever man and wife come together, it is advisable only to hang portraits of men of dignity and handsome appearance, for they say this may have a great influence on the fertility of the mother and the appearance of future offspring.[51]

Movement of the soul is also, in fact, one of the expressed goals of Renaissance *historia* painting. In his treatise *On Painting* (written in 1435 in Latin and 1436 in Italian), Alberti states,

> The *istoria* [sic] which merits both praise and admiration will be so agreeably and pleasantly attractive that it will capture the eye of whatever learned or unlearned person is looking at it and will *move his soul [animi motu / movimento d'animo]* (italics mine).[52]

These statements by Alberti are evidence that the idea of the soul's impressionability and motility (in addition to vision's affective power) endured into the early Renaissance. Alberti goes on to claim that the bodies depicted in paintings should be naturalistic and appropriate reflections of the internal states of the figures they represent in order to function successfully as moral exemplars and thereby serve the didactic and affective purposes of the *historia*:

> Then too, a *historia* will move the souls [*animos*] of the viewers when the persons who are depicted there show most clearly their movements of the soul. For it is decreed by nature, according to which nothing can be found that is not grasping of its like, that we mourn with those who are mourning, that we laugh with those who are laughing, we grieve with those who are grieving. But these movements of the soul [*hi motus animi*] are known from the movements of the body.[53]

---

[50] Augustine, *On the Trinity*, 11.2.5. This is also cited in Miles, "Vision," 130.

[51] Leon Battista Alberti, *Ten Books on Architecture*, 9.4, as quoted in Leon Battista Alberti, *On the Art of Building in Ten Books* (orig. 1452), 4th ed., trans. Joseph Rykwert, Neil Leach and Robert Tavernor (Cambridge, Mass. and London: The MIT Press, 1992), 299-300.

[52] Leon Battista Alberti, *On Painting*, 2.40, as quoted in the translation by John R. Spencer (New Haven and London: Yale University Press, 1966), 75. Cecil Grayson's English translation of Alberti's *On Painting* was recently re-edited and re-issued by Martin Kemp (London: Penguin Books, 1991), 75. Grayson's translation eliminates all mention of the soul from Alberti's text, which functions to divorce this quote from its theological roots. This is despite the fact that Grayson's transcriptions of the original Latin and Italian contain the phrases "*animi motu*" and "*movimento d'animo*," respectively. Grayson's translation reads: "A *historia* you can justifiably praise and admire will be one that reveals itself to be so charming and attractive as to hold the eye of the learned and unlearned spectator for a long while with a certain sense of pleasure and *emotion*" (italics mine).

[53] Alberti, *On Painting*, 2.41 (see also 2.42-3), as translated in Jack M. Greenstein, "Alberti on Historia: A Renaissance View of the Structure of Significance in Narrative Painting," *Viator* 21 (1990): 290. See also translations by Spencer, 77; and Grayson, 76. This is an argument that I am currently expanding upon for a separate publication. A similar Renaissance claim about the efficacy of images, especially those most "like" the viewer, can be found in the Florentine Dominican Fra Giovanni Dominici's *Rule for the Management of Family Care* (1403) in which Dominici recommends the possession of "paintings in the house of holy boys, or young virgins, in which your child when still in swaddling clothes may delight as being like himself, and may be seized upon by the like thing, with actions and signs attractive to infancy. And as I say for paintings, so I say for sculptures..." This is an excerpt of the larger passage quoted in David Freedberg, *The Power of Images: Studies in the History and Theory of Response* (Chicago and London: The University of Chicago Press, 1989), 4. See also Fra Antonino Pierozzi's admonition against monstrous images in St. Antoninus, *Summa theologica*, vol. III, 8, sec. 4, ch. 11, as quoted in Creighton Gilbert, "The Archbishop and the Painters of Florence," *Art Bulletin* 41 (1959): 79. For more on the affective power of image and the relationship between the exterior body's form and internal state of its soul, see Thomas Dale, "Monsters, Corporeal Deformities and Phantasms in the Romanesque Cloister of St. Michel de Cuxa," *Art Bulletin* 83 (2001): 402-30.

Bodies, therefore, could be read. The moral body (actual or depicted) could, thus, serve as instructional exemplar, able to effect a positive transformation within the soul of the beholder which would be mirrored in the beholder's bodily response. As a corollary, no sin could go unseen as the soul's condition was always apparent in the body. People who believed this must have been very aware of the images projected by their bodies and how they were perceived by others. Dallas Denery has recently claimed that, as a result, "seeing and being seen" were concerns "absolutely central to religious and spiritual life" in periods influenced by perspectivist optics.[54] As Denery has recently highlighted, Dominicans were especially aware that their sins were visible to all who could see their bodies, including when they were alone in the presence of God the omniscient.[55] Denery has argued that this greater visual awareness led to a Dominican culture of constant visual surveillance (as we are better at accurately viewing others than we are at viewing ourselves), within the monastery and when a friar moved beyond the convent's walls. Since one did not always have control over one's surrounding visual objects and the species they emitted (especially once outside the claustrum of the monastery), one had to be instructed or trained to either avoid unchaste visual stimuli by not allowing its species to enter the eye (the soul's "gatekeeper") or to filter out unchaste stimuli through the soul's faculties of judgment, both of which are advocated by Peter of Limoges. Within the church and monastery vision could be more easily monitored, regulated, and controlled.

Vision as Touch and Passion

> [Rays] shine through
> the eyes and touch whatever we see.
> – St. Augustine, *On the Trinity*, 9.3.3

According to current visual theory, vision requires distance between the eye and its object, therefore, vision is very different from the sense of touch which requires actual physical contact between the sense and its object. Baconian optics, however, describes vision as a more intimate sensory process that is almost tactile.[56] According to Bacon's optics, the object itself does not 'touch' the eye; however, it impresses its immaterial form (or species) into the medium of air, which gives (invisible) matter to the impressed form. Air, therefore, serves as the connective membrane that links the eye with its object.

Bacon also claims that as an object's species enter the eye and impress themselves into its matter the eye experiences both a pleasurable and a slightly painful sensation (or passion), most pronounced when looking at bright objects, such as the sun. Bacon states:

> [The *anterior glacialis*] must be somewhat thick, in order that it may experience a feeling from the impressions [*species*] that is a kind of pain. For we observe that strong lights and color narrow vision and injure it, and inflict pain...Therefore vision always experiences a feeling that is a kind of pain...[57]

The physicality of the visual process is thus indicated by the resulting pain and by the alteration

---

[54]   Denery, *Seeing and Being Seen*, 14.

[55]   Denery, *Seeing and Being Seen*, ch.1.

[56]   For a discussion of late medieval vision as "fleshy" and "tactile," see Biernoff, *Sight and Embodiment*, ch. 4. The idea that vision was tactile is rooted in Platonic theory and can also be found in the writings of St. Augustine. See Miles, "Vision," 127-8.

[57]   Bacon, *Opus Maius*, 2.445-6; 5.1.4.2, as quoted in Biernoff, *Sight and Embodiment*, 96. See also Bacon, *De multiplicatione specierum*, 19-21 / 1.1. Bacon's source appears to be Aristotle, *On the Soul*, 2.2.413b.

or 'movement' of the matter of the body and its soul. Bacon (like Augustine), therefore, suggests that when we perceive something we touch it with our eyes. It, then, physically enters the body and becomes a part of us.[58]

Consideration of the vision as an intimate and slightly painful act of physical contact (passion) with one's visual object makes one rethink claims about the eye's wounding power, statements such as St. Matthew's that "anyone who looks at a woman lustfully has already committed adultery with her in his heart,"[59] and the Dominican prohibition against fixing one's gaze on a woman. During the periods influenced by Baconian optics, desirous seeing was a form of carnal knowledge, involving desire, physical contact, and penetration, much more akin to our contemporary idea of the sexual act. It is no wonder that fixing one's eyes upon women was expressly prohibited by the Dominican Constitution that governed the friars at San Marco and necessitated their need for a certain degree of claustrum within the church, especially when female laity was present.

"Fixing the Eye": Gazing with Attention and Affection

As previously mentioned, the *Constitution of the Order of Friars Preachers* declares it a grave fault "If anyone going to a place where women are present '*fixes his eye*,' at least does so habitually, or if he speaks alone with a woman about anything other than confession or honest matters" (italics mine).[60] This regulation derives from the *Rule of St. Augustine* that warns:

> you must not *fix your gaze* upon any woman…. for it is not by thought or passionate feeling alone but also *by one's gaze* that lustful desires mutually arise. And do not say that your hearts are pure if there is immodesty of the eye, because the *unchaste eye carries the message of an impure heart* (italics mine).[61]

St. Augustine defined 'attention' (*aspectus*) as "the power that *fixes the sense of sight* on an object" (italics mine).[62] Augustine claimed that desire begins in the soul, which activates the will to move the body (in the case of vision this would include the eye) to 'grasp' its desired object by fixing its attention upon it.[63] According to Augustine and Bacon, the object in turn imprints itself upon the soul which animates the body, transforming them in its image. Augustine describes this assimilative process as one of love or affection, which he defines as a powerful concentration of the will's energy as generated by the soul's desire: "[The soul] binds itself to these images with so strong a love as ever to regard itself as something of the same kind… it is made like them."[64] It was, therefore, important for

---

58 See Biernoff, *Sight and Embodiment*, ch. 4; and Denery, "Seeing and Being Seen," 93-6. On this complete assimilation see Bacon, *De multiplicatione specierum*, 1.2.40. This idea of assimilation comes from Augustine, *On the Trinity*, 10.6.8. See Miles, "Vision," 128.

59 *Gospel of St. Matthew*, 5.28.

60 *Constitution of the Order of Friars Preachers*, 17. 42, as translated in Hood, *Fra Angelico at S. Marco*, 294.

61 *The Rule of St. Augustine*, 4.22.

62 Augustine, *On the Trinity*, 11.2.2. For most of the following discussion of St. Augustine I have primarily relied on Margaret Miles, "Vision: The Eye of the Body and the Eye of the Mind in Saint Augustine's *De trinitate and Confessions*," *Journal of Religious History* 63, no. 2 (1983): 125-42.

63 "Before the vision was produced, there already existed a will to form the sense attached to it for the body to be perceived." Augustine, *On the Trinity*, 11.5.9, as quoted in Miles, "Vision," 127. The soul "binds itself to these images with so strong a love as ever to regard itself as something of the same kind… it is made like them." Augustine, *On the Trinity*, 10.6.8, as quoted in Miles, "Vision," 128. St. Augustine also makes the analogy between sight and touch when he states: "[Rays] shine through the eyes and touch whatever we see." Augustine, *On the Trinity*, 9.3.3, as quoted in Miles, "Vision," 127.

64 Augustine, *On the Trinity*, 10.6.8, as quoted in Miles, "Vision," 128.

the soul's salvation that the eye did not fixate upon objects (such as women) that could lead the soul to a sinful response (such as lust), which would make itself apparent to others through the body.

For Augustine, it was not visible objects that were dangerous. Rather, what was potentially dangerous was the degree of the soul's investment of attention to them.[65] Augustine differentiates between the glance and the gaze, as the latter involves a greater investment of psychic energy or attention.[66] Augustine maintained that one could train the gaze of the eye and mind in order to achieve higher vision (Augustine is referring to inner vision of the mind, however, Margaret Miles notes that this follows the pattern understood for physical vision).[67] Conversely, the eye and mind could be trained not to devote attention to ("fix" upon) objects that could lead to sin. This training requires what Augustine called "continence," which he defines as a conscious concentration or redirection of the soul's energy.[68] If, according to Augustine[69] and Bacon, the will had the power to prevent the bodily senses from "combining" with sensible things, visual desire (a product of human will) could therefore be controlled, trained, or directed away from unchaste objects and redirected toward morally positive (external and/or internal) images, such as God or saintly exemplars. This could be done by controlling input from the external senses in order to concentrate and redirect the flow of the soul's energy towards physical or mental images that might lead to self-reflection and spiritual vision.

The San Marco Solution

At San Marco architectural barriers protected the friars from the potential dangers of gazing upon women and being the object of the female gaze. When seated in against the side walls of the choir, the friars would have had little chance of viewing women or being acted upon by their visual rays, as the friars were separated from their female congregants by two 16.5 feet *tramezzi* that served to maintain their ocular chastity. Michelozzo's solution, thus, prevented visual contact between friars and the female laity during mass; however it only reduced (but did not eliminate) visual contact between male and female congregants, who would have been able to freely gaze upon each other through the nave *tramezzo's* central opening, which was necessary to allow visual access to the high altar. Complete control over such gazing between the male and female laity may not have been possible at San Marco; however, there is evidence that non-architectural means were employed to reduce its occurrence. Sermons, such as those previously quoted by Peter of Limoges, Fra Antonino Pierozzi, and Fra Girolamo Savonarola contained warnings intended for the lay audience about the dangers of the gaze, teaching the visual awareness necessary for avoiding sin. These homiletical warnings may have been supplemented by pastoral recommendations for personal ocular control, as found in Fra Antonino Pierozzi's book of instructions written for Dianora Tornabuoni in circa 1450, in which he advises:

> And do this, go to the church and take good care of your sight, holding it well and mortified so as not to mar your spirit with scandal; and do this so that you yourself are not the reason, through incaution, of the loss in a

---

[65] Miles, "Vision," 133.
[66] Miles, "Vision," 136-7.
[67] Miles, "Vision," 130-3.
[68] The conservation of the soul's energy was called continence. Miles, "Vision," 133. Augustine, *Confessions*, 10.29.40.
[69] Augustine, *On the Trinity*, 336.

short time of what you have acquired only after a length.[70]

Antoninus further instructed Dianora that upon entering the church, after making the sign of the Cross with holy water, she must position herself "in that place where you believe you will make the least scandal with your sight or your sighting by others."[71] In these passages the female churchgoer is advised to practice visual self-restraint and vigilance. She is also denied the right to look and to be visible to others.

A variety of means were, therefore, employed by San Marco's Dominicans in order to control the gaze within the church, including tall architectural barriers (the tramezzi) to limit visibility, homiletical warnings about the dangers of the gaze, and pastoral instruction that encouraged visual self-awareness.

The Gaze Refocused

So far, this essay has primarily addressed where one was not supposed to look when attending Mass at San Marco. Where then was one supposed to focus the eye? In his *Moral Treatise on the Eye* Peter of Limoges recommends that one should redirect one's visual attention away from the potential dangers of the carnal body by meditating on morally and spiritually uplifting imagery; for example:

> The opening [*foramen*] that we ought to gaze upon most frequently is the wound of Christ who was pierced on the cross.... Anyone can enter into the interior of his conscience and meditate in his mind's eye on Christ's wound, so that he conforms to Christ's sufferings through his model.[72]

Although in this example Peter seems to be referring to meditation upon a mental image of Christ, it can be compared with the contemporary practice of affective devotion that required the contemplation of and assimilation with actual artistic images, such as painted or sculptural crucifixes, manuscript illuminations, and altarpieces depicting Christ or other moral exemplars. Recently, Robert Gaston has argued against the commonly-held belief that affective devotion was practiced primarily by the (more "sentimental") Franciscans, but only marginally by the (more "intellectual") Dominicans.[73] As evidence of

---

[70]   Antonino Pierozzi (St. Antoninus), *Opera a ben vivere con altri suoi ammestramenti* (orig. c, 1450), ed. Francesco Palermo (Florence: Cellini, 1858), 164, as quoted in Randolph, "Regarding Women in Sacred Space," 39.

[71]   Ibid, 39.

[72]   Peter of Limoges, VII. A vii, as quoted in Clark, 338. Also quoted in Biernoff, *Sight and Embodiment*, 123.

[73]   Robert W. Gaston, "Affective Devotion and the Early Dominicans: The Case of Fra Angelico," in *Rituals, Images and Words: The Varieties of Cultural Expression in Late Medieval and Early Modern Europe*, eds. F.W. Kent and Charles Zika (Turnhout: Brepols, 2005), 87-117. Gaston claims that in their desire to differentiate Dominican intellectuality from Franciscan spirituality scholars have intentionally ignored evidence that suggests that the Dominicans practiced similar image-instigated emotionally affective devotion as has been identified for Franciscans. Gaston (92-3) argues that "Dominican opinion that affective devotion was marginal in the early spirituality of the Order was shaped by developments in liturgical theory that inspired Vatican II, and has to be viewed in light of the consequences of that Council's liturgical reforms." Instead, he (105) concludes that "Dominican approaches to affective prayer, absorbed through many of the leading scholars, preachers and authors of devotional tracts for brethren and laypersons alike, would have influenced the ways in which the novices and friars used the frescoes for their private prayer." For related material on Fra Angelico's images and prayer see William Hood, "Saint Dominic's Manners of Praying: Gestures in Fra Angelico's Cell Frescoes at San Marco," *Art Bulletin* 68, no. 2 (1986): 195-206; idem, "Fra Angelico at S. Marco: Art and the Liturgy of the Cloistered Life," in *Christianity and the Renaissance: Image and Religious Imagination in the Quattrocento*, eds. Timothy Verdon and John Henderson (Syracuse: Syracuse University Press, 1990), 108-29; and idem, *Fra Angelico at S. Marco* (New Haven: Yale University Press), 1993. Gaston (102) notes that Hood "draws no conclusion regarding the nature of meditation that would have been directed at such pictures." Gaston (104) further criticizes Hood for suggesting that Dominic's meditation was intellectual, stimulated by texts and abstractions rather than by images. See also the discussion of the devotional practices of the Dominican Henry of Suso in Jeffrey Hamburger, *The Visual and the Visionary: Art and Female Spirituality in Late Medieval Germany* (Cambridge, Mass: MIT Press, 1998). Gaston (113-6) claims that Suso's writings were known to the Dominicans at Santa Maria Novella and San Marco and argues that Suso may, in fact, be relevant to our understanding of the works of Fra Angelico.

Dominican affective practice, Gaston cites St. Dominic's own devotional practices and several significant Dominican sermons and texts, including the following instructions from San Marco's Fra Antonino Pierozzi to Dianora Tornabuoni:

> I am comforted all the more [with] your charity in that every day you spend a bit in meditation upon the passion of our Jesus Christ [...] kneel before a Crucifix and with the eyes of the mind, more than with those of the body, consider his face. First, the crown of thorns, fit around his head [...] next the eyes, full of tears and blood; the mouth, full of bile and slobber and blood; the beard, similarly full of slobber and blood and bile, it has been all spit upon and torn; next the face, all obscured, and spit upon, and bruised from the blows to the cheeks and to the head, and all is bloody. And in reverence to all these things direct an Our Father with a Hail Mary.[74]

This quote reveals that San Marco's former prior (and patron of Fra Angelico) believed in the affective power of images (in this case a Crucifix). Gaston illustrates his argument in favor of Dominican affective devotion with images by Fra Angelico and suggests that Fra Angelico's frescoes in the convent of San Marco were intended to function affectively.[75]

Is it not also likely that artistic imagery (especially by Fra Angelico) within the church of San Marco served an affective function and that this function might have been supported by Michelozzo's architecture? In addition to being focused on each other (surveillance), the gazes of the friars when in their choir would have taken in the high altar with its new altarpiece containing saints and *beati* located on the front and sides of its frame and predella.[76] According to perspectivist optical theory, by directing visual attention to these images, the friars could have incorporated and assimilated with these moral exemplars in order to achieve a higher state of spiritual understanding.

From the transept and nave, the single opening in each of San Marco's *tramezzi* would have concentrated and, therefore, strengthened the effect of the laity's gaze by reducing the visual pyramid. The alignment of these openings in the center of the church framed a view of the primary object of visual desire during mass which was the body of Christ, present in the Eucharist and in the high altarpiece.[77] In fact, in the *San Marco Altarpiece* Christ's naturalistically depicted body appears three times—as an infant ruler, during his sacrificial death on the cross (including blood pouring and spurting from his

---

[74] This text is from Antonino Pierozzi, *Opera a ben vivere con altri suoi ammestramenti* (orig. c. 1450). It is quoted as follows by Gaston ("Affective Devotion and the Early Dominicans," 112, note 72): "Conforto anco la carità vostra che ogni dì pigliate una poca di meditazione della passion del nostro Gesù Cristo [...] inginocchiateve dinanzi ad un Crocefisso cogli occhi della mente, più che con quelli del corpo, considerate la faccia sua. Prima, alla corone delle spine, fittegliele in testa, insino ad célabro; poi gli occhi, pieni di lacrime e sangue; la bocca, piena di fiele e di bava e di sangue; la barba, similmente piena di bava e di sangue e di fiele, essendo tutta sputacchiata, e spelazzata; poi la faccia, tutta oscurata, e sputacchiata, e livida per le percosse delle gotate e delle coma, e tutta sanguinosa. E reverenzia di tutte queste cose direte un pater nostro con un avemaria." This quote also appears in Miklós Boskovits, "Arte e formazione religiose: Il caso del Beato Angelico," in *L'uomo di fronte all'arte: Valori estetici e valori etico-religiosi: Atti del 55o corso di aggiornamento culturale dell'Università Catolica, La Spezia, 8-13 settembre, 1985* (Milan: Vita e pensiero, 1986), 158.

[75] Gaston, "Affective Devotion and the Early Dominicans," 102-17.

[76] Hood (*Fra Angelico at San Marco*, 97-121) has previously claimed that the standing saints and *beati* in the altarpiece's frame and the miracles performed by Sts. Cosmas and Damian that appear in the side predella panels would have served as reminders to the Dominican friars of their institutional history and mission.

[77] For the body of Christ, especially on the Crucifix, as focus of meditation in later Middle Ages see Hahn, "Visio Dei," 49; and Biernoff, "Ocular Communion," in *Sight and Embodiment*, ch. 6.

wounds), and as deceased before the tomb with his wounds in prominent display—and in three different visual modes—*sacra conversazione*, icon, and narrative—in a vertical axis over the center of the mensa of the high altar (see Fig. 6). The axial arrangement of the openings and the high altar would have ensured that the species emanating from Christ's body could pass through them to hit the viewer's properly positioned eye, penetrate it, and pass to the internal senses so as to affect the soul and enhance the viewer's moral and spiritual transformation.[78]

From the lower church, the female congregation had the least visual access to the high altar as they were separated from it by two dividing walls. Any view they might have had of the high altar through the openings in the *tramezzi* would not have been easily obtained in a crowded church, when their vision would have been blocked by men and other women standing in front of the choir opening (see, for example, Fig. 5). The female congregation was likely presented with an alternative body of Christ in the Crucifixion rood located above the nave *tramezzo* (thereby functioning as a rood screen).[79] A Crucifixion rood would have directed the female laity's potentially harmful gazes upward and, therefore, away from people and objects in the church. Moreover, a rood slanted slightly downward would have radiated its strongest rays toward their bodies, impressing

Christ's body upon them with or without the engagement of the eye.

Conclusion

Consideration of how vision was believed to work in the early Renaissance period provides a deeper understanding of the fifteenth-century renovation of the church of San Marco and the viewer's experience within it. The architecture of San Marco was not an inert container of space. Rather, it should be considered part of an overall program intended to enhance one's devotional experience, which depended greatly on proper engagement of the eye. Architectural barriers sublimated the carnal gaze by obscuring the potentially corrupting corporeal body, while openings were designed to focus the lay viewer's attention by framing the body of Christ, in an attempt to direct the gaze toward the spiritual body.[80] Once the soul's attention was properly directed, the spiritual body had the power to impress itself on the viewer's body and move the viewer's soul to a higher spiritual state through affective devotion. In addition to visual censorship through the use of architectural barriers, San Marco's Dominicans seem to have employed pastoral strategies similar to those proposed by Peter of Limoges, namely sermons and written instructions that identified sinful imagery, advocated visual self-consciousness, and warned about the potential dangers of the gaze.

---

[78] I am currently working on a separate essay that addresses the visual and spiritual functions of the *San Marco Altarpiece* in greater detail.

[79] It is possible that the rood that stood atop the nave *tramezzo* was the School of Giotto Crucifix dated c. 1300 (currently in San Marco), which may have originally stood over the entrance to the Sylvestrine choir. The only mention I have found regarding a rood at San Marco concerns a later *Crucifix* painted by Baccio Montelupo in 1496 (currently in the Museo di San Marco), which is recorded as having been placed above the choir *tramezzo*. ASF, S. Marco 105, no. 73, c. 20 (16 October 1496) records payment for the Crucifix "*sopra il coro*" of San Marco. According to Giorgio Vasari (*Le vite...*, vol. 4, 541), "Mettendosi anco a lavorare il legno, intaglio Crocifissi grandi quanto il vivo; onde infinito numero per Italia ne fece, e fra gli altri uno a'frati di San Marco in Fiorenza sopra la porta del coro." Filippo Baldinucci (*Notizie Dei Professori Del Disegno Da Cimabue in Qua ... Opera*, orig. 1681-1728, Firenze: Eurografica, 1974, III, 146-7), who was in Florence at the time of the choir wall's removal also locates Baccio da Montelupo's *Crucifix* on the choir wall, suggesting that it remained on the choir wall from 1496 until the wall's removal in 1678.

[80] Biernoff (*Sight and Embodiment*, 125) states that St. Augustine, St. Bernard of Clairvaux, and Peter of Limoges all "approached the regulation or censorship of bodily sensation as a means of stimulating internal, spiritual sight."

FRANCISCANS AND THE MAN OF SORROWS IN FIFTEENTH-CENTURY PADUA*

William Barcham

his short paper discusses how the Order of the Friars Minor in fifteenth-century Padua employed, developed and interpreted the image of the Man of Sorrows. The subject, known in Latin as *Imago pietatis* and in Greek as *Akra Tapeinosis*, intimately focuses upon the dead Christ, his figure vertical but detached from the story of the Crucifixion (Fig. 1)[1]. Though the savior is essential to Christian redemption, his representation as Man of Sorrows did not always play a Eucharistic role in church. Indeed, the varying functions of the image within the Franciscan Padua in the Quattrocento are but one justification for this study. The objects under consideration here also responded to Minorite piety; they present a rich and impressive array of media and techniques, and most (but not all) of them originated in just two Franciscan churches, S. Antonio of the Conventuals and S. Francesco Grande of the Obser-

vants. Notwithstanding these rationales, the material has never before been considered as an interrelated group or even deemed possibly linked. It should be remembered, finally, that two important factors pinpoint the distinctive religious and cultural milieu of Padua: the city chose a Franciscan friar, St. Anthony, as its patron saint and centered its intellectual life on its famed university.

I. Background

To begin, we briefly survey the link between the Friars Minor and the Man of Sorrows in northern Italy before c.1400, that is, after its genesis in Byzantium in the late twelfth century and following upon its arrival on the Italian peninsula c.1260-75.[2] Surviving evidence establishes that indeed the bond between the Franciscans and the *Imago pietatis* was noteworthy from the outset.[3] Several of the first extant examples of the Man of Sorrows in Western European art, those dating to between c.1270 and

* Many thanks are owed, first, to Xavier Seubert for having invited the authors to participate in the conference leading to this publication and, second, to all the participants in the conference for their helpful and constructive criticisms of the initial talk. This study is part of larger and related projects: a book on the Man of Sorrows in Venetian and Veneto art, and an exhibition on the subject entitled *Passion in Venice*, see below, footnote 43. On the Man of Sorrows by the same authors, see "Gli esordi del *Cristo passo* nell'arte veneziana e la *Pala feriale* di Paolo Veneziano," in *Cose Nuove e Cose Antiche, Scritti per Monsignor Antonio Niero e Don Bruno Bertoli* (Venice: Biblioteca Nazionale Marciana, 2006), 403-429, and "Bernardino da Feltre, the Monte di Pietà and the *Man of Sorrows*: Activist, Microcredit and Logo," *Artibus et historiae* 57 (2008): 35-63.
[1] The English 'Man of Sorrows' and its modern European equivalents draw upon Isaiah 53,3: "To whom has the arm of the Lord been revealed? He grew up like a sapling before him, like a shoot from the parched earth; There was in him no stately bearing to make us look at him, nor appearance that would attract us to him. He was spurned and avoided by men, a *man of sorrows*, accustomed to infirmity."

Fig 1. Akra Tapeinosis (Utmost Humiliation), *or* Man of Sorrows *(reverse of two sided icon, second half of 12th century, 115 x 77.5 cm (45.27 x 30.5 in.), Byzantine Museum, Kastoria, Greece.*

(Photo: Museum of Byzantine Art, Kastoria)

Fig 2. Angel with Franciscan Coat-of-arms, c. 1450, marble, 81.6 x 55.5 cm (32.12 x 21.85 in.), Isabella Stewart Gardner Museum, Boston, S5w.
(Photo: author)

Fig 3. Icon, Man of Sorrows *(Crusader icon), 13th century, tempera on panel, 13 x 8.5 cm (5.1 x 3.3 in.), Mount Sinai, Monastery of St. Catherine. (Photo: Ann Arbor, The University of Michigan; Sinai Archives, Courtesy of the Michigan-Princeton-Alexandria Expedition to Mount Sinai, neg. #2511)*

Fig 4. Man of Sorrows *(right wing of diptych), c. 1260, egg tempera on wood, 32.4 x 22.8 cm (12.74 x 8.97 in.), London, National Gallery, NG6572.*
(© National Gallery, London / Art Resource, NY)

c.1320, boast a Franciscan origin or are associated with the Minorite Order. These Franciscan-related images total seven in number and exceed in quantity any other corporate or communal affiliation the figure appears to have enjoyed at the time. Furthermore, many later works of art—that is, those following in the course of the fourteenth century—exhibit the same link. Before identifying the works, however, two questions inevitably come to mind: why did the Man of Sorrows appeal in particular to the Franciscan community, and how did the friars encounter the subject before c.1260-75?

Francis' spiritual conformity with the crucified Christ was divinely sealed in his stigmata, the saint's mystical experience that led to his later renown as *alter Christus*, his *Christoformitas*, which is reflected in the Franciscan coat-of-arms (Fig. 2).[4] Francis taught the same virtues of poverty, humility and penitence that find expression in the abject and naked figure of the *Imago pietatis*, which exhorts the faithful to accept suffering and surrender to the divine plan of redemption. The Man of Sorrows promoted meditation upon Christ's anguish and death as one of its prime objectives and, accordingly, helped friars understand that just as Jesus willingly endured his earthly tribulations, so Francis submit-

ted to his. The figure also reminded the brethren at times of their twofold dedication to the stigmata, the Lord's and those of the Order's founder. But while Franciscans might be expected to revere the Man of Sorrows, the question nonetheless needles as to when and where they might have first caught sight of the Byzantine image. A definitive answer to that is not likely to emerge, but the early history of the Order offers plausible hypotheses we consider before examining the figure of the Man of the Sorrows in fifteenth-century Padua.

Members of the Franciscan Order resided in Constantinople by c.1220, and within two decades enjoyed close relations with the Latin court then reigning in the ex-Byzantine capital.[5] The friars' monastery had a famous library of Greek books, and individual brothers, one assumes, must have read the language. A few surely spoke it too: when friars traveled across Byzantine lands to visit Nicea, where the exiled Greek court waited while preparing to retake Constantinople, they negotiated for the possible Union between Catholic and Orthodox Christianity. By the first years of the 1260s, therefore, members of the brotherhood were familiar with Byzantine culture and had numerous occasions to see icons of the *Akra Tapeinosis* in the

---

[2]   The bibliography on the subject is now immense, but above all see Hans Belting, "An Image and Its Function in the Liturgy: The Man of Sorrows in Byzantium," *Dumbarton Oaks Papers* 34-35 (1980-81): 1-16, and idem, *The Image and Its Public in the Middle Ages, Form and Function of Early Paintings of the Passion*, trans. Mark Bartusis and Raymond Meyer (New Rochelle, NY: A.D. Caratzas, 1990). The issues of when, how and where the subject first arrived from the Byzantine East are complicated and cannot be addressed here; certainly drawings and pattern books may have been involved in the transmission. Paul Binski, in "The Faces of Christ in Matthew Paris's Chronica Majora," in *Tributes in Honor of James H. Marrow*, eds. Jeffrey K. Hamburger and Anne S. Korteweg (London: Harvey Miller, 2006), 85-92, rightly questions whether Paris's famous face of the dead Christ in his manuscript of the 1240s-50s is indeed that of the Man of Sorrows. The stylistic delineation of the face surely does not betray a Byzantine source, but Paris's private image nonetheless evokes a response similar to that of the Orthodox icon.

[3]   About a decade ago, the Franciscan scholar Mario Sensi named Angelo Clareno, a late thirteenth-century Friar Minor traveling in Greece, as the likely disseminator of the Man of Sorrows in central Italy; see his "*Imago pietatis* in ambiente francescano," *Il Beato Antonio da Stroncone*, vol. 3 (Atti delle giornate di studio, Stroncone, 4 May 1996 and 29 November 1997) (Assisi: Porziuncola, 1999), 257-338, and "Dall'*Imago Pietatis* alle cappelle gregoriane, Immagini, racconti e devozioni per la 'Visione' e la Cristomimesi," *Collectantana Francescana* 70 (2000): 79-148. Sensi's Franciscan-centric position regarding the intimate relationship between the Order and the image is surely correct, as is Belting's similar point of view in *The Image and Its Public*, p. 145 (above all).

[4]   The Franciscan coat-of-arms crosses the bare right arm of Christ held upwards (as if hanging on the cross) with the Francis' clothed left arm also held up. The palms of both hands bear stigmata. See Servus Gieben, *Lo Stemma Francescano, Origine e Sviluppo* (Rome: Istituto storico dei Cappuccini, 2009).

[5]   For the following material, see Martiniano Roncaglia, OFM, *I Francescani in Oriente durante le Crociate (Sec. XIII)*, vol. 1, and *Les Frères Mineurs et l'Eglise Grecque Orthodoxe au XIIIe Siècle (1231-1274)*, vol. 2 (*Storia delle Provincia di Terra Santa*) (Cairo: Centro di studi Orientali, della custodia Francescana di Terra Santa, 1954).

Latin Empire and nearby territories. The Order operated in still another geographical setting where friars might also have encountered the Man of Sorrows, in the Crusader Kingdom where they guarded several holy sites between the years 1244, when the Christians lost Jerusalem, and 1291, when their capital at Acre fell to Islam.[6] That same half-century witnessed an upswing in the creation of Crusader icons destined for the churches and resident armies of the Holy Land, and one of the most active Western ateliers in the Crusader capital of Acre produced images now characterized as Veneto-Byzantine in style. One such surviving icon even depicts the *Akra Tapeinosis* (Mt. Sinai, Monastery of St. Catherine), and others like it must have existed too (Fig. 3).[7] Hence, whether resident in Constantinople, traveling through Byzantine-held areas or posted to the Holy Land, members of the Franciscan Order had more than a few opportunities by c.1260-1270 to view the *Akra Tapeinosis* and appreciate its devotional appeal.

Even members of the Franciscan Order who never left Western Europe could have been acquainted with the Man of Sorrows too. In 1274 Pope Gregory X opened the Second Council of Lyon in order to discuss the Union of the Latin and Orthodox Churches, a point referred to in the preceding paragraph.[8] Emperor Michael Palaeologus (or Palaiologos), having already retaken Constantinople and re-establishing Greek rule there in 1261, sent ambassadors and clergy to Lyon from his distant capital, and many Franciscans, including St. Bonaventure, the general of the Order, also arrived

to participate in the council. Besides attending the formal meetings lasting through the summer, the prominent ecclesiastics of the Latin and Greek confessions attended the rites and ceremonies of their counterparts, Latin officials surely impressed by the complement of icons in an Eastern service. Like their brethren serving in the Holy Land, Franciscans at Lyon would unquestionably have taken note of an Orthodox *Akra Tapeinosis*—if indeed such a panel was present. An image of the abject and forlorn Christ would have strongly resounded with the values of Francis, their saintly founder.

Whether members of the Franciscan Order became familiar with the Man of Sorrows in the Greek East, the Holy Land or amidst Orthodox rituals in Lyon, evidence exists that the friars, or artists working for them, were responsible for introducing the subject onto Italian soil. The case rests on considering the Sinai icon, referred to above, vis-à-vis the ex-Stoclet diptych (Fig. 4), a work probably dating to the third quarter of the thirteenth century and pairing the Virgin and Child on its left wing with the Man of Sorrows on its right (London, National Gallery).[9] The latter figure is stylistically akin to its counterpart on the Sinai panel and may be regarded as descending from or related to a Crusader icon. The ex-Stoclet diptych also bears similarities with a second work, again of Crusader origin but now a diptych where the Crucifixion replaces the Man of Sorrows on the right valve (Chicago, Art Institute).[10] To be sure, the two images relate different subjects, and one cannot substitute for the other, but the visual connections between the diptychs are striking

[6] Valentino Pace, "Italy and the Holy Land: Import-Export. I. The Case of Venice," in *The Meeting of Two Worlds, Cultural Exchange between East and West during the Period of the Crusades*, ed. Vladimir P. Goss (*Studies in Medieval Culture*, XXI) (Kalamazoo MI: Medieval Institute Publishers, Western Michigan University, 1986), 331-345 (336, for the Franciscans especially within the context of the Crusades and the Holy Land).
[7] Belting, *The Image and Its Public*, 122.
[8] See Charles-Joseph Hefele, *Histoire des conciles d'après les documents originaux*, tome VI, part. 1 (Paris: Letouzey, 1914), 153-181, and Gilbert Dagron, "Byzance et l'Union," in *1274, Anne Charnieère, Mutations et Continuités* (Paris: Éditions du Centre national de la recherche scientifique, 1977), 191-202.
[9] Joanna Cannon, "The Stoclet 'Man of Sorrows': a thirteenth-century Italian diptych reunited," *Burlington Magazine* 141 (1999): 107-112.
[10] Christopher Lloyd, *Italian Paintings before 1600 in The Art Institute of Chicago, A Catalogue of the Collection* (Chicago and Princeton: Art Institute of Chicago and Princeton University Press, 1993), 131-135.

and several in number. The links comprise, obviously, size and format, but they encompass the more important particulars of the grieving angels gesticulating on either side of the superscriptions, the incised designs ornamenting the haloes and, notably, the raised borders that are also embellished with patterns.[11] In other words, the ex-Stoclet artist would seem to have known the Crusader artistic tradition in one way or another. Yet the diptych is not a product of the East but derived instead from a north Italian or even Umbrian source, this second option insinuating that it might have seen the light of day within the burgeoning Franciscan milieu. If such is the case for a work whose date may be as early as c.1270 and whose right-hand figure would have appealed to the Minorites, one may surmise that the Franciscans launched the Man of Sorrows on its Italian career.

Although no definitive conclusions regarding the appeal of the ex-Stoclet diptych to the Franciscan Order can be drawn, six other images of the Man of Sorrows dating between c.1290 and c.1320/30 do confirm the affiliation between image and Minorite piety. The patronage of the *Supplicationes variae*, a manuscript of the 1290s, has been ascribed to a Franciscan tertiary, and it contains two pertinent figures, one a Man of Sorrows within an initial ornamenting a folio with prayers associated with Bernard of Clairvaux, and the other a full-page Byzantinizing illustration emphasizing Christ's wounds (Florence, Biblioteca Medicea Laurenziana, Ms. Plut. XXV.3, fols. 183v and 387).[12] An *Imago pietatis* of c.1290 also crowns the central wall of a fresco cycle in the church of S. Francesco in Bolzano,[13] and a relief portraying the figure and dating to the first years of the ensuing century is immured in a pilaster to the right of the presbytery in S. Maria Gloriosa ai Frari, Venice.[14] The final works of our group also derive from northeastern Italy in the first decades of the fourteenth century: a relief of the Man of Sorrows that once sat within a roadside shrine decorated with the Franciscan coat-of-arms (Riva del Garda, Museo Civico; Fig. 5),[15] and an *Imago pietatis* that occupies one-half of the top register of the interior right valve of the famous S. Chiara Triptych originating in a community of Poor Clares outside Trieste (Trieste, Civico Museo Sartorio).[16] Spanning about a half-century in time and produced in media as diverse as manuscript illumination, panel and fresco painting and relief sculpture, these seven images were all likely connected with a Minorite ambience.

Given our intended aim to focus on fifteenth-century Padua, it would be tedious to prolong our

---

[11] A difference in height of 12 cm separates the ex-Stoclet (64 cm) and Chicago (76 cm) diptychs; a difference of 13 cm separates them in width (45 cm vs 59 cm).

[12] See Amy Neff, "A New Interpretation of the *Supplicationes Variae* Miniatures," in *Il Medio Oriente e l'Occidente nell'arte del XIII secolo. Atti del XXIV. Congresso Internazionale della Storia dell'arte*, ed. Hans Belting (Bologna: CLUEB, 1982), vol. II, 173-179; and Neff, "Byzantium Westernized, Byzantium Marginalized: Two Icons in the *Supplicationes Variae*," *Gesta* 38 (1999): 81-102.

[13] Sven Georg Mieth, *Das Franziskanerkloster in Bozen: Geschichte, Baugeschichte, Kunst, 1221-1514* (Bolzano: Athesia, 1998); *Trec3nto, Pittori gotici a Bolzano/Gotische Maler in Bozen*, exh. cat., eds. Andrea De Marchi, Tiziana Franco and Silvia Spada Pintarelli (Trent: Fotolito Longo, 2000); and *Atlante Trec3nto, Pittori gotici a Bolzano*, eds. Andrea De Marchi, Tiziana Franco, Vincenzo Gheroldi and Silvia Spada Pintarelli (Bolzano: Temi Editrice, 2002), and *Trec3nto, Pittori gotici a Bolzano*, eds. Andrea De Marchi, Tiziana Franco and Silvia Spada Pintarelli (Atti del convegno di studi) (Bolzano: Fotolito Longo, 2006).

[14] Isidoro Gatti, *S. Maria Gloriosa dei Frari, Storia di una presenza francesca a Venezia* (Venice: Edizioni delle Grafiche Veneziane, 1992), 136-137.

[15] Paolo Salvi, "Una Pietà di 'Rigino di Enrico' e alcuni aspetti del suo stile tra realismo e geometria," *Labyrinthos* 35/36 (1999): 81-116; and *Il Gotico nelle Alpi 1350-1450*, exh. cat., eds. Enrico Castelnuovo and Francesca de Gramatica, Trent, Castello del Buonconsiglio (Trent: Provincia Autonoma di Trento, 2002), 684-685, cat. 109.

[16] Maria Casotti Walcher, *Il Trittico di S. Chiara di Trieste e l'orientamento Paleologo nell'arte di Paolo Veneziano* (Trieste: Università degli Studi di Trieste, Facoltà di Lettere e Filosofia, 1961),16-17; Michelangelo Muraro, *Paolo da Venezia* (Milan: Istituto Editoriale Italiano, 1969), 139-141; and *Patriarchi: Quindici secoli di civiltà fra l'Adriatico e l'Europa Centrale*, exh. cat., eds. Sergio Tavano and Giuseppe Bergamini (Geneva and Milan: Skira, 2000), 288-289, n. XXI.5.

introduction and enumerate here the many instances in which the Man of Sorrows originated within a Franciscan milieu in northeast Italy during the Trecento. Suffice it to say that such works exist, though again their relationship to the Order is indisputable only at times; at others it is simply inferable. Within the first group, for example, a missal of c.1370 privileges Franciscan saints and places the Man of Sorrows in the initials of two Collects for different services observed during Holy Week.[17] The anonymous Piove di Sacco Altarpiece of c.1380-90, once in the local Abbey of S. Martino, fits into the second lot characterized by inference or implication: the polyptych formerly held the Man of Sorrows at its top center, and the presence of Saints Clare and Francis on the bottom register standing to the far left and right of four other saints hints that the work probably enjoyed a Franciscan origin.[18]

II. S. Antonio and S. Francesco Grande during the Quattrocento

A few decades after the now partially dismembered polyptych of Piove di Sacco was completed, nearby Padua—which had controlled the smaller provincial center since c.900— began enjoying a pictorial florescence of the *Imago pietatis*. Nine known representations of the figure once graced the two principal Franciscan churches in the university town, S. Antonio begun in 1232 and S. Francesco Grande in 1416. Yet another very special image likely originating in Padua portrays Francis himself with the Man of Sorrows, and still other Franciscan-related depictions of the Man of Sorrows were produced in the city at the end of the century. These last were neither the most expressive nor beautiful of the Paduan images but were indisputably the most easily accessible and popular of all, and they will bring our investigation to a close.

The figure of the Man of Sorrows very much altered in Quattrocento Padua despite its reiteration within the same spiritual milieu there. The change occurred not just because of the transformation from late Gothic to early Renaissance style, but also because context and function inflected the Man of Sorrows, as did what may be termed its 'framing effects' or how the image was expounded to viewers.[19] Of course such a mechanism was hardly new to fifteenth-century Padua. For instance, the *Imago pietatis* modifies when viewed in tandem with the *Madonna della Misericordia* on the S. Chiara Triptych, one inflecting the other, the two modulating each other so that mother and son together nourish Christian hope for earthly compassion and heavenly salvation. Over a century later, framing effects incorporated the Man of Sorrows into new artistic constructions in Padua to produce wide-ranging implications, the late medieval figure perhaps mitigated in its iconic force but its meanings augmented. Surely one of the most powerful transformative impulses to affect the *Imago pietatis* in the Renaissance was the changing assortment of its artistic contexts.

Michele Giambono's harrowing panel of the *Man of Sorrows with St. Francis*, c.1430 (New York, Metropolitan Museum of Art) opens this discussion, though whether the artist executed the painting

---

[17]   See Rosalie B. Green, "The Iconography of a Missal: Garrett Manuscript 39," *The Princeton University Library Chronicle* 27, no. 3 (1966): 159-165. The code numbers of the Index of Christian Art for these two illuminations in Ms. Garrett 39 are *32 P935 LUn 018*; and the system number of fol. 123r is *000121553* and that of fol. 383r is *000121995*.

[18]   See *Da Giotto al Mantegna*, exh. cat., ed. Lucio Grossato (Milan: Electa, 1974), cat. no. 11, and Cristina Guarnieri, "Per un corpus della pittura veneziana del Trecento al tempo di Lorenzo," *Saggi e Memorie di storia dell'arte* 30 (2006): 1-131 (p. 85, fig. 66). In 2002, the ex-Soprintendenza per il Patrimonio storico, artistico e demoetnoantropologico del Veneto removed the polyptych from the abbey church of S. Martino and temporarily placed it in the care of the Museo Diocesano, Padua, where it currently sits. We are grateful to the Director of the Museo, Andrea Nante, for his assistance.

[19]   For the term 'framing effects,' see the article by Nicholas Epley, Professor of Behavioral Science (University of Chicago Graduate School of Business) in the New York Times of January 31, 2008.

when working in Padua or responding to a commission in the city while residing elsewhere is unknown (Fig. 6).[20] Yet because he depicted the Man of Sorrows half a dozen times, in each instance varying the figure significantly by altering its framing devices, and because the New York painting is so insistently Franciscan in zeal, our inquiry into how the subject evolved in Quattrocento Padua would be poor indeed if this disturbing yet pictorially rich picture were ignored.[21] The presence of the little saint on the left clearly alters the late-medieval subject by leveraging the painting interpretively, not just establishing the Man of Sorrows within a specific spiritual milieu but also fine-tuning the image to focus the patron (him or her) on the source of Francis's stigmata. Giambono endowed his image too with exquisite details that manipulate or deepen its implications by alluding to the Passion story from the Bible. Christ's crown recalls Pilate's scorn; the crossbar and superscription evoke the Crucifixion; and the nails, wounds and copious blood summon forth Christ's physical agonies on the cross. The tomb, articulated with notions of correct foreshortening, has three panels of porphyry and *verde antico* in order to allude to ancient burial; the azurite fabric behind shows rising phoenixes alternating with elaborate floral designs, inside of which burst whirring flames—these symbolize the Resurrection.[22] Christ's open mouth suggests his reanimation; and, finally, the gorgeously embroidered Byzantine loincloth evokes a Eucharistic cloth. In other words, while painting a dead Christ detached from event and action, Giambono also encapsulated human sufferings and divine resurgence, providing a compelling example of how framing effects enhance our Franciscan-disposed subject. He thereby brought the patron forward in time to Francis who had died only two centuries before.

Franciscan dedication to the Man of Sorrows in fifteenth-century Padua is most apparent today in the church of S. Antonio, the Conventual establishment renowned for its relics of St. Anthony (1195-1231) and familiarly known as the Santo. By our reckoning the church claims at least seven representations of the Man of Sorrows dating to the years between c.1430 and '65.[23] Given the presence of so many works honoring the same subject and all executed within the span of one generation, the devotional accent in the church must have been intentional, although individual patrons and their artists surely would have exercised choice too. The works range in media from fresco and tempera to stone and bronze, and in dimension from diminutive to nearly life-size. Painters and sculptors now anonymous or scarcely known created a few as did others who were famous, the most exceptional being Donatello, the greatest artist of his century. S. Antonio also boasts another Man of Sorrows, however, one that fits into none of the aforementioned categories—neither date, media nor scale—but that still merits attention: a tiny silver figurine decorating the upper lunette of the Jawbone Reliquary of St. Anthony (Fig. 7).[24] The reliquary dates

---

[20] His family originating in Treviso, Giambono himself worked in Padua and Venice, and he received commissions from throughout the Veneto. See Tiziana Franca, *Michele Giambono e il monumento a Cortesia da Serego in Santa Anastasia e Verona* (Padua: Poligrafo, 1998).

[21] Four of the versions belong to the Metropolitan Museum of Art, New York; the Museo Civico, Padua; the Galleria Malaspina of the Musei Civici, Pavia; and a private collection in Milan. Giambono also painted two representations of the figure on liturgical vestments worn by saints: a panel showing St. Michael (the Bernard Berenson Collection, Villa I Tatti, Settignano), and one of St. Stephen (current whereabouts unknown).

[22] The intricate pattern has almost disappeared from the New York panel but was faithfully reproduced in a modern variant of c.1900 now in the Fogg Art Museum, Harvard University, Cambridge MA. Horace Morison bought the Fogg panel from a dealer in Naples at the same time that Roger Fry purchased the New York panel in the same city from Alba Barbato di Naduri.

[23] Other representations of the Man of Sorrows were made for, and still exist in, the churches of the Eremitani and S. Nicolò in the city.

[24] Our understanding of this complicated work is due to the generous help of Francesco Lucchini whose doctoral dissertation for the Courtauld Institute of Art, the University of London, deals with relics and reliquaries in S. Antonio.

Fig 5. Dead Christ with Mary and Saint John, *first quarter 14th century, polychromed and gilded marble, 93 x 64 cm (36.6 x 25.19 in.), Riva del Garda, Museo Civico.* (Photo: author)

Fig 6. Michele Giambono, Man of Sorrows, c. 1420-30, tempera and gold on wood, painted surface 47 x 31.1 cm (18.5 x 12.25 in.), New York, The Metropolitan Museum of Art, Rogers Fund, 1906 (06.180).

(Image© The Metropolitan Museum of Art.)

Fig 7. Giuliano da Firenze, Silver Reliquary, 14-15th century, Padua, Sant'Antonio, Museo del Santo. (Photo: author)

to 1349, and its original, lost Man of Sorrows was faithfully replaced in the nineteenth century. The possible relevance of the figurine to the succession of larger fifteenth-century sculpted and painted counterparts in the Santo lies in the patronage of the reliquary, the placement of the figure itself and its centrality to the church dedication. Taking these factors in reverse order: the jawbone is of course (allegedly) Anthony's; its housing is a precious and bejeweled object commissioned by the *Veneranda Arca del Santo*; and the Man of Sorrows is the highest image on the work's central axis. These elements, seen individually or even cumulatively, could not have determined *a priori* that the silver figurine would trigger the repeated appearance of the same subject in S. Antonio more than a half-century later, but when considered in terms of the ongoing popularity of the Man of Sorrows generally and its core relationship with Minorite piety, the little *Imago pietatis* likely created a devotional focus in the church engaging future generations.

The earliest of the works in the Santo adorns the tomb of Raffaello Fulgosio (b.1367), professor of Civic and Canon Law at the University of Padua from 1407 until his death in 1427 and whose sepulchral monument was commissioned in 1429-30 by his widow, Giovanna de' Beccaria, from the Florentine sculptor Pietro Lamberti.[25] Although no longer in its original setting in the Santo, the tomb has not been substantially altered: it is a double-sided structure, three levels high and surmounted by an imposing canopy represented as a draped alcove topped by a peaked gable. Apart from the recumbent Fulgosio, who lies like a Janus-like effigy facing each side of the uppermost level atop a bier supported by four lions, fifteen figures decorate the ensemble. Four of them represent Fulgosio's students, six his merits or Virtues and two small *spiritelli* carry a scroll with an inscription on one side of the sarcophagus.[26] On the reverse Mary and John flank the Man of Sorrows, each of the three enframed within a separate quatrefoil. Nothing iconographically distinctive or contextual characterizes the trio: Mary and John had long been associated with the Man of Sorrows, and the subject had already enjoyed a century-old tradition of presiding on a tomb.[27] No evidence exists, moreover, to suggest that the figural choice was expressly Franciscan. Like many of her time, Fulgosio's widow believed that in presenting the dead Christ synoptically on a funerary monument—that is, not full-length and hanging on the cross—the deceased and his surviving kin articulated their core belief that Jesus would raise the souls of the dead at the end of time.[28]

Despite its lack of Franciscan specificity, the Fulgosio Monument claims distinction in S. Antonio: for it heralded a triumvirate of Florentine commissions in the church, each bearing the *Imago pietatis*. In 1433 Filippo Lippi painted a panel likely destined as a reliquary cover (Esztergom, Keresztény Muzeum), and in 1448-49 Donatello sculpted his famous bronze relief for the high altar

---

[25] See Vittorio Lazzarini, "Il Mausoleo di Raffaello Fulgosio nella Basilica del Santo," *Archivio Veneto-Tridentino* IV (1923): 147-53; George R. Goldner, *Niccolò and Pietro Lamberti* (New York: Garland Publishing, 1978), 269-270; and Anne Markham Schulz, "Revising the history of Venetian Renaissance Sculpture: Niccolò and Pietro Lamberti," *Saggi e Memorie di storia dell'Arte* 15 (1986): 7-61 (esp. 24-29 and 47-49).

[26] Lazzarini first used the word *spiritelli* in his 1923 article; see note 26, 149.

[27] Three famous tombs in Verona, for example, are Guglielmo Castelbarco's (1319-20) outside the church of S. Anastasia, Cangrande's outside S. Maria Antica (c.1330-35) and that of S. Agata (1353) in S. Maria Matricolare, the cathedral. Writing of sepulchral imagery in *The Image and Its Public*, 2-3, Belting aptly notes that the Man of Sorrows "established a relationship between Jesus' redeeming death and the death of the person there interred."

[28] Two tombs with the Man of Sorrows dating from the same period are in Ss. Giovanni e Paolo, Venice, those of Doge Michele Steno (d.1415) formerly in S. Marina, and of Agnese and Orsola Venier (the wife and daughter of Doge Antonio Venier). And for more such tombs in Verona, see Tiziana Franco, "Tombe di uomini eccellenti (dalla fine del XIII alla prima metà del XV secolo)," *I Santi Fermo e Rustico, Un culto e una chiesa in Verona, Per il XVII Centenario del loro Martirio (304-2004)* (Verona: Parrocchia di San Fermo Maggiore in Verona, 2004), 247-61.

Fig 8. Fra' Filippo Lippi, Man of Sorrows with Two Cherubs, *c. 1430, tempera and gold on panel, 42.2 x 33.1 cm (16.61 x 13 in.) Esztergom, Keresztény Muzeum, Inv. 55.240.* (Photo: Keresztény Muzeum, Esztergom. Photograph by Attila Mudrák)

Fig 9. Donatello, Man of Sorrows with Two Cherubs, *1449-50, gilded bronze, Padua, Sant'Antonio.* (Photo: Giorgio Deganello)

of the basilica and still in situ (Fig. 8-9).[29] Resolving the enigmas and historical problems surrounding these two works lies well beyond the scope of this essay, as does the art historical issue of how the two great Florentines impacted generally upon Veneto art. Instead our concern focuses on the function of their works in S. Antonio, on how they portrayed the *Imago pietatis* anew and on how site and interpretation together can explicate Franciscan attitudes regarding choice of subject. Images destined for a reliquary and altar (indeed, the high altar!) were of special consequence, and if seen against the precedent of the Jawbone Reliquary, however small its figurine, the two commissions appear to connote an ongoing attachment to the Man of Sorrows on the part of the *Veneranda Arca del Santo*. Though this conclusion is far from certain, the originality of the two works is unquestionable; their exposition of the Man of Sorrows is thoroughly innovative when seen against the subject's history in the Veneto, arguing that the Conventuals enthusiastically embraced new religious imagery.

The novelty of the two representations lies in more than spatial illusionism and convincingly plastic figures, both elements of Florentine style and both of groundbreaking importance when seen against contemporary Paduan art. Lippi and Donatello also altered the Man of Sorrows by creating unified physical and emotional dramas wherein angels, heretofore used in local interpretations as observers or thurifers flanking the *Imago*

pietatis, dramatically suffer Christ's loss beside him.[30] Lippi's angels, rather than deferring hierarchically, sustain Christ even if from behind a parapet and outside the little tomb. Donatello's *spiritelli* do not support him, but they lament even more tragically than Lippi's. What's more, each rests a foot on the sarcophagus so that their flexed knees are proximate to Christ's elbows and nearly touch them. Working in different media, the two Florentines left the same pioneering mark upon the Veneto Man of Sorrows with Angels by synchronizing or coordinating space, emotion and composition. Such an approach had typified the Man of Sorrows with Mary and John, and two examples of affecting or poignant physical interaction between the living Mary and John and the dead Christ were already visible in Padua. The earlier is Nicoletto Semitecolo's panel of 1367 that served—exactly like Lippi's—as a reliquary cover.[31] The somewhat later example is Giusto de' Menabuoi's small representation of the *Dead Christ with Mary and St. John* on the central panel on the high altar predella in the Paduan baptistery, a building adjacent to the cathedral containing Semitecolo's painting.[32] Giusto was of course Tuscan like both Lippi and Donatello. Given the size of Padua, the consequence of its cathedral and baptistery, the location, placement and function of Semitecolo and Giusto's works— reliquary and altar predella—in their respective houses of worship and, once again, the historical relevance of the Man of Sorrows to Franciscan

---

[29]   The bibliography on these two artists working in Padua is immense: for Lippi, see Jeffrey Ruda, *Fra Filippo Lippi: Life and Work with a Complete Catalogue* (London: Phaidon, 1993); Megan Holmes, *Fra Filippo Lippi, the Carmelite Painter* (New Haven and London:Yale University Press, 1999); and Andrea De Marchi, "Un raggio di luce su Filippo Lippi a Padova," *Nuovi Studi, Rivista di arte antica e moderna* I (1996): 5-23. For Donatello, see John White, "Donatello's High Altar in the Santo at Padua," *Art Bulletin* 51 (1969): 1-14; and 119-141; and more recently, Creighton Gilbert, "The Original Assembly of Donatello's Padua Altar," *Artibus et Historiae* 55, XXVIII (2007): 11-22.

[30]   This stands in strong contrast, for example, with the same trio in the Certosa Altarpiece of 1450 by the Vivarini (Pinacoteca Nazionale, Bologna).

[31]   Semitecolo was active in Venice between 1353 and 1370; his painting, formerly on the altar of the Sacristy of Canons in the Cathedral of Padua, measures 60.4 x 78.4 cm and belongs to the Sorlini Foundation, Brescia. See *Da Bellini a Tiepolo, La grande pittura veneta della Fondazione Sorlini*, exh. cat., ed. Filippo Pedrocco (Venice: Marsilio, 2005), n. 1. Not coincidental in this context is that each of Donatello's two angels brings one hand to a cheek like Semitecolo's John.

[32]   Benjamin Kohl, "Giusto De' Menabuoi e il Mecenatismo artistico in Padova," and Anna Maria Spiazzi, "Giusto a Padova, La Decorazione del Battistero," in *Spiazzi, Giusto De' Menabuoi* (Trieste: Lint, 1989),13-30 and 83-127.

piety, it would seem apparent that, drawing upon a local tradition, the Conventuals at the Santo honored the subject in significant settings in their church and called upon renowned artists to interpret it inventively.

1450 was a memorable year for Franciscan Padua: on May 24, Pope Nicholas V canonized Bernardino da Siena, the renowned Observant friar who had preached in Padua fifteen years earlier. A few weeks later, in mid-June, the Conventuals at the Santo unveiled Donatello's immense altar complex in their church. A pair of noteworthy paintings quickly followed in both S. Antonio and S. Francesco Grande, each one destined for a highly visible site, only one of them depicting the Man of Sorrows however. The two apparently responded to the events of 1450, but each did so paradoxically. That is to say, the Conventuals produced a work reacting to the canonization of the Observant Bernardino, whereas the Observants commissioned a work responding to Donatello's altar complex for the Conventuals. The fresco of 1452 by the twenty-year-old Andrea Mantegna filled the lunette over the doorway to the Santo; it shows Bernardino's emblem of the sun radiating from Jesus' name, Bernardino and Anthony placed on either side of the motif and supporting it.[33] Bernardino had sought to reconcile the two Franciscan branches of Padua that had been competing against one another since the Observants' arrival in the city in 1425; their rivalry was based partly on the issue of which group more faithfully followed Francis' rule and, to a degree, on the question of which drew larger crowds and enjoyed a greater urban following.[34] Mantegna's fresco paid tribute to the Observant Bernardino's mediation but co-opted his canonization as a universally celebrated Franciscan feast.

The previous year, in 1451, the Observants at S. Francesco Grande also commissioned a painting for their church, a high altar polyptych surely geared as a response to Donatello's complex recently unveiled at the Santo. The Observant brothers implicitly reproached the Conventuals, for they invited Antonio and Bartolomeo Vivarini of Murano to execute a work with only eleven painted panels rather than selecting a famed foreigner to produce a lavish bronze ensemble with seven full-length, freestanding figures and over twenty reliefs.[35] Authentic to Francis' rule, the Observants opted for a less expensive and more traditional devotional monument. And they would have known the costs of their new altarpiece from the onset, for the Vivarini had already painted, separately or together, almost ten such polyptychs for churches in the vicinity, all with the Man of Sorrows on high.

The S. Francesco Altarpiece no longer exists as an integral work of art, but judging from other surviving Vivarini polyptychs of the period, it measured approximately eight feet in height by about ten feet in width and would have boasted a gilded wood frame. Initially, five full-length figures occupied the bottom register (one is now missing), four three-quarter length figures rose above them (two of these are lost), and the Man of Sorrows, still extant, crowned the top center (Fig. 10).[36] Two of the surviving figures portray two of the same Franciscan saints honored in the Santo: Anthony and Louis of Toulouse. Clare, John the Baptist, Peter and Paul—all extant—replace and increase by one Saints Prosdocimus, Daniel and Justina at the Santo, and the Madonna and Christ Child

33   *Mantegna e Padova, 1445-1460*, exh. cat., eds. Davide Banzato, Alberta De Nicolò Salmazo and Anna Maria Spiazzi (Milan: Skira, 2006), 192-193, cat. no. 5.

34   Regarding Observant and Conventual tensions and Santo interior: Geraldine A. Johnson, "Approaching the Altar: Donatello's Sculpture in the Santo," *Renaissance Quarterly* 52 (1999): 627-666.

35   *Mantegna e Padova, 1445-1460*, 168-172, cat. nos. 13-16.

36   The Man of Sorrows may well have been encased in a projecting tabernacle as in the Certosa Altarpiece.

Fig 10. Antonio and Bartolomeo Vivarini, author's partial reconstruction of San Francesco Grande Polyptych, 1451.

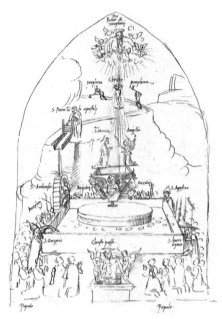

Fig 11. Attributed to Bartolomeo Sanvito, Mill of the Host, 1466, pen and ink, 300 x 213 mm (11.8 x 8.38 in.), J. Paul Getty Research Center, Los Angeles, CA, n.999255. (Photo: J. Paul Getty Research Center)

Fig 12. Antonio Maria da Villafora, Man of Sorrows with Mary and John, *101 x 41 mm (3.97 x 1.16 in.), miniature, folio ii, Statute Book of the Monte di Pietà of Padua, 1490s, Biblioteca Civica, Padua, inv. no. 103.* (Photo: Musei Civici degli Eremitani, Padova)

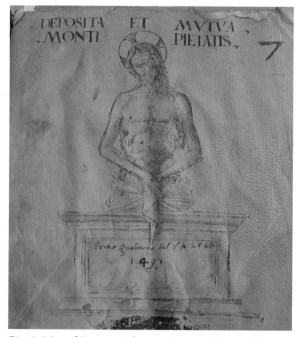

Fig 13. Man of Sorrows, *ink on parchment, Ledger of the Monte di Pietà of Padua, 1490s, Archivio di Stato.* (Photo: author)

occupied the center (in both works).[37] The identities of the two saints missing from the upper right at S. Francesco may be inferred: one was surely the Observants' own Bernardino who had just been canonized, and the other was perhaps the Magdalen, responding as a female hermit saint to Clare and John the Baptist, both on the left.

An eighteenth-century Paduan guidebook identifies the third lost panel—the central work on the bottom register—as St. Francis showing his stigmata.[38] Affirming the essential mystical experience of the church's dedicatory saint, both the panel's subject and its position in the ensemble likely carried a calculated and sharp retort to the Conventuals, particularly if the Vivarinis' Francis is compared with Donatello's. First, Francis's placement over the Santo altar enjoyed no exceptionality whatsoever. Furthermore, the Conventuals' Francis holds attributes just like his brother and sister saints on the altar, whereas the Observants' Francis displayed his defining singularity, his *Christoformitas*. But the visual conjunction between the Observants' Francis and the figure of the Man of Sorrows above must have attracted attention too. For while Francis presented his stigmata, the *Imago pietatis* also showed his, spreading his arms outward to display his palms. Hence, the Observants drew an analogy between Christ atop the polyptych and Francis as *alter Christus* below, each a framing device for the other and the two together establishing a one-to-one correspondence, at once spiritual and artistic, apparent to celebrant and worshipers alike. And just as the Vivarini designed Christ's diagonally outstretched arms to parallel the receding perspectival lines of his sarcophagus, and in precise concordance too with the actual incline of his angled pinnacle, so they created—we hypothesize—an identically oblique pattern on the bottom register by extending Francis' arms and hands.

Despite the size and ambition of the two Conventual and Observant altarpieces by Donatello and the Vivarini respectively, the Franciscan career of the Man of Sorrows had not yet reached its culmination in Quattrocento Padua. In the first years of the 1460s the Arca del Santo at S. Antonio produced a small silver navicella or incense burner portraying Saints Anthony and Stephen on one lid and the *Man of Sorrows and Two Angels* on the other, the figure of Christ closely following the outlines of Donatello's on his relief on the church's high altar.[39] Both Francesco Squarcione and his student Giorgio Schiavone, the Dalmatian Juraj Culinovic, have been proposed as the artist responsible for the preliminary drawing leading to the *nielli* on the two lids, but whether Squarcione's or Schiavone's, the work originated among the more forward-looking artists on the Paduan scene. The same was true for another and contemporary commission at the Santo, the much larger, more important and more complex work of the *Cappella del Corpo di Cristo*.

Begun by Bernardo de Lazara in 1466 as his burial chapel, the *Cappella del Corpo di Cristo* is one of the most enigmatic artistic enterprises in the Veneto but also one of the most fascinating.[40] Its altarpiece depicted the *Mill of the Host,* a Eucharistic subject based on exegeses drawn from the

---

[37] The panels with Anthony and Louis belong to the Fondazione Cavallini Sgarbi, Ferrara; those of Christ and Peter to the Národní Galerie, Prague; Clare and John the Baptist to the Kunsthistorisches Museum, Vienna; and the Virgin and Child to the Worcester (MA) Art Museum.

[38] Pietro Brandolese, *Pitture, sculture, architetture e altre cose notabili di Padova nuovamente descritte con alcune brevi notizie intorno gli artefici mentovati nell'opera* (Padua: P. Brandolese, 1795), 249.

[39] Marco Collarata, Giordana Mariani Canova and Anna Maria Spiazzi, eds., *Basilica del Santo, Le Oreficerie* (Padua: Centro Study Antoniani, 1995), 139-141, cat. 46 (Spiazzi); and Spiazzi, "Note sulla bottega di Francesco Squarcione: i disegni per l'oreficeria," in *Francesco Squarcione, PICTORUM GYMNASIARCHA SINGULARIS*, ed. Alberta De Nicolò Salmazo (Padua: Il Poligrago, 1999), 139-145.

[40] Raimondo Calligari, "Opere e committenze d'arte rinascimentali a Padova," *Arte Veneta* 49 (1996): 7-29; Michelle O'Malley, *The Business of Art, Contracts and the Commissioning Process in Renaissance Italy* (New Haven and London: Yale University Press, 2005), and *Mantegna e Padova, 1445-1460*, 266-267, cat. no. 58 (for the modern Paduan copy).

gospels.[41] Scarcely known in Italy, the theme is usually found in German speaking lands, one example painted in 1424 on a large retable (9 feet high by about 21 feet wide) for a Franciscan monastery in Göttingen and another depicted in the 1440s as a great stained-glass window in the Bern Münster.[42] De Lazara's Paduan altarpiece sadly no longer exists; both it and its chapel were destroyed by c.1550. The riddles surrounding the commission go well beyond its physical loss and the Italian realization of the *Mill of the Host*. According to the surviving contract, the painting was to follow a design by Nicolò Pizolo, another innovative painter of the period—indeed, Mantegna's colleague for the Ovetari Chapel in the local church of the Eremitani—but Pizolo had died in 1453, that is, thirteen years before the de Lazara contract was drawn up. His drawing, furthermore, has been lost. Another drawing, apparently reproducing the original, is attached to the 1466 contract (Los Angeles CA, The Getty Research Center, Fig. 11), and a later copy of that sheet survives too (Padua, Biblioteca Civica). Both show that the Man of Sorrows was one of the most important pictorial elements of the lost altarpiece and would have been seen in direct relationship with the chapel altar and confirming the miracle of transubstantiation. A discussion of the Santo's *Mill of the Host* is surely apt in the context of the *Imago pietatis* in fifteenth-century Franciscan Padua, the more so as the de Lazara family was one of the city's most prominent, their new burial chapel faced St. Anthony's own in the largest Franciscan

church in town and Bernardo employed the noted humanist scribe Bartolomeo Sanvito, famous as the creator of italic script, to write his contract.

Although the question of who brought the theme of the *Mill of the Host* across the Alps is irresolvable here, explaining the singularity of its Paduan interpretation is straightforward. Several of the peculiarities of the surviving drawing draw meaning from the *Imago pietatis* as the culmination, or rather conclusion, of the convoluted machinery Pizolo (supposedly) devised.[43] At the top center of the altarpiece, under its pointed Gothic arch, a glory of seraphim surrounds God the Father sending the Christ Child earthward and towards Mary and Gabriel. Further down but on the left, rainwater emerging from clouds flows down a channel tended by prophets. The water passes through a sluice, St. Peter meting it out into a waterwheel, while to the right and in the center, Christ's spirit emanates downward past the Annunciation, penetrating a large funnel adorned on its four sides with the evangelistic symbols, one of which faces outward towards worshipers—the lion of St. Mark. In a large vat below, a millstone powered by the waterwheel on the left produces little loaves or hosts. At the four corners of the vat stand the Four Doctors of the Church, only Gregory the Great at the front left stirring its contents.[44] The faithful kneel in adoration and adore the mill's miraculous harvest or yield, the Eucharistic wafers finding realization in the Man of Sorrows rising from the sarcophagus and held by angels.[45]

[41] John 6:31ff.: "Verily, verily, I say unto you, Moses gave you not bread from heaven; but my father giveth you the true bread from heaven. For the bread of God is he which cometh down from heaven, and giveth life unto the world."

[42] Peter Heimann, "Mola Mystica, Wandlungen eines Themas mittalterlicher Kunst," *Zeitschrift für Schweizerische Archäologie und Kunstgeschichte* 39 (1982): 229-252.

[43] See Catherine Puglisi and William Barcham in *Passion in Venice, Crivelli to Tintoretto and Veronese*, exh. cat., New York, Museum of Biblical Art (New York and London: D Giles Limited, 2011), 64-65 for a discussion questioning whether Pizolo alone was responsible for the final design.

[44] Wearing his papal tiara, Gregory the Great personally mixes the brew, so to speak, and his gesture stands out for its graphic individuality superimposed upon the previously drawn vat.

[45] The inscription *Christo passo*, a term identifying the figure still today in northeast Italy, identifies the Man of Sorrows. Our introductory essay in *Passion in Venice*, 13-14, explains the phrase.

Given that so many of the motifs noted in the de Lazara *Mill of the Host* are absent from depictions produced elsewhere, their possible meanings must be explored. The Paduan representation was the sole interpretation of the subject privileging the Annunciation and the Lion of St. Mark and distinguishing St. Peter and Pope Gregory the Great. The coupling of the first two, absolutely unique amidst the several versions of the subject, can only refer to Venice, to its legendary founding on the feast day of the Annunciation and its saintly founder, Mark himself.[46] Because the de Lazara family, Bernardo's father at its head, had been instrumental in ousting the local tyrants (the Carraresi) from Padua in 1405 so as to incorporate the city into the Venetian Republic, the Annunciation and the Lion of St. Mark together articulate dynastic pride and civic devotion. The prominence of St. Peter dispensing water and of Pope Gregory implementing communion leaves little doubt that the altarpiece emphasized that the Church alone had the authority to tender the *Corpo di Cristo* to the faithful and mediate between them and God.[47] But these two ideologies, Venetian loyalty and papal supremacy, seem to be at loggerheads with the political antagonism traditionally characterizing Venetian-Roman relations. Only the recognition that de Lazara's project dates to 1466 will bring the apparently opposing principles into harmony, for while the enterprise went forward, a Venetian patrician, Pietro Barbo, reigned on the Throne of St. Peter as Paul II (1464-71).[48] The Conventuals at S. Antonio unquestionably supported Bernardo's emphasis because of S. Antonio's role in Padua's civic life: that is, just as S. Marco was not the cathedral of Venice but the

governmental church safeguarding the relics of the city's patron saint, so the Santo was not the cathedral of Padua but the principal church of the city housing the relics of Padua's patron saint, a privilege the Franciscans were proud to expound upon. It is surely reasonable to read the de Lazara *Mill of the Host* as using its Franciscan site to draw attention to papal authority and boast of civic pride within the context of the Venetian State.

In the final decades of the century two more images of the Man of Sorrows joined those already in S. Antonio, and they comprised the eighth and ninth depictions of the subject to grace the church between c.1430 and c.1500. Despite the reappearance of the same theme in the same building time and again, the paintings demonstrate how artists and their ecclesiastical advisors might adapt or adjust visual form of the *Imago pietatis* to fit different locations and suit varying spiritual needs and thereby elicit different empathetic or spiritual responses. Anonymous artists working in fresco realized the two works, both showing the figure in conjunction with others but each one a different portrayal. One fresco is vertically formatted and depicts the Man of Sorrows holding a chalice and flanked by five grieving figures, Mary and John supporting him in the tomb (the front of which is adorned with the Veil of Veronica and before which stands the crowing cock), and the many *Arma Christi* appear like cut-outs applied onto the black background. The other fresco (now a fragment) is lunette shaped and depicts the Man of Sorrows again in the tomb. Though the left-hand figure has been lost (only its clothed elbow is extant), S. Chiara survives on our right.[49]

---

[46]   The lion is not a generically depicted beast but is one familiar from several Venetian formulations, for example on the façade of the fourteenth-century Palazzo Agnusdio.

[47]   Only the design of the Paduan *Corpo di Cristo* shows the millstone rotating because of St. Peter rather than being powered by the twelve apostles cranking a bar.

[48]   For our interpretation to hold that the drawing acknowledges the presence of a Venetian pope in Rome, one must explain how Pizolo who died in 1453 could have foreseen the election of Pietro Barbo to the Throne of St. Peter in 1464. This paper cannot examine the issue.

[49]   Raimondo Callegari discussed both paintings in essays gathered in the posthumous collection of his publications, *Scritti sull'arte padovana del Rinascimento* (Udine: Forum, 1998), 101-102 (fig. 39) and 238-241 (fig. 65).

The dissimilarity between the two works goes well beyond their dimensions, format and the number of figures. Painted at eye level on the concave wall of an interior niche close to the far right entryway of the Santo, the apparently earlier fresco is a striking interpretation of the traditional subject, converting it into a heart-rending and expressive picture that seeks to involve churchgoers directly before it. The six figures' haloes, Christ's included, are represented as foreshortened circles so as to render space dynamic and dramatize the ensemble. On the other hand, the Instruments of the Passion deployed synoptically around Christ on an absolutely black field and the Veronica and crowing cock at the bottom disengage the faithful from any possible realistic narrative, and the chalice in Christ's right hand, and into which his blood pours from his chest wound, transforms the affecting image into an emblematic performance of the Eucharist. The second fresco, unlike the first, ornamented an exterior wall over a doorway, perhaps in a cloister or open passageway. Its two surviving figures were viewed from below and, given their passivity and lack of expression, demand no emotional attachment and present the Man of Sorrows as a figure to cherish and adore. Following the fresco's lack of pictorial tragedy, Christ and Chiara's haloes are rendered as flat golden circles and deny all notion of drama. These two late fifteenth-century frescoes, when considered against the background of their thematic precedents in the Santo, show how the Conventuals not only employed and developed the *Imago pietatis* but also how they continually reinterpreted it, shifting it from one artistic context to another and framing it with and against many different motifs—figural and otherwise—so as to enrich its meaning, extend its spiritual possibilities

and intensify the image of the dead Christ for the church faithful.

III. Bernardino da Feltre and the Paduan Monte di Pietà

If the Conventuals and Observants were rivals—in that each branch sought to link itself more completely with Francis' strictures than the other—historical hindsight shows the Conventuals to have been the victors regarding which group more thoroughly exploited the Man of Sorrows in order to honor the *Christoformitas* of its saintly founder, not only to worship Christ. Nine representations of the *Imago pietatis* in the Santo between c.1430 and c.1500! But in point of fact the Observants proved to be the real champions of the subject in Quattrocento Padua, bringing its pathos into the streets and *piazze* of the city, transferring it into books and onto sculptures and processional standards and, most remarkable of all, extending its call to *pietas* into the unexpected world of finance. In 1453, just after Donatello unveiled his Man of Sorrows in the Santo and the Vivarini their polyptych in S. Francesco, the young Martino Tomitano left his home in Feltre and journeyed to nearby Padua to study at its university.[50] After two professors unexpectedly died, Martino sought solace and turned to James of the Marches, the Observant friar known in Italian as S. Giacomo della Marca, whose public sermons were then attracting attention in the city. Deeply moved and recognizing his call, Martino chose to enter the Observant Order, and on May 14, 1456, Giacomo della Marca formally accepted the youth into the monastery of S. Francesco as Fra' Bernardino, the name chosen to honor Bernardino da Siena. Giacomo personally bestowed the habit upon the young man.

---

[50] Much of the following material comes from our fuller discussion of the subject in "Bernardino da Feltre, the Monte di Pietà and the *Man of Sorrows*: Activist, Microcredit and Logo."

Within a few years, Bernardino da Feltre embarked upon a career of itinerant preaching, literally following in the footsteps of his revered namesake. During the '70s, '80s and '90s, he founded or revitalized more than thirty centers of the Monte di Pietà, a lending institution disseminated by the Observants that made loans to needy individuals pledging a small item or object, what was termed a *pegno*.

In 1491, responding to an urgent call from Bishop Pietro Barozzi of Padua to rally support for the institution of a local branch of the Monte, Bernardino visited the city and exercised his considerable local authority by launching a campaign to open local purses. He orchestrated a series of public events to generate crowds and capital; in other words, he arranged fundraisers. Bernardino's rousing sermons called thousands into the streets of Padua, hordes of people also thronging in from nearby villages and farms. He raised 5000 ducats, and the Paduan Monte opened for business. What exactly was Bernardino's choreography on July 31, 1491, when Bishop Barozzi presided over the opening ceremonies in Piazza dei Signori? According to contemporary accounts, Bernardino mounted a stage where he commanded an honored place among the gathered dignitaries; while holding his banner displaying the Man of Sorrows, he preached to crowds of Paduans congregating with visitors from surrounding towns. Following the concluding public mass, the friar offered Barozzi the Monte's newly made banner for an episcopal blessing, after which the bishop charged him to bear the standard to the nearby seat of the Monte. Declaring himself ready to die for Christ, Bernardino fixed his gaze upwards onto the *Imago pietatis* and led a slow, snaking procession to its final destination, the site of a former Jewish lending bureau where, setting down the banner, he claimed possession of the old building as the new Monte di Pietà.[51] Bernardino astutely used the standard to focus the marchers' attention, to drive home the association between Christ's compassion and donations to the Monte, and symbolically to evoke a Christian triumph over Jewish moneylenders.

The critical role the Man of Sorrows played while fluttering at the head of the Paduan procession of 1491 becomes vivid if one looks at the 1484 ceremonies instituting the Monte in Mantua and those of 1490 in Verona, Bernardino present in the first instance but absent in the second.[52] In the city of the Gonzaga where tapestry-bedecked streets resounded with trumpet music, Bernardino led an urban pageant from the Observant monastery to the new Monte, all the while "portando il stendardo della Pietà."[53] In Verona, however, neither Bernardino nor his banner was to be seen. Instead, the Observant Michele d'Acqui orchestrated the spectacle, and his principal imagery comprised *simulacra*, or effigies, representing Franciscan proto-martyrs and saints. Only later did a float pass by holding a three-dimensional dead Christ flanked by Mary and John with Virtues. A witness to the event hints that the ceremony was heavily laden with the imagery of the Friars Minor, whose insistence on Franciscan hagiography publicized the Observants' role in founding the bank, though Christ, Mary, John and the Virtues conveyed its spiritual rationale of course. Bernardino's presence in Mantua and

---

[51]   The original seat of the Monte was in the neighborhood of S. Lorenzo ai Portici; construction of the palace of the Monte di Pietà in the Piazza del Duomo began only in 1600. For the background on the activities of Jewish moneylenders in Padua and its region, see Vittorino Meneghin OFM, *Bernardino da Feltre e I Monti di Pietà* (Vicenza: L.I.E.F., 1974), chapter eight.

[52]   For Mantua, see Bernardino Guslino, "Vita del B. Bernardino (prima edizione integrale con note illustrative)," ed. P. Alberto Ghinato, *Le Venezie Francescane* XXVI, n.1-2 (1959): 1-47 (pp. 41-47 especially); and for an eyewitness account of Verona, see Guslino, "La Istituzione del Monte di Pietà di Verona nel racconto di un testimonio oculare," *Le Venezie Francescane* III (1934): 219-234.

[53]   Guslino, "Vita del B. Bernardino," *Le Venezie Francescane* XXVI, n.1-2 (1959): 46. Bernardino opened the Parma institution in 1488 with a Pietà standard too, for which see ibid., 23-24.

Padua (and elsewhere too) against his absence from Verona where no *stendardo della Pietà* seems to have been at hand indicates that his rich urban orchestrations were fundamental for the Monte. With time, Bernardino's processional banner of the Man of Sorrows became a regular fixture in the Monte protocol.

Bernardino's actual standard for the 1491 procession in Padua does not survive, but its general appearance emerges from a contemporary report written in Latin verse by Giovanni Barozzi, the bishop's cousin, who tells us that there was a *picta figura*, or painted figure, of the dead Christ on the edge of a tomb, his head crowned with thorns and his eyes closed.[54] The image hewed to its early tradition, but the anonymous artist acknowledged the latest artistic trends by lengthening the body, extending its arms so that, limp at his sides, they rested on his knees; and in order to magnify Christ's emotional and devotional impact, he highlighted Jesus' wounds with blood streaming downwards. More bloody than usual, this Man of Sorrows stimulated the crowd's empathy with Christ's suffering, and in the context of the anti-Semitic tirades the bishop had delivered that morning, the image would probably have encouraged the crowd to vilify Jewish moneylenders as the descendants of Christ's tormentors.[55] Bernardino too railed against Jews but justified his attacks by disavowing any general condemnation of the Hebrew community at large; he was merely censuring the oppressive practices of a few. Leaving aside this pernicious and all too familiar racist strategy, one may still admire the friar's wish to rally Padua—Jews excluded—so as to create a new social order that benefited the entire city (almost) and that united church with civic authorities.[56]

Although Bernardino's original standard is lost, two other images of the Man of Sorrows linked to the founding of the Paduan Monte still survive. The first is a miniature decorating the opening folio of the institution's 1491 Statute Book, a codex drawn up following Bernardino's specifications in which the communal authorities express their desire to assist the poor (Fig. 12).[57] The illustration shows the dead Christ within his tomb, his slender and outstretched arms supported by Mary and John who, seen before a verdant landscape promising regeneration, are illuminated in bright reds, greens and blues. The miniature exudes an engaging charm. Decidedly less delightful, the second Paduan *Imago pietatis* also takes its place at the opening of a foliated book, this time the 1491 ledger recording the Monte's first deposits and loans (Fig. 13).[58] Isolated, three-quarters in length and with his arms traditionally brought together at the wrists, the figure rises from the tomb. A skilled draftsman finely executed the drawing in pen and wash and added delicate touches in red for the blood dripping from Christ's side wound and to accent the nimbed halo.[59] Both miniature and drawing were likely

[54] Vittorino Meneghin OFM, "Il 'Mons Euganeus' di Giovanni Barozzi. Poemetto sull'erezione del Monte di Pietà di Padova (1491)," *Fonti e Ricerche di Storia Ecclesiastica Padovana* II (1969): 107-216, 180-182 especially, verses 49-54: "E tumulo nondum posito super hostia saxo/ Ut stas exanguis, membraque fessa tenes./Brachia dependent laterum incumbentia costis/ Porrectaeque manus ad genua ipsa iacent./ Cingit acerba caput foedum spinosa corona,/ Clausi oculi languent, undique sputa fluunt./ Barba bifurcato flavescens crine, comaeque,/ Oraque sunt sputis, tetra, veneniferis;/ Sanguine derorat facies et colla, sinusque,/ Et putrescenti membra cruore rigent."

[55] See Mitchell B. Meerback, "Fount of Mercy, City of Blood: Cultic anti-Judaism and the Pulkan Passion Altarpiece," *Art Bulletin* LXXXVII (2005): 589-642.

[56] On the association between public processions and the social order, see Sarah Beckwith, *Christ's Body: Identity, culture and society in late medieval writings* (London: Routledge, 1993), especially 33-34.

[57] Biblioteca del Museo Civico di Padova, B.P. 103, a ms. that is related to the work of Antonio da Villafora. Addenda to the original statutes of 1491 extend to 1507, suggesting that the miniature might date anywhere between 1491 and 1507.

[58] Padua, Archivio di Stato, Santo Monte di Pietà, reg. 19.

[59] The figure is close in style to a panel of the Man of Sorrows in the sacristy of San Giobbe, Venice, a work assigned to the circle of Vivarini.

commissioned by the Monte's officers, a twelve-man board that comprised prominent lay citizens only (nobles, merchants, notaries and members of the Confraternity of the Carità). In the months leading up to the Monte's inauguration, these Paduans had ample time to consult with Bernardino, on hand for a good part of the year, in order to select the appropriate emblem for the institution.

None of the early surviving images from the Paduan Monte depict Bernardino with the banner, but by the end of the 1490s, votive panels along with standards made for an individual Monte in the Veneto portray him just so, banner in hand.[60] Though difficult to date precisely, these portraits have a probable *terminus post quem* of 1494, the friar's death date, when the popular cult spontaneously inspired by the charismatic preacher must have begun. A canvas in the Pinacoteca Nazionale, Ferrara, exemplifies the many portrayals of Bernardino that date after c.1500, and it shows him with the standard rising from a mound (the *Monte*) and displaying the Man of Sorrows.[61] What is remarkable about this visual association is that it eventually came to be coupled with all establishments of the Monte di Pietà whether Bernardino generated them or not, and though each bank was a discrete civic entity, time and insignia together have created the mistaken impression that all the institutions were identically founded. The pennant and its Man of Sorrows have come to immortalize the friar as the architect of the Monte's success, the object and its image turning into his personal attributes and informing his iconography for posterity. In the more restricted context of the Man of Sorrows vis-à-vis fifteenth-century Franciscan Padua, Bernardino's significance lies in "urbanizing" the figure, taking it into the streets, and broadening its efficacy to address the problem of the urban poor, a burning social issue for the Franciscans. Initiating its chronological journey in Quattrocento Minorite Padua in the most traditional of ways, a half-length figure flanked by Mary and John on the Fulgosio Tomb, the *Imago pietatis* developed as a pluripotential image, assuming new meanings, adjusting to varied physical circumstances and enriching its spiritual milieu.

---

[60] For an illustrated repertory, see Meneghin, *Iconografia del B. Bernardino Tomitano da Feltre* (Venice, 1967).

[61] Tempera on canvas, 172 x 70 cm., assigned to the so-called "Vicino da Ferrara," and dated c.1494-1504, ex. Collection of the Monte di Pietà of Ferrara. This and many other images include banderoles inscribed with two phrases drawn from the gospels: *Habe Illius Curam* (Luke 10:35), and *Nolite Diligere Mundum* (John 2:15). Bernardino used the second verse as the theme of his Lenten sermons in Pavia in 1493; see Meneghin, *Bernardino da Feltre e I Monti di Pietà*, p. 463.

STANDING ON THE THRESHOLD:
BEHOLDER AND VISION IN THE ST. FRANCIS CYCLE
IN THE UPPER CHURCH OF SAN FRANCESCO, ASSISI

Beth Mulvaney

ntering the Upper Basilica of San Francesco at Assisi, the central church of the Franciscan Order, one crosses a literal and symbolic threshold (Fig. 1).[1] Colorful painted decoration covers every structural surface extending from the base of the walls to the soaring vaults overhead, wrapping the visitor within a completely Franciscan visual and material world. What some might see as an ironic and paradoxical twist to Francis's original dream, others might see as a mystical vision made concrete. To stand within this space, a sensate being submits to the dynamic relationship between the painted imagery and the spectator.[2]

The elaborate framing of the twenty eight individual scenes that create the cycle of St. Francis marks the threshold between the physical space occupied by a pilgrim in the nave and the fictional reality of the painted scenes drawn from Francis's life. Many of the images from the St. Francis cycle are spatially designed to actively invite the viewer into the represented space and time. As I examine the relationship between a viewer and the frescoes in the Upper Church there are three elements that I want to address: first, to analyze the "framing" of the St. Francis cycle and how it functions overall in relation to the decorative program in the nave of the Upper Basilica; second, to explore some of the inventive spatial and iconographic choices in the St. Francis cycle and their relationship to the beholder standing within the nave; and third, to investigate how iconographic and thematic parallels between scenes of the Francis cycle underscore how the individual act of viewing is used to shape devotional experience in a thoroughly Franciscan way.

"Framing" the Cycle

The structural clarity of the Upper Basilica is striking and ideal for mural painting. The open space of the nave is subdivided into four bays, each emphatically articulated by the clusters of brightly patterned colonettes marking each pier. Individual decorative patterns differentiate each architectural element, a choice that simultaneously defines the element and visually flattens it to become part of

---

[1]   Portions of this essay already have been published by this author: B.A. Mulvaney, "Standing on the Threshold: Beholder and Vision in the Assisi *Crib at Greccio*," in *Finding Saint Francis in Literature and Art*, eds. C. Ho, B.A. Mulvaney, and J.K. Downey (New York: Palgrave Press, 2009), 23-34.
[2]   My essay returns to some ideas that first emerged during a 2003 NEH seminar led by William R. Cook that focused on St. Francis in the thirteenth century.

Fig 1. Interior, Upper Basilica, San Francesco, Assisi Photo credit: © 1982-2001 ASSISI.DE

an all-over brocade of color and pattern that recedes in contrast to the larger fields containing the figural scenes.

Emerging from the shadows that gather below the stained glass windows, the frescoes forming the canonical cycle of Francis's life unfold to reveal a remarkable break from earlier medieval imagery. Prominently placed on the lower nave walls, the pictorial design of the St. Francis cycle is strikingly different from the Old and New Testament cycles located above. The cycle was completed as part of two different campaigns, and the difference in design is meaningful. Beneath the windows, the lower walls reveal a clever interplay between suggestively illusionistic spaces and sophisticated color choices that enhance the construction of a fictional reality.[3] The twenty–eight scenes from the life of Francis appear within an elaborate painted architectonic framework, analogous to a shallow loggia or porch. This shallow space appears to be supported by three-dimensional consoles running continuously below all the scenes while protected above by coffered ceiling squares, two rows in depth. This shallow loggia-like space is subdivided by regularly-placed, painted twisted columns that appear to sit on white marble plinths. The three-dimensional effect of the twisted columns is enhanced by the warm brick-red color field against which the columns project, aided even further by contrasting strips of yellow placed next to the sides of each column.[4] While these design choices do not mimic actual constructions, they are effective in suggesting space and depth. The same brick-red color, which visually helps the forward projection of the twisted

column, continues as a narrow band that surrounds each narrative scene. A second narrow band of turquoise, decorated with regularly-spaced lozenge shapes, is nested inside of the red band. The effect of these two contrasting square frames or bands gives prominence to each of the scenes. The scenes themselves are remarkable for their evocative spaces inhabited by volumetric figures that move and react in recognizable ways to the events pictured. The once-uniform cool blue background of all the scenes recedes into depth allowing these pictured figures and events to project strongly on their narrow stages framed as though through a loggia or window. Appearing immediately above the continuous fictive drapery that undulates along the lower walls, the device of the loggia–like frame bordering the Francis images implies a kind of passageway between the space of the beholder and the depth of the frescoes.

From this vantage point a viewer peers beyond the frame, as through a window or the openings of a loggia, at the unfolding events of Francis's life. This visual structure contrasts the Old and New Testament design directly above the Legend of St. Francis. The biblical cycles use decorative patterns to surround individual scenes, creating the effect of a series of tapestries with patterned borders laid flat against the wall surface. In addition, the upper walls are set back several feet from the lower nave walls, functionally forming the gallery within the nave elevation, while the frescoes' comparative distance from the viewer also figuratively underlines the sense of past history displayed in the Old and New Testament cycles.

---

3   Recent analyses of the cycle's pigments have been carried out and a team of researchers and restoration specialists have produced hypothetical reconstructions of the "original" colors and details of the Francis cycle in the Upper Basilica. See: Giuseppe Basile, Fabio Fernetti, Paola Santopadre, and Claudio Seccaroni, Sacro Convento di San Francesco, and Istituto Centrale per il Restauro Enea, *Giotto Com'era: Il Colore Perduto Delle Storie Di San Francesco Nella Basilica Di Assisi* (Rome: De Luca Editori d'arte, 2007). Following this publication, an exhibition was mounted of these digitally reconstructed images of the frescoes with an accompanying catalog, see: *I colori di Giotto: la Basilica di Assisi: restauro e restituzione virtuale*, ed. Giuseppe Basile (Milan: Silvana, 2010).

4   My description of the colors is based on what may be seen in the basilica today. The results published by Giuseppe Basile and others are different. Instead of the brick-red color field "behind" each twisted column, they suggest a much brighter, truer red. Despite these differences in colors, the effect produced is not unlike what I am suggesting in the essay.

Fig 2. Crib at Greccio, Upper Basilica, San Francesco, Assisi Photo credit: © 1982-2001 ASSISI.DE

In contrast, the elaborately constructed framework of the St. Francis cycle acts as a spatial intermediary between the physical nave space and the painted narrative space implying a sense of temporal present–ness in which the beholder becomes intimate witness to, and perhaps participant in, the unfolding events of Francis's life. Many of the images of the St. Francis cycle are spatially designed to actively invite the viewer into the represented space and time.

Relationship to the Beholder

Stepping across the threshold into the soaring and profusely decorated interior space of the Upper Church of San Francesco, a visitor might turn to the right and look up to find the *Crib at Greccio*, a wondrous image that inscribes an invisible and shifting threshold marking the difference between Medieval and Renaissance approaches to space and vision (Fig. 2). Framed by the architecturally–detailed cornices above and below with fictive columns on either side, the beholder's view mirrors that of the depicted women who stand at an opposite threshold gazing through an opening in the *tramezzo*, or choir screen, just below its molding. These women peer into the chancel from one opening, while the fresco's beholders peer into it from the opposite side. Framed by that doorway, one woman alone in the crowd stands on the threshold, as if to suggest viewing should be an *individual* experience for each beholder.

Or, stepping further into the nave, the visitor might glance to the left. Here, between the 3rd and 4th bays a complex reciprocity of meaning is created between the cycles in the nave.[5] Divided by the compound pier separating these two bays, Francis's gaze in the *Stigmatization* is directed not only to the vision of the Crucified Christ surrounded by Seraphim within this scene, but also implicitly to the image of Christ's *Crucifixion* in the upper register of the next bay. Immediately below the New Testament Crucifixion lies the Funeral and Apotheosis of Francis, which a contemplative beholder in the nave might also compare to the scene of Christ's *Lamentation* in the prior bay above the *Stigmatization* of Francis, thus setting up a series of diagonal relationships between the scenes of the New Testament and Francis's life in these two bays. Although the Francis cycle is distinctly separate from the biblical program, the fresco series of the saint's life is considerably enriched when regarded in connection with the larger salvation history pictured in the cycle above. A similar strategy is shared by the first biographer of Francis, Thomas of Celano, and the 1266 "official" biographer St. Bonaventure, who both embed references to the Old and New Testaments within the events of Francis's life. The relationship between the cycles is encouraged by the architectural elements of each bay, which create a defined frame that "packages" together individual components from the Old and New Testament scenes, the stained glass windows, and the frescoes from the life of St. Francis.

Indeed, to cross the threshold into the Upper Basilica of San Francesco at Assisi, is to enter another realm. It is a realm in which biography intersects salvation history and the individual beholder may join in the dialectic of private and public, inside and outside, present and past. The spatial organization of the decorative schemas, left to right, front to back, above and below, diagonal and parallel, circular and centered is dependent on the perception of the individual in relation to personal time and space as well as devotional frame of mind.

---

[5]   There are many books that contain images of the Upper Basilica and its frescoes. The most complete documentation found is: *Basilica di San Francesco ad Assisi*, 4 vols., *Mirabilia Italiae* 11, ed. Giorgio Bonsanti (Modena, Italy: Franco Cosimo Panini Editore, 2002). A more affordable guide using some of the same documentation is: *La Basilica di San Francesco ad Assisi*, ed. Gianfranco Malafarina, trans. Heather Mackay and Mark Roberts (Modena, Italy: Franco Cosimo Panini, and Assisi: Casa Editrice Francescana, 2005). Also, the catalog cited above, *I colori di Giotto*, edited by Basile has very good reproductions. A view of the 3rd and 4th bays bays is found in vol. 2 of the *Mirabilia Italiae* 11, 681.

Fig 3. Homage of a Simple Man, Upper Basilica, San Francesco, Assisi Photo credit: © 1982-2001 ASSISI.DE

To begin to understand the complexity of relationships as well as the inventive spatial and iconographic choices, I will move down the nave of the basilica to the beginning of the Francis cycle.

Iconographic Choices and Individual Devotion

The Francis cycle begins on the north wall, the right side of the nave, in the first bay, immediately below the Old Testament scenes of Creation and Noah and the Ark. These scenes and all those illustrating the Legend of St. Francis, are drawn from Bonaventure's *Legenda Maior*, the 1266 official biography of Francis paraphrased in Latin *tituli* on the wall below the scenes.[6] Like Celano, Bonaventure uses particular narrative techniques to reveal Francis to the wider public, such as appealing to the readers' realm of experience and invoking language from the growing urban merchant class, repeatedly calling Francis a "merchant of god." Both authors invoke chivalric language, referring to Francis as a "knight of Christ" as well as an "athlete of Christ." Writing for a rapidly expanding and increasingly divisive Order, Bonaventure codified the Franciscan narrative, selecting vignettes that not only outline the life of the man, but at the same time create a model of sanctity by expounding on his virtues. In Bonaventure's biography Francis will be presented as a new knight of Christ, as a new merchant of Christ, and will model humility and poverty in his actions, two virtues that emphatically counter the merchant's sin of avarice and the knight's of pride.

The three episodes within the first bay establish Francis as one who possessed attributes of grace before his conversion, an approach that closely follows Bonaventure's Chapter One, "Saint Francis's Manner of Life in the Attire of the World." Unlike Celano's first chapter of the *Vita Prima*, Bonaventure sets up Francis as a man naturally predisposed to good even though he had not begun his conversion. His text is sprinkled with quotations pulled from scripture, thus placing Francis within the larger history of salvation. In the scene *Homage of a Simple Man*, a scene for which there is no known visual precedent, a simpleton of the town, as instructed by God, laid down his cloak before Francis each time their paths crossed in recognition of Francis's special nature (Fig. 3). The scene's designer, unlike the biographers of Francis, could not list the virtues and moral nature of Francis's character, but like the writers, the painter describes particulars that allow for a growing understanding of Francis's nature. As is well known, the scene takes place in the Assisi Piazza Commune, before the Temple of Minerva, thus anchoring it within a recognizable location in Assisi. In depicting this town landmark, the artist has shown remarkable fidelity to appearance, even including two barred windows, perhaps as a reference to its thirteenth-century use as a prison. Yet the pediment decoration of a rose window centered between two angels is not at all accurate. Should the addition of this Christian detail on a former pagan temple be understood as a symbol of conversion? Does the prison additionally denote Francis's state before conversion? Is the prison a reminder of his life before his conversion when he was sick and imprisoned in Perugia?

Although haloed, the voluminously clothed state of Francis, recalling his status as the son of a cloth merchant, denotes his pre-conversion state, and unlike the description of Francis's youth in *I Celano*, he and his companions' dress is more restrained than the two men who witness the action of the simpleton. These two men standing beside

6   The translated text of Bonaventure is contained in: "The Major Legend of Saint Francis 1260-63," in *Francis of Assisi: Early Documents*, vol. 2: The Founder, eds. Regis J. Armstrong, J.A. Wayne Hellmann, William J. Short (New York: New City Press, 2000), 525-649. The Latin *tituli* are largely illegible today. The inscriptions and translations may be found in: Bruno Dozzini, *Giotto: The "Legend of St. Francis" in the Assisi Basilica*, trans. The New School—S. Maria degli Angeli (Assisi: Editrice Minerva, 1994).

Fig 4. Miracle of the Crucifix, Upper Basilica, San Francesco, Assisi Photo credit: © 1982-2001 ASSISI.DE

the simpleton, unlike those accompanying Francis, have fur collars and more extravagant hats, a mode of dress signifying scholars. A companion behind Francis who wears a scarlet cloak displays its inner, white lining, which is turned outward in his left hand. Visually this bright lining discretely draws attention to the joined hands of Francis's companions. Throughout the cycle, gestures play an important role; perhaps here their joined hands are a symbol of Francis's natural ability to bestow good will and peace, even before his conversion. While Celano and Bonaventure use language expressively to develop the character of Francis, the painter draws upon the iconographic prototype of an Entry into Jerusalem where the multitude is seen spreading garments before Christ. Bonaventure himself makes this connection between the recognition of Christ's and Francis's worthiness in his own text as he appropriates the phrase "spreading the garment" from Luke 19:36.[7] The two "scholar" onlookers to the spectacle play an analogous role to the Pharisees' bewilderment at Christ's reception at the Gate to Jerusalem.

The garment spread before Francis is rendered in a most spectacular way and stretches across the foreground linking the saint to the simpleton. The cloth is white and besides the meticulous modeling to suggest its three-dimensional properties, an open neck hole is prominently placed along the central vertical axis of the scene. Could this be a visual reference to Christ's "tunic without seam woven from top to bottom," (John 19:23), often understood to symbolize the Word of God to which Francis would devote his life after the conversion? In Bonaventure's "Prologue" to the life, he sets Francis up as a prophetic visionary, one whose mis-

sion is "of calling to weep and mourn, to shave one's head and wear sackcloth, and to sign the Tau on the foreheads of those moaning and grieving with a sign of a penitential cross, and of a habit conformed to the cross… ."[8]

In Celano's second Life, *The Remembrances of the Desire of a Soul*, he describes the conversion of a man who had "prostituted himself entirely to vanity."[9] Like the Simpleton, this converted Brother Pacifico, thus named by Francis because he had been returned to the *peace of the Lord*, was "allowed to see what was veiled to others. … he saw the great sign of the Tau on the forehead of blessed Francis, … ."[10] Francis himself saw the Tau emblazoned on military armor, depicted in the *Vision of the Palace*, the third scene of the first bay. Bonaventure tells us,

> …on waking up in the morning, since he was not yet disciplined in penetrating the divine mysteries and did not know how to pass through the visible appearance to contuit the invisible truth, he assessed the unusual vision to be a judgment of great prosperity in the future. For this reason, still ignorant of the divine plan, he set out to join a generous count in Apulia, hoping in his service to obtain the glory of knighthood, as his vision foreshadowed.[11]

The second bay of scenes represents the turning point in Francis's conversion where the image of the tau, the crucifix itself, urges Francis to heed his divine calling. Although he still misunderstands his mission, he has committed himself to God. This famous scene, the *Miracle of the Crucifix*, is the fourth

---

[7]   Bonaventure, *Francis of Assisi: Early Documents*, vol. 2, 531.

[8]   Bonaventure, *Francis of Assisi: Early Documents*, vol. 2, 527.

[9]   Thomas of Celano, "The Remembrance of the Desire of a Soul," in *Francis of Assisi: Early Documents*, vol. 2, 239-393.

[10]   Celano, *Francis of Assisi: Early Documents*, vol. 2, 317.

[11]   Bonaventure, *Francis of Assisi: Early Documents*, vol. 2, 532-33.

scene of the cycle (Fig. 4). Bonaventure tells us Francis was passing by the dilapidated church of S. Damiano when he was prompted by the spirit to enter the church and pray before the crucifix on the altar.

> While his tear-filled eyes were gazing at the Lord's cross, he heard with his bodily ears a voice coming from that cross, telling him three times: "Francis, go and repair my house which, as you see, is all being destroyed." Trembling, Francis was stunned at the sound of such an astonishing voice, since he was alone in the church; and as he absorbed the power of the divine words into his heart, he fell into an ecstasy of mind. At last, coming back to himself, he prepared himself to obey and pulled himself together to carry out the command of repairing the material church....[12]

In the biography and other writings, Bonaventure outlines a three-part process where souls are led to divine truth through what he called "contuition" or *contuitio*.[13] Bonaventure's stages of contemplation begin with sense knowledge, and proceed through intellectual understanding to finally reach a mystical experience of divine truth. In this fresco, Francis kneels before and gazes intently at the cross, presumably while meditating upon the divine words that instructed him to "go and repair my house." Even in the case with Francis, however, the communion with divine truth is not instantaneous. For Francis, although he was receptive, his intellectual comprehension faltered at understanding the divine message. The sensory cues provided in the Assisi frescoes allow for

viewers to become witnesses to the events of Francis's life, thereby opening the possibility for some to experience an intellectual comprehension, and perhaps the divine truth revealed in Francis's model of sanctity.

After "fortifying himself with the cross" Francis sold his father's cloth and even the horse he rode to town to fund repairs to the church. He sought refuge at the church hiding in a pit from his angry father. After some days, which were filled with tearful imploring of God to deliver him from those who tormented his soul, he emerged with great joy and resolved to face his father.

The scene of the *Renunciation of St. Francis* becomes a climax of dramatic tension when considered in its context as the central scene of the second bay (Fig. 5).[14] The scenes of *The Miracle of the Crucifix* and *The Dream of Innocent III* form a kind of framing device for the *Renunciation of St. Francis*, providing balance and an oblique perspective oriented to a spectator standing in the center of the bay, to give emphasis to the culminating moment symbolized by the literal and figurative chasm between Francis and his father. Yet, like the biographies of Francis where one event is seen as prescient prelude to another, the scene of the *Renunciation* creates a deliberate compositional and thematic counterpoint to the first scene of the cycle, *Homage of a Simple Man*. In the biographies, repeatedly Francis is invoked as the son of a wealthy cloth merchant. In the pictorial cycle, Francis is contextualized within the emerging urban merchant economy of the thirteenth century, revealed literally through the garments worn by characters in the frescoes as well as the social fabric in the visual description of contemporary urban structures. These garments are lovingly

12   Bonaventure, *Francis of Assisi: Early Documents*, vol. 2, 536.
13   Bonaventure, *Francis of Assisi: Early Documents*, vol. 2, 532, fn. d. Also see Ewert Cousins's analysis of Bonaventure's use of *contuitio*: Ewert H. Cousins, "Bonaventure's Mysticism of Language," in *Mysticism and Language*, ed. Steven T. Katz (New York, Oxford: Oxford University Press, 1992), 236-53.
14   For an eloquent analysis, see John White, *The Birth and Rebirth of Pictorial Space*, 2nd ed. (Boston: Boston Book and Art Shop, 1967), 40-2.

described to convey specific information about class and economy.

Both the *Homage* and the *Renunciation* split the scenes into two groups of figures leaving a centralized, open space. In the first scene, the open space is filled by the garment spread by the simpleton and the Temple of Minerva, and these elements connect Francis to the simpleton. In the *Renunciation* scene, the split between the two groups is left symbolically open or void. The garments cast off by Francis are gathered into the left arm of his father, Pietro Bernardone, whose right arm is restrained by a companion behind him. The restraint of his father's angry gesture contrasts with the gesture of friendship and accord of the joined hands of the figures behind Francis in the *Homage* scene. Francis's gesture, in both scenes, is one of submission.[15] In the first, his arms cross at the wrist, humbly submitting to the gesture of the simpleton. In the latter scene he raises his hands in prayer to the hand of God emerging from the heavens, a gesture Bill Cook has noted that is taken from the feudal system of social order indicating the vassal-to-Lord gesture of submission. Perhaps most significant is the reversal of Francis's position; instead of occupying the left side, he is placed on the right side, creating a visual halt to the left to right narrative compositional flow of the scenes. Francis strips off the rich fabrics of his former life and is symbolically reborn wrapped in the church.

Like each of the chapters in the written biographies, individual scenes are immeasurably enriched when considered as part of the whole, joining the thematic threads that link the scenes together. Immediately above in the Old Testament cycle are scenes from the Creation and Fall, as well as Noah and Abraham: in this context we understand Francis as another Adam, and Francis as an obedient follower of his faith. These first five scenes

of the Assisi St. Francis cycle use clothing, the fine fabrics associated with Francis's early life, to tie the scenes together as a chapter that prophetically precedes his later actions: they appeal to the senses, but become also understood as symbolizing greater truths. The closing of Chapter Two of Bonaventure's biography of Francis summarizes for the reader the meaning of these events (using Francis's relationship to the Portiuncula to link these early events leading to Francis's conversion and mission with the stages of mysticism):

> This is the place where the Order of Lesser Brothers was begun by Saint Francis under the prompting of divine revelation. For at the bidding of divine providence which guided Christ's servant in everything, he built up three material churches before he preached the Gospel and began the Order not only to ascend in an orderly progression from the sensible to the intelligible, from the lesser to the greater, but also to symbolize mystically in external action perceived by the senses what he would do in the future.[16]

This movement from the sensible to the intelligible to the mystical realm is also found in the fresco cycle. At the beginning of the series, Francis's special nature is sensed or suggested through symbolism, such as the garment spread before Francis in the *Homage of a Simple Man*, which is understood as the allusion to the Word of God by the visual reference to Christ's tunic and the crosses decorating the armor found in the windows of *The Vision of the Palace*. In the *Miracle of the Crucifix* Francis hears the cross speak to him but he doesn't fully understand yet what he hears. Later, after his

---

[15] This detail was pointed out by William R. Cook during the NEH Seminar, St. Francis in the Thirteenth Century, in the summer of 2003.

[16] Bonaventure, *Francis of Assisi: Early Documents*, vol. 2, 541.

Fig 5. Renunciation of St. Francis, Upper Basilica, San Francesco, Assisi Photo credit: © 1982-2001 ASSISI.DE

confrontation with his father in the *Renunciation*, he understands and he shows others how to reach an intelligible state, as in *The Dream of Innocent III, The Vision of the Fiery Chariot, or the Crib at Greccio*. Toward the end of the cycle, in the Stigmatization, Francis himself, is mystically transformed into the living seal, the "coat of arms" of the Lord. This kind of movement from the concrete to mystical also is found within individual scenes, such as the *Crib at Greccio*, where the image of the cross literally represents Christ, yet Francis's reenactment of the manger scene places him as the symbolic Christ.

Individual Act of Viewing

The suggestive spatial and iconographic choices in the *Crib at Greccio* and its formal and thematic relationship(s) to the *Verification of the Stigmata* and the *Mourning of the Clares* hold deep implications for the individual experience of viewing. While not part of a consecutive narrative grouping, these three scenes share a particularly Franciscan approach to the abstract and divine by appealing to the beholder's imagination in invoking the concrete and material as well as the more human realm of feelings and experiences. In each of these scenes, the artist summons the viewer's sense of temporal present–ness by using binary oppositions (of front/back, presence/absence, occupied/empty, three–dimensional/two–dimensional) that appeal to physical experience, and also to imitation and performance, which model the Franciscan, more personalized approach to spiritual apprehension and devotional practice.

The Assisi fresco representing the *Crib at Greccio* (Fig. 2) radically departs from the description supplied by Bonaventure's *Legenda Maior*.[17]

Bonaventure's text informs the reader that Francis obtained permission from the Pope to celebrate the memory of the Nativity "in order to arouse devotion." Bonaventure describes a forest night scene with Francis, dressed as a deacon, preaching the Gospel of Christ's birth.

> A certain virtuous and truthful knight, Sir John of Greccio, who had abandoned worldly military activity out of love of Christ and had become an intimate friend of the man of God, claimed that he saw a beautiful little child asleep in that manger whom the blessed father Francis embraced in both of his arms and seemed to wake it from sleep.[18]

Rather than surrounded by the forest at Greccio, a monumental *tramezzo* or choir screen spans the entire width of the image. During the Middle Ages *tramezzi* were erected to separate the sacred and lay areas of a church. Marcia Hall's study of Santa Croce in Florence shows that the *tramezzo* provided a way for the friars to pass from the monastery to the choir without being seen.[19] Learning from late medieval sources, including Durandus, the late thirteenth–century authority on ritual and the Church, Hall asserts that the chancel was divided hierarchically: the clergy occupied the immediate area around the altar, the friars the secondary area of the choir and during the mass male Christians might be permitted to cross over the *tramezzo* into the choir while women and those not baptized were relegated to the nave outside of the sacred area.[20] Indeed, this is precisely what is pictured within the *Crib at Greccio* where the

---

[17] Bonaventure, *Francis of Assisi: Early Documents*, vol. 2, 610-11.

[18] Bonaventure, *Francis of Assisi: Early Documents*, vol. 2, 610.

[19] Marcia B. Hall, "The *Tramezzo* in Santa Croce, Florence, Reconstructed," *Art Bulletin* 56 (1974): 325-41, at 337-40.

[20] See Durandus's 1286 treatise: W. Durandus, "The Symbolism of Churches and Church Ornaments," in *Rationale divinorum officiorum*, trans. J.M. Neale and B. Webb (Leeds: T.W. Green,1843), i-lix, at lvi-lvii. Also Donal Cooper, "Franciscan Choir Enclosures and the Function of Double-Sided Altarpieces in Pre-Tridentine Umbria," *Journal of the Warburg and Courtauld Institutes* 64 (2001): 1-54, at 51-4.

Assisi visitor cleverly has been transported behind the *tramezzo* to the sacred area of a church. Just as Durandus described, some devout laymen stand inside the tramezzo near the threshold of the chancel entrance in front of four friars who are elevated by the raised steps of choir stalls, their mouths open in song. In the foreground, the dramatic reenactment planned by Francis takes place. Vested as a deacon, the Saint kneels beside a manger placed in front of the altar where two other tonsured friars in priest's chasuble and subdeacon's dalmatic conduct the service. Forbidden to cross over the threshold of the *tramezzo*, the women are clustered within its doorway. Peering through the opening created by the painted framework, the Assisi visitor, by implication, "stands" in the chancel, an area that a *tramezzo* would have made invisible to a layperson in the nave. From this unexpected viewpoint, one that replicates the position of a friar, the beholder of this fresco is offered a most privileged position: an unobstructed view of the moment when Francis reaches into the crib to embrace the awakened child.

At the end of the thirteenth century, this is an astounding viewpoint rendered and offered by the artist—in effect, revealing a spectacle from "behind the scenes." Not only is the beholder led behind the *tramezzo*, but also offered the opportunity to gaze all around the sacred space and contemplate this panorama. On the left, the interior of an empty pulpit is partially visible, including its access stairway. Centered above the *tramezzo's* doorway opening is a monumental crucifix shown in perspective, its unseen painted face leaning forward toward the nave, away from the chancel; it is held in place by a chain connected to a tripod support firmly planted on the cornice. Like the pulpit, only the reverse side of the crucifix is visible, yet its distinctive silhouette serves to identify it. Its flatness is made more apparent by the shaded cross-bars and battens of its supports. With its obverse unseen, its function as a devotional object fades. From this point of view, which yields a meticulous scrutiny of its construction, its physical making is emphasized as a material object of mechanical representation; its inanimate nature contrasts the very human nature of Francis below.

Stepping over the threshold into this unexpected setting, we are shown a variety of elements from fundamentally different and distinct points of view. The pulpit is silent, the crucified Christ an inanimate outline. While an unusual view is rendered, always implicit is its more familiar binary opposite: the viewer has experienced the public space of the nave, the painted cross, the occupied pulpit. The women clustered within the *tramezzo* doorway, stand at this juncture between front and back, inside and outside, peering into the chancel toward the dramatic reenactment of the nativity, mirroring the position of the visitor standing in the Upper Church. The object of these gazes from within and outside the fresco is Francis, who kneels in the painted chancel lifting a baby from a manger. Shown in profile, Francis faces the covered altar and holds the swaddled infant just above the crib. He and the child gaze intensely at one another, seeming to share a psychological connection. Equally dramatic is the foreshortened head of the layman who looks down onto Francis and the child; he represents the knight mentioned in Bonaventure's text, who "affirmed that he saw a little Child" awakened by Francis. The knight's blue garments are depicted with bright, reflective surfaces to mark him visually as transfigured and enlightened by his experience of what he saw.

The altar is perpendicular to the nave and turned in a gentle oblique angle into depth, thus permitting us to see what transpires in front of it. Tightly surrounding the altar are friars and at least one other layman. Francis and two other friars are dressed in liturgical vestments; Francis wears the vestments of a deacon and the foremost friar wears the chasuble of the priest. The remaining four others, standing in the background parallel to the *tramezzo*, are dressed in Franciscan habits and have their mouths opened in song. Just to the left of the raised lectern, in an area behind Francis, stand a larger group of laymen dressed in an array of carefully differentiated garments. Some scholars have proposed that the fresco represents the recreation of Francis's Greccio sermon, which took place yearly in the Lower Church of San Francesco. In fact, as many have remarked, the marble choir screen that once divided the lay and liturgical spaces of the Lower Church, bears some physical resemblance to the one represented in this fresco. In short, the fresco displays a wealth of detail, extraordinarily rendered, including the most current liturgical furnishings within a distinctively Franciscan and Umbrian arrangement of the choir area.

This ahistorical appeal to the sensibility of a "witness" and/or "participant" within the drama is characteristic of the Franciscan experiential approach to devotional practice. Our ability to understand these practices in the late Middle Ages is aided by *The Meditations on the Life of Christ*, a text possibly written by a friar for a Poor Clare nun.[21] This exhaustive text follows the chronology of Christ's life and is interwoven with directives on proper meditation of the holy events as well as exhortations to imagine the sights and sounds of the events described, as well as the feelings of those involved in them. Repeatedly, throughout the *Meditations*, the author advises his reader to "see," to "behold," to "look" at the scene he is describing,

appealing to her imagination through visual imagery. He is outlining a practical guide to meditation that depends on a vivid amplification of the gospel narratives, often asking the reader to imagine herself present at the event. The reader is told to look closely at participants, to imagine their feelings and reactions to circumstances. The text, like the St. Francis cycle in the Upper Basilica, employs familiar sights or locations that appeal to the imagination of the reader allowing her to be "present" at the event while also bestowing a kind of witness–like authority on the description. For instance, in the *Meditations* the author describes the Virgin's distress at being unable to locate the twelve–year–old Christ before she finds him in the Temple with the Elders. He tells of her search in the neighborhood and appeals to the reader's realm of experience by observing that, as there is more than one route between Siena and Pisa, the Virgin searched alternate routes between Jerusalem and Nazareth.[22] This narrative device also is one used in the frescoes, found not only in the *Crib at Greccio*, but also in other scenes, perhaps most notably in the first scene of the cycle, *Homage of the Simple Man*, which places the still–extant Temple of Minerva as a backdrop to the protagonists of the drama. Besides using the familiar to engage the reader, the *Meditations* also uses vivid description and explicitly commands the reader to imagine herself present at the event described. For example, in recounting the Sermon on the Mount, he instructs his reader to "look and reflect" on the group assembling around Christ, as though observing from a distance. He then encourages her to "always try to look at the face of the Lord, and look also at the disciples as they gaze on Him with reverence, humility, and all intent-

---

[21]   Although dated to after 1346 and before 1364, this text summarizes devotional approaches dating to at least the thirteenth century. See: *Iohannis de Caulibus Meditaciones vite Christi: olim S. Bonaventurae attributae*, Corpus Christianorum 153, ed. M. Stallings-Taney (Turnhout, Belgium: Brepols, 1997). The frequently consulted translation is: *The Meditations on the Life of Christ*, trans. and ed. I. Ragusa and R.B. Green (Princeton, NJ: Princeton University Press, 1961).

[22]   *Meditations*, 89.

ness of mind, listening to those marvelous words and committing them to memory."[23] In effect, he encourages her to imagine moving closer and becoming a participant herself. Particularly noteworthy in regard to the *Crib of Greccio* is the encouragement by the author of the *Meditations* to assume several kinds of "viewpoints" within the Sermon on the Mount narrative. The painter, like the writer, approaches the *Crib of Greccio* in a typically Franciscan approach, persuading the beholder to experience the event as concretely as possible and from multiple perspectives.

Besides echoing the experiential devotional approach found in the *Meditations*, the ostensible subject of this fresco represents Francis's celebration of the nativity at Greccio, an event in which he imitated the gospels; the fresco itself recalls nativity reenactments that occurred in Assisi, perhaps in the Lower Church. While Francis's posture and role strongly recall that of Mary, certain figures within the chancel also echo, albeit faintly, other characters commonly seen in nativity or adoration plays. In this dramatic reenactment of the nativity, the layman with bowed head appears to imitate the pious and watchful role of Joseph. The singing friars might be compared to adoring angels, and the three prosperous citizens stationed in the foreground in front of the "heavenly chorus" might be compared to the three Magi. By contrast, the tonsured "celebrant" and two "acolytes" are more like adoring shepherds in their simplicity.[24] Seen in this way, the fresco may record the friars' and local townspeople's collaboration in sacred dramas. If so, the fresco involves imitation of more than one type of imitation of sacred event. Moreover, the devout woman framed in the doorway of the *tramezzo*, by virtue of her frontal, absolutely central position and the colors she wears, is faintly reminiscent of the

Virgin, particularly the Virgin as Ecclesia as she stands on the threshold of the chancel. The resemblance of figures in this fresco to nativity and adoration characters, whether intentional or coincidental, retains an indirect element of familiarity for a Greccio scene in which the accustomed setting and vantage point have otherwise been so unexpectedly inverted.

The artist employs a series of binary oppositions to summon up known experiences while also introducing an element of the unfamiliar; these binary pairings give concrete expression to the elusive "spiritual." In the *Crib at Greccio* there is a dramatic contrast in the scene between background absence and foreground presence. The emptiness of the pulpit and the blankness of the crucifix's back are contrasted with the occupied crib and with the altar that has been turned so that it offers its face to the visitor standing in the nave of San Francesco. The bodily three-dimensionality of the altar and its canopy contrasts with the more distant crucifix's flatness. Might the convergence of all these logically contradictory perspectives correspond to experience seen through not the bodily but the spiritual eyes, the very eyes required for our seeing so plainly the child in the crib? This idea also is found in the earlier image of Francis praying before the Cross of San Damiano: "While his tear-filled eyes were gazing at the Lord's cross, he heard with his bodily ears a voice coming from that cross...."[25]

A counterpoint experience is found on the opposite wall of the nave. As a viewer turns from the *Crib at Greccio* to begin moving closer to the altar, the *Verification of the Stigmata*, located on the opposite wall in the next bay, presents a more traditional viewpoint within a church. Whereas in the *Crib* the chancel was filled with participants and

23 *Meditations*, 153-55.
24 I am indebted to these insights offered by Dr. (James) Carlton Hughes during a conversation.
25 Bonaventure, *Francis of Assisi: Early Documents*, vol. 2, 536.

observers, while the nave remained unseen and perhaps empty, this time the action has shifted. The observers and participants are pressed together clustered at the juncture of the nave and chancel while the sacred area of the church remains an empty backdrop. Visually, the *Verification of the Stigmata* has reversed the perspective from the *Crib at Greccio*, but like the *Crib* (and the *Meditations'* descriptions of events) the beholder is offered various standpoints from which to examine the scene, ranging from a layperson, to a friar, to the knight probing the wound of Francis.

In this scene Francis's prone body lies parallel to the picture plane surrounded by officiating clergy, friars and other mourners. The officiating clergy's Franciscan habits are clearly visible beneath their surplices, reminding us of their fraternal vows and bond as well as the temporary roles they play within this service, and perhaps also those they might perform during a passion play. A kneeling knight, his hat removed, probes the side wound of Francis to confirm its authenticity. The actual physical position of the visitor in the Upper Church overlaps with the implied viewpoint, which is respectfully rendered from the nave looking toward a much simpler rood beam or iconostasis and the apse. The iconostasis consists of a simple wooden horizontal beam supported by consoles that connect the beam to the side walls, a choice that echoes the original arrangement in the Upper Church. In the fresco, the beam holds three shaped panels: an image of the Enthroned Madonna and Child on the left, a monumental painted crucifix in the center, and an image of Michael the Archangel on the right, all presenting their painted surfaces primarily toward Francis lying below and the beholder standing in the nave. Visible behind the wooden beam is the ghostly outline of the apse, articulated by a string-

course, the molding surround of the arch and the coffers in the apse vault. A variety of light fixtures are suspended on long cords, presumably from the ceiling, as is the forward–leaning Crucifix panel, which has been identified as representing the one commissioned by Brother Elias from Giunta Pisano in 1236 that later decorated the Upper Church.[26]

In this scene the more expansive threshold is marked by the body of Francis: the clergy and friars stand in the chancel while Francis and a few laypeople appear to be on the nave side, along with the beholder. The man kneeling in the foreground examining Francis's side wound was described by Bonaventure as "a knight who was educated and prudent, Jerome by name, a distinguished and famous man."[27] The knight pulls back Francis's robe with his right hand, while fingers of his left hand probe the wound. Besides this particular appeal to knowledge gained through touch and vision, auditory and olfactory cues are present: the friars chant, the few present laymen gesture and speak among themselves, incense and tapers burn. In some ways, the kneeling knight recalls the pose and gentle touch of Francis in the *Crib at Greccio*. Just as the sight of Francis awakening the Child stirred the sluggish faith of others, so the act of the knight Jerome serves to benefit many: "While he was examining with his hands these authentic signs of Christ's wounds, he completely healed the wound of doubt in his own heart and the hearts of others."[28] In the *Verification*, the knight Jerome gains knowledge and faith through touch, while in the *Crib at Greccio*, the knight John—who alone sees Francis awaken the sleeping child—gains knowledge through sight. The *Verification of the Stigmata* summons up how Francis received the stigmata, a scene represented in the bay immediately before this one. The representation of the painted cross mounted above Francis on the

---

[26] See: Dozzini, *Giotto*, 51.
[27] Bonaventure, *Francis of Assisi: Early Documents*, vol. 2, 646.
[28] Bonaventure, *Francis of Assisi: Early Documents*, vol. 2, 646-47.

wooden beam in the *Verification* becomes the visual substitution for his seraphic vision of the crucified Christ and his reception of the stigmata. Additionally, the artist evokes parallelisms to the disciple Thomas's doubting of Christ's resurrection and to the *Lamentation of Christ*, a scene represented above in the New Testament cycle. These visual and thematic parallelisms among the scenes help guide the faithful observer toward the connections between Francis and Christ, encouraging meditation on their shared humility and suffering, as well as recognition of Francis as *alter Christus*. Popular knowledge that Francis died on a wooden board also seems to be indicated in the fresco: Francis's thin, emaciated body lies upon a hard, cloth–covered surface. Like the *Crib of Greccio*, there are imitations of imitations in the *Verification*: the representation of the painted Crucifix, a simulacrum of Christ poised above the painted Francis who fashioned himself after Christ. Two similarly dressed men, each holding a shield and positioned at the head and foot of Francis, stand on the same plane as the kneeling Jerome. While the one positioned at the head of Francis stands facing the iconostasis and the crowd of mourners, the other one faces outward and gestures to the feet (and signs of the stigmata) of Francis. Placed directly beneath the painted representation of the militant Archangel Michael, this figure appears to replicate not only the stance and gesture of the painted image overhead, but also to guard entrance to the sacred space marked by Francis's body. Additionally, the *Verification* has affinities with the *Miracle of the Crucifix*, positioned on the opposite wall. In that early scene, Francis knelt before a cross in an empty dilapidated church and heard the cross speak to him; in the *Verification*, the knight kneels before the dead saint, seeing in Francis the mirror

of Christ. That experience before the cross of San Damiano led Francis to rebuild the church; the knight's experience kneeling beside the saint leads toward the healing of hearts. Now that Francis has rebuilt the Church, its space is filled with the faithful. These iconographic and thematic parallels between scenes of the cycle underscore how the individual act of viewing is used to shape devotional experience in a thoroughly Franciscan way: depending on imitation and concrete imaginative experiences to understand spirituality.

In the *Mourning of the Clares* the scene following the *Verification of the Stigmata*, a large crowd accompanying Francis's funeral cortege from the Portiuncula to Assisi has paused outside San Damiano so that Clare may bid him farewell.[29] Francis's prone body remains on the cloth–covered stretcher now moved in front of a large gothic church façade. St. Clare gently cradles him in a manner that echoes the Virgin Mary's embrace of the dead Christ in Lamentation scenes. Another sister kisses his left hand while still more sisters spill forth from the central and flanking doorways. Like the immediately preceding scene, this fresco strongly portrays Francis as *alter Christus* and now introduces Clare as *altera mater*. Of particular interest is the presentation of the Poor Ladies, who lived in strict *clausura* at San Damiano. Francis's death has pushed the women over the threshold that kept them invisible presences within the church. Thomas of Celano records in his first biography of Francis that the Saint's body was brought to San Damiano for Clare and her followers to mourn, and that the window or grate through which the cloistered nuns received the last sacrament was removed so that Clare could touch Francis in her grief.[30] The Assisi artist depicts the women stepping over the threshold in their "sorrow and joy" and in effect,

---

29 For illustrations of these two scenes, please consult *La Basilica di San Francesco ad Assisi*, 177-78.

30 This episode is found in Book II, Chapter X in: Thomas of Celano, "The Life of Saint Francis," in *Francis of Assisi: Early Documents*, vol. 1: The Saint, eds. Regis J. Armstrong, J.A. Wayne Hellmann, William J. Short (New York: New City Press, 2000), 284-87.

Francis as *alter Christus* becomes the substitute sacrament. Above the dense crowd of citizens and brothers accompanying Francis's body to its burial is a figure climbing a tree, an obvious reference to Zacchaeus from Christ's Entry into Jerusalem (Luke 19: 1–10). In death, Francis is headed to the heavenly Jerusalem represented in the fresco by the church façade.

Between these three scenes, the *Crib at Greccio*, the *Verification of the Stigmata*, and the *Mourning of the Clares*, the beholder has moved from the restricted space of the chancel to the more public space of the nave, and finally to the exterior of the church. In the *Crib at Greccio*, the alignment of the crucifix, lectern, and crib, sets up an axis of ontological hierarchy from Image to Word to Christ himself. The Franciscan "slant" of this axis is felt when one notices that it places the fullest manifestation of the Divine in the position most immediate to our own as viewers. The Greccio episode itself exemplifies the power of imitation on the collective and the individual levels. When the people replicated the scene of Christ's birth, then he indeed became manifest among them. And certainly, the more Francis imitated Christ, the more like Christ he became. In contrast to the *Crib of Greccio* where the women remained within the doorway, in the *Mourning of the Clares*, it is the sacral body of Francis that the women cross over the threshold to embrace. If in the *Crib at Greccio* the lone woman framed within the *tramezzo* doorway could symbolize Ecclesia, we now see the Church embrace Francis. Further, it is possible to infer from the Bonaventuran version of the *Crib at Greccio* that Francis and the Knight John were uniquely able to see Christ precisely because they had sought to imitate him in their lives.

Within the nave of San Francesco, the elaborate framing of the twenty eight individual scenes marks the threshold between the physical space occupied by a pilgrim in the nave and the fictional reality of the painted scenes drawn from Francis's life. These painted representations exhibit a break from earlier medieval approaches to images because they take on the challenge of constructing the reality of the material world while also suggesting that higher truths are discernible beyond the surface of appearances. The ability of the painter to invoke a coherent spiritual and spatial realm comparable to the viewer's physical world parallels contemporary persuasive elements contributed by authors of devotional manuals, such as *The Meditations on the Life of Christ*, literary forms like Thomas of Celano's and Bonaventure's biographies of Francis, and the performance and influence of developing sacred dramas. Through Francis the faithful beholder is reintroduced to the known and introduced to the unseen. From this position, standing on the literal and symbolic threshold, the beholder is encouraged to imagine participating in the spiritual pilgrimage of Francis, the *alter Christus*, and also is beckoned to join him, now and forever.

IMAGES OF FRANCISCAN HISTORY

David Flood

 spent a few days in Assisi in the fall of 1990. I stayed in the Chiesa Nuova of the Franciscans. The Father Guardian, Giovanni Boccali, gave me some material to read among which I found the thesis of Orietta Rossini on Angelo Clareno and his *History of the Seven Tribulations*. In the thesis Rossini describes a manuscript with an Italian translation of the *History* from the early fifteenth century. The manuscript contains fifteen miniatures illustrating the text. I soon secured myself slides of them. The miniatures do very well by the history.

The Author.

We do best to agree with those historians who say that Angelo Clareno, definitely a tribulant, was born around 1255 and became a Franciscan around 1270. In 1274 there arose a discussion in central Italy about the Franciscan order's poverty. Rumor had it that the fathers at the second council of Lyon were going to require that the order own property; the pope would absolve the brothers from the explicit determination of the rule against ownership. In the discussion some brothers said they could not, in conscience, accept papal release from the rule.[1] The minister provincials of the several provinces in central Italy, where the dissidence was broad and vocal, did not like the way some went on about Franciscan poverty. They ended up by throwing them into prison.

We do not know when Angelo Clareno joined the dissidents, but it seems he was among their number when, in 1290, the recently elected minister general of the order, Raymond Geoffroi, as his charge required, visited the friars of central Italy. He was schocked to find poverty's defenders in prison. He had them released. Hounded by their ministers, the dissidents eventually withdrew from the order and regrouped as their own entity, with the approval of Pope Celestine V. Pope Celestine's successor, Pope Boniface VIII, canceled the legitimation of the withdrawal and tribulation returned.

Around the council of Vienne, Pope Clement V tried to bring the dissidents and the ministers together. The dissidence was strong in southern France as well as in central Italy. In 1311, under the protection of Giacomo Cardinal Colonna, Angelo Clareno went to Avignon to represent his group's interests. The cardinal died in 1318. By then Angelo had his unease about the new pope abundantly confirmed;

---

[1] That had to do with the relationship between the rule and the gospel. The rule binds the two together. It opens with the line: "The rule and life of the lesser brothers is this: to observe the holy gospel of Our Lord Jesus Christ by living in obedience, without anything of one's own, and in chastity." In his final words to his brothers, Francis of Assisi said that God revealed to him that he was to live "secundum formam sancti evangelii."

he left Avignon and found safe residence with the Benedictines of Subiaco under Abbot Bartolomeo.

There, south of Rome, he conducted a large correspondence, wrote a commentary on the rule, and produced as well *A History of the Seven Tribulations* of the order in 1323-1326. It begins with Jesus' bestowal of the rule on Francis, enters rapidly into the plot to corrupt the rule, and then reports the successive defeats of the faithful. Angelo Clareno rooted his group's history in the struggle for fidelity that had begun early in the order. His account ends in the ambiguities intrinsic to the Joachimitic scheme of history's seven ages.[2]

The Manuscript

Angelo Clareno's history of the tribulations of the order has reached us in four Latin manuscripts and in nine Italian manuscripts. The Latin text has recently been twice edited. It has also been translated into English.[3] In preparation of one edition (1999) Orietta Rossini reviewed the manuscripts with the text.[4] There she devotes three-and-a-half pages to the manuscript with the miniatures: Ms. Vitt. Em. 1167 in the Biblioteca Nazionale Centrale "Vittorio Emanuele," Rome; measuring 284x194 (396-99, with bibliography). She dates it to the early fifteenth century. Under "Ornamentazione," she says the codex is illustrated by fifteen miniatures "a guazzo." One critic has called them primitive. She suggests he said that influenced by their context: Angelo Clareno and his brothers were not known for their learning. Put differently, they were not

clerics. For her part, she thinks several of them, though simple and poor of means, reveal a good hand; they attempt to characterize faces. I have found that Franciscans generally are enamored of them. Franciscans hesitate, however, to praise them as art, lacking the necessary aesthetic theory and vocabulary, but their response makes evident the miniatures' success in speaking to them.[5] They definitely do not laugh while looking at them. Two of the miniatures have recently graced the dust covers of two books. After her modest defence of the miniatures' artistic value, Rossini lists them. About the origins of the codex she does not have much to say, in spite of scrutinizing it for evidence.

The Miniatures

I pass through the miniatures rapidly, with the basic information about those portrayed.

Fig. 1.   Jesus Christ, accompanied by two angels, gives the kneeling Francis the rule. At the very beginning of Clarenus's account, Jesus says to Francis: "Take this book from my hand, the law of grace and humility, of poverty and piety, of charity and peace, the way of living which I followed with my disciples...." Jesus could have, but did not, referenced his words by Pope Nicholas III's bull *Exiit qui seminat* of 1279.[6]

Fig. 2.   Francis presents the rule to Honorius III, flanked by two cardinals. Chapter One has told Francis's story. Chapter Two relates the first tribulation.

[2]   On the apocalyptic expectations of Angelo Clareno and his associates, see the introduction to the English translation of the *History* in the following note, pages xxii-xxix.

[3]   *Angelo Clareno: A Chronicle or History of the Seven Tribulations of the Order of Brothers Minor*, trans. David Burr and E. Randolph Daniel (St. Bonaventure, NY: Franciscan Institute Publications, 2005). The worthy translation has a thirty-page introduction and a bibliography. Hereafter Burr-Daniel, *History*.

[4]   "I codici del Chronicon di Angelo Clareno," *Archivum Franciscanum Historicum* 87 (1994): 349-415. Rossini's edition: *Historia septem tribulationum Ordinis minorum* (Rome: Istituto storico italiano per il Medio Evo, 1999).

[5]   Their response validates A. Danto's remark on the different relation that arises between a viewer looking at a wall painting (Florence) and encountering a miniature on a folio (Siena). *Encounters and Reflections* (NY: Farrar, Straus, Giroux, 1990), 266.

[6]   In the introduction to his commentary on the rule, Pope Nicholas refers to the rule as "founded on the teaching of the gospel, confirmed by the example of Christ, and approved by the words and actions of his apostles..." The bull has been published in: K. Eubel, ed., *Bullarii Franciscani Epitome* (Quaracchi, 1908), 290-300.

Fig 1.

Fig 2.

On his return from the Orient (1220), Francis sees how some brothers have their plans for the order and are trying to win Cardinal Hugolino to their views. Francis rewrites the rule and brings it to Pope Honorius III. The pope examines it closely with his cardinals, and, in the spirit of his predecessor Pope Innocent III, confirms it.

Fig 3.

Fig. 3. Francis dying. In assistance, eight brothers, one writing. The rule lies open on the ground. When death approached, Francis called all those living with him (*in loco*) to his presence. He exorted them to life by the rule. Then, telling someone to take down his account, he blessed Bernard, the first of his brothers, and told how Bernard had joined him. He commanded that the ministers and the brothers honor Bernard in his place. Bernard and others were to suffer under the second tribulation.

Fig 4.

Fig. 4. Partisans of Brother Elias whip Anthony of Padua. Anthony visited Assisi to see the relics of Francis. Hefty henchmen of Elias seized him. They did not know him, nor did they examine him. It sufficed that he was, by accent, a foreigner, and they stripped and whipped him. This incident is related apart, for itself. It does not belong to the basic argument of Angelo Clareno's account.

Fig 5.

Fig. 5. A partisan of Elias pounds the holy pate of Caesar of Speyer, helping him pass to his heavenly reward. The incident occurs in the second tribulation, during which Brother Elias "persecutes the companions" of Francis.[7] Michael Cusato has written about the incident in his study on power in Franciscan history.[8]

Fig. 6. Thrown into jail by their brothers are: Gerard di Borgo San Donnino, Leonard, and Peter of Nubili. They lie dying on the ground. Or are two

Fig 6.

---

[7]   Burr-Daniel, *History*, 71ff. Re. Caesar of Speyer, 78.
[8]   Michael Cusato, "La renonciation au pouvoir chez les Frères Mineurs au 13e siècle," Manuscript (Friedsam Memorial Library, Saint Bonaventure University, 1990).

already dead, with a smile on their faces? The fourth tribulation centers on Bonaventure of Bagnoregio's punishment of Franciscan Joachimites.

Fig. 7.   Frater Petrus Ioannis Olivi, Brother Peter of John as many mansucripts call him. This son of the Midi was the theologian of the Franciscan conscience at the end of the thirteenth century. Of him Clarenus writes: "Peter of John, a pleasant and humble brother, was devoted to Christ and his mother and to Saint Francis. He was learned, both from study and by God's special grace. He spoke easily and well, better than most contemporaries and perhaps better than them all. He abounded in spiritual wisdom, in knowledge of God, in grace and truth, and in love for his order... He had the grace of foresight. His lessons explained well how to avoid spiritual dangers and how to reach the heights of truth and attain the final good. Many signs had foretold his coming, as with Dominic and Francis. Yes, the Abbot of Fiore had prophesied about him...."

Fig. 8.   Brother Pons Bautugat in prison. Brother Pons refused to hand over writings of Peter of John Olivi for burning. He was confined to a narrow, damp dungeon. In front of Pons, a snake, a frog, and a scorpion. "There he sat," writes Clareno, "half reclining under the weight of his chains, in shit and piss, buoyed up in spirit, afire with holy love, giving thanks to God. And there he died."

Fig. 9.   Five Italian ministers provincial gathered in secret to discuss criticism of large buildings, advanced study, and the search for ample funds. To quiet people, they decided to excommunicate those speaking up and throw them into prison. They decreed that once a week the judgment was to be

Fig 7.

Fig 8.

Fig 9.

read at chapter. Brother Thomas of Castel di Melo stood up and protested the injustice and the cruelty. He was thrown in prison, deprived of his habit, and burdened with chains. After a few months he took sick. Praising God and serene of spirit, he died.

Fig. 10. Seven brothers, Conrad of Offida, Peter of Monticello, Jacapone da Todi, Thomas of Trevi, Conrad of Spoleto, and two others, before Pope Celestine V, flanked by two cardinals. To escape the order's implacable hostility, Clarenus and Liberatus asked Pope Celestine for juridical separation from the order. They received it. The operation was labeled the Celestine maneuver.

Fig. 11. Conrad of Offida. In 1295, Peter of John Olivi wrote a letter to Conrad, defending the validity of Pope Celestine's withdrawal from the papacy and criticizing the disturbances caused by the Italian dissidents. Conrad was older than Peter, though he did not die until 1306. A man of prayer and of spiritual counsel, he became associated with the dissidents while living on Mount Alverna. He supported the Celestine maneuver.

Fig. 12. Arnald of Villanova, a medical doctor, favored the Franciscan dissidents. Here he pleads their case before King Charles of Sicily. He urged the king to write letters to the minister general, to have him end the unjust persecution of the Spirituals of southern France. Charles did write, adding that if the minister general did not comply, he, the king, would seek the pope's help. Charles and his family often used their royal influence in the interests of Clareno and his friends.

Fig. 13. Francis and Dominic. Joachim of Fiore wrote in a way which allowed the Franciscans to interpret his words as a prophecy of Francis and Dominic and their two orders. The two men would

Fig 10.

Fig 11.

Fig 12.

initiate the passage of the church out of the fifth into the sixth age of history. Whereas the fifth age had been and still was one where the church settled too comfortably into the ways of the world, the sixth age would be a time of spiritual renewal. The two orders would bring Christendom through the tribulation into an age of spiritual abundance.

Fig 13.

Fig. 14. The Four Martyrs of Marseille. The fight over Franciscan discipline in southern France, between the Community and the Spirituals, entered its decisive phase when sixty-three brothers journeyed to Avignon to plead their case before Pope John XXII. He, of course, sided with the order's administration against the Spirituals. Prison and threats wore down the opposition until only five remained. One, given his family connections, was consigned to life in prison. The final four were declared heretic by a commission of theologians and burned in Marseille, May 7, 1318.

The four made the mortal error of challenging church power within reach of papal vengeance. They refused to submit to John XXII's bull *Quorundam* of October 7, 1317, and its principle: Poverty is great, chastity is greater, greatest of all is obedience. By obedience John XXII meant in good part a respectful interiorization of the reality of papal power.

Fig 14.

Fig. 15. Bernard Délicieux before an inquisitor. Bernard was an intrepid opponent of the Inquisition in southern France. He had come to Avignon with the sixty-three to represent their case. Given his learning and eloquence, he was immediately separated from them and made a case apart. Separated from the others, he slipped away. He was caught and after a series of trials condemned to life in prison. Trembling from weakness though still clear of mind, he managed to win freedom from chains in his prison cell. Pope John XXII revoked the clemency, the chains were laid back on, and Bernard died soon after.

Fig 15.

Angelo Clareno wrote a partisan account of Franciscan history, as historians today know so well. Good that he got it down, I say, for it was his Franciscan story, and he could not expect that he would get a fair hearing from the order's learned friars. And though partisan, Angelo succeeds in getting onto the record the historicity of "the tribulations." It was not all a bad dream of Angelo's tormented mind. Lydia von Auw, a pioneer in research on Angelo Clareno, who edited his correspondence, remarked once that his many years in prison cast a pall of sadness over his life. There is ruin and tragedy in Franciscan history.

Art from Below

I propose bringing our miniatures into the history of art by playing them off against the art then coming about at Santa Croce in Florence. At about the time Angelo Clareno was writing his history, the Franciscans in Florence and their benefactors were deciding on the appointments of the new church's chapels.[9] We have an account of the windows for two chapels of the church paid for by one of Florence's leading families.[10] The Bardi family set up and sustained the Compagnia dei Bardi, a banking and trading business. The family had funds. When the transept of the new church was completed in 1310, it became known that the papacy favored with indulgences those who helped decorate the transept's chapels. The chapels needed frescos, panel painting, and stained glass. The Bardi family were already great patrons of the friars, Nancy Thompson tells us, and assumed responsibility for two chapels:

one dedicated to Francis of Assisi, the other to Louis of Toulouse. Louis was the son of King Charles II of Naples, the scion who renounced succession, became a friar, and died young, as bishop of Toulouse. He was canonized in 1317.

The artistic results of Bardi patronage did honor to the church, as well as the saints, and made the Bardi family's politics clear, as well as its wealth, and certainly its piety. Giotto did the frescos, Giovanni di Bonino was responsible for the stained glass. The frescos in Santa Croce looked to those in Assisi for leads. The work in the two chapels acquired cultural importance, an importance acknowledged by historians of art. The windows of the Francis chapel show Francis, Anthony of Padua, and Louis of Toulouse, each facing a pope in the parallel window, with papal hands extended towards them in blessing.[11] The figures were visible from far off in the church, as Thompson explains, above the rood screen between the choir and the lay area of the church. The close association between saints and popes made the family's politics clear. The Bardi also manifested their alliance with the Angevins by promoting the new saint in Florence. Nancy Thompson sees advantage for both Bardi and Angevins in devotion to the young saint. Bardi business was looked on favorably in Angevin lands, while Saint Louis's visibility in Florence's new church promoted the dynasty of the Angevins. As for piety, the Bardi had reason to feel at home in Santa Croce and expect prompt satisfaction when they knelt to beg forgiveness of their sins. They had already paid for indulgence.

---

9   The church had been built against strong criticism from the friars' ranks, among them the formidable Ubertino of Casale. The critics cited the order's constitutions, which spoke clearly against the building plans. They could as well, and perhaps did, cite Bonaventure of Bagnoregio's first letter to the order as minister. Bonaventure called for such criticism as theirs. The friar critics of Santa Croce said their peace, were not heard, and left the friary in protest.

10   N. Thompson, "Cooperation and Conflict: Stained Glass in the Bardi Chapels of Santa Croce," in *The Art of the Franciscan Order in Italy*, ed. W. Cook, The Medieval Franciscans 1 (Leiden: Brill, 2005), 257-77.

11   It is not easy to draw from the papal figures stained in glass, as Thompson wishes, a message about where the Santa Croce friars stood in the controversy between Pope John XXII and the order. There was a lull in the tensions in the middle 1320s. Michael of Cesena seized upon it to let the waters settle, only to witness the pope's wrathful resurrection of the differences in the spring of 1328. Anyway, as a body, the order supported Michael of Cesena, reelecting him as minister, against the wishes of the pope. That was not going to get a window.

When we talk about Franciscan art in Italy towards the end of the Middle Ages, we enter a world of wealth and power. The splendid church of Santa Croce offered the artists of the day a showcase for their talent and the rewards of good work. It invited them to show what they could do for the age's foremost public. The artists responded well. Whatever their sentiments, political and religious, they used the church space to make beauty and suggest the sublime, while seeing to it that they made do at home and even lived well. They left their labor behind. Great art drifts upward, socially, rewarding the artist, as those of means and of place readily claim it as theirs.[12] Santa Croce began to shine, thanks to the artists' efforts, and however critical some of the friars in the house might still consider the whole enterprise, they did not hesitate to look with pleasure on the results of the artists' labor. Those in charge of convent and church, the guardian and his men, belonged to proud and ambitious Florence in a way that invited agreement and support; the city applauded the architectural action so well performed and then saw to the splendor of its furnishings.

When we glance at our miniatures and then look to the architectural and pictorial art of the basilica of Assisi and Santa Croce, we tend, I propose, to set the miniatures aside, which we can look at and enjoy easily, and concentrate on the task of taking in and enjoying, in some way, Giotto and Giovanni di Bonino and the sacred space of Santa Croce. Before we do, though, I think it good to point out some of successes of the miniatures. The miniature of Peter of John Olivi does not set the friar in the halls of learning, for he did not belong there. However well-trained and gifted a theologian, he did not operate in the privileged sites of late thirteenth-century knowledge. The four friars burned in Marseille, May 18, 1318, play with the fire that consumed them; they have floated to the top left corner of the folio on which they appear and hang there suspended in a lightness that suggests spirit. Pons Bautugat raises a problem. How does an artist bring Pons into the associations of great art without robbing him of his witness? The series opens with Jesus addressing Francis. The figures are humble; they are also complete and well-placed. The miniature says, in sum, that the history enjoys divine blessing, which is good to know as one begins reading. Angelo's history is subjective; it is also wrong; but it is right in its judgment on the administrators (ministers) of the order. They are also the ones who got and committed the funds for any great art in which the order was involved.

True Franciscan art gets no further than the miniatures. It is intrinsically, if Franciscan, art-from-below.[13] Nor can the miniatures go far. If they lose their proximity to the story to which they belong, the miniatures begin showing whatever primitiveness we see there, for we are socioculturally bound to the world of wealth with its art, and that affects our vision. From-below has to speak as art can; it has to be more than illustration, and *Tribulations'* miniatures pass the test. Good Franciscan work can, at one moment, knock timidly at great art's portal. Can, but it's a bad move.

---

[12] The association carries over into learned discussion of such art, as David Carrier notes: "How Can Art History Use Its History?," *History and Theory* 46 (2007): 473.

[13] On history-from-below see E. Clark, *History, Theory, Text* (Cambridge: Harvard University Press, 2004), 80.

ARTISTIC DIVERSITY IN COLOR AND STYLE OF THE HABIT IN PAINTINGS OF ST. FRANCIS OF ASSISI IN THE THIRTEENTH, FOURTEENTH, AND FIFTEENTH CENTURIES *

David Haack

Judging by the textual sources from the history of the Franciscan Order, its many statutes consistently recommended a prescribed style of habit.[1] The uniformity of statutes suggests that the appearance of the habit was strictly regulated. The concern of the governing body of the Franciscan Order regarding conformity in the style of habit is understandable, considering the number of heretical groups of men wearing similar garments throughout northern Italy.[2] However, the history of the Order told in images which were not regulated presents a very different story. The paintings of St. Francis wearing the habit are diverse in style, color, and fullness of cloth. Thus many of the fourteenth and early fifteenth century depictions of St. Francis's habit suggest that the statutes were not strictly enforced.

Within a reliquary in the Basilica di San Francesco in Assisi is a small grey garment without a *capuche*,[3] ragged and heavily patched, the habit St. Francis of Assisi wore when he died.[4] The Sacro Convento at the same Basilica di San Francesco has another relic of St. Francis, a *capuche* which is round, rather than pointed, and grey in color. The Church of Ognissanti in Florence claims another

---

* The initial impetus for this paper was provided by a chapter in my doctoral dissertation: David J. Haack, "Content and Controversy in Choir and Convent. Images of St. Francis of Assisi 1300-1450" (Ph.D. diss., Syracuse University, 1999), 186-201.

[1] E.g. see a recent edition of the 13th-century statutes in C. Cenci and R.G. Mailleux, eds., "Constitutiones generales Ordinis fratrum minorum I (saeculum XIII)," *Analecta Franciscana* 13 (2007), among them those produced at the General Chapters at Narbonne in 1260 (65-103), Assisi in 1279 (105-148), and Paris in 1292 (277-364). Sections regulating habits are present in all these (and more) sets of statutes: Narbonne 1260, 71-73; Assisi 1279, 112-13; Paris 1292, 289-91. See an older edition of the same statutes: M. Bihl, ed., "Statuta generalia Ordinis edita in Capitulis generalibus celebratis Narbonae an. 1260, Assisii an. 1279 atque Parisiis an. 1292," *Archivum Franciscanum Historicum* 34 (1941): 13-94; 284-358 (sections on habits are on 42-45).

[2] In fact it has been suggested that the uniformity of the habit was a sign of a unified Order, and that the role of the Franciscan habit in the thirteenth century was much more important than has been previously thought. Particularly, the habit has been a highly contested issue between conventual and spiritual Franciscans. See Cordelia Warr, *Dressing for Heaven: Religious Clothing in Italy*, 1215-1245 (Manchester and New York: Manchester University Press, 2010), 110-11; David Burr, *The Spiritual Franciscans. From Protest to Persecution in the Century after Saint Francis* (University Park, PA: Pennsylvania State University Press, 2001), 171-2, 181. On Franciscan habits also see a catalog of a recent exhibit on habits which was held in Rome, Museo nazionale di Castel Sant'Angelo, in 2000: *La Sostanza dell' Effimero. Gli abiti degli Ordini religiosi in Occidente*. Catalogo a cura di Giancarlo Rocca (Rome: Edizioni Paoline, 2005), 97-101, 319-354.

[3] The capuche, or cowl, was an unattached head piece. For written descriptions, drawings, and etchings of the various parts of Franciscan habits utilized in art, see A. Jameson, *Legends of the Monastic Orders as Represented in the Fine Arts*, 6th ed. (London: Longmans, Green, and Co. 1880), 236, 238, 294; for woodcut ill. 45-51; for etchings, plates VIII, IX. For another group of depictions, see "Spanish Sayal," http://floridafriar.weebly.com/1/category/habit/1.html. Accessed October 29, 2012.

[4] See *La Sostanza dell' Effimero*, 319.

Fig 1. Margarito d'Arezzo. St. Francis. 13th c.
130x53 cm. Tempera on panel. Arezzo Pinacoteca,
Arezzo. Public domain.

habit of St. Francis, a brownish-grey habit showing the placement of the side wound resulting from the stigmata. Another habit, or garment, is found in the Basilica di Santa Chiara. However, controversy surrounds this garment, as it is considered a penitent's tunic from the thirteenth century, which some historians believe to have been worn by St. Francis; yet no proof exists. The Basilica di Santa Chiara does have an embroidered alb, worn by St. Francis of Assisi as deacon, that St. Clare had spun for him.[5]

In the Rule of 1223, St. Francis refers only to the quality of garments given to novices, two tunics without the *capuche*, a cord, breeches and a *caparo* (a covering for the head, shoulders and part of the chest and back, sometimes referred to as a cowl or shorter cape, reaching down the back to the cord).[6] The *caparo* and the *plica*, or fold of fabric over the waist, were abandoned during the generalate of St. Bonaventure, and the novices received instead a *caputium*[7] *probationis*[8], which they wore with their habit until solemn profession when they received the *capuche*. Garments were not to be of costly material and when torn, were to be repaired with sackcloth and other patches. St. Francis expected the friars to clothe themselves no better than local peasants.[9] With the exception of panel paintings by Bonifacio Bembo, (Fig. 7) all painted habits considered in this essay look new or nearly new, with no patches, stains, or worn spots. Therefore, the habit employed in most paintings was meant to represent the ideal style of

habit worn at the local convent level at the time the painting was produced.

Generally, all professed friars had one tunic with a *capuche* and another without a *capuche*.[10] In the early days there was no uniformity in the style of the *capuche*. St. Bonaventure may have brought about uniformity,[11] decreeing that the *capuche* not be pointed, but rounded at the back, and the cowl be orbicular, in the form of a collar not reaching further than halfway between the shoulder and the elbow.[12] The early Tuscan paintings by Margarito d'Arezzo, (Fig. 1) Cimabue, and Giotto show the hood or cowl attached to the habit. When the *capuche* was worn over the head, with arms extended, the general shape of the habit reminds one of the tau or cross of Christ. Salimbene wrote of a long pointed *capuche* being worn in the Order already during the generalate of Elias. However, the long *capuche* was considered a sign of punishment and mark of shame for some offense committed.[13] Nevertheless, examples of the long *capuche* described by Salimbene were not depicted in painting, perhaps because of its negative connotations. The General of the Order in 1245, Crescentius of Jesi, condemned the use of the short mantel by the Spirituali friars of the Marches.[14]

The cord made of either hemp or flax, in contrast to the cloth or leather belt worn by other religious orders and mendicants of St. Francis's time, became one of the distinguishing features of the Franciscan habit. The three knots in one end

---

[5]   Ingrid J. Peterson, *Clare of Assisi, A Biographical Study* (Quincy, Ill: Franciscan Press, Quincy University, 1993), 201.

[6]   Peasants and coachmen of that time used a caparo for rainy weather. Chapter II of the Rule of 1223.

[7]   *Caputium* refers to the probationary headpiece that symbolized the loss of status, political and social rights. From the Latin word *caput*.

[8]   *Caputium probationis* was originally part of the Benedictine rite of passage for novices, adopted by the early Franciscans.

[9]   Désirée Koslin, in "The Robe of Simplicity: Initiation, Robing, and Veiling of Nuns in the Middle Ages," in *Robes and Honor: The Medieval World of Investiture,* ed. Stewart Gordon (New York: Palgrave, 2001), 262-3, attributes the mendicant insistence on "the simplest locally available cloth" to the Benedictine ideal of "undyed, local woolen cloth cinched with a rough, knotten hempen rope."

[10]   Raphael M. Huber, *A Documented History of the Franciscan Order* (*1182-1517*) (Washington: The Catholic University of America Press, 1944), 670.

[11]   Huber, *History*, 13-4.

[12]   Huber, *History*, 680.

[13]   Huber, *History*, 689.

[14]   See "Chronica XXIV Generalium Ordinis Minorum," *Analecta Franciscana* 3 (1897): 263.

Fig 2. Master of Monte Oliveto and Italian Sienese Painter. Detail from the center panel of Triptych: Crucifixion. 1300-1325. Size unknown, tempera and oil on panel. Metropolitan Museum of Art, New York, 41.190.31 Author's photo.

of the cord extending from the waist represent the Franciscan vows of poverty, chastity, and obedience. In early frescoes and paintings the cord is usually shown hanging down the center of the habit, the tying knot at the waist and two knots hanging down the front from the same length of cord.[15] (Fig. 1)

The early habit also had a plica or fold of fabric over the cord as can be seen in most early paintings of St. Francis. (Fig. 2) Since many habits for living friars were inherited from deceased friars, they were at times too long giving reason for the variations of overhang at the waist over the cord, the *plica*. Many painted habits consulted for this study display no *plica*, indeed they appear to have been designed anew expressly for the model in the painting, (Fig. 10) indicating again the need for repeated mention of a standardized habit in many statutes of the Order. The standardized habit was mandated to be of a specific length and fullness according to the papal bulls of Clement V and John XXII discussed below.

Painters of any given period commonly depict St. Francis of Assisi and other Franciscan saints in the style of habit in vogue at the time of painting the work. By looking at the life-period of the painter, Raphael Huber establishes the style, color, position of cord and shape of the habit of that period.[16] I agree, but propose that the friars of a specific convent dictated to the painter the intended stylistic differences needed for identification by a particular convent of friars. In a broad sense the *Spirituali*, intending to visually define themselves as different from the *Frati*

della Comunità, were reprimanded for wearing habits that were too short and frayed,[17] while the *Frati della Comunità* friars were chastised for habits of new sumptuous cloth and style. (Fig. 6, 9) John Moorman notes the habits of friars in paintings of the latter part of the thirteenth century as "much fuller and of better cloth with long sleeves to cover the hands, and a large *capuche*."[18] In paintings consulted for this study, sumptuous cloth and fuller design appears to have been the norm. All other examples appear to exhibit quality cloth, but less of it.

Generally, friars had two habits, a work habit and a ceremonial habit. They were replaced when beyond repair or when new cloth was acquired. Sizing of the habit appears to have been irrelevant regarding width, as the pattern of the habit was to be cut resembling a tau, or cross shape. Climate and seasonal changes may account for some variations in the weight of material used for habits in northern Italy, reflected in the diversity of appearances of painted drapery in this study.

The first mention of habits in governing documents of the Franciscan Order can be found in the *Constitutions of Narbonne* (1260) which demanded that uniformity in the color of habits be stringently enforced. Friars were ordered to wear habits of an approved color, neither completely white or light colored, nor black, and made from rough, uncarded cloth bought by the guardian of the convent to which they belonged.[19] Later, one under-garment was permitted and shoes could be worn, rather than going barefooted, if given permission.[20]

---

[15]　On the significance and symbolism of the cord, see Elisabetta Gulli Grigioni, "Cordigli francescani. Valenze spirituali, protettive, decorative," *Il Santo* 43 (2003): 857-74.

[16]　Huber, *History*, 669.

[17]　See footnote 27.

[18]　John R. H. Moorman, *The History of the Franciscan Order From Its Origins to the Year 1517* (Chicago: Franciscan Herald Press, 1968), 185.

[19]　Moorman, *History*, 149-50. See Narbonne statutes, ed. Cenci, *Analecta Franciscana* 13 (2007): 71-73; or ed. Bihl, *Archivum Franciscanum Historicum* 34 (1941): 42-44.

[20]　See Narbonne statutes, ed. Cenci, *Analecta Franciscana* 13 (2007): 72; or ed. Bihl, *Archivum Franciscanum Historicum* 34 (1941): 42-43.

Fig 3.   Taddeo Gaddi. The Stigmatization of St. Francis. c. 1325-30. 83 1/2" x 58 7/8". Tempera and gold on panel. Harvard Art Museums/Fogg Museum. Copyright: Public domain.

Fig 4.   School of Giotto and others (1266-1337). Allegory of Poverty. Undated. Size unknown. Detail of fresco in the Basilica of St. Francis, Lower Church Franciscan Allegories, vault of rt. transept. Basilica of St. Francis of Assisi, Assisi. Copyright 1993 Scala.

Fig 6. Giovanni di Paolo. St. Matthew and St. Francis. c 1436. Right hand panel of a major altarpiece. 52 7/8" x 33 1/2", Tempera on wood, gold ground Metropolitan Museum of Art, New York, 88.3.111 Author's photo.

Fig 5. Mariotto di Nardo. Detail of "St. Francis" from The Coronation of the Virgin Altarpiece. 1408. Size unknown, oil on panel S. Stefano in Pane, Florence. Author's photo.

Statutes referring to habits are restrictions or formulas that were to be honored by the entire worldwide Franciscan Order.[21] In painted panels, the habit reflects a wide range of color and texture. Regional differences in color and quality of fabric used in sewing the habit could signal that regional preferences and development of subtle changes in how the habit was worn were common. Adjustments of cord placement and *plica* excess, as well as pleat direction at the waist, are subtle changes that may have been favored by one province or convent or another. Papal bulls and chapter statutes were not always consistent, and appear to address excesses only.[22]

Obviously the problem of uniformity of habit continued to be a concern for the legislative body of friars. It was advantageous for the continued success of the Franciscan Order to form universal statutes that would be read and honored by all friars. Considering the digressions from the grassroots friars in their interpretation of poverty and adherence to the *Rule* of life, it becomes apparent that groups of like-minded friars intentionally adapted or took liberties with General Chapter statutes, both in living their Franciscan lives and in paintings portraying the habit of their Order. Many paintings in this study depict the diversity of habit styles of the fourteenth and early fifteenth centuries, thus allowing the adaptations to be considered somewhat successful. If the purpose of the habit on the painted figure of St. Francis is to represent the actual habit of St. Francis, none of the paintings appear to be accurate, with the possible exception of a painting by Bonifacio Bembo, (Fig. 7) now located in the Bergamo Museum in Bergamo, Italy.

The fact that habit statutes were reformed and adjusted by several General Chapters clearly points out a recurring problem for the Order, and the possibility that the paintings examined represent St. Francis wearing the contemporary habit of the fourteenth and early fifteenth centuries. For example, in 1279, the General Chapter at Assisi forbad wearing of belts with knives and purses.[23] The papal bull, *Exiit qui seminat* (1279), specifically warned the *Spirituali* to conform to the type of habit worn by the entire Order.[24] Other statutes pertaining to the habit were drawn up in Paris in 1292. Again, the decree bans belts with knives and purses.[25] The Franciscans were chastised and a ban issued against wearing superfluous clothes at the General Chapter at Padua in 1310.[26]

The tunics adopted by the *Spirituali* and other Franciscan reformers were generally tight-fitting and short,[27] for which Clement V and John XXII reproached them in their bulls *Exivi de Paradiso* (1312) and *Quorumdam exigit* (October 7, 1317) respectively.[28]

Friar Michael of Cesena, the General, was to insist on uniformity throughout the Order regarding the shape of the habit. Between the death of Pope Clement V (1314) and the election of John

---

[21]   Statutes concerning the habit were not directed to an individual province or convent until the year 1500.

[22]   For another relatively new source of the development of the habit's color and shape as it applies to all the branches of the Franciscan Order, see Servus Gieben, "Per la Storia dell'abito Francescano," *Collectanea Francescana* 66 (1996): 431-78.

[23]   See Assisi statutes, ed. Cenci, *Analecta Franciscana* 13 (2007): 113; or ed. Bihl, *Archivum Franciscanum Historicum* 34 (1941): 45.

[24]   Moorman, *History*, 310.

[25]   See Paris statutes, ed. Cenci, *Analecta Franciscana* 13 (2007): 291; or ed. Bihl, *Archivum Franciscanum Historicum* 34 (1941): 45.

[26]   See "Die Erlasse der Generalminister und die Beschlüsse der Generalkapitel vor dem Jahre 1316," *Archiv für Literatur- und Kirchengeschichte des Mittelalters* 6 (1892): 69-70.

[27]   Although we were unable to locate a suitable contemporary image, later manuscript illuminations depicting habits of the *Spirituali* provide some idea of what they might have looked like; see fig. 13-15 to the essay by David Flood in this volume. Cf. *La Sostanza dell' Effimero*, 331-2, which uses some of the same images as David Flood on the habits of the various groups of the spirituals. Also see David Burr, *The Spiritual Franciscans*, 171-2, 181, on the controversy about the "ugly" habits of the spirituals and papal injunctions against them.

[28]   Huber, *History*, 680.

XXII (1316) the recalcitrant *Spirituali*[29] again introduced a shorter, narrower habit in order to display outwardly their dissatisfaction with the rest of the Order.[30] The desire for uniformity again meant that all friars were required to wear the habit that was the same in color, length, width, and price.[31] In 1316, the General Chapter at Assisi decreed that uniformity of friars' clothes be maintained and the *mantellus*, or cloak, could be worn if it was plain and simple.[32] To my knowledge, there are no extant paintings of St. Francis wearing a *mantellus*. The same Chapter ordered that all poor friars within local convents be given a habit once a year by their local guardian.[33] Fifteen years later, the Constitutions of Perpignan (1331) decreed that, when the head was covered with the cowl, the *capuche* must not reach to the cord.[34] (Fig. 10) It appears that as more restrictions were placed upon the wearing and design of the habit, the more liberties were taken by the local communities of friars. The repeated injunctions indicate that the need for correction was ongoing.

Issues concerning uniformity of the habit were again part of the agenda of the Provincial Chapter of Assisi in 1334.[35] Apparently, there were still *Spirituali* who had not conformed to the edicts concerning the habit. Authorities feared schism within the Order even then, as reflected in clauses of the statutes of 1346, 1351, and the following excerpt

from 1354: "Again since our Order...is held to be one and indivisible, the General Minister, in accord with (the entire) General Chapter, forbids that in the future any sect be allowed to arise among the brothers...which, by separation of clothing, looks likely to become separate in spirit, especially as such a sect is adjudged presumptuous and rash by the declaration of the lord Pope John XXII and the lord Pope Benedict XII."[36]

Clearly, the possible separation of spirit was considered in relation to the separation of clothing, meaning the continued preferences in style and color were becoming more noticeable. The papacy obviously was in favor of continuity in the style of habit throughout the Franciscan Order.

Similarly, the General Chapter of Venice in 1346 concerned itself with quality of the habit. Statutes decree habits of friars should "be not so good as to arouse curiosity nor so bad as to create disgust."[37] The decree also prescribed that the exact length of the habit should be no more than five digits, or fingers, of the hand longer than the friar who wore it, thus allowing the friar to make a fold over the cord at the waist (the *plica* mentioned above) and again that all habits should be of uniform color, neither tending toward black nor white. The Farinerian Statutes of 1354 condemned the wearing of excessive or idiosyncratic clothing.[38] The statutes of 1354 and subsequent statutes prescribe

---

[29] The *Spirituali* habit is described in friar Angelo Clareno's description of friar Conrad of Offida, who was content for more than fifty years with a single tunic of old and shabby cloth, patched with sacking and other rags and always barefoot. See Duncan Nimmo, *Reform and Division in the Franciscan Order* (1226-1538) (Rome: Capuchin Historical Institute, 1987), 95-6. For an image, see fig. 11 to the essay by David Flood in this volume and *La Sostanza dell' Effimero*, 331.

[30] Huber, *History*, 680.

[31] A. Carlini, ed. "Constitutiones Generales Ordinis Fratrum Minorum anno 1316 Assisii conditae," *Archivum Franciscanum Historicum* 4 (1911): 278-9.

[32] Ibid.

[33] Ibid., 530.

[34] Huber, *History*, 680. Referring to the v-shaped back of the capuche that ended at a point.

[35] Huber, *History*, 245-48.

[36] Nimmo, *Reform and Division*, 356. Also see M. Bihl, ed., "Statuta generalia Ordinis edita in capitulo generali an. 1354 Assisii celebrato communiter Farineriana appellata," *Archivum Franciscanum Historicum* 35 (1942): 35-112, 177-253.

[37] Moorman, *History*, 359. Also see F.M. Delorme, ed., "Acta Capituli Generalis anno 1346 Venetiis celebrati," *Archivum Franciscanum Historicum* 5 (1912): 699-700; cf. *Farineriana*, ed. Bihl, *Archivum Franciscanum Historicum* 35 (1942): 87.

[38] Cf. *Farineriana* II, n. 7, 10, ed. Bihl, *Archivum Franciscanum Historicum* 35 (1942): 87-88; also see *Bullarium Franciscanum*, ed. C. Eubel, vol. 6, 655.

Fig 7. Bonifacio Bembo. St. Francis Stigmatized. c. 1450-77. Size unknown. Oil on panel. Prov. Unknown. Now in Bergamo Museum, Bergamo Author's photo.

Fig 8. Domenico Veneziano. St. Francis and St. John the Baptist (detail). 1454. 190 x 115 cm. Detached fresco. Museo dell Opera di Santa Croce, Florence. Author's photo.

Fig 10. *Pietro Paolo Agabiti da Sassoferrato. St. Francis between Sts. Anthony and Bernardine. Undated. Size unknown. Oil on canvas. Prov. Della Chiesa di S. Francesco ai Monte, Iesi. Now in Iesi Pinacoteca, Iesi.* Author's photo.

Fig 9. *Francesco and Bernardino Zaganelli. Detail La Madonna col Figlio e Santa. 1504. Size unknown. Oil on panel. La Brera Gallery, Milano. Inv. 458* Author's photo.

that the *plica* must not fall over the cord at a greater length than the width of four fingers, and not be so short as to not be able to cover the cord.[39] Riding horses and wearing shoes were also forbidden.

Regulations on clothing were not followed with any regularity. Some friars managed to make their cord display a curiosity, and wore cloaks in the form of 'curling' (*crispos*), or pleating (*rugatos*) at the neck or wore multi-colored habits.[40] Some friars were wearing linen shirts next to the skin, and sleeping on linen in feather-beds, and others giving up the habit altogether in favor of secular garb.[41]

The Franciscan friars after 1354 were expected to supply their own needs, while those in authority had secular servants.[42] Contrary to the practice of the mid-thirteenth century, many friars in the fourteenth century were encouraged to be self-supporting. John Moorman explains that the individual Franciscan friar was encouraged to seek financial self-support from his relatives and friends in order to purchase habits, pay for medical attention and personal expenses.[43] Gifts of cloth for habits required approval of the local guardian in an attempt to ensure uniformity in color and value.

The chroniclers of the *Osservanti con vicari* report that the *Fraticelli*[44] in Perugia, circa 1370, mocked the *Frati della Comunità* in the streets, pouncing on them, and revealing several layers of comfortable clothing. They jeered at them, asking if that was how St. Francis had taught them to dress. Some Perugians supported the *Fraticelli* and lost respect for some *Frati della Comunità* friars. To calm the people, friars from Paoluccio Trinci's congregation, the *Zoccolanti*[45], were called in to prove that the *Rule* was observed within the official Franciscan Order.[46]

Friar Bartholomew Rinonico of Pisa had written that Joachim of Fiore prophesied the rise of the Franciscan Order dressed in the color of doves. Bartholomew described the habit of St. Francis as "ashy, pale and earth-coloured," like the habit displayed in Assisi.[47] He presented his book on the 'conformities' between the life of St. Francis and the life of Christ (*De Conformitate Vitae Beati Francisci ad Vitam Domini Jesu*), which he had begun in 1385, to the General Chapter at Assisi in 1399. He received a gift of a habit supposedly worn by St. Francis for his efforts.[48]

At the time of the Western Schism, 1378-1417, the Franciscan grey color habit tended more toward white. Franciscan friars who became prelates of the church, such as bishops and cardinals, tended to wear grey.[49]

---

[39]   Huber, *History*, 672.

[40]   Cf. *Farineriana* II, n. 7, 10, ed. Bihl, *Archivum Franciscanum Historicum* 35 (1942): 87-88. Cloaks were an innovation introduced in the Constitutions of 1316 (Moorman, *History*, 358 n. 9).

[41]   For pleated cloaks, see *Farineriana* II, 10 (ed. Bihl, 88), multi-colored habits, *Farineriana* II, 7 (87), linen undergarments, *Farineriana* II, 12 (88-89), feather-beds, *Farineriana* II, 15 (89) and M. Bihl, ed., "Memorialia seu Definitiones Capituli generalis anno domini 1354 Assisii celebrati," *Archivum Franciscanum Historicum* 35 (1942): 222 (*Memorialia* n. 15); secular garb, *Farineriana* IV, 5 and Nimmo, *Reform and Division*, 214-15.

[42]   Nimmo, *Reform and Division*, 214-15.

[43]   Throughout this period, criticism against the Franciscans contended that the friars had collected rents on houses bequeathed to them as commercial ventures, and had personal money and opened bank accounts.

[44]   The *Fraticelli* were constant critics of the Franciscan Order and were unsuccessfully suppressed by the papal bull *Sancta Romana* of December 30, 1317 (Herbert Holzapfel, *The History of the Franciscan Order*, trans. Antonine Tibesar and Gervase Brinkman [Teutopolis, Ill.: St. Joseph's Seminary, 1948], 52). Also see Dominic V. Monti, *Francis & His Brothers* (St. Anthony Messenger Press, 2009), 78-9.

[45]   An eremitical sect founded by Paoluccio Trinci that ate bread, herbs, and wild fruit; drank only water, and wore clogs, wooden shoes with irons fitted to them (See Moorman, *History*, 372).

[46]   Nimmo, *Reform and Division*, 407-08.

[47]   Bartholomaeus de Pisa, "De conformitate vitae beati Francisci ad vitam Domini Jesu," *Analecta Franciscana* 5 (1912): 104.

[48]   The work is printed in *Analecta Franciscana* 4 (1906) and 5 (1912), totaling 1,136 pages.

[49]   The *Frati della Comunità* wore the grey habit until the beginning of the eighteenth century, when they changed their habit color to black. One reason for the diversity in color was explained by the fact that often cloth came from benefactors (See Huber, *History*, 683).

By the end of the fourteenth century the cost of the habit material had increased substantially and tunics became more elaborate and voluminous, (Fig. 6, 9) as can also be seen in a painting by Mariotto di Nardo, ca. 1408 (fig. 5), and in a work by Domenico Veneziano, ca. 1454 (Fig. 8).

The *Constitutiones Barchinonenses* promulgated by the first General Chapter of the *Osservanti con Vicari*, which was held at Barcelona in 1451, recommended the use of the grey, then ash-grey, for the habit of the new Reform friars.[50] In this investigation, only a few paintings depict a grey habit color, (Fig. 4) while all others display various shades of grey/brown or ashen/brown.

If the habit's evolution was now recognized as a reality, it is possible to suggest paintings of the habit express that same evolution. It appears as if the Franciscan hierarchy was now ready to admit and allow local friar communities the right to create or maintain a favored style of habit. In other words, the contemporary habit of the day was accepted and was to become the model habit for artistic representations of friars of the Order and even of St. Francis of Assisi.

The color of Franciscan habit worn by St. Francis of Assisi was not as important to him as the weave of cloth, patched areas, and economic use of fabric. Yet color and amount of dry goods (fabric) used in the production and design of the habit was one of the deciding factors that appeared in many statutes of the Order. The habit in the painted images of St. Francis in the fourteenth and early fifteenth centuries testified to all designs and color choices noted above. Painted panels, in general, that display the habit of St. Francis of Assisi appear to be more brown than grey. (Fig. 2, 3, 9, 10) Although no documentation is available, the habits in paintings of St. Francis in the fourteenth- and fifteenth centuries may, as above, simply reflect the available cloth offered in a specific locale to be used in the sewing of new habits.

Literature on Franciscan art habitually rewards altarpieces and painted panels by known favored artists, rather than discussing and publishing secondary works of Franciscan art that may have originated in convents and choirs where friars, following the ideal of poverty, could have been reluctant to hire expensive primary artists. The confiscation and/or destruction of choir and convent paintings during the Napoleonic regime did not help the situation. Additional problems are presented due to the absence of artists' contracts either in the local Franciscan convents or local *archivio di statos* in central Italy. Yet the visual history of the Franciscan habit suggests that scholars of the Franciscan tradition will be well advised to pay attention to such secondary works from the context of convents, as well as generally to visual, and not only verbal evidence. The case of the Franciscan habit suggests that the images had been reflecting variations within the Order long before the separation was officially acknowledged in textual sources such as the Bull of 1517.

---

[50] Huber, *History*, 685.

FROM CONVERSION TO RECONVERSION: ASSESSING FRANCISCAN MISSIONARY PRACTICES AND VISUAL CULTURE IN COLONIAL MEXICO

Cristina Cruz González

hey began to view her for long periods of time, gazing in suspense...at that portrait of the Queen of Heaven and Earth...Admiring her overwhelming beauty, love entered them through the eyes, seeing and admiring so much loveliness and majesty in that marvelous image that it won't be the first or last time that the eyes are the instruments by which the heart surrenders.

—Hermenegildo Vilaplana, *Historico y sagrado novenario de la milagrosa Imagen de Nuestra Señora del Pueblito*, 1761[1]

Reading Franciscan miracle narratives from seventeenth- and eighteenth-century Spanish America, one regularly encounters objects that convert, bleed, sweat, heal, and generally assist the faithful in a number of ways. The Pueblito icon, referenced above, performs all of these feats and much more: according to the earliest accounts, this arresting sculpture of the Immaculate Conception reconverted lapsed Christians in 1632. Franciscan friars first began missionary activity in el Pueblito—a small community located on the outskirts of Querétaro—in the 1530s.[2] Yet over the next century, native Otomies began congregating at the nearby pre-Hispanic temple mound, allegedly offering gifts of incense and flowers to their idols, crying for the protection and aid of their gods, and dancing at the foot of the man-made shrine. The burning of incense and the veneration of demonic idols, especially by a people who had accepted the sacrament of baptism, left the Franciscans alarmed and frustrated. Blinding ignorance and the traps of sin had led the Indians astray, misdirecting the native eye. Friars responded by crafting a sculpture of the Virgin of the Immaculate Conception and installing it at the offensive site. The icon was so potent, so the story goes, that when the idolaters beheld the sculpture, they underwent a profound spiritual change and embraced Christianity. Privileging the sense of sight, the foundational text stresses the process of reconversion through vision. The natives may have listened to the words of mendicant catechists for years, but it was only through the faculty of sight that they were truly able to absorb faith and convert to Christianity.

[1]   Vilaplana, *Sagrado novenario de la milagrosa imagen de Nuestra Señora del Pueblito…* (Mexico: Biblioteca Mexicana, 1761), 15-16.
[2]   Fernando de Tapia and Nicolás de San Luís Monañés founded Santa Maria del Pueblito in 1531. Rafael Ayala Echavarri, "Relación Histórica de la Conquista de Querétaro," *Boletín de la Sociedad Mexicana de Geografía y Estadística*, Mexico 66, nos. 1-2 (1948).

Images were critical to conversion and reconversion campaigns in New Spain. This essay gages the difference between the two processes—conversion and reconversion—vis à vis Franciscan image theory and missionary history in the New World. Seeking to interrogate both the theoretical and historical distance between the two positions, I begin by examining the status of the image for missionaries in sixteenth-century Mexico before evaluating the order's changing approach to images in general and animated images specifically.[3] I argue that the rhetoric of reconversion in the eighteenth century can be understood as one facet of a broader Franciscan project of transvaluation regarding the order's presence in Spanish America. For the Franciscan friars who come to Mexico as part of the Congregation for the Propagation of the Faith (arriving in 1682), spiritual reparation, religious renovation, and ethical restitution formed a lexicon aimed at sustaining long-term projects of instauration. The late colonial promotion of sacred images was crucial to a buoyant Franciscan ontology: miraculous images reconverted lapsed communities, spiritually renovated ailing cities, battled devils in Christian bodies, and announced mendicant piety and sanctity. As the reader will discover, icons could also aid in the construction, negotiation, and dissemination of a late colonial Franciscan identity.

The Art of Conversion: The Franciscan Order in Sixteenth-Century Mexico

Led by Fray Martín de Valencia, head of the Observants of San Gabriel de Extremadura in Spain, twelve Franciscan missionaries landed at San Juan de Ulua (Veracruz) on May 13, 1524.[4] To these pioneering friars, the instructional image was crucial to both the Christian conversion and education of native communities. Franciscan chroniclers explicitly describe and illustrate the early mendicant treatment of images, offering multiple justifications for the didactic image. By far, the most common defense was related to the language barriers faced by friars throughout the sixteenth century: linguistic obstacles made images essential for the conversion of souls. Indeed, this appears as a pedagogical maxim in all subsequent Franciscan historical accounts. Aside from invoking Gregory the Great's adage—the image is the Bible of the illiterate—friars also attest to the native 'fascination' with the image, a visceral reaction they trace back to a pre-Hispanic past.

Franciscan friars not only wrote about their use of instructional images in sixteenth-century New Spain, they also illustrated their pedagogical approach to visual representations. The value of the didactic image for the Franciscan Order in New Spain is made most apparent in the copper engravings accompanying Diego de Valadés' *Rhetorica Christiana*. Expert in Latin and trained as a draftsman and artist in the Franciscan school adjacent to the Chapel of Saint Joseph in Mexico City, the mestizo Valadés served as Peter of Ghent's secretary prior to becoming a Franciscan delegate to the Vatican. While in Italy, he published his monumental treatise with 27 engravings in 1579. Chief among *Rhetorica's* engravings is the depiction of a friar speaking to a native audience from the heights of a Renaissance-styled pulpit (Fig. 1). Stirring his audience with dramatic pictures and fiery words, he brandishes his pointer and motions towards images of the Passion, Crucifixion, and Resurrection of

---

[3]   Animated images are those that are filled with life or contain the deity itself. I follow Moshe Barasch's use of the term. Barasch, *Icon: Studies in the History of an Idea* (New York: New York University Press, 1992).

[4]   Although the friars were not the first Franciscans to arrive in the New World—that honor belonged to the famed lay brother Peter of Ghent and two other religious—the arrival of the Twelve officially marked the order's American enterprise. For the initial decades of Franciscan evangelization in the New World, see Robert Ricard's classic *The Spiritual Conquest of Mexico*, trans. Lesley Byrd Simpson (Berkeley and Los Angeles: University of California Press, 1966).

Fig 1. Franciscan preaching from a pulpit. Diego Valadés, Rhetorica Christiana *(Perugia 1579). Courtesy of the Getty Research Institute, Special Collections, Los Angeles, California.*

Fig 2. Ideal atrium, Diego Valadés, Rhetorica Christiana *(Perugia 1579). Courtesy of the Getty Research Institute, Special Collections, Los Angeles, California.*

Christ. This engraving by Valadés would prove popular among the Franciscans to come—Gerónimo de Mendieta and Juan de Torquemada include it in their own works— stressing not only the order's use of didactic images, but implying a proprietary attitude towards the pedagogical use of images.

A second copper engraving in *Rhetorica* complements our previous illustration and includes an ideal Franciscan monastery in New Spain (Fig. 2). The descriptive image shows the religious use of space, focusing particularly on the activities that took place within the Franciscan atrium. At center, Saint Francis and friar Martín de Valencia—with the aid of the famous Twelve—support the church in the New World. Christian instruction surrounds the central scene: friars teach native children and adults, administer the sacraments, discuss Christian doctrine, perform religious rites, and engage in language training. In the upper left, Peter of Ghent instructs neophytes by pointing to objects pictured on a large canvas and, on the opposite right, another friar points to a picture illustrating the creation of the world (*creatio mundi*) while his pupils watch from below.[5] A Franciscan cord frames the entire composition, as occurs with the majority of the illustrations.

We see in Valadés' engraving the didactic image in action, including the large canvases and pointer-wielding friars so colorfully described by Franciscan historians. But the engravings also advance the notion that it was first and foremost the order of Saint Francis that offered a viable architectural and philosophical platform for Christianization in the New World: if there was a built environment that best symbolized the 'architecture of conversion' in the sixteenth century, it was not the cathedral or parish church, but the Franciscan monastery (Fig. 3).[6] Monumental mendicant structures—whether the initial three-aisled basilica plan used at early Franciscan foundations or the mid-century "fortress monastery" that replaced it— served as sites for liturgical and paraliturgical actions, heralded utopian missions, and effectively converted pre-Hispanic space into a colonial built environment. Architectural features such as immense atria, corner posa chapels, and open chapels (also known as *capillas de indios*) appear as willing concessions on the part of friars rather than evidence of an anxious power struggle. The order touted an architecture of conversion rather than of conquest, as the explicit intention was to transform rather than destroy— the existing order.

Friar Diego Valadés goes to such great lengths to emphasize the power of the instructional image for Franciscan conversion efforts in New Spain that it is sometimes easy to forget that it was more than simply Christian iconography that was being taught by friars to native artists. European aesthetics and a Western visual culture were also being grafted onto a new landscape. The Franciscan art school for native youths in Mexico City reputedly "fashioned the statues and retables for churches and furnished them with ornaments, crosses, candelabra, holy vessels, and the like."[7] Juan de

---

5　A tribute to his teacher, Valadés names Peter of Ghent in the engraving and associates him with all forms of knowledge (*discunt omnia*). In the accompanying text, Valadés writes: "he taught them all the arts, he was, indeed, ignorant of none of them." Diego de Valadés, *Rhetorica Christiana ad concionandi et orandi vsvm accommodata, vtrivsque facvltatis exemplis svo loco insertis; qvae qvidem ex Indorvm maxime depromta svnt historiis…* (Perugia 1579). For the facsimile edition with Spanish translation, see Valadés, *Retórica Cristiana*, trans. Tarsicio Herera Zapién, introd. Esteban Palomera (Mexico: Fondo de Cultura Económica, 2003). For a discussion of the engravings, see Francisco de la Maza, "Fray Diego Valadés, escritor y grabador franciscano del siglo XVI," *Anales del Instituto de Investigaciones Estéticas* 13 (1945): 15-44.

6　On the relationship between the "spiritual conquest" in New Spain and sixteenth-century mendicant architecture, particularly the notion of a "fortress monastery," see Clara Bargellini, "Representations of Conversion: Sixteenth-Century Architecture in New Spain," in *The Word Made Image*, Fenway Court, v. 28 (Boston: Isabella Gardner Museum, 1998), 91-102. More recently, Jaime Lara's *City, Temple, Stage: Eschatological Architecture and Liturgical Theatrics in New Spain* (Notre Dame: University of Notre Dame, 2004) expertly examines monastic architecture against the backdrop of specific eschatological and missionary concerns in New Spain.

7　Gerónimo de Mendieta, *Historia ecclesiastica Indiana* (Mexico: Porrúa, 1971), Book 4, Chapter 13.

Fig 3. Huejotzingo Monastery façade. Huejotzingo, Puebla, 16th century. Photo by author.

Fig 4. Virgin of Los Angeles. José de Molina,
c. 1798. Courtesy of the Getty Research Institute, Special
Collections, Los Angeles, California.

Fig 5. Virgin of Los Angeles. José de Nava, c. 1730.
Courtesy of the Getty Research Institute, Special Collections,
Los Angeles, California

Torquemada stresses the success of the undertaking, the art school producing "the images and altarpieces for all the country's temples."[8] Aside from creating works for mendicant spaces and parish churches, native artists from Saint Joseph were also supplying images to modest and elite confraternities, convents, and hospitals. Just as Franciscans in early colonial Mexico were willing to exploit artworks above and beyond the boundaries of the painted pictograph and printed page, the artistic output reached past the realm of the monastery and profoundly influenced colonial visual culture in general.

Despite a great investment in visual representations, sixteenth-century friars were cautious regarding the native understanding of thaumaturgic objects and generally thought it best to not propagate miraculous images within indigenous communities. The Franciscan position regarding the Virgin of Guadalupe most clearly reveals the order's reticence. In a sermon delivered on September 6, 1556, the archbishop of New Spain—a Dominican named Montúfar—advocated the numinous qualities of the Guadalupe painting. Comparing the image to the great icons of catholic Europe, including Our Lady of Antigua, Our Lady of Montserrat, and Our Lady of Loreto, the archbishop recounted the miracles recently performed by the Mexican image and urged the faithful to place their trust in the wondrous icon.[9] He especially encouraged the Spanish community to show due devotion to the miraculous image and, thus, be an example for natives to follow. The Franciscan houses in Mexico City and nearby Tlatelolco were quick to respond: one friar stressed that promotion of the image would upset the native community; unable to distinguish between icons and idols, neophytes would surely commit idolatry. Another friar referred to the popular devotion at Tepeyac as "a cult we all deplore."[10] Franciscans had purposely discouraged the icon's devotion amongst the Indians because, as friar Antonio de Huete argued, the natives "believed that the painting at Tepeyac was the Virgin herself, whom they worship as an idol."[11] Yet the biggest backlash came when Francisco Bustamante, the Franciscan provincial in New Spain, criticized the archbishop in a sermon delivered in the Chapel of Saint Joseph in Mexico City. Bustamante charged that the Guadalupe cult had no foundation since it was "just yesterday" that an Indian "named Marcos" painted the image of the Mexican Virgin. He further criticized archbishop Montúfar for his blind support of the devotion— the supposed miracles were unapproved—and insisted the cult was disguised idolatry. Taking a proprietary attitude toward Christian evangelization and the eradication of idolatry, Bustamante considered the archbishop's sermon to be a direct attack on Franciscan goals and triumphs in the New World.[12] It was with much effort that friars had convinced the Indians to not adore material images, the provincial added, that encouraging numinous objects would be counterproductive to the evangelization project. Lastly, Bustamante was openly suspicious of the church's intention to collect tithing in the name of the image. Natives should remain exempt from giving tithes, he argued, lest they doubt

[8]   Serge Gruzinski, *Images at War: Mexico from Columbus to Bladerunner* (Durham and London: Duke University Press, 2001), 76.

[9]   Following the textual evidence, a supernatural apparition involving an Indian named Juan Diego was not to be counted among the icon's miracles circa 1556. Edmundo O'Gorman, *Destierro de Sombras* (Mexico: IIH, UNAM, 2001), 69. O'Gorman's work provides an excellent account of the 1556 events and expertly analyzes the evidence at hand. For an intellectual history of the icon's controversies and keen analysis of the historiography, see David Brading's *Mexican Phoenix: Our Lady of Guadalupe* (Cambridge: University of Cambridge, 2001). A valuable discussion of the icon, sixteenth-century debates, and authorship of the image appears in Jeanette Peterson's "Creating the Virgin of Guadalupe: the Cloth, the Artist, and Sources in Sixteenth-Century New Spain," *The Americas* 61, no. 4 (April 2005): 571-610.

[10]   Quoted in Ricard, *Spiritual Conquest*, 190.

[11]   Ibid., 189.

[12]   Ibid.

the genuine advantages of religious conversion and the sincerity of the first missionaries.[13]

I recount these facts and notions regarding the Guadalupe case in order to make clear that Bustamante was not aghast at a painting made of the Virgin Mary. Franciscan friars had prepared the artist, and others like him, for such religious images. Rather, according to the witnesses, Bustamante complained that the Indian faithful were confused about image and prototype—the "cloth, paint or wood" on the altar and the "true Mother of God who is in heaven"—and, so, should not be encouraged to worship a miracle-working icon. For Bustamante, the viewer's ethnic identity was directly related to the image's dangers; promotion of a miracle-working icon adversely affected a people who were only recently persuaded to reject idolatry by religious friars. It is for this reason that Bustamante threatened to stop preaching to natives should the church advance the icon's miraculous reputation. In Bustamante's sermon, there is neither recrimination of the image nor a categorical rejection of miracle-working icons.

The antagonism between the Franciscan Order and the archbishop of New Spain went beyond the efficacy of a cult of images. A cold disabuser of utopian illusions, Montúfar challenged the pretense of a Franciscan monopoly over native communities, openly criticized renowned Franciscan projects—such as the elite trilingual college at Tlatelolco—censored the order's efforts to understand native languages and religious customs, and mocked the Franciscan dream of a primitive church in the New World. Yet it would be a mistake to argue that the mid-century Franciscan position on images—as expressed by Bustamante and his associates in Mexico City—was solely motivated by their deep disdain for the archbishop and his politics.[14] The challenges posed by sacred images and Precolumbian idols were critical themes thoughtfully explored by the Franciscans themselves.[15]

Franciscan chronicler Juan de Torquemada, working in New Spain in the mid-seventeenth century, is a key figure in understanding the theoretical turn that occurs in terms of Franciscan image-theory in late colonial Mexico. The author clearly departs from earlier friars who redeem the image in the New World if only for its didactic merits; for Torquemada, the susceptible viewer is no longer confined to the neophyte or the illiterate. The friar considers the effects of the image on a general Christian population, one that finds images necessary for the configuration of beliefs and the practice of faith. In his historic work, *Monarquia Indiana*, the friar fears the dangers of the Christian icon—"a malicious and misleading mask"—while accepting the human need (and weakness) for a visual religion. Believing the visible image was an impossible but necessary operation, Torquemada considers man's vulnerability on two levels: the need to materialize divinity and the craving to put one's faith in miracle-working objects. Once the invisible was made visible, albeit imperfectly, a trusted image was consolation for the frail human condition: "…by seeing it with bodily eyes a person might have faith in (the icon) during a conflict when he feels insurmountable anguish and hardship."[16] Challenged

---

[13] All of the mendicant orders protested the Church's position on taxing Indians, although the Franciscans were probably the most vocal. On this topic, see Ricard, *Spiritual Conquest*, 252. Indeed, the Second Provincial Council (1565) agreed with the religious, as Chapter 16 specifically states that the giving of tithes only applies to Spaniards and not indigenous parishioners. Francisco Lorenzana, *Concilios provinciales primero, y segundo, celebrados en la muy noble, y muy leal ciudad de México…dalos a luz el Illmo. Sr. D. Francisco Antonio Lorenzana* (Mexico: Hogal, 1769), 203.

[14] For a lively account of regular/secular struggles in sixteenth-century New Spain, see Ricard, *Spiritual Conquest*, 242-7.

[15] A contemporary of Bustamante expresses many of the same concerns regarding sacred images. The 1559 dialogue by friar Maturino Gilberti, *Diálogo de doctina Christiana en lengua de Mechuacan* (Mexico 1559), reveals an author who was suspect of hybridity, cautious of devotion, and perpetually concerned that natives not substitute icons for idols.

[16] Torquemada, *Monarquía Indiana*, 3 vols. (Mexico: Porrúa, 1969), vol. 3, 106.

with a feeble-minded population, then, the icon's benefits outweighed its detriments. In the event that one might confuse the icon with the idol, Torquemada added: "The image is the semblance of another thing which is represented in its absence," noticeably paraphrasing Saint Basil's adage.

If the honor rendered the image is transferred to the prototype, it follows that the production of—and devotion to—sacred images should be encouraged. And indeed, this is what the Council of Trent (1545-63) mandated in its 25th session:

> And they must also teach that images of Christ, the Virgin mother of God and the other saints should be set up and kept, particularly in churches, and that due honor and reverence is owed to them, not because some divinity or power is believed to lie in them as reason for the cult, or because anything is to be expected from them, or because confidence should be placed in images as was done by pagans of old; but because the honor showed to them is referred to the original which they represent: thus, through the images which we kiss and before which we uncover our heads and go down on our knees, we give adoration to Christ and veneration to the saints, whose likeness they bear.

Although both the First and Second Provincial Councils in Mexico (1555 and 1565) encouraged devotion to Mary and the saints, prostrating in front of paintings and kissing sculptures were not common Franciscan lessons to be learned by natives in sixteenth-century New Spain. The threat of idolatry was too real, the Christianization process still incomplete.

A Spiritual Conquest Reconsidered

Bustamante's suspicion that Guadalupe was a church ploy to bring in native funds not only reveals a standard religious complaint following increased clerical power, but also affirms the fact that sanctuaries housing popular, miraculous images were quickly becoming chief nodal points of economic and religious influence and authority in Spanish America. Indiscriminately drawing viewers from colonial society at large, these fast emerging nuclei emphasized the precarious construction of the mendicant edifice in New Spain, a utopian structure designed to keep the native masses under the spiritual tutelage of friars alone. During the late sixteenth century, the Crown began the process of transferring economic, religious, and political clout from monastic centers to the diocesan Church, a sharp and unforgiving strategy that would greatly intensify in the eighteenth century and culminate in the nineteenth. Secularization policies supported the Crown's intention to centralize and standardize political authority and supervise the clergy more closely. In the words of William Taylor, "The members of religious orders in pastoral service were far too independent for the regalists' taste…."[17]

What can only be described as a tense landscape was punctuated with dramatic, violent encounters: In 1559, seculars attacked a monastery in Puebla, harming the friars and sacking the church.[18] Around the same time, Franciscan friar Maturino Gilberti tells us that seculars entered the Franciscan monastery in Pátzcuaro, smashing the baptismal fonts and expelling friar Jacobo Daciano by force.[19] The religious fought back: in

---

[17]   William Taylor, *Magistrates of the Sacred: Priests and Parishioners in Eighteenth-Century Mexico* (Stanford: Stanford University Press, 1996), 83.

[18]   Francisco Morales to Las Casas, September 1, 1559, in *Colección de documentos inéditos para la historia de Ibero-América*, ed. S. Montoto (Madrid: Editorial Ibero-Africano-Americana, 1927), 231.

[19]   Francisco Fernández del Castillo, ed., *Libros y libreros en el siglo XVI* (Mexico: Tip. Guerrero, 1914), 27.

response to bishop Palafox's efforts to secularize more than 30 Franciscan churches in Puebla (c. 1641), twelve friars, armed with sticks and knives, caused damage throughout the town of Cholula and violently took possession of the parish church before fleeing with an image of the Virgin.[20] Other friars advised their native congregation to boycott secularized churches and urged the removal of priests. Most impressively, friars Francisco de Ribera and Juan Quijano gathered up six hundred natives in the Toluca region and demolished the church of Saint Peter Calimaya. Their companion, friar Antonio de Torrijos, confessed that he had also burned a church.[21]

Adding insult to injury, the Franciscan Order's early achievements were also challenged: when the First Provincial Council of 1555 barred baptism for adults who 'had not completely and definitely abandoned idolatry,' the measure was a thinly veiled critique of the Franciscan practice of 'baptizing by squadrons.'[22] While the Franciscan "spiritual conquest" was under attack, either emanating from intra-order rivalries or stemming from the Church and Crown's desire for increased clerical control, a colonial cult of images was deepening its roots—in no small part due to Jesuit activity. By the late seventeenth century, Franciscan friars, too, began to actively nominate particular images in their cultural and political strongholds, detailing

their histories and emphasizing their popularity in publications bound for mass distribution. Complementing these activities, a different kind of Franciscan chronicle began appearing by the end of the seventeenth century, one that not only emphasized the order's illustrious role in the evangelization of the New World, but also delineated the friar's role in the propagation of numerous devotions within a miraculous landscape. The most influential Franciscan text of this type is Agustin de Vetancurt's *Teatro Mexicano* (1697-1698).

Vetancurt's opus contains an enlightening section on sacred objects—mostly Marian images related to Franciscan monasteries—explaining both their miraculous achievements and devotional following.[23] His Marian cartography includes sections on the Virgin del Valle (San Cosme), the Virgin of Tolantonco (Texcoco), La Conquistadora (Puebla), the Virgin of Tepepan (Xochimilco), the Virgin of Tecaxic (Toluca), and many other sacred objects.[24] Our author, however, begins his section on sacred images with the most celebrated icon of late colonial Mexico, the Virgin of Guadalupe. The centrality of the Virgin of Guadalupe is noteworthy. Despite evidence of sixteenth-century dissent, the Franciscan Order was carefully woven into the tapestry of the most important seventeenth-century apparition narrative. Initially a 'doubting Thomas,' the archbishop Juan de Zummaraga (a Franciscan)

[20] Antonio Rubial García, *Santa María Tonantzintla: un pueblo, un templo* (Mexico: Universidad Iberoamericana, 1991), 28.

[21] Mariano Cuevas, *Documentos inéditos del siglo XVI para la historia de México* (Mexico: Museo Nacional de Arqueología, Historia y Etnología, 1914), 260-61.

[22] Lorenzana, *Concilios provinciales*, 42-3.

[23] Agustín de Vetancurt, *Teatro mexicana: Descripción breve de los sucesos ejemplares de la Nueva-España en el Nuevo Mundo Occidental de las Indias*, 4 vols. (Madrid: J. Porrúa Turanzas, 1960). Vetancurt's project would have stunned friar Gerónimo de Mendieta, the sixteenth-century Franciscan historian who often lamented the lack of miracles in his age. According to Mendieta, New Spain was anything but a prodigious landscape: neither visions of virgins nor saints on horseback appeared before this friar's eyes. Although perplexed by the absence, Mendieta ultimately reasons that the colony is better off without numinous phenomena: "And there could be no other reason for it, since miracles are meant for the unfaithful and the incredulous (as Saint Paul would say) and not for the faithful." Mendieta, *Historia ecclesiastica*, 297.

[24] Vetancurt was no doubt influenced by the work of his fellow historian and friend Francisco de Florencia. The Jesuit had already published several monographs on miraculous Christian images in Italy and New Spain (Loreto, Remedies, Guadalupe, Chalma) and was completing his tour de force, *Zodiaco Mariano* (published posthumously by Juan de Oviedo in 1755), while Vetancurt was compiling his own compendium. Florencia, in turn, may have used a recent publication by the Italian Giovanni Felice Astolfi as a model. Florencia and Oviedo, *Zodiaco Mariano en que el Sol de Justicia Cristo…* (Mexico: Antiguo Colegio de San Ildefonso, 1755). Astolfi, *Historia universale delle imagini miracolose della gran Madre di Dio riverite in tutte le parti del mondo* (Venice: Sessa, 1623).

becomes a key witness to the *acheiropoietos* icon.[25] Furthermore, Vetancurt emphasizes the Franciscan monastery in Tlatelolco, stressing its role in the legend. It was in the Tlatelolco church that the Indian Juan Diego was first converted, attended mass, traveled to on the day of the first apparition, and was eventually persuaded—by Motolinía, no less—to take a vow of chastity. In Vetancurt's time, the annual December 8 mass and sermon dedicated to Guadalupe took place at the church, recognizing the site's relationship to the Indian seer. If the Franciscan presence in the historiography of the Guadalupe narrative was significant, the aporias were even greater: Didn't the Franciscan provincial speak out against church support for the miraculous icon in 1556? Didn't friars refer to it as "a cult we all deplore?"

Reconverting Image, Space, and Place in New Spain

The crafting of a numinous landscape would become a standard element in Franciscan chronicles by the end of the seventeenth century.[26] Popular icons were documented and disseminated through such texts; as importantly, the official literature constructed an orthodox account of particular cults, replacing infelicities in unofficial narratives and solidifying the importance of mendicant friars in the founding of devotions and the building of their corresponding sanctuary structures. Close analysis

of the Virgin of Tecaxic (near Toluca) reveals a variegated strategy defined mostly by its purported echo: the (re)crafting of an image, the (re)building of a hermitage, are elements of a new devotional matrix linked to most religious groups—the Franciscan Order chief among them—vying for power in late colonial Mexico.

The seldom-studied icon from Tecaxic—rarely published and virtually unknown outside of the area of Toluca—was miraculously well preserved in the seventeenth century despite being placed in an extraordinarily harsh environment for many years. As is typical for colonial icons in general, its history is scattered and thin, even non-existent for many decades. It was likely identified with the Franciscan Order and propagated by friars starting sometime between 1650-1660. The first published history is a monograph by Juan Mendoza de Ayala (Franciscan guardian of the monastery at Atengo) entitled *Relación del santuario de Tecaxic* (Mexico 1684).[27] Mendoza's study was fairly accessible in its time and both Vetancurt and Florencia cite extensively from it.[28] Published with the express approval of Juan de Luzuriaga, the Franciscan provincial in Mexico City, it may have inspired further Franciscan monographs including Luzuriaga's own work on the Virgin of Aranzazu.[29]

According to Mendoza, the Franciscans stationed at the monastery in Toluca had the task of evangelizing the natives from the nearby colonial pueblo of Tecaxic in the first decades following the

---

[25]   By the time of Vetancurt's publication, the narrative involving the Virgin's apparition to a docile Indian named Juan Diego was firmly in place and the icon was touted as being "not made by human hands."

[26]   Aside from Vetancurt's *Teatro Mexicano*, see Alonso de la Rea's *Crónica de la orden de nuestro seráfico padre San Francisco, provincia de San Pedro y San Pablo de Michoacán en la Nueva España* (Mexico: Por la Viuda de Bernardo Calderon, 1643) and Baltasar de Medina's *Chronica de la Santa Provincia de San Diego...* (Mexico: Juan de Ribera, 1682).

[27]   Juan de Mendoza de Ayala, *Relación del santuario de Tecaxic, en que esta colocada la milagrosa imagen de Nuestra Señora de los Angeles...* (Mexico: Juan de Ribera, 1684). Mendoza published several sermons contemporaneous with his Tecaxic history, most of these dedicated to his order and/or its chosen devotions.

[28]   Vetancurt, *Teatro Mexicano*, vol. 3, 241, 367-8; Florencia and Oviedo, *Zodiaco Mariano*, introd. Antonio Rubial (Mexico: CONACULTA, 1995), 173-8.

[29]   Juan de Luzuriaga, *Paranympho Celeste, Historia de la mystica zarza, milagrosa Imagen, y prodigioso Santuario de Aranzazu de Religiosos observantes de N. Seraphico Padre San Francisco en la Provincia de Guypuzcoa de la Region de Cantabria....* (Mexico: Herederos de la Viuda de Bernardo Calderon, 1686).

Conquest. A hermitage was built in the area and a painting of the Virgin of the Assumption—painted on local cotton—installed above the main altar. Soon, an epidemic ravaged Tecaxic and the humble hermitage and image fell into disuse. The Marian painting lay in its dilapidated and abandoned structure until two neighbors, hearing 'angelic music,' were drawn to it and discovered that the icon was miraculously preserved. Thereafter, celestial music continued to be heard every Saturday and the image began to respond to the needs of villagers. Mendoza's history states that on one occasion, two brutes from the city of Toluca decided to stage a duel within earshot of the hermitage. As they were about to begin, they were drawn to the angelic music inside. Finding themselves alone, with only the image of the Virgin of the Assumption before them, they became mesmerized by the icon, laid down their arms, made peace, and concluded that the music could only have come from a heavenly source. They alerted the guardian from the Franciscan monastery in Toluca and fame of the image thereupon spread. Florencia confirms fervent devotion: the faithful come to the sanctuary and take exact measurements of the icon, touch the image with flowers that they will then take home, and even collect the melted wax and burnt remains from the candles and flames that once illuminated the image. These "ashes" (*cenizas y pavesas*), our source states, were considered relics and were dissolved into water and given to the sick to drink with favorable results.

True to her avocation, the icon appears as a Virgin rising up from the tomb, ascending into heaven. Apostles and holy women stand on either side of the tomb, bearing witness to her Assumption. Two of the Apostles gaze down at the empty sepulcher, astonished by the absence of a body. The Virgin is shown with fairly typical Immaculist attributes: she wears a deep red tunic and a star-studded blue cloak, she is sustained by angels, enveloped by golden rays of light that emanate from her body, and her feet rest on a crescent moon. Contemporary scholars have dated the painting to the sixteenth century, noting a Renaissance-like handling of the figures, but the image could well be an early seventeenth-century creation.[30] The style is a local one and, in fact, the iconography is typical for the area.[31]

Several aspects of the icon's history follow Byzantine tropes and practices concerning miraculous images in general. For instance, the doctrinal devotion—the Virgin's Assumption—is linked to the object's most famous trait: the Mexican icon was able to produce 'sweet, celestial music.' Although such music often guides seers to hidden numinous objects, here the detail is especially appropriate. John of Damascus, writing on the ancient tradition of the Assumption affirms that the Apostles heard angelic music during Mary's entombment in Gethsemane and for three days after. The apotropaic property of the Tecaxic icon—the ingestion of physical pigmentation by those seeking supernatural protection from some ill or evil—is also reminiscent of a central function of early Byzantine images. The Seventh Ecumenical Council (A.D. 787) relates a case involving a gravely ill woman who, praying before her household icons of Saint Cosmas and Saint Damian, scraped off bits of their surfaces and, mixing the particles with water, proceeded to drink the concoction. She, too, was miraculously healed.[32] Fast forward to fifteenth-century Castile and one finds a similar religious practice: pilgrims at the shrine of Guadalupe in Extremadura "not only

---

[30]   María Eugenia Rodríguez Parra and Mario Ríos Villegas date it to the sixteenth century in *Catalogo de Pintura Colonial en Edificios Religiosos del Municipio de Toluca* (Toluca: Estado de México, Universidad Autónoma del Estado de México, 1984), 98.

[31]   A similar painting appears in the old refectory of the Tecaxic convent and a nearly identical version graces the main altar of Our Lady of the Angels in Huitzila (bordering Toluca). Ibid., 102 and 155.

[32]   Leslie Brubaker and Robert Ousterhout, eds., *The Sacred Image East and West* (Urbana-Champaign: University of Illinois Press, 1995), 7.

kissed the slab of marble on which the image was discovered, some of them were cured by drinking scrapings of the rock with water."[33]

Mendoza notes that, with the encouragement of the Franciscan guardian of Toluca (friar José Gutiérrez), the inhabitants of the area began building a new sanctuary for the image. In 1651, a subsequent guardian (friar Diego de Amaya) prepared a special sermon for the Feast of the Assumption and dedicated it to the Tecaxic icon. So moving was his panegyric for the nearby image, that a great amount of money and building material was collected for the completion of the structure and its attached (Franciscan) monastery. In 1665, Tecaxic received its own guardian and construction continued on the church. By 1676, the church was finished except for its retablo, for which the new Tecaxic guardian (friar Juan de Valdez) hired "a master artist." Following the retablo's completion, leftover monies were used for a *portería*, a baptistery, and additional works for the new monastery.

The incorruptibility of the painting, despite its location in a supposedly ruined hermitage for decades, mimics a traditional sign of piety displayed by a holy body or saintly corpse. In New Spain, it is not uncommon for such a trait to be ascribed to icons and for this to be seen as a sign of the divine. The Virgin of Los Angeles from Tlatelolco is a case in point. The icon's major chronicler, Pablo Antonio Peñuelas, describes how in 1580 a canvas of the Virgin of the Assumption was carried away in a flood and ended up in the neighborhood of Coatlán (now within present day Tlatelolco).[34] There, an Indian cacique named Isayoque built a small adobe chapel for it but the paint began to flake off. The Indian devotee then ordered that a "faithful copy" be painted onto the adobe wall of the hermitage. The eighteenth-century history by Peñuelas claims that friars from the Franciscan convent at Tlatelolco took charge of the adobe site as early as 1595 but no documentation regarding the image from this period remains. Devotion declined, the adobe chapel fell into ruin, and more floods came. The image miraculously survived and again the adobe structure was rebuilt in 1607; this time a confraternity was organized to maintain proper devotion. The new adobe hermitage was apparently shoddily built and began to crumble; yet again the image survived. Finally, with the powerful support of the archbishop of Mexico and a generous donation by José de Haro, construction began on a new, attractive, and well-built sanctuary in 1780.[35]

The Virgin of Los Angeles is officially lauded for having survived countless floods, daily weather exposure for over two centuries, and the two-time collapse of the adobe structure (a hermitage) on which it was painted. In a 1798 engraving by José de Molina, the inscription proudly notes the object's miraculous survival: "Copy of the Image of Our Lady of Los Angeles, painted on a crude adobe wall and conserved for the span of two centuries and venerated in its sanctuary *extramuros* from Mexico City. Touched by the Original" (Fig. 4).[36] An earlier engraving by José Nava (c. 1730) provides other specifics, stating that the image is venerated in the "barrio de Santiago de Tlatelolco" and has been "miraculously conserved for more than

---

[33]   William Christian, Jr., *Apparitions in Late Medieval and Renaissance Spain* (Princeton: Princeton University Press, 1981), 88. Scraping the encasing or pedestal of the icon, as in this Castilian case, likely follows the tactile approach to saint's tombs in early Christianity, as William Christian has also suggested.

[34]   Pablo Antonio Peñuelas, *Breve Noticia de la Prodigiosa Imagen de Nuestra Señora de los Ángeles* (Mexico: Felipe de Zuñiga y Ontiveros, 1781). Reprint 1805.

[35]   According to other accounts, abuses were being committed in the 1607 adobe structure and so the archbishop responded by sealing off access to the image and covering the adobe wall in 1746. See Joseph Cassidy, *Mexico: Land of Mary's Wonders* (Patterson, New Jersey: St. Anthony Guild Press, 1958), 53.

[36]   Getty Research Institute, Special Collections, Los Angeles, California.

200 years against the injuries of time, hurricanes, floods, and earthquakes" (Fig. 5).[37] Both Tecaxic and Los Angeles make important claims to religious renewal. With both devotions, however, it was not simply the case that inspirational paintings led to church repairs. Rather, the icons found themselves in ruined hermitages, structures physically unsuited for spiritual devotion. That such "fallen spaces" were leveled and (re)built as new structures with new functions—official sanctuary spaces are licensed by the Church, overseen by religious friars or secular clergy, and follow the Church's liturgical calendar—significantly points to the power politics at play in seventeenth-century Mexican religiosity.

As with the adobe structure from Tlatelolco, we know little about the actual construction, maintenance, and condition of the adobe hermitages at Tecaxic. Some archival documents attest to the existence of the painting in a hermitage but contradict the existence of an abandoned ruin. An inhabitant of Toluca left a will dating from 1668-1670 in which he listed a number of tithes and Masses granted to the Virgin of Tecaxic in her hermitage; it remains unclear whether he was referring to the earlier hermitage or to the new sanctuary sans altarpiece.[38] Whatever the case, the information makes no mention of the image's miraculous survival in a dilapidated structure—the detail emerges only with Mendoza's text in 1684. If the hermitage and image existed in the area in the 1670s but the structure was not in ruins, how and

why did the Franciscan Order attach itself to the site, rebuild it, and validate devotion to the image contained within it?

The colonial and contemporary literature involving Mexican sanctuaries often misleads, drawing us to the fascinating—if misguided—notion that Marian sanctuaries somehow replace the temples of pagan goddesses; yet our real focus should be the rapid rate at which officially recognized sanctuaries were replacing illegitimate, Christian spaces. Tepeyac, Los Angeles, and Tecaxic are just three of many examples. To fully understand the growing secular and religious tendency to replace 'falling' hermitages with proper sanctuaries, we should remember that oratories, hermitages, and hermits fill the pages of the First Provincial Council in Mexico City (1555): Chapter 25 warns against the use of personal homes and unsanctioned spaces as religious places; doing so, the council stresses, neglects and belittles the church structure and the Mass performed therein, setting a bad example for the newly converted Indians to follow.[39] The same council, in its 35th chapter, prohibits, under penalty of excommunication, the construction of unlicensed oratories and hermitages and bans friars and priests from performing religious rites within such spaces.[40] Furthermore, the chapter outlaws hermits or persons wishing to retreat and lead an alternative and singular lifestyle outside of an approved, religious monastery.[41] The reason for these edicts is clear: unlicensed religious structures and those who will inhabit them are literally and

---

[37] The engraving attests to the image's popular devotion in its last home prior to the building of the new c. 1780 sanctuary. Getty Research Institute, Special Collections, Los Angeles, California.

[38] "Testamento de Miguel García Figueroa, San Jose de Toluca, Mexico (1668-1670)," Ms., Biblioteca Nacional de México. Similar documents speak to the cult's popularity in the eighteenth century: Fray José Varela, "Noticia de las obras pías del convento de Nuestra Señora de los Ángeles de Tecaxic (1772)," Ms. Biblioteca Nacional de México; and Fray Francisco García Figueroa, "Revisión del archivo del convento de Santa María Tecaxic y reforme de sus escrituras y demás instrumentos (1773-1774)," Ms. Biblioteca Nacional de México. For a description of the monastery and sanctuary after secularization, see "Informe del estado de algunos conventos luego de secularización (c. 1774)," Ms. Biblioteca Nacional de México.

[39] Lorenzana, Concilios provinciales, 80.

[40] Ibid., 92-94.

[41] Ibid., 94.

spiritually outside of the sanctioned religious culture of the colony. Hardly veiled is the fact that the Church found these places and people difficult to control; hermits and hermitages were, in more ways than one, potentially hostile to religious orthodoxy and ecclesiastical (and, hence, political) hierarchies. When Archbishop Francisco Lorenzana publishes the councils in the eighteenth century, he offers even more explicit advice: do not let the Indians, he warns, construct hermitages or neighborhood chapels since these lead to misguided simulacra, scandalous religious practice, and the abandonment of parish churches.[42] Here it's the parish church, not the hermitage, which fears collapse.

The Propagation of Faith and Image in Eighteenth-Century New Spain

We return to the Virgin of el Pueblito, a sculpture of Mary Immaculate lauded for her miraculous deeds and one of many images crafted and championed by the Franciscan Order in the eighteenth century.[43] Although the Virgin of el Pueblito reconverted lapsed natives outside of Querétaro, the sculpture proved to be a wonder-working object in the colonial city of Querétaro as well. In fact, her biggest fan base in the eighteenth-century—when the figure began appearing in colonial documents—consists of well-heeled residents in Querétaro.[44] If the Franciscan Order rediscovered the sway of the miraculous icon in the seventeenth century, it discovers something much more powerful in the eighteenth: a rhetoric of perpetual conversion, spiritual renewal, and religious rebirth.

Hermenegildo Vilaplana, a Franciscan friar and prolific historian, provides us with the most complete colonial history of the icon in 1761, including its foundation, appearance, miraculous feats, and devotional following.[45] To be sure, Vilaplana writes from a different vantage point than Mendoza de Ayala and even Vetancurt. A Franciscan attached to the apostolic College of the Propagation of the Faith in Querétaro (the celebrated Colegio de Santa Cruz), he has no illusions about the status of religious clergy under the Bourbon regime. In 1749, friars in New Spain were ordered to abandon monasteries in Indian towns.[46] There were 251 monasteries in 1746; a mere forty years later, only 125 remained.[47] Historian Francisco Morales, O.F.M., describes the damage:

---

[42]   Ibid., 389.

[43]   The Virgin of Macana from New Mexico is a comparable case study. For an expert account of how the Marian cult was solidified by late colonial Franciscans wishing to stress the order's past and present achievements in light of an unstable political and socio-religious climate, see Ilona Katzew, "The Virgin of Macana: Emblem of a Franciscan Predicament in New Spain," *Colonial Latin American Review* 12, no. 2 (December 2003): 169-98.

[44]   The devotional Virgin of el Pueblito is one of many icons discussed by Esteban Gómez de Acosta in his 1743 report to King Philip V of Spain. He states that a rich confraternity from the city of Querétaro attended to both image and shrine. Esteban Gómez de Acosta, *Querétaro en 1743. Informe presentado al rey por el corregidor Esteban Gómez de Acosta*, trans. and ed. Mina Ramírez Montes (Querétaro: Talleres Gráficos del Gobierno del Estado, 1997), 140-41.

[45]   Gómez de Acosta's brief report on the sanctuary and Marian sculpture at el Pueblito makes no mention of the icon's miraculous reconversion of the area's population nor does the author attribute the sculpture to the artist-friar Sebastian Gallegos. Juan Antonio Oviedo adds a small section on the Virgin of el Pueblito to Francisco de Florencia's *Zodiaco Mariano* in the mid-eighteenth century, specifically noting the sculpture's many miracles and Franciscan following. Florencia and Oviedo, *Zodiaco Mariano*, 193-6. Less than a decade later, Vilaplana's account—a lengthy panegyric in typical Baroque style—becomes the definitive record on the subject, including a detailed account of the sculpture's reconversion of natives in 1632 and the sumptuous sanctuary structure. It was republished several times during the colonial period and most recently in 1954. Vilaplana, *Historico y sagrado novenario de la milagrosa imagen de Nuestra Señora del Pueblito* (Pueblito, Querétaro: Ediciones Paz y Bien, 1954).

[46]   King Ferdinand VI signed the royal decree on October 4, 1749. "Real cédula de Fernando VI, el Buen Retiro, October 4, 1749," Archivo General de la Nacion (Mexico), Reales Cédulas, vol. 69, exp. 103 and 104.

[47]   Francisco Morales, O.F.M. "Mexican Society and the Franciscan Order in a Period of Transition, 1749-1859," *The Americas* 54, no. 3 (Jan., 1998): 325, fn. 3.

Apart from the loss of their monasteries and the inconvenience of moving entire communities to their new residences, the friars saw the destruction of their last remaining link with their founding fathers, namely their strong relationship with the Indian population…The abrupt change from the ample freedom with which they had exercised their pastoral activities in rural Mexico to the narrow confines of conventual life in urban centers was an impact from which the Provinces would never recover.[48]

Although the state of affairs was even more dramatic from 1786 until 1859, the year male religious orders were suppressed in Mexico, the traumas of the eighteenth-century were lessened by two factors: 1) the need for the order to occupy the majority of missions vacated by the Jesuits following their expulsion from Spanish America (1767)[49] and 2) the founding of additional Propagation of the Faith colleges and their corresponding missions.[50]

After fierce lobbying, the heroic Antonio Linaz received Papal authorization to establish the first American missionary college for the Propagation of the Faith in 1682; in 1683 the Franciscan friary for Recollects in Querétaro was claimed by the newly arrived apostolic missionaries and became known as the College of Santa Cruz of the Propagation of the Faith. After the College of Santa Cruz, the most important colleges to follow were the College of Guadalupe in Zacatecas and the College of San Fernando in Mexico City (from which would hail the founders of all the California missions). The Propagation of the Faith had clear objectives in Spanish America—to produce professional missionaries, evangelize amongst still unconverted heathens, continue exploration into the farthest reaches of New Spain (north and south), and make strict Christians out of Spanish and Creole sinners.

The Propagation of the Faith introduced New Spain to friars who were orthodox in their religious views, unapologetic about the virtues of icons and relics, and convinced that the mendicant congregation would finish the mission begun a century and a half earlier by Martín de Valencia. Upon arrival in Querétaro, friars addressed a Spanish, Creole, and mestizo population. The economic, ethnic, and social diversity of the flock distinguished the Propagation of the Faith friars from their earlier missionary counterparts. It was the city as much as the countryside—and the Spaniard as much as the native—who were in need of spiritual repair. A portrait of Antonio Linaz, painted in the eighteenth century for the College of San Fernando in Mexico City, emphasizes the heterogeneity of the audience (Fig. 6). In it, the zealous missionary is surrounded by indigenous and non-indigenous men, women,

---

[48] Ibid., 328. Yet Morales' research is exceptional precisely because it moves beyond secularization in understanding the decline of the order from 1749 to 1859. Refusing to see Mexican society as historically static, he investigates the decrease of religious vocations in city and countryside, the impact of radical politics within the order itself, and the transformation of colonial society in general (independent of Crown policies).

[49] Franciscans were entrusted with the majority of Jesuit missions in northern New Spain, the society's stronghold at the time. For missionary changes in Sonora and Arizona, see Kiernan McCarty, *A Spanish Frontier in the Enlightened Age. Franciscan Beginnings in Sonora and Arizona* (Washington D.C.: Academy of American Franciscan History, 1981). For Baja California, see Lino Gómez Canedo, *Un lustro de evangelización franciscana en Baja California* (La Paz, Baja California: Dirección de Cultura, 1983).

[50] Beginning with Santa Cruz in Querétaro (1683), the colleges were founded in the following order: Cristo Crucificado in Guatemala (1700), Guadalupe de Zacatecas (1704), San Fernando in Mexico City (1733), and San Francisco in Pachuca (1733). The colleges in Orizaba, and Pachuca were founded after 1786. The best colonial source for the apostolic colleges in New Spain is friar Isidro Félix de Espinosa, *Crónica de los Colegios de Propaganda Fide de la Nueva España…* (Mexico: Joseph Bernardo de Hogal, 1746). A comprehensive study on the apostolic colleges and their functioning in Spanish America is found in Félix Saiz Diez, *Los Colegios de Propaganda Fide en Hispanoamérica* (Madrid: (s.n.), 1969).

and children. The picture of conversion is no longer the Valadesian image of a mendicant proselytizing among semi-nude Chichimecs or imparting of Christian instruction via visual narratives drawn on monastic walls (Fig. 7). Instead, friar portraits—especially those forming part of the fascinating and understudied martyr series—tend to emphasize both the order's value to colonial society at large and the pronounced relationship between missionary activity and animated images (Fig. 8).[51]

Reconversion was on display in late colonial Querétaro. Within a year of founding their first missionary college, friars preached fire and brimstone daily for an entire month in Querétaro's parish church. Shortly thereafter, they began a proselytizing tour, visiting cities such as Mexico City, Puebla, Merida, and Morelia. In their religious marathons—sometimes preaching for 40 hours straight—friars were able to convince elites to give up their errant ways, encourage women to adopt conservative dress and lead modest lives, and even prompt the guardian of the Franciscan monastery in Mexico City to renounce his post and join the college of apostolic friars.[52] Bullfights, plays, and festivals came to a halt; parties, dances, and comedies all ceased. "Querétaro is not what it used to be," our primary chronicler friar Isidro Félix Espinosa boasted. No doubt his detractors were lamenting the same point. Says one critic: "Friars have arrived who are so impertinent that we no longer have the festivities we once had; now it is all very sad, one hears neither a harp nor a guitar, it's all prayer and sermons, so much so that the place has lost all sense of happiness."[53]

Relentless sermonizing made an impact, to be sure. The dramatic displays of mortification exercises in public spaces must have been equally impressive. Although flagellation and self-mortification practices were common enough since the arrival of the religious order in the sixteenth century, the Propagation of the Faith friars took the tradition beyond a monastic arena, and onto the very public, colonial urban stage. They publicly traced the Via-Sacra each and every Friday and they led penitential processions in every city they entered. "Devoted to the Cross and to the crucified Christ, they devised new ways of copying the sorrowful image onto their own bodies," says Espinosa.[54] Linaz had novices publicly flog him on a daily basis, friars Frutos and Jorge de Puga would scourge their flesh in city streets and in route to their missions, the illustrious Margil de Jesus and the great apostle to California, Junipero Serra, would publicly torture their own bodies beyond the prescribed regulations. In one spectacular religious demonstration in Morelia, apostolic friars led a procession that included brothers from the Third Order, members from the Franciscan monastery in Morelia, secular priests, and the illustrious cabildo (municipal council). All were barefoot and mortifying their flesh—some wore iron collars and some were led by ropes. One witness marveled at a scene in which the council members humiliated their bodies with such devotion that they were indistinguishable from the apostolic friars.[55]

Fanning the flames of religious fanaticism, the college in Querétaro openly argued that demonic

---

[51]   Antonio Rubial and María Teresa Suárez Molina have lucidly examined Franciscan pictorial strategies within the complex socio-political and religious landscape of the northern frontier. Rubial and Suárez, "Mártires y Predicadores: La Conquista de las Fronteras y su Representación Plástica," in *Pinceles de la Historia: De la Patria Criolla a la Nación Mexicana* (Mexico: MUNAL, INBA, 2000), 50-71.

[52]   Franciscan guardian Antonio de Escaray temporarily joined the College of Guadalupe in Zacatecas. Isidro Félix de Espinosa, *Crónica de los Colegios de Propaganda Fide de la Nueva España*, ed. Lino G. Canedo, O.F.M. (Washington, D.C.: Academy of American Franciscan History, 1964), 182, 184, fn. 3.

[53]   Espinosa dismisses the description as the sinful desires of a vulgar man and reminds the reader that, thankfully, Querétaro is no longer what it once was: "Due to the moderation exhibited and the frequency of the sacraments, (the city) can now be counted as one of the most exemplary cities in the world." Ibid.

[54]   Ibid., 174.

[55]   Ibid., 189.

Fig 6. Portrait of Antonio Linaz. Anonymous, 18th century. Museo Regional de Querétaro.

Fig 8. Portrait of friar Silva. Anonymous, 18th century. College of Guadalupe, Zacatecas.

Fig 7. Indoctrination of the Chichimecs. Diego Valadés, Rhetorica Christiana (Perugia 1579). Courtesy of the Getty Research Institute, Special Collections, Los Angeles, California.

currents threatened Christian life. There was no better proof that the Devil had returned to the New World, if he ever left at all, than the bizarre case of the Querétaro demoniacs. In the early 1690s, friars from the College of Santa Cruz worked feverishly to exorcise devils from the (usually female) bodies. Using relics, images, and other types of sacred objects, they were so successful in performing exorcisms—and they conducted so many of them—that the Holy Office of the Inquisition eventually chastised the college and began to restrict the practice.[56] The timing of the demonic possessions with the presence of the passionate friars was not coincidental, as historian Fernando Cervantes has noted:

> There can be little doubt that the most important factor leading to the growth of an awareness of the diabolic at this time was the missionary activity of the newly arrived Franciscans of Propaganda Fide, who founded their first college in Querétaro in 1683.[57]

Thus, as friars were discovering idols in native communities, demons were being discovered in non-Indian bodies in the most Christian of cities.

Accompanied by a discernable conviction in the power and merits of the sacred image—and given the socio-political and religious landscape in eighteenth-century New Spain—it is little wonder

the apostolic friar Vilaplana lauds the Pueblito icon and propagates her cult throughout Querétaro and beyond. The sculpture is the picture of Mary Immaculate—her hands closed in prayer, her body framed below by a Crescent moon and above by a diadem of twelve radiating stars—she is a Virgin conceived without sin. An elaborately dressed Christ Child stands on a cushioned cloud beside her. The Madonna iconography, however, is only a portion of the sacred object: a kneeling Saint Francis supports three spheres and serves as the pillar for both Virgin and doctrine. Sharing with Mary the ability to heal, protect, and respond to prayer, the seraphic saint forms an integral part of the numinous object.

The iconography of the Pueblito image has a remarkable source: an oil sketch by Peter Paul Rubens and an associated print by the Flemish engraver Paul Pontius (Fig. 9).[58] Rubens paints the theme once, in 1630-1632, and never returns to the iconography again. Yet the composition is soon engraved and issued as a print by Rubens' assistant, the young Paul Pontius.[59] A "finished" European painting was never produced and it is quite likely that Rubens created his oil sketch solely as a model for Pontius to follow. The Pontius print would have been an ideal illustration—both in format and subject—for a Franciscan thesis defending the doctrine of the Immaculate Conception.

Once in New Spain, the imported image was copied, adapted, and transformed. Consistently

56 At least one resident found the order's use of relics and sacred objects in Querétaro suspect. In a letter dated October 5, 1691, the municipal magistrate of Querétaro, José Pozuelo, conveyed this worry to Inquisitors: "…all I know is that the Church's relics and sacred objects are being abused…(and therefore) I ask that a dispassionate person be sent to examine the matter, so that your lordships may prescribe a convenient remedy and with the sickle of your holy zeal mow the darnel that the enemy seeks to plant amidst the Christian wheat." Archivo General de la Nación (Mexico), Inquisición, 527.8, fols. 465r-v. Inquisitors also took issue with the quantity of cases, finding it unlikely that the Devil would bother with so many residents in a single city. An edict from 1692 banned the college from performing further exorcisms. Fernando Cervantes, *Devil in the New World: The Impact of Diabolism in New Spain* (New Haven: Yale University Press, 1994), 98-124.
57 Cervantes, *Devil in the New World*, 113.
58 Peter Paul Rubens, *Franciscan Allegory in Honor of the Immaculate Conception*, 1631-1632, John G. Johnson Collection, Philadelphia Museum of Art. For a brief commentary on the work, see Julius Held, *The Oil Sketches of Peter Paul Rubens: A Critical Catalogue* (Princeton: Princeton University Press, 1980), 526-28.
59 Pontius (b. 1603) began as a student of Rubens and then, later, became his chief engraver. At some point between 1632 and 1658 (the year of his death), he was charged to produce an engraving modeled on Rubens' oil sketch. For discussion of the print, see Richard Judson and Carl van de Velde, *Book Illustrations and Title Pages*, vols. 21-22 of the *Corpus Rubenianum Ludwig Burchard* (London, New York: Phaidon, 1968-).

Fig 9. Allegory of the Immaculate Conception. Peter Paul Rubens, c. 1632. Philadelphia Museum of Art.

Fig 10. Franciscan allegory of the Immaculate Conception. Baptistery, Santa María Tonantzintla, 18th century. Photo by author.

appearing in Franciscan settings, the iconography became closely associated with Franciscan ideas of conversion and evangelization particular to the New World. It appears as the principal sculpture in the chapel of the Third Order in Tlaxcala, a central architectural emblem on the façade of the Basilica of the Virgin of Ocotlan in Tlaxcala, an important image in the *porteria* of the Franciscan monastery in Ozumba, and a prominent feature in the baptistery of the Franciscan church in Tonantzintla (Fig. 10).[60] In the case of el Pueblito, the allegorical image ceased to function solely as illustration and attained the status of a holy image—charged with the ability to heal, protect and, of course, reconvert.

According to eighteenth-century chronicles, the earliest historical and devotional texts that we have for the Virgin of el Pueblito, friar Sebastian de Gallegos sculpted the icon in 1632.[61] Made of *caña de maíz*, the Marian image is consistent with a mid or late seventeenth-century sculptural tradition.[62] Yet the Christ Child and Saint Francis were added later, perhaps in the same period that Vilaplana wrote his history of the image. The friar's 1761 publication carries the oldest engraving of the Mexican icon (Fig. 11). Created by Antonio Onofre Moreno, the sacred image—supported by the saint and flanked by two manicured trees—is represented within an architectural frame. An inscription follows the form of the arch and reads: 'True portrait of the miraculous image of Our Lady of el Pueblito who is venerated in her sanctuary *extramuros* from the

city of Querétaro.' Onofre's rendition became the orthodox representation of the sacred image—the "true copy"—and would be reproduced throughout central Mexico and as far north as California and New Mexico (Fig. 12).

The portrait of Saint Francis sustaining the Immaculate Conception may have reminded viewers of the order's traditional support of the controversial doctrine, but the Marian icon's fusion with the Seraphic Atlas also provided a convenient idiom for the promotion and glorification of the Franciscan Order as a whole. However far from the realities of the secular consensus, the propaganda issued by the congregation conveyed a tone of unchallenged supremacy and signaled the importance of the order's missionary activity and its continued relevance in the New World. The holy image is an icon, yes, but it is also a self-portrait, a propagandistic weapon in the Franciscan struggle to endure.

We have explored the Franciscan investment in images on multiple levels, attempting to examine it alongside the order's missionary history in New Spain: from the challenges of the spiritual conquest in the sixteenth century to the more disturbing historical realities of the seventeenth and eighteenth centuries. Initially, images were both viable didactic tools and aesthetically powerful objects well suited for the conversion and indoctrination of a native population. By the seventeenth century, as society was in the throes of chronic secularization, cultural heterogeneity, and religious hybridity, the order was clearly attaching itself to a powerful

---

[60]   The iterations are many. For a concise review, see my article "The Circulation of Flemish Prints in Mexican Missions and the Creation of a New Visual Narrative, 1630-1800," *Boletín: The Journal of the California Mission Studies Association* 25, no. 1 (2008): 5-34.

[61]   Florencia and Oviedo, Zodiaco Mariano, 194; Vilaplana, *Historico y sagrado novenario*, 10.

[62]   In the area of Michoacan-Patzcuaro, artists typically employed corn stalk paste as a sculptural material. An early and still valuable study of this method was provided by Andrés Estrada Jasso, *Imaginería en caña: estudio catálogo y bibliografía* (Monterrey: Ediciones al Voleo, 1975). More recent examinations have added to our knowledge of this tradition: Antonio García Abásolo and Gabriela García Lascurain, *Imaginería indígena mexicana: una catequesis en caña de maíz* (Córdoba, Spain: Publicaciones Obra Social y Cultural Caja Sur, 2001); Sofía Irene Velarde Cruz, *Imaginería Michoacana en caña de maíz: estudio histórico y catálogo de imagines en Morelia, Tupátaro, Pátzcuaro, Tzintzuntzan, Quiroga y Santa Fe de la Laguna…* (Mexico: CONACULTA, 2003); and Leonor Labastida Vargas, "El empleo videoscopia en el estudio de la imaginería ligera o de pasta de caña," *Anales del Instituto de Investigaciones Estéticas* 27, no. 87 (2005): 199-207.

Fig 11. Virgin of el Pueblito. Antonio Onofre Moreno,
18th century. Published in Vilaplana, Histórico y Sagrado
Novenario... *(Mexico 1761).* Courtesy of Biblioteca Nacional (México).

Fig 12. Virgin of el Pueblito. Anonymous, 18th century.
Mission Inn, Riverside, California.

cult of images and dotting the landscape with official sanctuary spaces, from the Virgin of Los Angeles to the Virgin of Tecaxic. With the propitious arrival of the Propagation of the Faith friars in 1682, the missionary panorama of colonial Mexico broadened. In city and countryside, epicenter and periphery, friars constantly reminded authorities and the general public of their paramount value in the New World. The (re)conversion of lapsed Christians and the reorganization of a native population within a larger colonial society were presented as ongoing efforts, not projects limited to an earlier age. The foundation narrative for the Virgin of el Pueblito, crafted in the mid-eighteenth century, communicated these ideals. The image itself—Saint Francis as an Atlas sustaining three spheres and Mary Immaculate—championed a timeless mission, one that would successfully chart the impetuous course ahead.

THE 1472 *TRANSLATIO* OF THE RELICS OF ST. BERNARDINE OF SIENA: A NEW INTERPRETATION OF A FRESCO BY PINTURICCHIO IN THE BUFALINI CHAPEL IN SANTA MARIA IN ARACOELI IN ROME

Trinita Kennedy

n 1481–82 the Perugian painter Bernardino Pinturicchio was in Rome assisting his older compatriot Pietro Perugino on frescoes commissioned by Pope Sixtus IV for the Sistine Chapel.[1] Pinturicchio soon parlayed that experience into his first major independent commission in Rome: the fresco cycle in the family chapel of Niccolò di Manno Bufalini, a papal bureaucrat and fellow Umbrian who hailed from Città di Castello. The Bufalini Chapel is the first in a series of private chapels built along the south side of the nave of the Observant Franciscan church of Santa Maria in Aracoeli, which is prominently located on the highest summit of the Capitoline Hill.[2] No documents for the chapel are known to survive, but it was most likely founded and constructed circa 1480.[3] At the time the Observant Franciscans were adapting the fabric and decoration of the church to suit their needs. In 1445 the reform-minded Pope Eugenius IV had installed them at the Aracoeli in place of the unreformed Conventual Franciscans who had been

there since the mid-thirteenth century. Pinturicchio frescoed the Bufalini Chapel with scenes from the lives and miracles of the two most important saints to the Observant Franciscans: St. Francis of Assisi, the founder of the Franciscan order whose core values they sought to revive, and St. Bernardine of Siena, the first of the Observant Franciscans to be canonized.

Pinturicchio harks back his experience in the Sistine Chapel in the fresco on the lower tier of the east wall of the Bufalini Chapel (Fig. 1). As in Perugino's masterful depiction of *Christ Giving the Keys to St. Peter* (Fig. 2), the composition centers on a polygonal domed temple set far in the distance. In the carefully measured space of the piazza, the protagonists act out the drama in the foreground while figures in the middle ground participate in secondary episodes. Pinturicchio adopts the compositional framework of Perugino's papal fresco, but introduces important changes to it. With this scene in particular, Pinturicchio must have sought to engage and beguile members of the papal court and thereby win their admiration. The

---

[1] Giorgio Vasari, *Le Vite de' più eccellenti pittori scultori e architettori nelle radazioni del 1550 e 1568*, eds. Rossanna Bettarini and Paola Barocchi (Florence: Sansoni, 1966), 573. On Pinturicchio's role in the Sistine Chapel frescoes, see L. D. Ettlinger, *The Sistine Chapel before Michelangelo: Religious Imagery and Papal Primacy* (Oxford: Clarendon Press, 1965), 19–42.

[2] C. Gennaro, "Niccolò dei Bufalini," in *Dizionario Biografico degli Italiani* (Rome: Istituto della Enciclopedia Italiana, 1976), 14: 802–03.

[3] For the building history of the church, see Ronald E. Malmstrom, "S. Maria in Aracoeli at Rome" (Ph.D. diss., New York University, 1973).

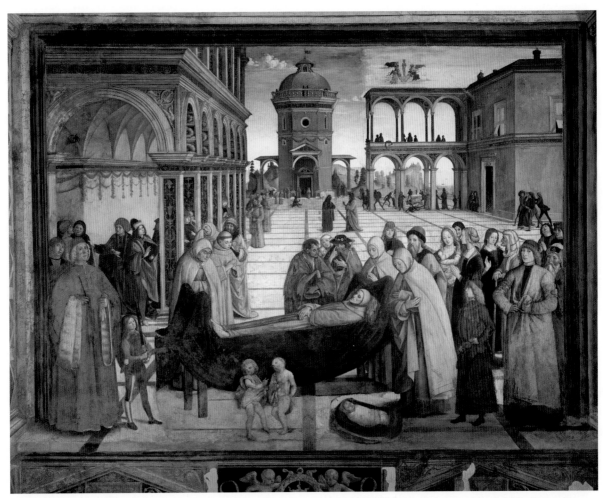

Fig 1. Bernardino Pinturicchio. The Translation of St. Bernardine of Siena *(formerly identified as* The Death of St. Bernardine *or* The Funeral of St. Bernardine*), early 1480s. Fresco. Bufalini Chapel, Santa Maria in Aracoeli, Rome. © Scala / Art Resource, NY

subject matter of this important scene is typically identified as St. Bernardine's death or funeral, both of which occurred in L'Aquila in 1444. In the discussion that follows, I will argue that it is instead a more recent event: the 1472 ritual translation, or *translatio*, of St. Bernardine's relics to San Bernardino in L'Aquila, his burial church.[4]

Understanding the placement of this fresco within the chapel is fundamental because it affects how we read and interpret it. From the nave of the church, one enters the Bufalini Chapel through an arched opening. The chapel is square in plan; it measures approximately five by five meters and is crowned by a groin vault. A simple altar, which lacks an altarpiece and is not known to have ever had one, is placed opposite the entrance on the south wall. Light is admitted to the chapel through the double lancet on the west wall. The tomb of Niccolò Bufalini and his family, which is inscribed "Nicolai de Castello et suorum," is installed below that window, and Niccolò was buried there in 1506.[5] All three walls of the chapel and the ceiling are frescoed.[6] The scene under discussion occupies a large rectangle on the east wall that is separated from the lunette above by a fictive cornice; there is also a frescoed dado below. Photographs of the scene are most frequently taken directly in front of the wall, yet it is important to realize that the ideal viewing point—the place where Pinturicchio's carefully calculated perspective fully coheres—is from an oblique angle at the threshold of the chapel. From there, the orthogonal lines rush out of the painting and draw the viewer into it. This distinguishes the painting in an important way from the perfectly balanced composition of Perugino's *Christ Giving the Keys to St. Peter.*

Pinturicchio's scene is composed of an expansive paved piazza framed by three elegant Renaissance buildings. On the left there is an arcade with six bays ornamented with festoons and on the right there is a stately two-story family palace with a coat of arms above the portal and a bench that wraps around the exterior. Perpendicular to the palace is a two-story loggia with three bays. At the center of the composition is a tall, thin octagonal church with a golden dome and three portals, each with a portico set before it. Just as Leon Battista Alberti recommends in his mid-fifteenth-century architectural treatise *De re aedificatoria*, the temple is free on all sides, elevated on a high base, and well ornamented.[7]

In this cityscape, St. Bernardine is represented in three different states of being. On the ground floor of the loggia on the right, he is alive; in the foreground he is deceased, with his body extended horizontally on a bier; in the upper-right corner, his soul is surrounded by a mandorla and carried to heaven by angels.

In the foreground scene, St. Bernardine's diminutive and emaciated body is dressed in a hooded Franciscan habit and lies on a cloth-covered bier with a red pillow placed beneath his head. Men and women, the young and the old, religious and lay people gather around him. The exotic costumes indicate that foreigners as well as locals are present. Funneling through the loggia on the left are men of various ages who approach

---

[4]   Relic translations, in addition to funerals, were popular subjects in pictorial narratives of the lives of saints; see Barbara Abou-El-Haj, *The Medieval Cult of Saints. Formations and Transformations* (Cambridge and New York: Cambridge University Press, 1997), 48–49.

[5]   For the Bufalini family members buried in the chapel, see BAV MS Ott. Lat. 2548, D. Iacovacci, *Repertorii di familie*, fols. 791–96.

[6]   Important discussions of Pinturicchio's entire cycle include Corrado Ricci, *Pinturicchio* (London: W. Heinemann, 1902), 36–53; Priscilla Seabury Albright, "Pintoricchio's Frescoes in the San Bernardino Chapel in Santa Maria in Aracoeli, Rome" (Ph.D. diss., University of California, Berkeley, 1980); Marilyn Aronberg Lavin, *The Place of Narrative. Mural Decoration in Italian Churches, 431–1600* (Chicago and London: University of Chicago Press, 1990), 215–22; Holly Rarick, "Pinturicchio's Saint Bernardino of Siena frescoes in the Bufalini Chapel, S. Maria in Aracoeli, Rome" (Ph.D. diss., Case Western Reserve, 1990).

[7]   Leon Battista Alberti, *On the Art of Building in Ten Books*, trans. Joseph Rykwert, Neil Leach, and Robert Tavernor (Cambridge, MA and London: M.I.T. Press, 1997), 194–97.

Fig 2. *Pietro Perugino.* Christ Giving the Keys to St. Peter, *ca. 1481–1482. Fresco. Sistine Chapel, the Vatican. © Scala / Art Resource, NY*

the foot of the saint's bier; at the head of the procession is a young page holding a simple wooden processional cross of the kind which had been used in translation ceremonies since at least the fifth century.[8] Behind the page is a distinguished looking gray-haired man with strongly individualized features; he is almost certainly the patron Niccolò Bufalini. He wears a luxurious brocaded robe with wide, fur-lined sleeves and a red beretta. He has taken off one of his white gloves to hold a lit taper; he is in fact the only one in the entire scene bearing a candle and, along with his particularly fine clothing, which gives him unusual prominence in the composition. Flanking the bier on both sides are Franciscan friars, one of whom openly mourns for St. Bernardine. These five friars wear the typical dress of the Observant Franciscans in the fifteenth century: an ash-gray habit tied with a knotted cord, plus a cloak and a cowl, or *capuche*. All the friars except the youngest one, who must be a novice, have their hoods up. Their habits are distinctly different from the Franciscan friars who assemble in the procession outside the portico on the left in the middle ground. Those friars, who are dressed in brown and wear their cowls around the neck, are most likely Conventual Franciscans.[9] On the right side of St. Bernardine's bier there is a larger, less orderly crowd approaching the body with reverence and devotion. So portrait-like are the

depictions of the two well dressed young laymen in the foreground that it is tempting to identify them as Bufalini's offspring.[10]

Pinturicchio represents four of St. Bernardine's miracles. The saint's exceptional miracle-working powers contributed to his remarkably speedy canonization, which occurred just six years after his death.[11] Historian Philippe Jansen has shown that these miracles fall into a small number of categories, the most important of which were exorcisms, the resurrection of children, and the healing of the blind, deaf, and maimed—the same kind of miracles performed by Christ.[12]

The earliest miracles in the scene appear to be the ones taking place under the loggia connected to the palace. St. Bernardine stands in the central bay of the loggia and holds a tablet with the letters IHS, an emblem for the Holy Name of Jesus. The saint famously incorporated IHS tablets into his preaching, and simply by displaying them he often effected miracles.[13] Here St. Bernardine is about to heal a boy being gored by an angry bull; this occurred in Prato in 1425 and was one of the most frequently represented of all the saint's miracles.[14] Pinturicchio shows another miracle that seems to occur simultaneously. A female demoniac who stands in front of the palace is being exorcised. Three men support her body so that the devil can escape. St. Bernardine performed this

---

8   Kenneth G. Holum and Gary Vikan, "The Trier Ivory, 'Adventus' Ceremonial, and the Relics of St. Stephen," *Dumbarton Oaks Papers* 33 (1979): 117, 123.

9   More work remains to be done on the ways Franciscan Conventuals and Observants distinguished themselves with dress, but see David Haack, "Content and Controversy in Choir and Convent Images of St. Francis of Assisi, 1300–1450" (Ph.D. diss., Syracuse University, 1999), 186–200, 272; Ronald Lightbown, *Carlo Crivelli* (New Haven and London: Yale University Press, 2004), 243.

10 Albright 1980, 226, suggests they may be Giovanni Pietro and Ventura Bufalini.

11 For St. Bernardine's canonization process, see *Acta Sanctorum* (Paris and Rome: V. Palmé, 1866), 18: 87–148.

12 Philippe Jansen, "Un exemple de sainteté thaumaturgique à la fin du Moyen Âge: les miracles de saint Bernardin de Sienne," *Mélanges de l'école française de Rome* 96, no. 1 (1984): 129–51.

13 Loman McAodha, "The Holy Name of Jesus in the Preaching of Bernardino of Siena," *Franciscan Studies* 29 (1969): 37–65; Daniel Arasse, "Iconographie et évolution spirituelle: la tablette de saint Bernardin de Sienna," *Revue d'histoire de la spiritualité* 50 (1974): 433–56; idem, "Entre dévotion et hérésie. La tablette de saint Bernardin ou le secret d'un prédicateur," *Res* 28 (1995): 118–39; Lina Bolzoni, *The Web of Images. Vernacular Preaching from its Origins to St. Bernardino da Siena* (Aldershot and Burlington: Ashgate, 2004), 168–77.

14 The episode is also depicted, for example, in the cycle of panel paintings attributed to the Workshop of 1473 in the Galleria Nazionale dell'Umbria in Perugia. On the popularity of this miracle, see also Iris Origo, *The World of San Bernardino* (New York: Harcourt, Brace, & World, 1962), 180.

type of miracle many times during and after his life and therefore it is difficult to pinpoint exactly the instance Pinturicchio represented.

The other miracles take place beside the corpse and thus, following the internal logic of the painting, happen more recently in time. Directly in front of the bier are two toddlers and an infant; these babies presumably were ill or dead before coming into contact with the relic but are now full of life.[15] The toddlers dance with joy while the infant rests peacefully in a bassinet. Behind the bier are two adult male pilgrims with beards who are dressed in rags. The one on the left doffs his cap in the presence of the saint's body and holds out his maimed hand in the hopes of it being healed. The pilgrim on the right holds a staff and still wears his cap, which is covered with badges from the shrines he has already visited, including a scallop shell from Santiago de Compostela in Spain. This man points with his right index finger to his eyes, likely indicating that he was a blind but now could see thanks to St. Bernardine's thaumaturgic powers.

Like Perugino in *Christ Giving the Keys to St. Peter*, Pinturicchio takes great pains to emphasize the foreground scene above the subsidiary ones and to connect it to the octagonal temple in the background. Most importantly, the artist has painted a dark, wide gridline that extends from St. Bernardine's body all the way to the church.[16] Particularly when seen from the ideal viewpoint in the chapel, a sense of movement is created by this perspectival construction; the viewer understands

that the body, once pilgrims have had a chance to venerate, touch, and be healed by it, will be transported to the church located at the vanishing point. Indeed, a crippled man can even be seen awaiting the arrival of the wonder-working corpse on the steps of the building. The protagonists of the picture therefore are St. Bernardine's body and the temple.

Given its significance to the narrative, this temple is worthy of close consideration. Art historians often describe it as a pagan temple, when in fact it most closely resembles a martyrium—a type of monument built between the fourth and sixth centuries throughout the Christian world to mark the sites in the life and Passion of Christ, the tomb of a saint, or a place of a saint's suffering or testimony.[17] Of the various shapes used for these buildings, octagons were among the most popular and distinctive. They were first used at sites related to Christ, including the Church of the Ascension in Jerusalem; the eight sides of these monuments refer to Christ's Resurrection on the eighth day after his entry into Jerusalem and even symbolized Christ himself. By extension, octagons came to be used in the architecture of early saint's shrines, since as martyrs saints were witnesses to Christ's mission of incarnation, sacrifice, and salvation.[18] An important example is the fifth-century martyrium at Qal'at Sim'ān in Syria. The octagon at its center originally enshrined the column upon which the famous ascetic St. Simeon Stylites the Elder spent the last four decades of his life. The

---

15 For the large number of infants brought back to life by St. Bernardine, see Jansen 1984, 137–38. For the importance of this type of miracle, see Diana Webb, "Friends of the Family: Some Miracles for Children by Italian Friars," *The Church and Childhood. Studies in Church History* 30 (1994): 183–95.

16 In *Christ Giving the Keys to St. Peter*, Perugino similarly used the lines of the pavement to emphasize the principal figures. Two lines frame Christ, St. Peter, the keys to the church, and the church door.

17 For this building type, see André Grabar, *Martyrium: Reserches sur le culte des relques et l'art chrétien antique*, 2 vols. (Paris: Collège de France, 1943–46); Richard Krautheimer, *Early Christian and Byzantine Architecture* (Harmondsworth: Yale University Press, 1986). See also idem, "Review of *Martyrium: Reserches sur le culte des reliques et l'art chrétien antique* by André Grabar," *Art Bulletin* 35, no. 1 (March 1953): 57–61.

18 Richard Krautheimer, "Introduction to an 'Iconography of Medieval Architecture,'" *Journal of the Warburg and Courtauld Institutes* 5 (1942): 11.

octagon was where pilgrims were able to vener-ate and touch the miracle-working relic.[19]

This observation that Pinturicchio's painted temple resembles an early Christian martyrium substantiates my theory that the principal event de-picted in his fresco is the translation of St. Bernar-dine, since in 1472 his body was deposited in his tomb church of San Bernardino in L'Aquila, the form of which recalls an early Christian martyrium. The church was badly damaged in an earthquake in the eighteenth century, but its original form was recorded in the early seventeenth century in an il-lustration (Fig. 3) to Luke Wadding's *Annales Mino-rum* for the year 1472. The building consisted of a domed octagon appended to a long nave with two side aisles. San Bernardino in L'Aquila was designed as a major pilgrimage shrine capable of holding large crowds, and St. Bernardine's original burial site was in the crypt below the dome.[20]

Based on this evidence, it is clear that Pinturic-chio took some liberties when he depicted San Bernardino in L'Aquila as a free-standing, centralized structure without a nave. Yet the essence of the building and its most significant part was of course the domed octagon, for this was where St. Bernar-dine's tomb was located until the body was translated

a second time to a marble tomb in a chapel off the nave in 1505. The octagon was the most symbolic part of the building as well because of its mar-tyrium-like form. Burying St. Bernardine, a new saint, in the style of early Christian martyrs and confessors, served as a tangible sign of the spiritual regeneration of the church in the fifteenth century thanks to the reform efforts of the popes.[21]

The events leading up to the translation of St. Bernardine's relics to this church were particularly dramatic.[22] The wheels were first set into motion during Lent of 1472 with the sermons of the pow-erful and controversial but highly persuasive Ob-servant Franciscan preacher Michele da Carcano from Milan.[23] When he took the pulpit in L'Aquila's main piazza to preach to the people at the beginning of Lent, he found there a rival performer, the Do-minican preacher Giovanni da Pistoia.[24] So that he could be heard, Michele da Carcano moved and the new site he picked was the piazza directly in front of San Bernardino in L'Aquila, which was then under construction. This change in venue turned out to be fortuitous. With the incomplete church as his backdrop, Michele da Carcano's sermons gained new purpose. He began calling for the translation of St. Bernardine's body to the church.[25] By this date,

---

[19]   On pilgrimage to this shrine, see Gary Vikan, *Byzantine Pilgrimage Art* (Washington, DC: Dumbarton Oaks, Trustees of Harvard Uni-versity, 1982).

[20]   See also Umberto Chierici, *La Basilica di S. Bernardino a L'Aquila* (Genoa: Casa di risparmio dell'Aquila, 1964), 21–33; Damiano V. Fucinese, "La riedificazione di San Bernardino all'Aquila e il problema della pianta quattrocentesca," *Opus* 4 (1995): 125–61. On the crypt, see, Nunzio Faraglia, "La chiesa primitiva e il monastero di S. Bernardino in Aquila," *Rassegna pugliese di scienze, lettere ed arti* 27 (1912): 255.

[21]   The building can be connected to a larger early Christian revival in fifteenth-century Italy, for which see Irving Lavin, "Donatello's Bronze Pulpits in San Lorenzo and the Early Christian Revival," in *Past-Present: Essays on Historicism from Donatello to Picasso* (Berkley and Los An-geles: University of California Press, 1993), 1–27; Linda A. Koch, "The Early Christian Revival at S. Miniato al Monte: The Cardinal of Portugal Chapel," *Art Bulletin* 78, no. 3 (September 1996): 527–55; Marvin Trachtenberg, "On Brunelleschi's choice: speculation on medieval Rome and the origins of Renaissance architecture," in *Architectural Studies in Memory of Richard Krautheimer*, ed. Cecil L. Striker (Mainz: Von Zabern, 1996), 169–73. For other octagonal "martyria" built in central Italy during the Renaissance, see Hans Ost, "Santa Margherita in Montefiascone: A Centralized Building Plan of the Roman Quattrocento," *Art Bulletin* 52 (December 1970): 373–89; Paul Davies, "The Tempietti on the Ponte Sant'Angelo and the Renaissance of Architecture in Rome," in *Ashes to Ashes: Art in Rome between Humanism and Maniera,* eds. Roy Eriksen and Victor Plahte Tschudi (Rome: Edizioni dell'Ateneo, 2006), 11–40.

[22]   Ugo Speranza, "La traslazione del corpo di S. Bernardino da Siena avvenuta nell'anno 1472 (con documenti inediti)," *Deputazione di storia patria per l'Abruzzo* 16 (1935): 81–86.

[23]   Roberto Rusconi, "Michele da Milano," in *Dizionario Biografico degli Italiani* (Rome: Istituto della Enciclopedia italiana, 1976), 19: 742–44.

[24]   Paolo Sevesi, "Un sermone inedito del B. Michele Carcano su S. Bernardino da Siena," *Studi francescani* 3 (1931): 73.

[25]   Faraglia (1912), 338.

Fig 3. San Bernardino in L'Aquila in the early seventeenth century, as represented in Luke Wadding, Annales Minorum, *first published in 1625–54 (Florentia: Ad Claras Aquas, 1932, vol. 14, unnumbered plate).*

several decades had passed since the saint's death and canonization and his body still had not been deposited in the church. Compare this, for example, to St. Francis's burial church, San Francesco in Assisi, which was begun in 1228, the year of the saint's canonization, and had progressed far enough already by 1230 that the saint's body could be translated there.[26] San Bernardino in L'Aquila, on the other hand, was repeatedly beset by earthquakes, plagues, and financial difficulties. St. Bernardine was canonized in 1450 and still in 1472 no part of his burial church appears to have been completed and the entire structure lacked a roof.[27]

Michele da Carcano continued preaching in L'Aquila every day even after Lent ended in 1472. With an ever greater sense of urgency, he emphasized that the time had come for St. Bernardine's body to be brought to San Bernardino in L'Aquila. Even though the building was not yet finished, it had evidently reached a stage where the body could be safely entombed there. Bringing the relic to San Bernardino in L'Aquila was undoubtedly meant to stimulate the floundering construction. Peter Brown, Patrick Geary, and other historians who study relics have noted that translations helped to dramatize the cult of a saint and usually provoked an outburst of popular enthusiasm for it. For this reason, these splendid ceremonies and the miracles that often accompanied them were particularly important to cults that had begun to wane, which at least to some extent, St. Bernardine's had.[28] With this renewed enthusiasm for the saint, it was hoped that pilgrims would donate the money needed to bring the shrine to completion after much delay.

To translate the body, the Observant Franciscans needed the permission of Pope Sixtus IV, who was himself a Franciscan. Despite belonging to the rival Conventual branch of the order, he responded favorably to this request, for he naturally favored Franciscan saints and sought to enhance Franciscan shrines.[29] On May 1, 1472 the pope issued a bull in which he granted the Observant Franciscans permission to hold their general chapter in L'Aquila on May 15 and afterward to bring St. Bernardine's body to his burial church. The pope designated May 17, the Feast of Pentecost, as the date for the translation to take place.[30] On May 4 Sixtus IV issued another bull in which he expressed his love and continued support for the Observants and renewed all privileges accorded to them by his papal predecessors.[31]

Wadding states that more than 2,000 Observant Franciscans made the journey to L'Aquila to witness St. Bernardine's translation;[32] in all

[26]   Elvio Lunghi, *The Basilica of St. Francis in Assisi* (New York: Scala / Riverside, 1996).

[27]   Maria Rita Berardi, "Esigenza religiose ed egemoni politiche nella fabbrica di San Bernardino all'Aquila," in *Luoghi sacri ed spazi della santità*, eds. Sofia Boesch Gajano and Lucetta Scarffia (Turin: Rosenberg & Sellier, 1990), 512–13; Simonetta Ciranna, "La costruzione della cupola di San Bernardino all'Aquila tra XV e XVIII secolo," in *Lo specchio del cielo: forme significati tecniche e funzioni della cupola dal Pantheon al Novecento*, ed. Claudia Conforti (Milan: Electa, 1997), 151–65.

[28]   Peter Brown, *The Cult of the Saints: Its Rise and Function in Latin Christianity* (Chicago: University of Chicago Press, 1981), 88–105; Patrick Geary, *Furta Sacra: Thefts of Relics in the Central Middle Ages* (Princeton: Princeton University Press, 1978), 10–15; Jonathan Sumption, *Pilgrimage: An Image of Medieval Religion* (London: Faber & Faber, 1975), 149–50; Louisa Bourdua, "Displaying the Body of Saint Anthony of Padua," in *Bild und Körper im Mittelalter*, eds. Kristin Marek, Raphaèle Preisinger, et al. (Munich: Wilhelm Fink, 2006), 243–55.

[29]   For an overview of the relationship between the Franciscan Conventuals and Observants in the fifteenth and sixteenth centuries, see John Moorman, *A History of the Franciscan Order from its Origins to the Year 1517* (Chicago: Francis Herald Press, 1968), 441–500; 569–88. Rona Goffen, "Friar Sixtus and the Sistine Chapel," *Renaissance Quarterly* 39, no. 2 (Summer 1986): 218–62; Jill Elizabeth Blondin, "Pope Sixtus IV at Assisi: the Promotion of Papal Power," in *Patronage and Dynasty: the Rise of the della Rovere in Renaissance Italy*, ed. Ian Verstegen (Kirksville: Truman State University Press, 2007), 19–36; Sarah Blake McHam, *The Chapel of St. Anthony at the Santo and the Development of Venetian Renaissance Sculpture* (Cambridge: Cambridge University Press, 1994), 17–20.

[30]   Speranza (1935), 82.

[31]   Luke Wadding, *Annales Minorum* (Florentia: Ad Claras Aquas, 1932), 14: 5.

[32]   Ibid.

likelihood this was the largest gathering of the friars that had occurred since St. Bernardine's canonization twenty-two years earlier at Old St. Peter's in Rome.[33] The translation was pivotal for them because it finally meant that St. Bernardine's body would be housed in a church of their own. Until then, the body had been entombed in the Conventual Franciscan church of San Francesco a Palazzo in L'Aquila. Pinturicchio seems to allude in his fresco to the transfer of the relic from the Conventual Franciscans to the Observant Franciscans by showing the Conventual friars in the distance and the Observant friars in the foreground. Wadding tells us that prior to giving up the body the Conventual Franciscans invited the Observant Franciscans to their church for a special viewing of the corpse.[34] When St. Bernardine's coffin was unearthed and opened his body was found not to be a heap of bones. Rather it was fragrant and incorrupt just as it had been left twenty-eight years before—a miracle in itself and a sign of Bernardine's sanctity.[35]

The translation ceremony was conducted with great solemnity. Sixtus IV granted a plenary indulgence to all who attended the event and visited San Bernardino in L'Aquila.[36] To maximize attendance and donations, the city of L'Aquila announced the festivities and the indulgence to the rest of the Abruzzo and other regions in Italy.[37] In attendance were at least 40,000 lay people and 1,500 members of other religious orders or confraternities.[38]

St. Bernardine's body was taken from San Francesco a Palazzo and carried through the streets of L'Aquila to its special burial church with a procession of people behind it. The body was dressed in a silk habit tied with a cord of golden threads. Once the body reached San Bernardino, it was placed in a crystal casket ornamented with gold and installed in the mysterious darkness of the crypt.[39] The casket, which cost 3,000 *scudi*, was surrounded by protective iron bars of the kind often found at saint's tombs.[40] Michele da Carcano then celebrated Mass outside the church. Sermons were a traditional part of relic translations and Michele da Carcano gave a particularly long and eloquent one that took the form of a biography of the saint which concluded with St. Bernardine's death in L'Aquila, his canonization, and an account of his many posthumous miracles.[41] Donations to the church poured in, just as the pope and the Observant Franciscans had surely hoped.[42]

Sixtus IV did not attend the translation ceremony. Other people from Rome with strong links to the pope, however, are known to have been present. They include Queen Catherine of Bosnia, who lived in Rome in exile as a guest of the pope after the Ottomans conquered her homeland in 1461.[43] Pinturicchio's fresco seems to suggest that Niccolò Bufalini also made the journey to L'Aquila to witness the translation, which brings us to the question of who exactly he was. His principal role in the curia was papal abbreviator. He was one of many in the apostolic chancery who drafted and prepared

[33] For the canonization ceremony, see ibid., 12: 68–70
[34] Ibid., 14: 5.
[35] Note, however, that the body seems to have been embalmed; for the preservation of holy bodies in this way, see Katherine Park, "The Criminal and the Saintly Body: Autopsy and Dissection in Renaissance Italy," *Renaissance Quarterly* 47, no. 1 (1994): 1–33.
[36] Wadding (1932), 14: 7.
[37] Speranza (1935), 82.
[38] Faraglia (1912), 338.
[39] Ibid., 339.
[40] Ibid.; Speranza (1935), 85.
[41] The sermon is transcribed in full in Sevesi 1931.
[42] Berardi (1990), 512–13, 522.
[43] Ludwig Pastor, *The History of the Popes from the Close of the Middle Ages* (London: J. Hodges, 1894–1951), 3: 264–67.

bulls, briefs, and consistorial decrees before they were written out *in extenso* by *scriptores*.[44] In the fifteenth century these abbreviators were becoming increasingly prominent and important. Pius II organized them into their own college with a chapel and their own statutes and put them under the governance of a Cardinal Vice-Chancellor.[45] Paul II suppressed the college, but Sixtus IV reestablished it in 1479 and limited the number of abbreviators to seventy-two. Twelve of these men were *abbreviatores de parco majori*, or abbreviators of the upper presidency, who reported directly to the Cardinal Vice-Chancellor, and Bufalini was one of them. In addition, by 1484 Bufalini had also been named a Consistorial Advocate and was teaching law at the University of Rome.[46] During the Renaissance, cardinals and bankers, not papal abbreviators or concistorial lawyers, were typically patrons of chapels in major Roman churches, which tells us that Bufalini was unusually ambitious for a man of his station.[47] His position as papal abbreviator is most interesting in light of the fresco in his private chapel depicting St. Bernardine's translation. It is possible that Bufalini was involved in the composition of Sixtus IV's bull issued on May 1, 1472 permitting the Observant Franciscans to take St. Bernardine's body to his burial church in L'Aquila. The fresco therefore may commemorate the patron's involvement in this major bull for the Observant Franciscans.

While more documentary research is needed to know for sure what Bufalini's involvement was in the bull and ceremony related to Bernardino's 1472 translation, it is clear that Pinturicchio's fresco was a particularly well placed piece of papal and Observant Franciscan propaganda. Santa Maria in Aracoeli was a stop on virtually every pilgrim's itinerary in Rome because of its miracle-working icon of the Virgin known as the *Madonna advocata*.[48] Pinturicchio's fresco, which can be seen by anyone who enters the church and walks down the nave, shows St. Bernardine's body in the incorrupt state in which it was found when it was unearthed for the translation and attests to the relic's continued efficacy as a miracle-worker long after his death. Bufalini, with the insertion of his own likeness in the scene, shows himself to be, at the very least, a believer in St. Bernardine's thaumaturgic powers. In this way, the patron encourages viewers of the fresco to believe as well. The representation of the apotheosis of Bernardino's soul in the upper-right corner of the composition provides assurance that the saint was in heaven and could be called upon to intercede on behalf of the faithful.[49]

In its insistence on the holiness of St. Bernardine's body and his miracles, Pinturicchio's fresco is analogous to thirteenth-century *vita* panels

---

44   For papal abbreviators, see "Abbreviatores ou abbreviateurs de lettres apostoliques," *Dictionnaire de droit canonique* (Paris: Letouzey, 1935–65), 1: cols. 98–106.

45   John F. D'Amico, *Renaissance Humanism in Papal Rome: Humanists and Churchmen on the Eve of the Reformation* (Baltimore: Johns Hopkins University Press, 1983), 29.

46   Gennaro (1972), 802.

47   Bufalini, however, set an important precedent. His son-in-law, Antonio Caccialupi (1453–1518), who was also a papal abbreviator and consistorial lawyer, followed in his footsteps and acquired a chapel in the Augustinian church of San Salvatore in Lauro in Rome; Bufalini's daughter and Caccialupi's widow Maria commissioned Parmigianino to paint the *Vision of St. Jerome* (1526–27; National Gallery, London) for the chapel's altar. See Mary Vaccaro, "Documents for Parmigianino's 'Vision of St. Jerome,'" *Burlington Magazine* 135, no. 1078 (January 1993): 22–27; Sandro Corradini, "Parmigianino's Contract for the Caccialupi Chapel in S. Salvatore in Lauro," *Burlington Magazine* 135, no. 1078 (January 1993): 27-29.

48   On this icon, see most recently, Claudia Bolgia, "The Felici Icon Tabernacle (1372) at S. Maria in Aracoeli, Reconstructed: Lay Patronage, Sculpture and Marian Devotion in Trecento Rome," *Journal of the Warburg and Courtauld Institutes* 68 (2005): 27–72.

49   For more on this imagery, see Robert Mode, "Saint Bernardino in Glory," *Art Bulletin* 55 (1973): 58–76.

made for St. Francis. These panel paintings promoted Assisi as a great pilgrimage shrine.[50] Nearly two centuries later, Pinturicchio's fresco uses similar means to publicize the Franciscans' newest healing shrine, San Bernardino in L'Aquila, and to encourage pilgrims to visit it. In general, Sixtus IV sought to encourage the pilgrimage of the faithful. He was responsible for building new Marian shrines and pilgrimage hospitals in Rome and enhancing Franciscan shrines in Assisi and Padua; he also lavished attention on the Basilica della Santa Casa in Loreto.[51] The translation of St. Bernardine's body was one of many things the pope did to revive the popularity of pilgrimage.

While a full analysis of the Bufalini cycle is beyond the parameters of this study, the recognition that one of its scenes refers directly to papal concerns helps us to see other scenes in the chapel in this way as well. Take, for instance, the scene of *St. Francis Receiving the Stigmata* on the west wall. Sixtus IV staunchly defended the Franciscans'

claim that St. Francis and only St. Francis could be represented that way in art, and the pope issued a series of bulls to that effect between 1472 and 1478.[52]

Most importantly, Pinturicchio's cycle signals a reawakening of St. Bernardine's cult in the late fifteenth century and a new phase in its history and development. After having been buried for twenty-eight years in a Conventual Franciscan church, St. Bernardine's body was exhumed and discovered to be incorrupt. The saint then worked new miracles as his body was carried through the streets of L'Aquila on the way to the martyrium-like burial church being constructed for it by the Observant Franciscans. Pinturicchio's composition—a clever adaption of Perugino's *Christ Giving the Keys to St. Peter* in the Sistine Chapel—publicizes the thaumaturgic power of St. Bernardine's corpse and celebrates its arrival at its purpose-built shrine. This fresco, paid for by the papal abbreviator it depicts, represents a recent event and attests to the dynamic ways that the Franciscan order was promoted during the papacy of Sixtus IV.

[50] Gregory W. Ahlquist and William R. Cook, "The Representation of the Posthumous Miracles of St. Francis of Assisi in Thirteenth-Century Italian Painting," in *The Art of the Franciscan Order*, ed. William R. Cook (Leiden and Boston: Brill, 2005), 211–56. See also Klaus Krüger, *Der Frühe Bildkult des Franziskus in Italien: Gestalt- und Funktionswandel des Tafelbildes im 13. und 14. Jahrhundert* (Berlin: Gebr. Mann, 1992).

[51] For an overview of these projects, see *Sisto IV: Le Arti a Roma nel Primo Rinascimento*, ed. Fabio Benzi (Rome: Edizioni dell'Associazione culturale Shakespeare and Company 2, 1997).

[52] See André Vauchez, "Les stigmates de Saint François et leurs détracteures," *Mélanges de l'Ecole française de Rome* 80 (1968): 1011–12.

GENDER, IMAGE, AND DEVOTION IN ILLUSTRATED MANUSCRIPTS OF THE *MEDITATIONES VITAE CHRISTI*

Holly Flora

he famous Franciscan devotional text known as the *Meditationes Vitae Christi*, or *Meditations on the Life of Christ*, has long been cited by historians for its impact on late medieval and early Renaissance iconography. Composed by a Franciscan friar, perhaps John of Caulibus, for a Clarissan nun,[1] the *Meditationes* retells the Gospel stories in charming and often emotionally charged details, and many such details have been connected to new types of images that emerged in late medieval art. Depictions of the Virgin Mary kneeling as she accepts Gabriel's message during the Annunciation, as seen for example in the chancel frescoes of the Arena Chapel in Padua, correspond to a lengthy passage in the *Meditationes*. Looking for textual sources for such novel imagery, art historians suggested that Giotto and other artists must have known the *Meditationes* and based these new motifs on it. Despite the fact that some scholars now believe the *Meditationes*

was actually composed no earlier than 1336, a full thirty years after Giotto's frescoes of 1306, the *Meditationes* continues to be considered a key influence, if not a direct inspiration, for iconographic innovations.[2]

Because of the now-disputed date of the composition of the *Meditationes*, the study of illustrated manuscripts of this text is all the more important, for these are the only works of art certainly based on it. Until recently, however, these manuscripts remained largely understudied. In this essay, I will explore two of the earliest known illustrated copies of the *Meditationes*, both made in Italy around the middle of the fourteenth century, as evidence for the ways in which the *Meditationes* text was adapted visually. These manuscripts are Ms. ital. 115 now in the Bibliothèque Nationale in Paris, and Snite 85.25, currently housed at the Snite Museum of Art at the University of Notre Dame. Dianne Phillips has convincingly established general aspects of the context and patronage of the Snite

---

[1]   Sarah McNamer has recently proposed that a shorter version of the *Meditationes* text was first written by a nun, but the version I discuss in this essay seems to have at least been compiled and augmented by a friar. See Sara McNamer, *Affective Meditation and the Invention of Medieval Compassion* (Philadelphia: University of Pennsylvania Press, 2010), 86-115. It should also be noted, however, that McNamer's theories about the origins of the *Meditationes* have recently been challenged; see Péter Tóth and David Falvay, "New Light on the Date and Authorship of the *Meditationes Vitae Christi*," in *'Diuerse Imaginaciouns of Cristes Life': Devotional Culture in England 1300-1550*, eds. Ryan Perry and Stephen Kelly (Turnhout: Brepols, forthcoming).

[2]   Sarah McNamer, 'Further Evidence for the Date of the Pseudo-Bonaventuran *Meditationes Vitae Christi*', *Franciscan Studies* 50 (1990): 235-61 (235, n. 1).

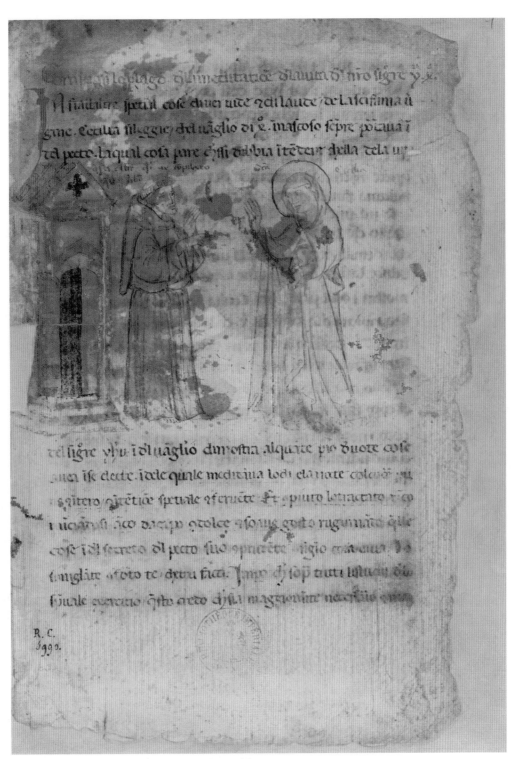

Fig 1. Paris, Bibliothèque Nationale Ms. Ital. 115, folio 1 recto

manuscript.[3] I will rely on her work extensively here, but I also wish to take her arguments about its text and image program a step further to suggest possible interpretations in light of evidence provided by the Paris manuscript.

Despite the fact that they are based on the same text, the pictorial programs in the Paris and Snite manuscripts are very different, and each contains clues as to how the text and images were tailored very specifically for each book's readers. It is my hope that a comparative study of these two manuscripts will cast new light on aspects of their patronage, strengthening Dianne Phillips' contention that the Snite manuscript was likely commissioned by a lay patron in Bologna, and further supporting arguments I have made elsewhere that the Paris manuscript was probably made for a group of Poor Clares in Pisa.[4] Deliberate inflections in the text and image program of each of these books relate specifically to the gender and vocation of each manuscript's intended readers. My analysis of the Infancy cycles in these two manuscripts will suggest that the visual exegesis of the *Meditationes* text was anything but a straightforward translation from text to image; instead, the text was inherently malleable and even in its earliest history was adapted in widely divergent ways to address the interests of its diverse audiences.

I have chosen to focus on the Paris and Snite manuscripts because they are two of the earliest *Meditationes* manuscripts known, and they are among the most extensively illustrated copies of

this text. Based on stylistic evidence, the Paris and Snite manuscripts are both dated to c. 1340-50, shortly after the proposed post-1336 date of composition of the text. Isa Ragusa has even tentatively suggested that the Paris manuscript may be the very first copy of the *Meditationes*.[5] While this point remains uncertain, what is clear is that if the new dating of the text is correct, in its very earliest days the *Meditationes* was being adapted beyond its initial Clarissan, Tuscan audience and known and read by lay and monastic audiences alike. These two manuscripts are also important because illustrated manuscripts of the *Meditationes* are extraordinarily rare, a fact that is surprising given the very visual language used in the text and its long association with images. Out of about two hundred and twenty known manuscripts of the *Meditationes*, only five contain illustration cycles. The Paris manuscript is both unfinished and incomplete, but even so contains 198 images on its 206 surviving folios, while the Snite manuscript, missing only two folios, features forty-eight illustrations.

The illustrations in the two manuscripts are vastly different in terms of style and technique. The Paris manuscript features drawings in a very Tuscan style, with elongated, swaying, very "Gothic" figures typical of Siena and Pisa in the mid fourteenth-century, and they are painted in an unusual tempera wash technique on the equally rare support of paper. By contrast, the Snite manuscript features the characteristically Bolognese style of illumination, with squat, compressed figure types,

---

[3]   See Dianne Phillips, "*The Meditations on the Life of Christ*: An Illuminated Fourteenth-Century Italian Manuscript at the University of Notre Dame", in *The Text in the Community: Essays on Medieval Works, Manuscripts, Authors and Readers*, eds. Jill Mann and Maura Nolan (South Bend, IN: University of Notre Dame Press, 2006), 237-80.

[4]   See Holly Flora, "Paris Bibliothèque Nationale ital 115: A Pisan Trecento Manuscript", *Bollettino Storico Pisano* 74 (2003): 353-59; Holly Flora, "A Book for Poverty's Daughters: Gender and Devotion in Paris Bibliothèque Nationale ital. 115", in *Varieties of Devotion in the Middle Ages and Renaissance*, Arizona Center for Medieval and Renaissance Studies, vol. 7, ed. Susan Karant-Nunn (Turnhout: Brepols, 2003), 61-85; Arianna Pecorini Cignoni and Holly Flora, "Requirements of Devout Contemplation: Text and Image for the Poor Clares in Trecento Pisa," *Gesta* 45 (2006): 61-76; Holly Flora, "The Charity of the Virgin Mary in the Paris *Meditations on the Life of Christ* (BnF, ital. 115)", *Studies in Iconography* 29 (2008): 55-89, and Holly Flora, "Tensions in Textual Exegesis: Word and Picture in an Illustrated Manuscript of the *Meditationes Vitae Christi*", *Ikon* 1 (2008): 123-32.

[5]   See Isa Ragusa, "L'autore delle *Meditationes vitae christi* secondo il codice ms. Ital. 115 della Bibliothèque Nationale di Parigi", *Arte medievale*, Second Series 11 (1997): 145, and "La particolarità del testo delle *Meditationes Vitae Christi*", *Arte medievale*, New Series 2 (2003): 79.

and its rich colors and gold on parchment are typical of luxury book production in that university city. Despite these obvious differences, the Paris and Snite manuscripts are the only early illustrated copies in Italian, the hypothesized original language of the text, and they therefore stand to reveal the most about its earliest pictorial exegesis.

Evidence indicating the original readers of these manuscripts can be found on the frontispieces to each book. The first folio of the Paris manuscript (Fig 1) depicts a tonsured man, his brown robe and rope belt indicating him as a Franciscan, conversing with a haloed female figure. Inscriptions in the image denote the male figure as "The friar who compiled this book" and the female figure as "St Cecilia."[6] This picture corresponds to a portion of the text's prologue, where Cecilia is praised because of her devotion to the life of Christ. As the friar faces Cecilia with an open, raised left hand and his right hand pointing at her, she holds up her right hand in response while her left hand points downward toward the text below her. Because no book is depicted in the image, the inscription above the friar noting him as the compiler of "this book" indicates that the book in the reader's hands, the text Cecilia points to, is the one that he has compiled. Cecilia is thus presented as a direct model for the reader, and male to female advisor-advisee relationship is implied. This type of advisory relationship is the exact circumstance under which the *Meditationes* was originally created, written by a Franciscan friar for a Poor Clare nun under his spiritual direction. The image therefore points toward a similar situation of patronage for the Paris manuscript: that is, the book was made for a female Franciscan audience, likely also under

the direction of a friar. The second image in the manuscript, St. Francis (Fig 2), who is the only non-biblical saint besides Cecilia depicted, also points strongly toward a Franciscan context.

In the Snite manuscript, the situation of patronage is at once more straightforward and frustratingly enigmatic. The badly abraded frontispiece features Christ enthroned with two kneeling book owners, one male and one female (Fig 3). The figure on the viewer's left is the apparent male patron, whose costume indicates a layperson of knightly status. The female figure at right wears a blue garment and a mantle, clothing likewise indicative of lay rather than religious vocation. Dianne Phillips has suggested that the male figure, kneeling at Christ's right, is the most probable primary patron and most likely to have had agency in the creation of the manuscript's program, but that the presence of the kneeling woman points to a female reader for the manuscript as well.[7] It is unclear whether or not these two are a couple, but their kneeling postures declare them both as probable book users or owners, which points to the likely situation of a single household.[8]

A number of other aspects of each manuscript concur with these hypotheses about their original owners. The Paris manuscript features the so-called long version of the *Meditationes*, which contains an extended narrative of the ministry of Christ and a lengthy treatise on the active and contemplative lives. The Snite manuscript has the "short" version of the *Meditationes* text, narrating only the Infancy of Christ and his Passion. The lay patrons of the Snite manuscript were perhaps more interested in this abbreviation, while the longer version containing the treatise on the active and contemplative

---

6   Ms. Ital. 115, folio 1 recto. The inscription above the male figure reads: "questi è il frate che àe compilato questo libro."

7   Phillips, "The *Meditations*", 237-81.

8   As Kathryn Smith has established in regard to devotional books produced in England, it was not at all uncommon for fourteenth-century families to share in the reading of their devotional books, and supplicant figures such as these often indicated a book's intended readers. See Kathryn A. Smith, *Art, Identity, and Devotion in Fourteenth-Century England: Three Women and their Books of Hours* (London: British Library, 2004).

Fig 2. Paris, Bibliothèque Nationale Ms. Ital. folio 2 verso

Fig 3. Notre Dame, Snite Museum of Art 85.25, folio 1 recto

Fig 4. Paris, Bibliothèque Nationale Ms. Ital. folio 28 verso

lives lends itself more obviously to a monastic setting. The colors, gold, and parchment of the Snite manuscript likewise suit a wealthy layperson, while the watercolors and paper of the Paris manuscript, while certainly not cheap by medieval standards, are relatively humble, and are perhaps deliberate nods to the Franciscan poverty of its reader.

I would now like to examine the Infancy of Christ cycles in each of these manuscripts in depth as indicators of the original context and use of each. I am using the Infancy narratives for several reasons. One is that the Paris manuscript is incomplete, and does not contain the Passion section, and the Snite manuscript contains the shorter version of the *Meditationes* without the ministry of Christ narratives. Thus the Infancy sequence is the only portion of the text that is elaborated in both manuscripts, and so it offers the best basis for comparison. More importantly, however, the Infancy narrative in the *Meditationes* is set apart from the rest of the text in structure as a lesson on devotion for the reader. It therefore offers the most useful clues as to how a reader would be taught to use it.

The Paris *Meditationes*

I will begin by taking an in-depth look at the Paris manuscript. The layout and text-image structure of the manuscript itself is suggestive of the book's original purpose as a book for nuns living an enclosed life of meditation. The Infancy narrative is presented in an extensive, indeed almost exhaustive, series of eighty nine images. The story of the Virgin's youth and of Christ's youth are therefore given detailed treatment, and broken down into minute moments of time, allowing the reader to experience these stories intimately. You can see this structure well in the Adoration of the Magi sequence, broken up into two distinct moments, the approach of the Magi and their entourage on the

left, and their approach to the Virgin and Christ on the right (Fig 4 and 5). This thoroughness in illustrating the text allows for an almost cinematic feel to the image program; following the pictures "frame by frame" a reader could proceed from one image to the next while following the description of the scene very closely. A reader's imagination would therefore be stimulated and a visionary experience of the text would be encouraged. This visual absorption of the text would further be prompted by the way the images interrupt the text block on each page, essentially taking over each folio in at least one if not two images. No frames, borders, or even historiated initials or rubrics set the text apart from the images, and as this structure would imply, the images and text are presented in close proximity on the page, so that a reader could read the words and then immediately visualize them. Arguably, a reader could also rely solely on the pictures, skimming or even ignoring the text, an exercise facilitated by the presence of detailed captions in each of the images, sometimes so detailed as to almost obviate the text altogether.

Such a structure of text and image therefore allows for multiple ways of use, which might be suitable for the varying levels of literacy one might find in a typical Clarissan convent in Trecento Italy. Although most Poor Clares in this period did not come from poor families—in fact quite the contrary—levels of education for noble women varied greatly. That flexibility in devotional instruction was desirable is implied even in the earliest literature written for the Poor Clares, including Urban IV's Rule, which dictates that the sisters who do not know how to read are to recite the Our Father, while those who can are to sing the Divine Office.[9] One can imagine that if such a book was shared in a convent as most were, nuns with varying reading abilities could use the Paris manuscript. Adaptability in use is also prescribed in the *Meditationes*

---

[9]   *Rule of St. Clare*, in *Francis and Clare: The Complete Works*, trans. R.J. Armstrong and I.C. Brady (New York: Paulist Press, 1982), 214.

itself. The *Meditationes* text is neatly structured with each episode from Christ's life described in a detailed narrative followed by a moralizing sermon or lesson frequently paraphrased from Bernard of Clairvaux. The author tells his Clarissan reader that she is to read through the narratives of Christ's life on a weekly basis, but that the "morals and authorities" at the end of each story need only be used when the reader might need help with a particular vice or sin.[10] The Paris manuscript, with many illustrations contained within the narrative passages and almost none in the moralizing sections, likewise would allow for visionary, imaginative reflection on Christ's life using the image-laden narrative sections, as well as a more conceptual approach using the text-only passages.

It is while using the Infancy section that the reader would learn how to use the Paris manuscript's narratives in this highly imaginative, participatory way facilitated by the text-image structure. In both the text of the *Meditationes* and in the image cycle of the Paris manuscript, the Infancy narrative functions as a lesson on devotion. Imperative commands for the reader gradually intensify in this section of the text. The reader is encouraged to emulate Mary as she enters the temple as a young girl, following her example in knowledge of the scriptures and devotion. The reader is then told to follow the Holy Family through the birth of Christ, and to interact with the holy figures firsthand. At the Nativity, for example, the reader is told to:

> Kiss the beautiful feet of the infant Jesus . . . and beg his mother to offer to let you hold Him a while. Pick Him up and hold Him in your arms. Gaze on his face with devotion and reverently kiss

Him and delight in Him. You may freely do this, because He came to sinners to deliver them, and for their salvation humbly conversed with them.[11]

The Infancy image cycle in the Paris manuscript, with its detailed, play-by-play presentation of the narrative, would help to encourage the vivid devotional imagination of the reader to enter into the narratives in the way the author prescribes here. The Nativity of Christ is elaborated in six different images, revealing the Virgin and Joseph in a variety of devout postures at various moments, for example both kneeling in front of the manger (Fig 6). These would encourage the reader, as the *Meditationes* author implores, to "linger" at the manger, and stay awhile.

Further, the creators of the Paris manuscript went beyond the text to include other details that would offer a connection to a Clarissan reader specifically. Uniquely, the Paris manuscript features repeated images of veiled women clad in light brown tunics presented as companions to the Virgin. These figures occur not only in scenes where traditionally the Virgin is shown with companions, as in the sequence of her youth while enclosed at the temple, but also in much of the sequence of the Holy Family's exile in Egypt, where the text does not mention their presence (Fig 7). The Paris manuscript contains instructions to the artists in the margins, and these specify that companions or "other women" are to be included in the images. I believe these figures are intended to refer to the readers of the manuscript, who are particularly encouraged to emulate Mary in the nun-like lifestyle she embraces in the *Meditationes*, where she is portrayed not only as celibate but also prayerful and an assiduous worker at spinning and needlework.

---

[10] *Meditations on the Life of Christ: An Illustrated Manuscript of the Fourteenth Century*, trans. Isa Ragusa and Rosalie Green (Princeton, NJ: Princeton University Press, 1961), 387. I have chosen to use this older translation as opposed to the more recent one completed by Taney and others because it is based on the text of Ms. ital. 115.

[11] *Meditations*, 38.

Fig 5. Paris, Bibliothèque Nationale Ms. Ital. folio 29 verso

Fig 6. Paris, Bibliothèque Nationale Ms. Ital. folio 19 verso

Fig 7. Paris, Bibliothèque Nationale Ms. Ital. folio 41 recto

Fig 8. Paris, Bibliothèque Nationale Ms. Ital. folio 24 verso

These labors mark her as the new Eve, but more importantly connect the Virgin's life to that of a Clarissan reader, who would be engaged in similar pursuits every day in her convent.

The readers of the Paris manuscript would be encouraged to interact in the events of the Infancy narrative on the level of observation, and to go beyond looking to become involved emotionally as well. The best example of this encouragement of affective devotion is in the Circumcision of Christ in the Paris manuscript (Fig 8), a presentation particularly shaped by a desire for an intense emotional experience of this event consistent with Clarissan spirituality. The text of the *Meditationes*, most unusually, declares that the Circumcision was actually performed by the Virgin herself. The illustration of this detail is unique to the Paris manuscript. It is emphasized as the first violent event to be described in detail by the *Meditationes*, offering the reader a powerful lesson on affective devotional prayer. The author prepares his audience, just before describing the event of the Circumcision itself, by asking her to get emotionally involved in the narrative: "feel compassion for him and weep with Him, for perhaps he wept today."[12] This is the first time the text commands the reader to "weep," and it is the first time it describes Mary in pain and sorrow as well, for she had not felt physical pain at the birth of Christ. The *Meditationes* author explains that Mary's sorrow stems from empathy:

> But when he cries, do you think the mother will not cry? She too wept, and as she wept the Child in her lap placed His tiny hand on his mother's mouth and face as though to comfort her by His gestures ... Deeply stirred, in sorrow

and tears for her Son, she in turn consoled Him with gestures and words.[13]

This textual description vividly recalls devotional imagery, such as painted panels of the Virgin and Child featuring the child touching his mother's face or veil, which would have been known in Italy in the thirteenth and fourteenth centuries. Likewise, the image accompanying the Circumcision scene on the facing page shows the Christ Child reaching his hands towards the Virgin's face (Fig 9). The artists' instructions for this depiction specify that the Child is to touch the Virgin's mouth and face, and the image was apparently deemed powerful enough on its own that no caption was needed.[14]

The various theological nuances implied by this anomaly of text and image are the subject of a different study, but for my purposes here, it is sufficient to note that all other images I have found depicting women (although not the Virgin) circumcising the Christ Child have been in female Franciscan contexts. This detail seems to have had particular meaning for the Poor Clares, and I would argue that its importance stems in part from the reader's empathetic response to Christ's physical pain and suffering. This lesson on Christ's humanity, occurring in the Infancy section, would prepare the reader for the more intense modes of affective devotion prescribed in the Passion narratives to come. The Circumcision narrative is thus an important example of the way the Paris manuscript's imagery is uniquely and specifically shaped for a Clarissan audience.

Another aspect of the Paris manuscript targeting a female Franciscan audience is its presentation of the Virgin. She is the primary role model for the reader not only as an example of monastic life, but as a paradigm of Franciscan charity. A number of

---

[12]   *Meditations*, 43.
[13]   *Meditations*, 44.
[14]   *Meditations*, 44.

images show the Virgin in various acts of charitable giving: while enclosed at the temple as a young girl, she gives her bread away to the poor, and, later, scorning the gifts of the Magi as against poverty, she also immediately donates them (Fig 10). The Virgin is also made out to be the primary bread-winner when the Holy Family is in exile in Egypt, and must work to have the means to survive. Though Joseph is also shown working in one image, more images depict Mary as the key wage earner of the household, a presentation that is consistent with Joseph's portrayal as "old" and essentially a recipient of the Virgin's charity, in the text. Her evident devotion to poverty and her diligence in work mark her as a relevant role model for a female Franciscan reader.

The Snite *Meditationes*

By contrast, the Snite manuscript presents the Infancy of Christ as a lesson on familial duty and family propriety, without any obvious visual references to poverty. More importantly, Joseph is portrayed quite differently than in the Paris manscript, and functions, as much as if not more than the Virgin, as a model for the reader. But before analyzing the Snite images in depth, I want to point out how different this manuscript is in general. The Snite manuscript is traditional in its use of fine parchment and gold leaf, techniques more typical of luxury book production in Trecento Italy. The liberal use of expensive blue and red pigments, and the careful detailing seen for example in the gold-leaf patterning used to adorn the background of each miniature, for example, attest to the care lavished in its creation. The layout of the Snite manuscript is also much more conservative. On each page containing an illustration, the miniature is neatly confined to the portion of the page just above the chapter the image illustrates. In the line just above or just below each miniature, a rubric and an historiated initial introduce the text to which the image corresponds. Although as in the Paris manuscript, the miniatures do sometimes occur in the middle of textual passages, they always occur at the beginning of the chapter in question, and so are less intrusive in terms of the flow of text. This placement of text and image in the Snite manuscript is consistent with that of other types of manuscripts produced in Trecento Bologna, including law manuscripts. In reading the Snite manuscript, a reader would view the pictures as a prelude to the textual passage. Thus, the images, while also probably intended as aids to visualization as in the Paris manuscript, offer far less scope and detail for the devotional imagination.

As I mentioned previously, the Snite manuscript is the shorter version of the *Meditationes* text, and it has a more limited pictorial program; indeed the entire image cycle in the Snite manuscript is only equal to the number of images in the Infancy section of the Paris manuscript. Most of the scenes chosen for illustration are those found in other pictorial life of Christ cycles, and many of these correspond to the liturgical calendar. Thirteen images out of the total of forty-eight in the Snite manuscript illustrate the Infancy cycle, and most of these are standard, such as the Presentation of the Virgin in the Temple, the Annunciation, Visitation, Nativity, Annunciation to the Shepherds, Adoration of the Magi, Circumcision, Presentation in the Temple, and Flight into Egypt.

The Snite manuscript is remarkable, however, in terms of certain choices made in the image program. The common subject of the marriage of the Virgin is not depicted, while the more rare image of Joseph pondering whether he should leave the Virgin when he learns of her pregnancy is included, as well as the Bathing of the Christ Child and a scene showing the Holy Family renting a house during return from the Flight into Egypt.

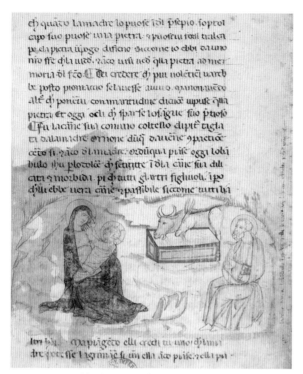

Fig 9. Paris, Bibliothèque Nationale Ms. Ital. folio 25 recto

Fig 10. Paris, Bibliothèque Nationale Ms. Ital. folio 30 verso

Fig 11. Notre Dame, Snite Museum of Art 85.25, folio 12 recto

Fig 12. Notre Dame, Snite Museum of Art 85.25, folio 10 verso

All three of these atypical scenes emphasize Joseph, and it is this presentation of Joseph that is one of the most remarkable and telling aspects of the illustration sequence. The *Meditationes* text praises Joseph frequently, but the images in the Snite manuscript emphasize him even more; throughout the Infancy cycle, he is as present and as central to the images as the Virgin.[15] Whereas in the Paris manuscript Joseph plays an important role but is often shown off to the side, relatively inactive or aloof as in many Trecento depictions of him, the Snite manuscript allows him center stage in many compositions. One example is this image of Joseph thinking about leaving Mary but then being reassured by an angel in a dream, a selection that offers a pointed lesson on Joseph's integrity, propriety, and his obedience to God (Fig 11).

Another example is the Visitation image, (Fig 12) a scene that more typically features only the Virgin and Elizabeth, where Joseph stands front and center.[16] The repeated image of Joseph is significant because, as Dianne Phillips has convincingly argued, his costume is distinctive from that of the other Biblical figures shown.[17] Rather than wearing typical and generalized "holy figure" robes, he wears a gray tunic with an elbow-length capelet and a jaunty hat trimmed in luxurious black fur. This garb is contemporary fourteenth-century dress typical of a prominent urban layman, perhaps a merchant or other professional. The gray color may be, as Phillips suggests, a particular concession to his humility and his piety, but the other details of his costume make clear that he is not a member of a religious order. This marked presentation of Joseph as a contemporary layman is perhaps intended to offer a figure the lay male patron depicted in the frontispiece to the manuscript could identify with.

Throughout the Infancy sequence, Joseph continues to be emphasized and presented as the proper *paterfamilias* in the Holy Family. He is especially attentive during the Nativity sequence, reverently adoring the Christ Child after the birth and during his first bath, which is often interpreted as an event revealing the truth of the Incarnation (Fig 13). In stark contrast to the unusual, highly emotional scene of the Circumcision in the Paris manuscript, the Snite Circumcision shows the event taking place in public at the temple, with Joseph holding the child while the operation is performed by a male mohel (Fig 14). His prominence here is remarkable because he is not even mentioned in the chapter on Circumcision in the *Meditationes*. His presence at the Circumcision is implied, however, because it was at the Circumcision that Jesus was named, a task assigned to Joseph, according to Matthew's gospel.[18] Joseph's prominence in this scene in the Snite manuscript indicates his leadership in the family and his proper role as head of household, a role the male book owner might also have played in his own family.

The presence of Joseph is likewise asserted in the Annunciation to the Shepherds and Adoration of the Magi miniatures (Fig 15), where Joseph and Mary are presented together, as a visual unit, a compositional departure from most Trecento images, where he sits apart from Mary, often with his head in his hands, pondering the mystery before him, as in the Paris manuscript. Also a departure from the Paris manuscript are the images of the Flight into

[15] Phillips, "The *Meditations*", 248-54.
[16] The standard visitation iconography features Mary and Elizabeth alone, but ital. 115 (folio 13v) and CCC 410 (folio 10r) feature Joseph and Zaccarias also, whereas Snite 85.25 has Joseph at the center of the composition with three male figures behind him (folio 10v).
[17] Phillips, "The *Meditations*", 237ff, points to the cult of Joseph as it was developed in Trecento Bologna. Joseph has also been seen as both a positive and, at times, a negative model in other contexts; see Pamela Sheingorn, "Joseph the Carpenter's Failure at Familial Discipline", in *Insights and Interpretations: Studies in Celebrations of the Eighty-Fifth Anniversary of the Index of Christian Art*, ed. Colum Hourihane (Princeton: Princeton University Press, 2002), 156-67.
[18] Matthew 1:25.

Fig 13. Notre Dame, Snite Museum of Art 85.25, folio 15 recto

Fig 14. Notre Dame, Snite Museum of Art 85.25, folio 18 recto

Egypt, where a male figure traveling with the Virgin, Christ, and Joseph is included, perhaps intended to be one of his sons, as in other examples of this scene from the period (Fig 16).[19] The inclusion of this figure reminds the reader again of Joseph's role as proper caretaker of his family, providing for and protecting them along their journey.[20]

The particular depiction of Joseph in these images points to concerns with which a male, married patron in medieval Bologna may have identified strongly in his own role in the family and community. Consistent with this pictorial emphasis is a unique passage in the text of the Snite manuscript digressing from the *Meditationes*' description of the Holy Family's journey into Jerusalem. This passage instructs the reader as to what to do when visiting a city: first, one is to visit a church, and then upon returning to your own town, immediately visit your oratory.[21] The Snite manuscript's text and image program thus exhibits an awareness of its lay patron's lifestyle, and seeks to help a male patron in particular identify personally with the piety of the Holy Family as described in the *Meditationes*.

Conclusion: Patronage and Identity

As these images attest, Dianne Phillips is absolutely correct in her assertion that the Snite miniatures and text contain "concessions to male concerns," and the manuscript thus stands in many ways in stark contrast to the Paris manuscript. But

I would take Phillips' argument a step further to suggest instead that the manuscript reflects *familial* concerns, and specifically those of a prosperous urban family in medieval Bologna. In many of the scenes where Joseph is emphasized, visual importance is placed not only on Joseph himself but on him as Mary's chaste partner, Christ's foster father, and ideal *paterfamilias*; thus on the entire Holy Family.[22] The way the Virgin is portrayed also hints at the concerns of the other probable patron of the Snite manscript: a laywoman. Emphasis on the role women play in the education of their children and their importance in the domestic sphere can be seen in several of the Snite miniatures. In the scene of the Virgin's Presentation in the Temple, for example, her mother Anna is shown very actively guiding her daughter toward the priests, while Mary's father Joachim stands behind Anna, barely noticeable in the composition (Fig 17). This image is quite different from the more common iconography of the scene, which shows the Virgin ascending a flight of steps to the Temple as a sign of her willingness to enter it, while her parents look on. Because a prosperous laywoman in medieval Bologna most likely was entrusted with her family's spiritual instruction and care in their home, perhaps expected to teach her children to read or at least to develop a certain level of "devotional literacy," the emphasis on Anna's similar role is telling.[23]

---

[19]   The Protoevangelium of James mentions Joseph's sons by a former marriage, and one or two of them are depicted in many Trecento Italian scenes of the flight into Egypt, including the Arena Chapel. For the apocryphal text see James, *The Life of Mary and the Birth of Jesus: the Ancient Infancy Gospel of James*, ed. and trans. Ronald Hock (Berkeley: Ulysses Press, 1997), 51.

[20]   On the iconography of Joseph and late-Medieval exegetical traditions, see Cynthia Hahn, 'Joseph as Ambrose's "Artisan of the Soul", in the Holy Family in Egypt by Albrecht Dürer', *Zeitschrift für Kunstgeschichte* 47:4 (1984): 515-22. See also Paul Payan, *Joseph: Une image de la paternité dans l'Occident medieval* (Paris: Aubier, 2006).

[21]   Dianne Phillips, "The Illustration of the *Meditations on the Life of Christ*: A Study of an Illuminated Fourteenth-Century Italian Manuscript at the University of Notre Dame" (unpublished doctoral dissertation proposal, Yale University, n.d.), 4.

[22]   On the holy family unit as a marriage model for devout laypeople in the late Middle Ages, see Cynthia Hahn, "'Joseph Will Perfect, Mary Enlighten, and Jesus Save Thee," The Holy Family As Marriage Model in the Mérode Triptych,' *Art Bulletin* 68:1 (1986): 54-66.

[23]   On the concept of 'devotional literacy,' see Margaret Aston, "Devotional Literacy," in *Lollards and Reformers: Images and Literacy in Late Medieval Religion* (London: Hambledon, 1984), 101-33. On Anna as teacher to Mary as a role model for literate laywomen, see Pamela Sheingorn, "'The Wise Mother": The Image of St Anne Teaching the Virgin Mary,' *Gesta* 32:1 (1993): 69-80, reprinted in *Gendering the Master Narrative: Women and Power in the Middle Ages*, eds. Mary C. Erler and Maryanne Kowaleski (Ithaca and London: Cornell University Press, 2003), 105-34.

Fig 15. Notre Dame, Snite Museum of Art 85.25, folio 20 recto

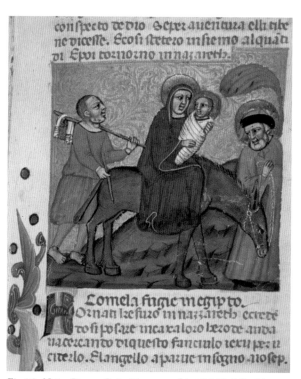

Fig 16. Notre Dame, Snite Museum of Art 85.25, folio 26 recto

Fig 17. Notre Dame, Snite Museum of Art 85.25, folio 5 verso

It is also significant that the Virgin is presented multiple times reading, another marker of her piety and her education. The right half of the same miniature shows Mary studiously enclosed at the temple, reading (Fig 17). This image differs from her depiction contained in the Paris manuscript, where she is repeatedly shown working alongside companions, and much more often kneeling in prayer, but not herself reading a book. A companion sits with her, recalling the companions in the Paris manuscript, but in this instance, the companion wears distinctly secular dress, and also seems to be adoring the reading Virgin by her side. I would suggest that, similarly to the situation suggested by the Paris manuscript, she may be intended as a figure of identification for the book's female reader. The two companion figures shown in the scene of Joseph's dilemma, both shown with hands clasped as if in prayer and one gazing at Mary, perhaps also functioned the same way, allowing the female book owner to imaginatively enter her world as prescribed in the *Meditationes* text. The Snite manuscript's imagery thus suggests multivalent readings and an intentional shaping of its pictorial program for more than one reader with different devotional interests.

These companion figures and also the unique presentation of Joseph in the Snite manuscript were probably intended to aid the devotional imagination of the book's owners in the same way that the companions and the presentation of Mary in the Paris manuscript did for its owners. However, a few key differences reveal the clearly different lifestyles and devotional interests of the owners of these two books. The Paris manuscript's emphasis on Franciscan poverty, for example, is entirely absent in the miniatures of the Snite manuscript. Instead of portraying the dire poverty of the Holy Family and their generosity to the poor, the Holy Family's propriety in ritual and societal function is highlighted. And while the Snite manuscript has a particular, and very vivid urging of its readers to participate emotionally in the narratives, the Snite manuscript instead emphasizes proper outward action and duty. Such a dichotomy can be explained in part based on the vocational differences between the lay owners of the Snite manuscript, whose concerns were perhaps more worldly and that of the *vita activa*, while the Clarissan readers of the Paris book sought the *vita contemplativa*, taught to desire introspection and an intense inward experience of the life of Christ. The creators of the Snite manuscript, like those who planned the Paris manuscript, thus seem to have been acutely aware of the lifestyles of those commisioning the book, and were equally interested in providing visual and textual devices that allowed readers to make the leap from the page to their own devotional imaginations.

The very different interpretations in word and image in the Paris and Snite manuscripts illustrate how far reaching the practice of piety prescribed by the *Meditationes* was even in its earliest incarnations. The text had almost immediate appeal for lay audiences, male and female, and it could be easily adapted for different contexts; as such it might be thought of not as a text but as a template designed to be read differently by different audiences. A large part of the appeal of the *Meditationes* comes from its use of affective devotional vignettes and anecdotal details that provided a means for readers to identify with Christ and his human sufferings. Scholars have long assigned credit to the Franciscans for developing such a device, although the recent study by Sarah McNamer cited above argues that women, rather than the Franciscans, invented medieval affective compassion literature, including the core text of the *Meditationes*.[24] Regardless of its origins the *Meditationes* as it is presented in the fourteenth-century manuscripts I have analyzed here certainly depends on modes of devotion the Franciscans promoted. The Franciscans capitalized on the late-medieval cultural longing for a new, more personal experience of Christ's life, one all the more real to them as it was made directly relevant to their own lives, as in the diverse image programs of these manuscripts. We should perhaps then think of the *Meditationes* not as static *inspiratore* for late medieval Christian iconography, but as fuel for artistic and devotional imaginations shaped by a new worldview centered on a very human Christ and Mary, whose experiences could be seen in the light of each life lived on earth.

---

[24] McNamer, *Affective Meditation*, 86-115.

THE EYES HAVE IT: THE QUESTION OF REDEMPTIVE VISION IN THE *VERGER DE SOULAS* (PARIS, BIBLIOTHÉQUE NATIONALE DE FRANCE, MS fr. 9220)[1]

Lynn Ransom

he role of imagery in medieval devotional practice is an exceptionally rich area for study, especially in regard to medieval theories of vision, but it can be difficult to show a precise correlation between what is written about the role of imagery in devotion and the actual production of devotional art. Medieval artists did not write in theoretical terms about the art they produced, and those writings that do address the use and contemplation of art are usually written by theologians and mystics who likely did not produce art themselves.[2] There are, however, examples in medieval art that clearly demonstrate instances of artists and theologians working together. My study of the illumination program of one manuscript in particular has drawn me into this line of inquiry as it provides a compelling example of such collaboration. The iconography of the program manifests a profound reliance on specifically Franciscan approaches to the devotional image as they existed in the late thirteenth century. It is the closest that I have come to seeing theological speculation on the role of imagery in devotion and actual craft intersect on the same page, and I would propose that it is no coincidence that this intersection occurs in a book designed specifically for Franciscan devotional practice.

The manuscript in question is an unusual picture book produced at the end of the thirteenth century, as I have argued elsewhere, by a Franciscan for a lay person under his spiritual care.[3] Now in the Bibliothèque nationale de France under the shelfmark MS fr. 9220, the manuscript is known as the *Verger de soulas*, or "Orchard of Solace," from an inscription on the first folio. To the best of my knowledge, it is utterly unique in its contents, conception, and design. It is a large volume, roughly the length of a forearm, and comprises sixteen folios containing eight pairs of facing illuminated

---

[1]   Portions of this essay have already been published previously; see Lynn Ransom, "The Bernardian Roots of Bonaventure's *Lignum vitae*: Visual Evidence from the *Verger de soulas*," *Ikon* 1 (2008): 133-42. I would like to thank Professor Marina Vicelja for giving permission to republish these portions here.

[2]   For an excellent summary of the problems in interpreting the role of imagery in medieval art, see Lawrence J. Duggan, "Was Art Really the 'Book of the Illiterate'?," *Word & Image* 5 (1989): 227-51.

[3]   My argument for a Franciscan designer is more fully laid out in a previous essay; see Lynn Ransom, "Innovation and Identity: A Franciscan Program of Illumination in the *Verger de soulas* (Paris, Bibliothèque nationale de France, MS fr. 9220)", in *Insights and Interpretations: Studies in Celebration of the Eighty-fifth Anniversary of the Index of Christian Art*, ed. Colum Hourihane (Princeton, NJ: Princeton University Press, 2002).

pages with blank openings between each pair.[4] With one exception, all of these illuminations are full-page miniatures. The exception is a uniquely illustrated hymn, which will be discussed in more detail below.

The *Verger de soulas* belongs to a group of similar diagrammatic collections that have been identified and given the name "*Speculum theologie*," based on an inscription found in some of the manuscripts. Nearly all copies of the *Speculum theologie* are found in manuals for preaching and confession and are not illustrated or illuminated; most are scribal productions lacking any aesthetic refinement.[5] Unfortunately, no documentary evidence survives to give any indication of the circumstances of production of the *Verger de soulas*, though it was likely not intended for a clerical audience given the extent and opulence of its illumination and other reasons discussed below.

Through its complicated play of diagrammatic text and imagery, the *Verger de soulas* offered its medieval reader a compelling program of catechetical instruction and a manual for penitential devotion in the context of Franciscan spirituality. Though a full explanation of the program is beyond the scope of this essay, it will suffice here to focus on the illustrated hymn and one of the full-page miniatures containing the diagram known as the *Lignum vitae* for the purpose of defining this context (Fig 1 and 2). In both the hymn and the *Lignum vitae*, layers of iconography produce guided narrative meditations on the events of

Christ's life. In these meditations, the reader undertakes a devotional practice in which seeing the suffering Christ—first on the page and then in the mind—begins a process of compassionate devotion. Through this process, the penitent imaginatively and actively participates in Christ's pain and humiliations. He or she co-suffers with Christ in order to attain conformity with him because it is only through utter conformity, and therefore true understanding of his suffering, that the soul can find redemption as the example of St. Francis so aptly demonstrated for the believer.

That imagery played an important role in Franciscan devotional practice is commonly accepted. Those who study Franciscan devotional literature consistently remark on the emphatic visual quality of the order's meditative practice.[6] Indeed, Franciscan devotional writings such as the well-known *Meditationes vitae Christi* are often credited with the explosion of devotional narrative art seen in the last centuries of the Middle Ages. But as William Cook observed in his introductory essay to this volume, we do not really know precisely why narrative becomes the conduit for religious experience in much of Franciscan devotional literature and art. Nor do we yet fully understand the relationship between the written words that evoke mental images and the artifactual images that sometimes accompany them. The two miniatures under discussion here, however, provide some insight. In both, the intersection of written word and painted image demonstrate how at least one creative Franciscan

---

[4] Two of these otherwise blank openings do contain texts: the first opening, fols. 2v-3r contain French verses on the Throne of Wisdom, the subject of the preceding miniature of fol. 2r; the second opening, fols. 6v-7r contain French verses on the Twelve Pains of Hell, which are depicted in the following opening. Distinct ruling patterns for each text, ruled to ensure that each text fits into the space of the opening, indicate that both texts were additions to the manuscript rather than part of its original design.

[5] The term "copy" is used loosely here: no two examples of the *Speculum theologie* are alike in content, order, or number of diagrams. In addition to the *Verger de soulas*, there are three other illuminated copies. Two are in the Howard Psalter and the Psalter of Robert de Lisle, which are bound together as London, British Library, MS Arundel I & II. The third is in Paris, Bibliothèque de l'Arsenal, MS 1037. The *Speculum theologie* group was first identified by Lucy Freeman Sandler in *The Psalter of Robert de Lisle in the British Library* (London: Harvey Miller, 1983, rev. ed. 1999). For a complete list of known copies, see the appendix to the revised edition.

[6] For a discussion of imagery in Franciscan spirituality, see David L. Jeffrey, *Early English Lyric and Franciscan Spirituality* (Lincoln, NB: University of Nebraska Press, 1975), 83-117; and Denise Despres, *Ghostly Sights: Visual Meditation in Late Medieval Literature* (Norman, OK: University of Oklahoma Press, 1989), esp. 19-51.

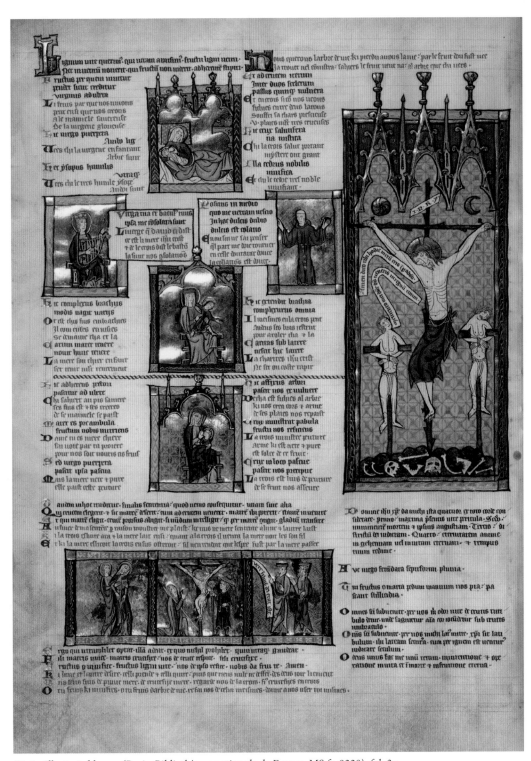

Fig 1. *Illustrated hymn (Paris, Bibliothèque nationale de France, MS fr. 9220), fol. 3v.*

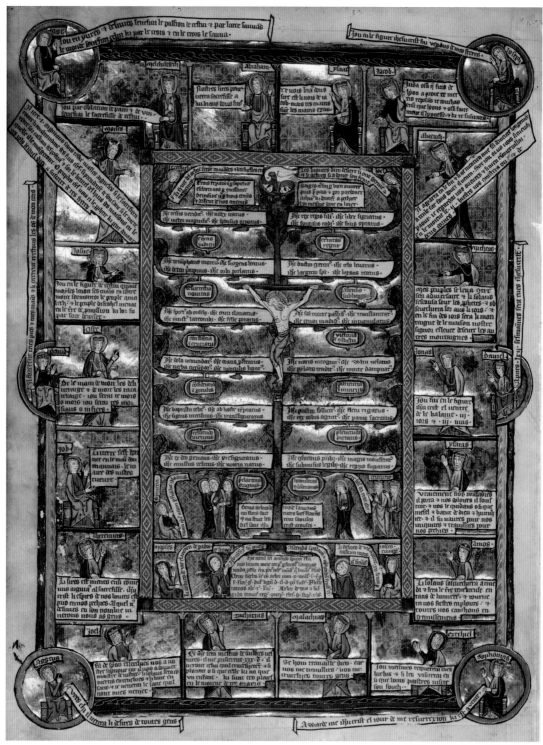

Fig 2. Lignum vitae (Paris, Bibliothèque nationale de France, MS fr. 9220), fol. 9v.

viewed the artifactual image as fundamental to the process of the soul's redemption. His program is a highly sophisticated interpretation of his order's understanding of the power of both visualization and vision in the process of redemption.

First, however, it will be necessary to outline briefly the argument that the program was designed by a Franciscan for a lay person under his spiritual care. The argument is based primarily on linguistic evidence: there is a judicious use of the vernacular against the standard Latin of many of the diagrams. The diagrams are mostly catechetical in content; however, at any point where the Latin did not reflect basic doctrine that any Christian would know, a French translation was provided alongside the Latin text. For example, the diagrams of the Trees of Virtues and Vices, the Tables of the 12 Articles of Faith, 10 Commandments and the 7 Acts of the Passion—all taken from basic catechetical instruction—have only Latin inscriptions. Another diagram known as the *Arbor amoris*, an exposition on divine love, only circulated in a monastic context prior to the *Verger de soulas*. Its Latin inscriptions are therefore accompanied by French ones in order to make the difficult Latin comprehensible.[7] The two leaves under discussion, the illustrated hymn and the *Lignum vitae*, provide other examples of the use of French as translation for unfamiliar Latin or as explanatory text as in the words "spoken" to the reader by the prophets and Old Testament figures surrounding the *Lignum vitae*.

Turning to the identity of the designer, the argument for a Franciscan affiliation is based largely on iconographic evidence. The manuscript contains two pictorial signatures of the order in the form of "portraits" of Franciscans, both of which appear in the illustrated hymn and the *Lignum vitae*. In the illustrated hymn, the small miniature forming the right arm of the cross composed by the five miniatures on the left of the page contains a friar, identified as Franciscan by his habit. In the *Lignum vitae*, St. Francis, the founder of the order, appears in the register below the base of the Crucifixion (Fig. 3).

These signatures do not *de facto* prove that the manuscript was designed by a Franciscan, but other elements teased out of an examination of these two folios come straight out of the spiritual aims for the Order as expressed in the writings of St. Bonaventure. His many devotional and theological writings were fundamental in shaping Franciscan spiritual practice. In them, one finds the basis for the type of affective devotion to the humanity and Passion of Christ as a result of which the soul is led to Christ by the emotions and the senses.[8] One also finds there the significance of living the penitential life in which conformity to Christ's suffering grants the reward of redemption. This concept is expressed most fully in St. Francis's stigmatization, the reward for his utter conformity to Christ. Bonaventure's writings also speak to a theology of the devotional imagination in which the visualization of Christ's suffering and humanity lead to understanding and knowing and, from there, redemption.[9] This theology is grounded in the classical understanding of vision and imagination as expressed in the fourth century by St. Augustine. In his *De Genesi ad litteram*, Augustine classified vision into three categories with the lowest being corporeal vision, the sight of the eyes; the next highest being spiritual

---

7   For a discussion of the history and context of this diagram, see Lynn Ransom, "Cultivating the Orchard: A Franciscan Program of Devotion and Penance in the *Verger de soulas* (Paris, Bibliothèque nationale de France, fr. 9220)" (Ph.D. diss., University of Texas at Austin, 2001), 167-9.

8   Bonaventure, *Opera Omnia*, ed. Collegium S. Bonaventurae, 10 vols (Quarracchi: Collegium S. Bonaventurae, 1882-1902).

9   For a thorough examination of the role of imagination in late medieval theology and literature, see Michelle Karnes, *Imagination, Meditation, and Cognition in the Middle Ages* (Chicago: University of Chicago Press, 2010). In Chapters 2 and 3, Karnes examines, in particular, Bonaventure's understanding and use of imagination as the basis for her argument that the theory of imagination as expressed in his theological and devotional writings was fundamental to shaping the experience and practice of late medieval narrative devotions on the life of Christ.

Fig 3. Lignum vitae (Paris, Bibliothèque nationale de France, MS fr. 9220), fol. 9v, detail.

vision, the vision of things recalled by memory or of things imagined in the mind's eye; and finally intellectual vision, the imageless vision of rational thought.[10] His schema of vision and cognition held throughout the Middle Ages and in itself proposed a theology of vision. If the natural, hence suspect, world of the senses was perceivable by the lowest form of vision, the highest level perceived the imageless vision of the divine. As did many theologians before him, Bonaventure adhered to this basic concept, but he worked it into a devotional science in which the corporal image became the first step in accessing the vision of imageless divinity, which he equated to spiritual union with God. For Bonaventure, sight was the most important sense in leading the devotee to God because the natural world presented the vestiges of divine reality. From this level, one could ascend through understanding to direct knowledge of Divine Being. This idea is most clearly laid out in his treatise *Itinerarium mentis in Deum* in which the 'mind' is understood to be the soul.[11] In this treatise, Bonaventure describes six stages of illumination divided into three pairs, following Augustine's Trinitarian framework. In the first two stages, the soul is purged of distracting visions and thoughts by contemplating God in the sense world and his image stamped on a person's sensual perceptions. Then, in the next two steps the soul is "illuminated" by the contemplation of the image of God in one's mind, in both its natural and reformed states. Finally, the soul is united with God through the contemplation of his abstract essence and goodness above one's mind.

In reconciling Bonaventure's cognitive theology with devotional art, one has first to admit that in his system the image in question is not an artifactual one. When Bonaventure writes about images in this context, he is not referring to what we call art but what is seen through the eyes in the natural world or images that are seen by the mind's eye. When he writes about artifactual religious art, which he does in his Commentary on Peter Lombard's *Sentences*, he defends religious imagery on three points: first, religious art instructs those who cannot read, which applies to the laity; secondly, it arouses the emotions which lead to compassion, "for emotion is aroused more by what is seen than by what is heard," and finally, it aids the memory in recollection because "those things that are heard, fall into oblivion more easily than those things which are seen."[12]

Bonaventure's attitude to the religious, artifactual image as it is expressed here has too often been used to draw a rather simplistic conclusion about the role of art in devotional practice as opposed to the role of image in meditation: whereas the cognitive image is part of the apparatus of divine contemplation, religious art is a mere prop for assisting the illiterate and aiding memory. A close reading of the illustrated hymn and miniature of the *Lignum vitae* in the *Verger de soulas*, however, presents a more complicated view of how religious art was used to mediate between the world of sense perception and the contemplation of the imageless divine.

The illustrated hymn reads like an introduction to the process of redemptive seeing that will be more fully developed in the *Lignum vitae*. The premise of the hymn is deceptively simple as is the relationship between the text and the miniatures.

---

10   For a fuller discussion of Augustine's theory of vision and its relation to later medieval thought, see Sixten Ringbom, "Devotional Images and Imaginative Devotions: Notes on the Place of Art in Late Medieval Private Piety," *Gazette des Beaux-Artes* 73 (1969): 162-3.

11   For a revised and expanded edition and translation of this text, see St. Bonaventure, *Itinerarium mentis in Deum*, ed. and trans. Philotheus Boehner, O.F.M., and Zachary Hayes, O.F.M., in *Works of St. Bonaventure*, II (Saint Bonaventure, NY: Franciscan Institute Publications, 2002).

12   See Bonaventure, *Commentarii in IV libros Sententiarum*, lib. III, dist. IX, art. I, quaest. II, concl., in vol. 3 of *Opera omnia* (Quarrachi: Collegium S. Bonaventurae, 1882-1902), 203; these statements are cited and discussed in Duggan, "Was Art Really the 'Book of the Illiterate'?," 232.

The page is really an exquisitely choreographed dance between word and image. The verses, written in Latin in black ink with French translations in red ink, comprise the hymn to the Holy Cross and the Virgin, which has been attributed to Franciscan authorship.[13] The hymn draws a parallel between the Virgin as the *lignum* that bears the fruit of the Christ Child and the *lignum* to which Christ in his agony is affixed. She is portrayed as a participant in the redemption of mankind because, as the hymn explains, it is through her breasts that the Christ Child was nourished for us, just as Christ's blood nourishes us in return. The imagery on this folio confirms and demonstrates the parallel suggested in the hymn.

The first two verses of the hymn begin in the first column and then are translated into French in the second column. Translated, they read: *We desire the tree of life/ we who have lost life because of the fruit of the forbidden tree / But one will not recognize what one finds unless s/he sees the fruit clinging to the branch.* The fruit is Christ and the Tree of Life is the Cross, as depicted in the Crucifixion where the cross is made of green branches in reference to the legend of the True Cross according to which the wood was said to be made from the Tree of Life that grew in the Garden of Eden.

At this point the verses literally and thematically bifurcate to begin a comparison of the Virgin's role in the redemption of mankind with Christ's role. The next two verses set forth the comparison. Verse 3—inscribed to the left of the miniature depicting the Nativity with the Virgin suckling the Christ Child—reads: *The fruit, thanks to which we have life, /Hangs, we believe, at the breast of the Virgin.* Verse 4—to the right—reads: *And on the cross again between criminals, having suffered five wounds.* Here, the author alludes to the comparison between the Virgin and the cross. The comparison is then explicitly stated in the next two verses.

Unlike the previous two verses, both verse 5 and verse 6 start to the left of the Nativity scene and continue on the other side, thus dividing the text of the verses across the miniature. In verse 5, this division serves a metaphorical purpose. It begins: *Here is the child-bearing Virgin* (hic virgo puerpera), and then continues with the next to the right of the miniature: *Here is the healing cross* (hic crux salutifera). Then, the third line of the verse—which reads *Both are the mystical trees/wood* (Ambo ligna mistica)—is divided so that it frames the Nativity. Not coincidentally, the division occurs within the word *ligna* (wood). Not only does it make sense metrically, but it also literally frames the image of the Virgin within the word signifying what the Virgin represents—the *lignum*. In verse 6, the text is again divided in the miniature, but this time it is done so without the metaphorical implications of the previous verse.

The following verses and the two miniatures continue the choreography. Set apart from the columnar flow of the others, these verses are inscribed in expanded scrolls signifying direct speech to the reader. The verse inscribed on the left scroll is actually not from the hymn but is taken from the Psalms. David, identified by his harp, holds the scroll inscribed with Psalm 22:4: *Thy rod and thy staff have comforted me.* Whereas the red text of the other verses indicates a translation of the preceding line, here the psalm is not translated by the red text but gives commentary explaining that the rod is the Virgin and the staff is the cross.

The verses inscribed on the second scroll, held by the Franciscan in the center of the page, return us to the hymn. These are verses 7-8. Scrolls were a common iconographic device used to signify speech, and here the device is used to indicate the friar's speech to the reader. Again, as in verse 5, the placement of the verses is critical to the interpretation of the page. The verses begin: *Placed in the*

---

[13]   *Analecta hymnica*, vol. 54, 203, where Franciscan authorship is ascribed. See Appendix for transcription.

middle, I do not know where to turn / In this sweet moment of doubt, sweet is the comparison. The choice, the moment of doubt, for this friar is which to choose: the Virgin or Christ? The choice here is not only a reference to the theme of the text, but also to the visual presence of the friar, speaking to the reader through the scroll as he encourages the reader to see that the choice is there on the page.

The friar's position on the page is important. Centrally located, he stands between the cross of the Crucifixion scene on the right and the three miniatures of the Virgin with the Christ Child, whose alignment forms the vertical axis of the cross completed by the horizontal axis formed by the miniatures depicting David and the friar. The friar becomes a bridge, as it were, between the parallel of the Virgin and the cross of the Crucifixion, and through his direct address to the reader, he becomes a bridge between the reader and the meditations visualized on the page.

Verses 9-18 continue the hymn with verses comparing the nurturing attributes of the Virgin, underscored in the two miniatures of the Virgin and Child to those of the crucified Christ. Then, finally, verses 19-26 are written in single lines and frame a more fully conceived Crucifixion scene presented in three registers. On the left, the evangelist John supports the swooning Virgin, whose heart is pierced by a sword. This iconography is known as the Sword of Compassion. It developed from Simeon's prophecy during Christ's presentation in the temple that "a sword will also pierce the Soul of the Virgin" (Luke 2:35). The image of a sword piercing the Virgin's breast became popular in the twelfth and thirteenth centuries as an example of the doctrine of the *compassio*, literally translated as "co-suffering." The Virgin thus became the co-sufferer with Christ and the perfect model for compassionate devotion.[14] In the central register, the crucified Christ is flanked by Longinus and Stephaton. On the right, the Centurion, with another figure, holds a scroll inscribed *Vere filius dei erat iste* (Matthew 27:54), which signifies his conversion brought about by the act of witnessing, or more emphatically seeing, Christ's death.

The text concludes the comparison by stating in verses 19-22: *At the end, the essential meaning is revealed in this, that namely no one seeks one to the exclusion of the other. Whoever chooses to follow the cross and thus to disregard the mother, when they come to the cross, they will be able to find the mother standing there. And who chooses the mother completely rejects the cross if they do not yet understand that it happens that the sword also passes through the mother.* The verses below the miniature explain that whatever choice is made, the reader will rejoice in both the Virgin and Christ. Finally, there is a short prayer asking Christ for his nourishment. The triptych thus offers the reader not only an example of compassionate devotion in the figure of the Virgin but also a demonstration of redemptive vision in the figure of the Centurion. With this demonstration together with the larger Crucifixion above, the reader is thus able to realize the promise set forth at the beginning of the hymn: *We desire the tree of life / we who have lost life because of the fruit of the forbidden tree / But if anyone finds it (the tree of life), he will not know it unless he sees the fruit clinging to the branch.*

This hymn thus introduces the notion of redemptive vision to the reader, that through seeing the Fruit hanging from the cross, he or she is somehow transformed and in the process conformed to Christ. How vision should be employed in this process continues to be explored in the miniature containing the illustrated *Lignum vitae* diagram,

---

14   See C. Schuler, "The Sword of Compassion: Images of the Sorrowing Virgin in Late Medieval and Renaissance Art" (Ph.D. diss., Columbia University, 1987), esp. 28-67. Though Gospel accounts identify the instrument as a "lance," medieval authors and artists identified it as "gladius," or "sword."

which in the original order occurred on the next opening of illuminated pages following the opening with the illustrated hymn.[15] Unlike the unique example of the illustrated hymn, the *Lignum vitae* diagram is more common. It appears in manuscripts as well as in wall and panel paintings, frequently in Italian art, from the middle of the thirteenth century through the fourteenth.[16] The example in *Verger de soulas*, however, stands apart from many others in its density of secondary iconographic and textual detail. As with other diagrams in this picture book, the designer overlaid the diagram with an elaborate iconographic scheme, including the historical narrative of the Crucifixion with witnesses from the Biblical past as well as the more contemporary witnesses of St. Francis and St. Bernard. The iconographic association of the Crucifixion with the *Lignum vitae* is typical and is, in fact, made in other instances of the diagram in several other *Speculum theologie* manuscripts. Nor is the inclusion of St. Francis unusual.[17] St. Bernard's presence, however, is unique and, at first thought, unexpected. Yet, it proves to be one of the most provocative iconographic additions in the manuscript for the implications it bears on the role of image devotion in Franciscan devotional practice.

Before continuing with this point, it would be useful to describe more fully the content of the *Lignum vitae* in general and its treatment in the *Verger de soulas* in particular. The diagram is based on a devotional meditation composed by Bonaventure sometime before his death in 1274. Bonaventure construes a systematic meditation on the life of Christ around the form of a tree. He begins the meditation by asking his reader to picture in his mind a tree (*Describe igitur in spiritu mentis tuae arborem*) and explains:

> Since imagination aids understanding, I have arranged in the form of an imaginary tree the few items I have collected from among many, and have ordered and disposed them in such a way that in the first or lower branches, the savior's origin and life are described; in the middle his passion; and in the top, his glorification. In the first group of branches there are four stanzas placed opposite each other; so, also in the second and third group of branches. From each of these branches hangs a single protuberance in the likeness of a fruit. So there are, as it were, twelve branches bearing twelve fruits according to the mystery of the Tree of Life.[18]

---

[15] A description of the manuscript in an inventory of the library of Philip the Bold, dated 1420, identifies the last miniature as beginning with the seventh pain of hell, which now occurs on fol. 8r. During a later rebinding of the manuscript, what was originally the last of four gatherings was misplaced, and is now the second gathering; for details, see Ransom, "The Orchard of Solace," 17-19, and Appendix A. For the inventory description, see Patrick M. de Winter, *La Bibliothèque de Philippe le Hardi, Duc de Bourgogne, 1364-1404: Étude sur les manuscrits a peintures d'une collection princière a l'époque du "style gothique international,"* in *Documents, études, et répertoires publiés par l'Institute de Recherche et d'Histoire des Texts* (Paris: Éditions du Centre National de la Recherche Scientifique, 1985), cat. no. 7, 201.

[16] On the history of the diagram, see R. Ligtenberg, "Het *Lignum vitae* van den H. Bonaventura in die ikongrafie der verrtiende eeuw," *Het Gildeboek* 11 (1928): 15-39.

[17] St. Francis can be found at the base of a *Lignum vitae* diagram in a roughly contemporary manuscript, a bible now in Berlin, Staatliche Museen, MS 78 E 2, fol. 1. Other examples can be found more commonly in Italian painting. Two well-known examples are a panel painting featuring the *Lignum vitae* in the Accademia in Florence and a fresco of the same theme by Taddeo Gaddi in the basilica of Santa Croce.

[18] *Et quoniam imaginatio iuvat intelligentiam, ideo quae ex multis pauca collegi in imaginaria quadam arbore sic ordinavi atque disposui, ut in prima et infima ramorum ipsius expansione Salvatoris origo describatur et vita, in medio passio, et glorificatio, in suprema. Et in prima quidem ramorum serie quatuor altrinsecus secundum alphabeti ordinem ponentur versiculi, similiter ita secunda et tertia, ex quorum quolibet instar fructus unica pullulatio pendet, ut sic sint quasi duodecim rami afferentes duodecim fructus iuxta mysterium ligni vitae.* Bonaventura, *Opusculum III. Lignum vitae. Prologus,* in *Opera omnia,* vol. 8 (Quarrachi: Collegium S. Bonaventurae, 1898), 68; trans. E. Cousins, Bonaventure (Mahwah, NJ: Paulist Press, 1978), 120.

Bonaventure divides his mentally-conceived "tree" into three stages, represented by three sets of four branches, for a total of twelve branches. These are clearly delineated in the branches of the diagrammatic tree. From each branch grows a single fruit, each of which expresses one of twelve aspects of the truth of Christ. Each fruit offers four points of meditation on that aspect of Christ's life represented by the branch. For example, the first fruit, His Distinguished Origin, begins four meditations on Christ: "Jesus generated by God," "Jesus heaven-sent," "Jesus prefigured," and "Jesus born of Mary." The second branch continues with the fruit described as the "Humility of His Mode of Life," and the points of meditation are "Jesus conformed to his forefathers" (through circumcision), "Jesus shown to the Magi," "Jesus submissive to the Law" (through the Purification of the Virgin and his Presentation in the Temple), and "Jesus exiled from his kingdom" (signified by the Flight into Egypt). The branches continue upward so that the events of Christ's life are laid out from his infancy to his public life, passion, death, and resurrection up to the Second Coming. Each stage of his life advances to the next in the boughs of the tree forming a path leading to the centerpiece of Bonaventure's meditation, the Crucified Christ, so that the reader can say in fulfillment of Bonaventure's opening words to the meditation: *Christo confixus sum cruci* ("with Christ I am crucified to the Cross"), taken from Paul's letter to the Galatians (2:19).[19]

This same passage is inscribed on Francis's scroll in the *Verger de soulas* diagram. In the miniature, Francis gazes upward to the center of the composition, the crucified Christ hanging from a cross created by the vertical stem of the diagram and a horizontal bar just below the fifth row of branches (Fig. 3). Below him are two figural groups placed in two registers at the base of the Tree, creating a narrative representation of the Crucifixion within the diagram. In the upper register of this detail, the Virgin swoons again but this time into the arms of her sisters as the sword that pierced her son's side now turns to pierce her own breast in fulfillment of Simeon's prophecy according to the medieval iconographic tradition of the sword of compassion.[20] The prophecy itself is inscribed on the scroll held by Simeon to the left. Opposite her is the Evangelist John, Christ's beloved disciple, who, weeping, raises his hand to his face. Behind him stands the Centurion who, converted upon witnessing Christ's death, proclaims for the second time in this manuscript and by way of his scroll that "Christ truly is the Son of God." In the register below are four figures, sitting or kneeling beneath the base of the cross. The two outermost figures are Moses and the Evangelist John (shown again). Their scrolls are inscribed with French texts making scriptural references to the mystical Tree of Life. The scrolls read "The Tree of Life is in the middle of paradise" (*Li arbres de vie el moien de paradis*, from Gen. 2:9) and "The Tree of Life bears twelve fruits" (*Li arbre de vie aport xii fruis*, from Rev. 22:2), respectively. Between them are two tonsured figures identified by inscriptions as Francis of Assisi, on the left, and Bernard of Clairvaux, on the right. Francis holds a scroll inscribed *Christo confixus sum cruci*, the same passage from Galatians that Bonaventure cites at the beginning of his *Lignum vitae*. Bernard's scroll contains a verse taken from Canticles 7:8, "I will go up into the tree and will take hold of the fruit thereof" (*Ascendam in palmam et apprehendam fructus eius*). Both figures flank a lengthy passage of Latin text inscribed

---

19   Bonaventure, *Opera*, vol. 8, 69.
20   The silver leaf used to depict the sword is now tarnished and thus difficult to see in the photograph.

within a rectangular box. This text is a conflation of verses taken from two hymns, the *Pange lingua gloriosi praelium certaminis* and the *Vexilla regis*.[21] Both hymns are praises to the cross and the Crucifixion, and the verses make special reference to the redemptive and salvific power of the cross.

This *Lignum vitae* diagram within which these figures and texts reside is a thoroughly Franciscan composition. The iconography of the sword of compassion and the stigmata visible in Francis' side and on his raised hand are allusions to the type of compassionate, penitential devotion that the friars preached. Given the authorship of the meditation, the Franciscan associations are to be expected. The inclusion of St. Bernard in the iconographic program, as stated earlier, is more surprising. Nowhere in his meditation does Bonaventure refer to Bernard, nor does Bernard appear in any other illustrated *Lignum vitae* diagrams. His appearance here raises two questions: 1) why is this Cistercian saint given pride of place beside the founder of the Franciscan order, and 2) what does it mean that the theologian who deplored art as a distraction to the spiritual life is shown here worshipping an image of the Crucified Christ?

The answer to the first question is fairly straightforward. Bernard's influence on Franciscan spirituality has long been recognized. Indeed, Bonaventure's method of devotion to the Crucified Christ aided by meditation on the events of Christ's life as it is laid out in the *Lignum vitae* has its roots in the teachings of Bernard who most influentially formulated the aims of the new spirituality developing in the twelfth century that would fundamentally

shape the spirituality of the later Middle Ages. This spirituality is characterized by the practice of highly emotional and affective Christocentric devotion as a means to redemption. In his theological writings, Bonaventure borrows passages from Bernard extensively and formulates his theology based on many of Bernard's arguments. This is no less true in the text of *Lignum vitae*, which was, in fact, inspired by Bernard's forty-third Sermon on the Song of Songs.[22]

The *Lignum vitae* is generally considered to be one of the most influential Gospel harmonies to provide a structured serial meditation on the life of Christ; it is also the basis of the later *Meditationes vitae Christi*. The roots of the *Lignum vitae*, however, go deep into the affective spirituality that centered on devotion to the humanity of Christ first promoted by Bernard in the twelfth century. Bonaventure's debt to Bernard, and especially to the sermon mentioned above, is easy to trace within the words of the *Lignum vitae*. Bernard's sermon parses the verse from Canticles 1:12: "A bundle of myrrh is my well-beloved unto me. He shall lie between my breasts" (*Fasciculus myrrhae dilectus meus mihi, inter ubera mea commorabitur*).[23] For Bernard, myrrh is bitter (*amara*) and therefore "signifies the hard and rigorous facts of trouble and sorrow" that the bride keeps close to her breast to endure for the sake of her Beloved.[24] Further on, Bernard addresses his audience directly:

You, also, if you are wise, will imitate the wisdom of the Bride; you will not allow that bundle of myrrh, which you hold so dear, and which is the fellowship

21 For the hymns, see *Pat. Lat.* 53, col. 785, and *Pat. Lat.* 101, col. 1389, respectively.
22 This is first noted in Patrick F. O'Connell, "Aelred of Rievaulx and the '*Lignum vitae*' of Bonaventure: A Reappraisal," *Franciscan Studies* 48 (1988): 54.
23 For the complete text, see Bernard of Clairvaux, *Sermo XLVIII super Cantica Canticorum*, in *Opera*, vol. 2, eds. J. LeClercq, C. H. Talbot, and H. M Rochais (Rome: Editiones Cistercienses, 1958), 41-44.
24 *Myrrha amara res, dura et aspera tribulationum significat.* Bernard of Clairvaux, *Opera*, vol. 2, 41, line 10-11; trans. S. J. Eales, in St. Bernard, *Cantica Canticorum. 86 Sermons on the Song of Songs* (London: Eliot Stock, 1895), 266.

you have with the sufferings of your master, to be torn away from your heart even for an hour; you will retain always in your memory all the bitter pain which he bore for you, and meditate upon them continually, so that you too may say with the bride: a bundle of myrrh is my well-beloved unto me; he shall lie between my breasts.[25]

In the next paragraph, Bernard elaborates on what this bundle of myrrh is. He tells his brothers:

> I, brethren, from the beginning of my conversion, set myself, in place of all merits in which I knew that was wanting, to bind up this little bundle of myrrh for my individual needs, collected from all the cares and bitter experiences of my Lord and to keep it always close upon my breast; in the first place of the privations of his infant years, then of the labors he underwent in preaching, his fatigues in journeying to and fro, his watching in prayer, his fastings and temptations, his tears of compassion, the snares laid for him in discourse; and, lastly, his perils among false brethren, of insults, spitting, blows, abuse, scorn, piercing by nails, and other such things, which he suffered for the salvation of our race,

which in the Gospel history, as in a forest, may abundantly be gathered.[26]

In this passage, Bernard effectively lays the groundwork for what would become Bonaventure's serial meditation based on the events of Christ's life, the *Vita Christi*. That Bonaventure is consciously adapting Bernard's sermon to this end is made explicit in the prologue to the *Tree of Life* in which Bonaventure writes:

> The true worshiper of God and disciple of Christ, who desires to conform perfectly to the Savior of all men crucified for him, should above all strive with an earnest endeavor of soul to carry about continuously both in his soul and in his flesh, the cross of Christ until he can truly feel in himself what the apostle said above [referring to Gal. 2:19]. Moreover an affection and feeling of this kind is merited to be experienced in a vital way only by one who, not unmindful of the Lord's passion nor ungrateful, contemplates the labor, suffering, and love of Jesus crucified, with such vividness of memory, such sharpness of intellect and such clarity of will that he can truly say with the bride: A bundle of myrrh is my well-beloved unto me; he shall lie between my breasts.[27]

---

25 *Tu quoque, si sapis, imitaberis sponsae prudentiam, atque hunc myrrhae tam carum fasciculum de principali tui pectoris, nec ad horam patieris auferri; amara illa omnia quae pro te pertulit, semper in memoria retinens, et assidua meditatione revolvens, quo possis dicere et tu: Fasciculus myrrhae dilectus meus mihi, inter ubera mea commorabitur.* Bernard of Clairvaux, *Opera*, vol. 2, 42, lines 12-15; trans. Eales, p. 276.

26 *Et ego, fratres, ab ineunte mea conversione, pro acervo meritorum quae mihi deesse sciebam, hunc mihi fasciculum colligare et inter ubera mea collocare curavi, collectum ex omnibus anxietatibus et amaritudinibus Domini mei, primum videlicet infantilium illarum necessitatum, deinde laborum quos pertulit in praedicando, fatigationum in discurrendo, vigiliarum in orando, tentationum in ieiunando, lacrimarum in compatiendo, insidiarum in colloquendo, postremo periculorum in falsis fratribus, conviciorum, sputorum, colaphorum, subsannationum, exprobrationum, clavorum horumque similium, quae in salutem nostri generis silva evangelica copiosissime noscitur protulisse.* Bernard of Clairvaux, *Opera*, vol. 2, 42, lines 18-27; trans. Eales, 268.

27 *Verus Dei cultor Christique discipulus, qui salvatori omnium pro se crucifixo perfecte configurari desiderat, ad hoc potissimum attento mentis conatu debet intendere, ut Christi Iesu crucem circumferat iugiter tam mente quam carne, quatenus praefatum Apostoli verbum veraciter valeat in semetipso sentire. Porro huiusmodi affectum et sensum is duntaxat apud se vivaciter experiri meretur, qui, dominicae passionis non immemor nec ingratus, laborem et dolorem amoremque crucifixi Iesu tanta memoriae vivacitate tanto intellectus acumine tanta voluntatis caritate considerat quod veraciter illud sponsae proferre potest eloquium: Fasciculus myrrhae dilectus meus mihi inter ubera mea commorabitur.* Bonaventure, *Opera*, vol. 8, 68; trans. Cousins, 119.

Not only does Bonaventure use the same verse from the Canticles that provided the basis of Bernard's sermon on the devotion to the human sufferings of Christ, he also borrows Bernard's language in the next passage in describing the Gospels as a *silva*, a forest, from which the bitter myrrh has been gathered. Bonaventure writes: "To enkindle in us this affection, to shape this understanding, and to imprint this memory, I have endeavored to gather this bundle of myrrh from the forest of the Holy Gospel, which treats at length the life, passion, and glorification of Jesus Christ."[28]

Although Bonaventure never makes a specific allusion to his debt to Bernard, these passages make very clear that the *Lignum vitae* grows out of this sermon, a connection that the designer of this miniature is quick to make by placing Bernard at the base of the tree beside Francis, giving us the answer to my first question of why Bernard appears at the base of the tree.

The second question—what does it mean that the theologian who famously promoted the ideal of imageless devotion is shown here worshipping an image of the Crucified Christ—raises several issues that have concerned many art historians in regard to the role of the image in devotion.[29] Although Bernard ultimately believed in an ideal of imageless devotion, he nevertheless understood that image-based devotion was a necessary means to an end. In another sermon on the Canticles, he advises that a soul at prayer should have before it a "sacred image [*sacra imago*] of the God-man, in his birth or infancy, or as he was teaching, or dying, or rising, or ascending."[30] Bernard follows this by claiming that the *sacra imago* binds the soul

to virtue and expels vice because by *seeing* Christ in the flesh, humanity could converse with him and be drawn first to the salutary love of his humanity and then to spiritual love.

With this sentiment, Bernard, as Jeffrey Hamburger has put it, "opens the door to the visual arts," a door that the designer of this miniature working over a hundred years after Bernard was happy to step into.[31] It must be emphasized, however, that when Bernard speaks of the *imago*, he is referring not to an artifactual image but to a mental image, and he speaks of it in a way that suggests a point somewhere between the second and third levels of vision in the classical Augustinian scheme of corporal, spiritual, and intellectual vision. The designer, a Franciscan well-versed in the theology of his day, would have been aware of this distinction and would not have considered his artifactual image the goal of spiritual and intellectual contemplation of the Cross but a *means* to that goal. In this respect, one can turn again to Bernard's forty-third sermon on the Song of Songs in order to place the designer's motivations. Near the end of the sermon Bernard writes: "My dear brethren, do also gather for yourselves each a bundle so precious and beloved, give it a place in the depths of your heart, fortify it with the portal of your breast, that it may abide between your breasts also. Let [Jesus] be borne, not behind you and on your shoulders as a burden, but in front of you and before your eyes...." After describing how the Virgin, Simeon, and Joseph all took up Christ, bore him, and gazed upon him, he exhorts his audience to "do likewise; for if you have him whom you are bearing always before your eyes,

---

[28] *Ut igitur praefatus in nobis accendatur affectus, formetur cogitatus, imprimatur memoria ex sacri Evangelii silva, in qua de vita, passione et glorificatione Iesu Christi diffuse tractatur, colligere studui hunc myrrhae fasciculum ...* Bonaventure, *Opera*, vol. 8, 68; trans. Cousins, 119.

[29] See Bernard of Clairvaux, *Sermones super Cantica Cantorum*, LII.iii.5, *Opera Omnia*, vol. 2, 93.

[30] *Adstat oranti Hominis Dei sacra imago, aut nascentis, aut lactentis, aut docentis, aut morientis, aut resurgentis, aut ascendentis ...*, from S. Bernardus, *Sermo XX super Cantica Canticorum*, in *Opera*, vol. 1, 118; also cited and discussed in Jeffrey Hamburger, "The Visual and the Visionary: The Image in Late Medieval Monastic Devotions," in *The Visual and the Visionary: Art and Female Spirituality in Late Medieval Germany* (New York: Zone Books, 1998), 121.

[31] Hamburger, 121.

it is certain that, beholding the pains and troubles which the Lord endured, you will more easily and willingly bear your own...."[32]

By including Bernard in his configuration of witnesses to the Crucifixion taking place above, the designer is not only giving credit to Bernard for sowing the seeds of the *Lignum vitae* under which he stands, but he is supplying a model of imaginative devotion, to use the terminology from Sixten Ringbom's important essay on the subject.[33] Bernard's presence provides authority, giving weight to the power of the image in what I am calling "redemptive vision," in which the act of seeing Christ in his suffering begins the transformative process of redemption in the viewer's soul.

The concept of redemptive vision is enforced by other figures in the composition. I have already noted the Centurion who also appears in the illustrated hymn. As a soldier of Pilate and a non-believer, his conversion upon witnessing Christ's death demonstrates to the viewer the power of the sight, or visual experience, of the Crucifixion.

Francis is another model of redemptive vision. Like the Virgin with whom he is visually aligned, his offers another model of compassionate devotion through contemplative viewing. His stigmatization was his reward for his complete conformity to Christ, but it only occurred, as Bonaventure writes in his biography of the saint, when he saw the vision of the crucified Christ appearing between the wings of the Seraph. Bonaventure writes:

> Eventually he understood by a revelation from the Lord that divine providence

had shown him this vision so that, as Christ's lover, he might learn in advance that he was to be totally transformed into the likeness of Christ crucified ... As the vision disappeared, it left in his heart a marvelous ardor and imprinted on his body markings that were no less marvelous.[34]

The designer is thus not only presenting the stigmatization reenacted on the page for the viewer but also demonstrating how contemplation of the image of the crucified Christ gives spiritual reward. At the same time, he offers the viewer the same vision that Francis saw historically and sees perpetually in this miniature. Bernard is also much more than a witness to the Crucifixion. Like Francis, he communicates with the viewer through the inscription on his scroll. As noted above, the words inscribed on the scroll, *Ascendam in palmam et apprehendam fructus eius*, are from Canticles 7:8; but they do not appear to have been used in Bernard's writings. Rather, the intention behind the verse is to instruct the viewer in how to approach the vision inscribed on this page: one should climb up mentally in the tree with the eyes and take hold of Christ through the faculty of spiritual vision. The viewing of the *Lignum vitae* thus becomes an interactive spiritual exercise in which the viewer's response is conditioned not only by the image on the page but also by the visual responses enacted by the figures below.

The designer of this *Lignum vitae* diagram intentionally employs various levels of visuality to engage the experience of the viewer and to mediate

---

[32] *Habete illum semper non retro in humeris, sed ante prae oculis ... Exemplo ergo sint vobis, ut et vos similiter faciatis. Si enim ante oculos habueritis quem portatis, pro certo, videntes angustias Domini, levius vestras portabitis ....* Bernard of Clairvaux, *Opera*, vol. 2, 44, lines 1-9; trans. Eales, 270.

[33] S. Ringbom, "Devotional Images and Imaginative Devotions: Notes on the Place of Art in Late Medieval Piety," *Gazette des Beaux-Arts*, 6th ser., 73 (1969): 159-77.

[34] *Intellexit tandem ex hoc, domino revelante, quod ideo huiusmodi visio sic divina providentia suis fuerat praesentata conspectibus, ut amicus Christi praenosceret, se non per martyrium carnis, sed per incendium mentis totum in Christi crucifixi similitudinem transformandum. Disparens igitur visio mirabilem in corde ipsius reliquit ardorem, sed et in carne non minus mirabilem signorum impressit effigiem.* S. Bonaventura, *Legenda Sancti Francisci*, cap. XIII, in *Opera omnia*, vol. 8, 543; trans. Cousins, 306.

between the spiritual image of the divine and the painted images on the pages. The complexity of the visual relationships suggests a level of sophistication in the perception of the artifactual image that can be applied to less obvious examples. These artifactual images are not simply there to illustrate and to aid corporal vision. Rather, the designer invests his images with much more power, as much I would say as he gives his words.

We can look back to the way in which Bonaventure constructs certain forms of devotion in words that are reminiscent of the way in which our designer constructs the devotion of his reader/viewer with images. In his meditations on the life of Christ that form the *Lignum vitae*, Bonaventure appeals to the spiritual vision of the mind's eye so that the images of the events of Christ's infancy, public life, passion, death, and resurrection become present in the eye of the beholder. He does this by calling for the active participation of his reader in the events related to each meditation, so for example, in the meditation on the First fruit, recalling the Nativity, Bonaventure first describes what happens at the Nativity in prose, then adds: "Now, then, my soul, embrace that divine manger; press your lips upon and kiss the boy's feet. Then in your mind, keep the shepherd's watch, marvel at the assembling host of angels, [and] join in the heavenly melody."[35] The prayer guides the devotee in making herself present at the event. Bonaventure does this, he explains, so that in mentally re-living the event, it will be impressed upon the interior of the mind. Essentially, what he is asking the reader to do is to make an

image in her mind's eye to gaze upon in the second level of vision in the Augustinian scheme, that is, spiritual vision.

What Bonaventure is asking his reader to do using words, the designer of the *Verger de soulas* is asking his viewer to do by seeing his imagery depicted on the page in front of her. The artifactual images do not in themselves transport the reader to a higher level of knowledge but give the viewer the ability to make that leap, just as Bonaventure's words do. In Franciscan devotional practice, vision, whether gained through word or image, was thus inextricably linked to understanding.

In conclusion, the illustrated hymn and the *Lignum vitae* describe and demonstrate a process of redemptive vision and show that Franciscans did not simply use art to advertise the Order or to promote its saints, history, and agenda. They also actively employed it to engage the medieval viewer in a process of realization and redemption. While the example of the *Verger de soulas* provides here only one example, the brief conclusions drawn from its pages could be applied to future studies of Franciscan art. Although one can argue, and I would not disagree, that the devotional purposes of the artifactual image intended by the designer of the *Verger de soulas* existed at least since the teachings of Bernard of Clairvaux, the Franciscans brought the earlier developments in monastic spirituality promoted by Bernard out into the open and made efforts to incorporate them into the spirituality of the laity through the art produced under their influence.

---

[35]   *Complectere itaque nunc, anima mea, divinum illud praesepe, ut pueri pedibus labia tua figas et oscula gemines. Deinde pastorum excubias mente pertracta, Angelorum mirare concurrentem exercitum, caelesti melodiae tuas interpone partes....* Bonaventure, *Opera*, vol. 8, 68; trans. Cousins, 129.

Appendix: Transcription of the illustrated hymn in Paris, BNF, MS fr. 9220, fol. 3v.[36]

1) Lignum uite querimus
qui uitam amisimus
fructu ligni uetiti

Nous querons larbre de vie
ki pierdu auons la uie
par le fruit dou fust uee

2) Nec inuentum nouerit
qui fructum non uiderit
adherentem stipiti

Ia trouet nel connistra
sahiers le fruit veut na
al arbre que chie vees

3) Fructus per quem uiuitur
pendet sicut creditor
virginis ad ubera

4) Et ad crucem iterum
Inter uiros scelerum
passus quinque uulnera

Li fruis par que nos uiuons
pent ensi que nos creons
a le mamiele sancreuse
de la uirgene glorieuse

Et en crois si comme nos ueons
fichies entre deus larons
souffri sa chars prescieuse
v plaies mult tres crueuses

5) Hic uirgo puepera
        Ambo lig (…)
Tres chi la uirgene enfantant
        Arbre sunt (…)

5) Hic crux salutifera
        na mistica
Chi la crois salut portant
        mystere ont grant

6) Hec ysopus humilis
        Vtraque (…)

6) Illa cedrus nobilis
        uiuifica

Tres chi leurs humle ysope
        Andoi sunt

Et chi le cedre tres noble
        uiuifiant

Virga tua et baculus tuus
ipsa me consolata sunt [Psalm 23:4]

7) Positus in medio
quo me uertam nescio

8) In hoc dulcis[37] dubio
dulcis est collatio

---

[36]   Verse numbering follows the standard edition in *Analecta hymnica*, vol. 54, 203.
[37]   Scribal error. *Analecta hymnica* gives "dulci" (vol. 54, 203).

Li uierge que David ci dist
ce est li mere ihesu Christ
et de le crois dist le baston
la sunt nos consolations

En mi sui ne sai penser
quel part me doie tourner
en celle doutance douce
la collations est douce

9) Hic complexus brachiis
modis uagit uariis

10) Hic extendit brachia
Complexurus omnia

Or est chis fuis embrachies
Il com eufes en iusies
se demaine cha et la

Il meismes en la crois pent
andens ses bras restent
pour acoler cha et la

11) carum mater tenere
nouit hunc tenere

12) caritas sub latere
nescit hic latere

La mere sou chier enfant
Set tenir mult tenrement

La charites ihesu christ
ne set ou coste tapir

13) Hic adherens pectori
pascitur ab ubere

14) Hic affixus arbori
pascit nos ex uulnere

16) Mater est preambula
fructum nobis nutriens

15) crux ministrat pabula
fructu nos reficiens

Dame tu es mere chiere
sai uote par ta proiere
pour nos soit nouris cis fruis

La crois ministre peuture
arme ki est nete et pure
est solee de ce fruit

18) Sed uirgo puerpera
pascit ipsa pascua

17) crux in loco pascue
pascit nos precipue

Mais la mere nete et pure
elle paist ceste peuture

La crois est lius de peuture
de se fruit nos asseure

(19-22) Tandem in hoc traditur . finalis sententia . quod nemo consequitur . unam sine alia . qui crucem elegerit . et sic matrem deserit . cum ad crucem uenerit . matrem ibi poterit . stantem inuenire
Et qui matrem eligit . crucem prorsus abigit . si nondum intelligit . quod per matrem contigit . gladium transire.

Au finer de ma sentence per raison moustre me plaist . ke nus ne mete sentente a lune et lautre laist
Ki la crois esliute ara et la mere lait ensi . quant a la crois en sus osteroit . sil nen tendoit que lespee fust par la
mere passee.

(23-26) Ergo qui utramlibet optat . illam adeat . ex quo nichil prohibet . quin utraque gaudeat
Fili martris unice . matris crucifixe . nos de cruce respice . fili crucifixe
Fructus o uiuifice . fructus ligni uitae . nos te ipso refice . nobis da frui te . Amen.

Ki lune et lautre desire . celli prende et celli quire . puis que riens nule ne defft. des deus ioir le ement
Uns s--- fuis de pruue mere . de crucifije mere . regarde nos de la crois . fius crucefijes en crois O tu fruis ke
uiufies o tu fruis darbre de uie refai nos de celui meismes . donne a nos user toi mismes.

[In lower right corner, below Crucifixion]
Domine ihesu christe da michi ista quatuor ex toto corde considerare . primo . maxima presentis uite per-
icula . Secundo . imminentem mortem et ipsius angustiam . Tertio . districtum dei iudicium . quarto . eter-
nitatem anime in gehennam uel in uitam eternam et tempus tuum redime.

Ave uirgo fecundata septiformi pluuia

Tui fructus o maria pedum manuum nos pia pascant stillicidia

Omnes sancti subuenite . per vos michi odor uite . de crucis turibulo . detur unde saginetur . anima cor
iocundetur . sub crucis umbraculo.
Omnes sancti subuenite . per uos michi latus mitte . christi sit latibulum . ibi lateam securus . cum per
ignem est uenturus . iudicare seculum.
O deus unus fac me unum rerum . in intentione et operatione in uita et in morte et in fruitione eterna.

THE PLACE OF AESTHETICS AND THE ARTS IN MEDIEVAL FRANCISCAN THEOLOGY

Oleg Bychkov

hile it is common to find some connections between medieval practical theology and the use of aesthetic forms of expression such as painting or architectural space, scholars have struggled to find similar links between the arts and medieval speculative theology. Erwin Panofsky's study of medieval scholasticism and Gothic architecture is one example of a failed attempt to find a definitive connection.[1] The root of the problem is that few art historians have the knowledge of medieval speculative theological texts, and vice versa, few textual scholars of medieval theology have a solid background in the arts. Another factor is that the situation was exactly the same in the Middle Ages and therefore there are hardly any direct links to be found in the first place. One valid approach would be to investigate whether a certain tradition in medieval speculative theology is *supportive* either of artistic expression in general or even of a particular kind of artistic expression. This essay is a modest attempt to provide textual resources from Franciscan speculative theology for scholars studying links between Franciscan art and Franciscan theology. It ventures no

further than to show whether there was any theoretical support in speculative texts for the sort of art practices that existed in the medieval artistic traditions that were associated with the Franciscan movement.

1. The aesthetic way of grasping reality

The medieval Franciscan theological tradition, from Alexander of Hales and Bonaventure to Duns Scotus, is firmly rooted in Augustine and therefore in a late ancient Christian form of Neoplatonism. Thirteenth-century Franciscans also use the works of Cicero, such as the *De officiis* (*On Duties*), where he expresses Stoic views on ethical issues. Augustine, as many other early Christian thinkers, is also heavily influenced by Stoicism, which, in turn, inherits many ideas from Plato. The importance of this historical-textual observation lies in the fact that both the Platonic and the Stoic traditions rely heavily on aesthetic perception in constructing the picture of our interaction with reality, and in particular with the "ultimate" reality, be it the realm of the divine, the ideas, or generally the "nature of the universe." According to Plato, the realm of the ideas, and in particular the idea

---

[1]   See O. Bychkov, "Theology, Aesthetics, and the Gothic Space: Does Scholastic Theology have Anything to do with the Gothic?" in *Theology in Built Environments*, ed. S. Bergmann (New Brunswick, NJ/London: Transaction, 2009), 39-58.

of the "beautiful," expressed by the Greek term τὸ καλόν, which refers equally to both aesthetic and moral excellence, is revealed to us initially through our experience of the aesthetic forms of bodies. The fusion between aesthetic and moral excellence in Greek thought ensured that by becoming aware of the aesthetic nature of reality we are at the same time attaining moral standards. The Stoics took this theory one step further: a move captured by Cicero's *On Duties*. The two main principles of ethical behavior, the noble or excellent (τὸ καλόν, *honestum*), and the fitting (τὸ πρέπον, or *decorum*), are in fact also aesthetic, in the sense that they can be immediately perceived in the person's behavior or appearance, not grasped by logical reasoning. Augustine's writings are the pinnacle of late ancient aesthetic thought. Such depth of speculation on the nature of aesthetic experience is subsequently achieved only in Kant. According to Augustine, aesthetic experience is transcendental, in Kant's sense of the term, in that it makes us immediately aware of the transcendent laws of proportion and equality; the latter two in ancient thought, as they are still today, were closely associated with the aesthetic principle of beauty.[2]

Thirteenth-century Franciscan thought simply takes over Augustine's aesthetic theory, the most striking example being Bonaventure's *Journey of the Mind into God*, Chapter 2, which is mostly a paraphrase of Augustine's works *On Order* 2, *On Music* 6, *On Free Choice of the Will* 2 and *On True Religion*,

often in the same words, where Augustine outlines the Neoplatonic theory of the ascent to the divine principle through aesthetic experience.[3] Since Bonaventure's account is both well known and not very original let us turn to the most formidable Franciscan speculative theologian at the turn of the fourteenth century, John Duns Scotus, who neither is particularly known for artistic and aesthetic parallels nor would accept any train of thought unless it was absolutely essential to his theoretical constructs. Does the aesthetic moment play an important role in his theology? In Book 1, Distinction 2 of his Commentary on the *Sentences* of Peter Lombard, in both Oxonian and Parisian versions of it, Scotus reexamines the validity of Anselm's *Proslogion* proof of the existence of God, i.e., that the existence of God is evident simply from the concept that we have of God.[4] It is well known that as an utter Augustinian, but also as an admirer of Stoic ideas found in Cicero's texts, Anselm often turns to what we can call "aesthetic" proofs in his theology, so Scotus here is forced to examine this area.[5] One of the steps in proving that God exists is simply to prove that some infinite being necessarily exists (in Anselm's words, "something greater than which nothing can be conceived"). Scotus proceeds by way of proving that the concept of "infinite" is not incompatible with that of "being": our intellect clearly perceives that there can be "infinite being." Moreover, our intellect always strives beyond any finite being, which means that it is clear to our

2   On Platonic and Stoic aesthetics, see O. Bychkov, *Aesthetic Revelation: Reading Ancient and Medieval Texts after Hans Urs von Balthasar* (Washington, D.C.: Catholic University of America Press, 2010); and O. Bychkov and A. Sheppard, *Greek and Roman Aesthetics*, Cambridge Texts in the History of Philosophy (Cambridge: Cambridge University Press, 2010).

3   See O. Bychkov, *Aesthetic Revelation*, 268ff.

4   See O. Bychkov, "'Aesthetic' Epistemology: Parallels between the Perception of Musical Harmony and the Cognition of Truth in Duns Scotus,' in *John Duns Scotus 1308-2008. Investigations into his Philosophy*. Archa Verbi, Subsidia 5 (Münster: Aschendorff, 2010), 345-56. The same texts are discussed in O. Bychkov, *Aesthetic Revelation*, 282ff and idem, "The Nature of Theology in Duns Scotus and his Franciscan Predecessors," *Franciscan Studies* 66 (2008): 43.

5   The texts quoted below are from *Reportatio* I-A, Dist. 2, Part I, q. 1-3, n. 71-73 (Wolter/Bychkov, vol. 1, 136-7). The text of the *Reportatio* is quoted according to the edition-translation: Allan Wolter and Oleg Bychkov, eds. and trans., *John Duns Scotus. The Examined Report of the Paris Lecture* (*Reportatio* I-A), vols. 1-2 (St. Bonaventure, NY: The Franciscan Institute, 2004, 2008). A similar account is found in the *Ordinatio*. The key parallel text is in *Ordinatio* I, Dist. 2, d. 2, p. 1, q. 1-2, n. 136 (II, 208; translated in A. Wolter's *Duns Scotus, Philosophical Writings* [Indianapolis/Cambridge: Hackett, 1987], 72-3).

intellect that there is something more to reality than finite being, since it certainly wouldn't strive after something it doesn't think exists (*Rep.* I-A, loc.cit., n. 71). Suddenly Scotus realizes, just like the Stoics before him, that he also needs to prove why we should trust our intellect when it thinks that something is "clearly" the case. What if it is continuously deceived? Amazingly, the Subtle Doctor comes up with the following way to root the certainty of our intellectual cognition (loc.cit., n. 72):

> The sense faculties which are less perfect cognitive powers than the intellect immediately perceive any lack of harmony in their object, as is clear from the case of auditory perception of dissonance. Therefore, if 'infinite' were repugnant to 'being,' the intellect would immediately perceive this repugnance and lack of harmony and then, because of the repugnance, it could not grasp 'infinite being' as its object—just as it could not have something contradictory, like 'man is irrational,' as its object. But everyone experiences the opposite, since the intellect never rests with finite being.

Thus the proof of certainty of our intellectual cognition rests on a purely aesthetic argument. In our perception of the arts (in this case music but it could have easily been visual arts) our senses indicate the presence or absence of proportion or harmony with a pinpoint and never-failing accuracy, which can be independently verified afterwards, for example, with the help of measuring instruments. Why, then, not trust our intellect, which is a faculty that is not inferior to our senses? The main objection to Anselm's argument is resolved in the same

way (cf. loc.cit., n. 73-74). If one objects that we can easily think of something that definitely does not exist, for example, of absurd things such as chimaeras, Scotus answers that we do not actually have clear and certain ideas of such things. That is, it is already in our intellect that these things lack reality and certainty. On the other hand, if our intellect does see or perceive something clearly, as it happens in aesthetic perception, it is necessarily the case.

No doubt, another famous view of Duns Scotus helps his assertion that we can clearly and quasi-aesthetically perceive certain things about divine reality. Scotus held that in the most general sense being is predicated of both God and creatures univocally, and not by analogy. This view is formulated concisely in this form:[6]

> Every intellect that is certain about one concept and dubious about other concepts,[7] has the concept about which it is certain as other than that about which it is dubious ... But the intellect of the pilgrim is certain that God is a being, doubting whether it be a created being or uncreated, and the being is saved univocally in both; therefore the concept of being is other than both and is preserved in both; therefore it is a univocal concept. For it is certain that some having a dubious concept assumed God to be the sun, and the like, and nevertheless they did not doubt that God was a being, therefore etc.

Scotus further expands his view on univocity: it is not only 'being' in its most general sense that can be predicated of both God and creatures univocally, but also the transcendental properties

---

[6]   *Rep.* I-A, d. 3, q. 1, n. 28 (Wolter/Bychkov, vol. 1, 193); a similar formulation is found in *Ord.* I, d. 3, p. 1, q. 1-2, n. 27 (translated in A. Wolter's *Duns Scotus. Philosophical Writings*, 20).

[7]   Reading "other concepts" is taken from the *Ordinatio* version.

of being (such as unity and goodness), as well as "pure perfections" such as 'power' or 'greatness,' so a rather detailed picture of what God is like can be gleaned from creatures.[8] It is clear, additionally, that Scotus proves the univocity of being in the same way that he proves Anselm's argument for the existence of God, i.e., aesthetically: the intellect clearly sees whether this is the case or not, without any discursive deduction.

However, one may ask, what is it exactly that we grasp with such certainty, even about divine realities, as a result of this quasi-aesthetic seeing? Duns Scotus discusses this issue in the context of God's omnipotence. The problem is as follows. If God can produce anything, then he can produce, for example, a subject without its attributes or an attribute without its subject, for example grass without greenness or greenness without grass. But this will destroy the certitude of human knowledge, because we could never be sure if what we are seeing is merely greenness or greenness with grass underneath it: the classic example is eucharistic bread and wine that only appear as bread and wine, but are actually flesh and blood. Scotus admits that this is indeed the case with proper attributes of things, but not with a separate class of attributes: relational attributes, which he calls *habilitates*. These can be known with certainty no matter what God decides to do about things and their proper attributes:[9]

Indeed, [a proper attribute] is not always present in its subject as in its immediate cause, from which it originates, but this is only known [to happen] in most cases, because it is only 'in most cases' that an attribute originates from the principles of its subject, but not always. Indeed, the first cause, on which

any absolute being directly depends, can cause a certain attribute not to follow or originate from a certain subject. ... At the same time, a relational attribute, which implies a certain aptitude (*habilitas*) in or as regards its subject (and which is perhaps nothing else but its [i.e., the subject's] essence), can be known of the subject in an absolute sense and with necessity. For aptitude implies a relation, nor can it be separated from that whose aptitude it is, and therefore such an attribute is necessarily known as regards its subject. Hence in the whole of geometry there is not a single query about an absolute or actual attribute in its subject, but only about aptitudinal attributes that include relations. For example, the 'ability to have three [angles] equal to two right angles' is appropriate for a triangle. Indeed, even if no two right angles were ever found in actuality, the attribute 'to have three [angles] equal to two right angles' would still be proper for a triangle. Now this could not be true if actual equality to two actually existing right angles were meant. This, furthermore, is the case with all mathematical conclusions.

So what are those *habilitates* or relational properties that can be known with certainty under any circumstances through a type of intellectual seeing? Most likely Scotus speaks of certain 'eternal' characteristics of beings that go beyond such attributes as quantity or quality. Such characteristics, which played a crucial role in the Pythagorean, Platonic, and Neoplatonic traditions, including Augustine (and in

---

8   See references to texts from the *Reportatio* in O. Bychkov, "The Nature of Theology in Duns Scotus...," 47ff; and J.A. Aertsen, "Scotus's Conception of Transcendentality: Tradition and Innovation," in *John Duns Scotus 1308-2008. Investigations into his Philosophy*, 107-23.

9   *Rep.* I-A, Dist. 42, q. 2, n. 32 (Wolter/Bychkov, vol. 2, 517-18).

modern times also in Kant), do, indeed, tend to be of a relational kind: for example, proportions, which seem to transcend size, scale, place, and time. As Scotus himself observes, such characteristics are more likely part of the essence of the thing than its 'attributes.' Indeed it seems that, for example, the knowledge of the ratio of 2 to 1 will be true under any circumstances at any period in time and does not depend on the size of objects, or even the type of intelligence, for example Martian as opposed to human. At the same time, even an uneducated person can detect this ratio, which means that perceiving it is an aesthetic, not intellectual process. Augustine, following the long standing Platonic-Pythagorean tradition, already gave us a complete description of this phenomenon in application to Christian theology: the very fact that we are naturally able to perceive visual proportions and musical intervals, which seem to be eternal and free from change, reveals to us both the realm of the divine and our ability to connect to it, i.e., the divine element in us. For Duns Scotus, such universal relational structures are essentially permanent and eternal, and they can be detected aesthetically, as we perceive consonance in music. Thus it is evident that in Franciscan theology the aesthetic or artistic way of knowing reality is either as important or even more important than the conceptual mode.[10] It is difficult to imagine how such a position on aesthetics would not validate an approach to theology through the arts.

2. Aesthetics and the Trinity

The discussion of relational properties such as proportion brings us directly to a theological subject that is undisputedly prominent in speculative Franciscan theology: that of the Trinity.[11] In medieval Franciscan theological circles, from Alexander of Hales to Duns Scotus, differences between the persons of the Trinity were perceived to be of a purely relational kind: for example, as that of a begetter to someone begotten, or that of a spirator to someone spirated. In terms of their substance and all "substantial" qualities, or "pure perfections" such as power, goodness, and so forth all persons were considered perfectly equal. However, according to Duns Scotus, from the point of view of relational properties, that is, their standing as regards their origin—either as originators or those who are originated—the divine persons are not entirely equal but some are in a position of greater authority. For example, the Father possesses greater authority as regards the Son, who is in a "subordinate" position. These two types of relational properties possessed by the divine persons, "common" relations of equality shared by all, and "personal" relations of origin that are specific to individual persons and differentiate them as far as their "authority" is concerned create two models of the Trinity. Both models can be interpreted in terms of aesthetics. The first model, where the relation between the three persons is perfect equality, can be seen in an aesthetic light because according to Augustine and subsequently all medieval Franciscans the main principle of beauty is the proportion of equality. From this point of view one can call the Trinity "beautiful" as a quintessence of equality, with all three persons being equal between each other (Fig. 1). The other model is "subordinationist," where the relations are not those of equality but those of procession, which invest some persons with greater "authority": the Son proceeding from the Father, and, according to the Western model, the Holy

---

[10]   H. Möhle demonstrates definitively that "conceptual being" and "real being" are not predicated univocally, i.e., they cannot be reduced to a single univocal concept and there is therefore a conceptually unbridgeable gap between them: see H. Möhle, "Metaphysik und Erkenntniskritik. *Prima scientia est scibilis primi,*" in *John Duns Scotus 1308-2008. Investigations into his Philosophy,* 82ff; he refers to the text of *Rep.* I-A, d. 29, q. un., n. 19 (Wolter/Bychkov, vol. 2, 243). What aesthetic experience perceives, however, is precisely real, and not conceptual being!

[11]   Since this subject is covered at length in my "What does Beauty have to do with the Trinity? From Augustine to Duns Scotus," *Franciscan Studies* 66 (2008): 197-212, I will not discuss it here except very briefly.

Fig 1. The Trinity, by Andrej Rublyov, cca. 1411; Moscow, The Tretyakov Gallery

Spirit proceeding from both the Father and the Son, and according to the Eastern, proceeding from the Father through the Son (Fig. 2). How this model can be interpreted in aesthetic terms will be explained below in the section on Christology.

3. Artistic image and imaging

So far these observations on aesthetics in Franciscan theology have concerned general issues and could be applied as much to natural beauty as to aesthetic art objects. Does Franciscan speculative theology say anything about the issues pertaining more directly to the arts, in particular to visual art? At the center of ancient and medieval discussions of visual art was the status of the image. How much value should be assigned to producing a visual image of something? In his notorious denunciation of art in Book 3 of the *Republic*, Plato characterizes the artistic image as an imitation that is "twice removed" from the original in the ideal realm, and therefore not worth very much. This attitude persists in the Platonic and early Christian tradition without much change, except that subsequent Hellenistic and Roman thought elevates the role of the image slightly by pointing out that artists often imitate not material reality but ideas in their mind.[12] The truly fundamental discussion of the role of the image, in particular in religion, comes during the iconoclastic disputes in Byzantium in the eighth and ninth centuries, with repercussions in the West. Iconodules such as John Damascene espoused what was later styled the "theology of glory." It is expressed well by the phrase in Rom. 1:20 "the invisible things of God, since the creation of the world, have been clearly perceived through the things that have been made," which seems to sanction the use of worldy objects for the purpose of gaining some insight into the divine. Although

Damascene convincingly shows both the legality and the value of the use of images in Christian religion, his defense of images centers on the symbolic, memorial and revelatory function of representations. All this is aptly summarized in a well-known saying from Basil the Great used by Damascene: "For the honor given to the image passes to the archetype."[13] Images of Christ and the Saints remind us of these persons and direct our mental gaze at them. The use of imaging activity is thus warranted, and the license is given to use our sense perception and imagination in visual art. However, still nothing is said directly about the aesthetic qualities of the image.

All the more interesting, then, is a gloss that Bonaventure puts on the medieval iconoclastic dispute in his Commentary on the *Sentences* (*Sent.* I, d. 31, p. 2, a. 1, q. 3 ad 2-4; my translation):

> Therefore it is clear why Hilary attributes to the Son the name [of beauty] rather than another one: because he can define the image by this name even better than by any other.
>
> As for the objection that the beauty of the image refers back to the prototype, one must say that this is true. However, honor and beauty 'refer back' in different ways. Indeed, honor in an image or painting refers back to the prototype in such a way that there is no honor as such in [the picture] itself: a clear example is when an icon of St. Nicholas is being venerated or honored. At the same time, beauty refers back to the prototype in such a way that beauty is still in the image, and not only in him whose image this is. Moreover, one can find two

---

12   See selections from Cicero, Seneca and Plotinus in O. Bychkov and A. Sheppard, *Greek and Roman Aesthetics*.

13   *On the Holy Spirit* 18.45, quoted by John Damascene in *On the Divine Images*, Treatise I.21 (John of Damascus, *Three Treatises on the Divine Images*, trans. A. Louth [Crestwood, NY: St. Vladimir's Seminary Press, 2003], 35).

Fig 2. Divine Fatherhood, The Novgorod School, beg. 15th c.; The Tretyakov Gallery, Moscow.

principles of beauty in [the image,] while only one principle is found in him whose picture this is. Clearly, the image is called 'beautiful' both when it is well shaped and also when it represents well him, of whom it is. It is obvious that this is a different principle of beauty, because it can exist without the other. In this sense, a picture of the Devil is called "beautiful" when it represents well the repulsiveness of the devil, i.e., when it is [formally] ugly! Therefore Hilary, when he attributes *species*[14] or beauty to the Son, mostly attributes it to him insofar as he is the 'Image,' rather than insofar as he is the 'Son.'

First of all, the fact that Bonaventure interprets St. Basil's famous pronouncement about the role of images[15] means that he was in general familiar with the Byzantine theory of the image and prototype in the context of the use of icons. What is interesting is his discussion of beauty contained in the image. The second principle of beauty, when a picture is called beautiful if it is a good likeness of something, clearly stems from the meaning of both Greek and Latin terms for 'beautiful': as was mentioned before, both terms can be used simply in the sense of positive evaluation, instead of 'excellent.' It is the first principle of beauty, however, that is more important. To be sure, the criterion of visual beauty here, being "well shaped" or "well proportioned" (*bene protracta*), is common to almost all traditions. Bonaventure speaks of the beauty of form. However, this formal beauty contained in the image is precisely the one it shares with the formal beauty of the prototype. Bonaventure alludes to this formal beauty by stating that

this is the only type that the prototype has, because it obviously lacks the specifically artistic beauty in the sense of skillful imitation. Indeed, if the prototype is formally ugly, a skillfully made image of it will be formally ugly as well. Thus the beauty of the prototype is seamlessly transferred to and preserved in the image, and it can be traced back from the image to the prototype.

The view of visual art as a process of truthfully capturing and preserving the form of the prototype, which still remains beautiful in the image, clearly validates the use of the image as revealing some features of the prototype. Furthermore, if one looks at this position through the lens of Duns Scotus, Bonaventure's observation becomes even more important. First of all, both God and creatures are 'beings' in the same most general sense. Second, our mind is capable of detecting most general characteristics of beings, their relational properties such as proportions, with absolute certainty. This means that the beautiful form that we see in the image does not always have to be merely analogical to the beauty of the prototype: in fact it can be *exactly that very beauty* of the prototype!

4. Aesthetics and Christology

It has been pointed out on many occasions that medieval Franciscan theology, in addition to its particular interest in Trinitarian relations, is also heavily Christocentric.[16] In fact, Bonaventure discusses the status of the image and beauty precisely in a Christocentric context, when he examines the second person of the Trinity, the Son. The second person of the Trinity is important for aesthetics for two reasons. First of all, the Son is seen as the perfect *image* of the Father. Second, the Son's regular

---

[14]   The Latin term *species* means both 'shape' or 'form' (as in 'outward form' but also as the Aristotelian inner form or essence of things) and 'beauty,' the last meaning being quite prominent.

[15]   Although Bonaventure does not mention Basil's name, the line "honor in an image or painting refers back to the prototype in such a way that there is no honor as such in [the picture] itself" is a very close allusion to Basil's formulation quoted above.

[16]   The material contained in this section is presented in more detail in my *Aesthetic Revelation*, 268ff.

attribute in medieval theology is beauty (*species* or even *pulchritudo*). The Western medieval tradition of viewing the Son as beauty goes back to Augustine who in *De Trinitate* 6.10.11[17] interprets a brief and unclear passage from Hilary of Poitiers. The passage from Hilary, *De Trinitate* 2.1,[18] reads as follows: "in the Father, the Son, and the Holy Spirit [there is] infinity in the eternal, beautiful form (*species*) in the image, and use in the gift." The expression "beautiful form in the image," Augustine explains, refers to the second person of the Trinity. He continues:

> For an image (*imago*), if it expresses perfectly him of whom it is an image, is itself equated to [its prototype], not [the prototype] to its image. Now in that statement about the Image he used the name *species*, I believe, on account of beauty (*propter pulchritudinem*), [for in this Image, that is, in Christ as the Image] there is already great harmony, and equality of the first rank, and likeness of the first degree, disagreeing in no respect, and in no manner unequal, and in no part dissimilar, but continually corresponding to him of whom it is the Image.

Unlike in the case of Trinitarian beauty, which consists in the proportion of equality that is characteristic of all persons, Augustine here attributes the relation of equality, which according to him is the essence of beauty, specifically to the Son. In other words, beauty in this case acts as a personal property of the Son that is specific to the Son as an individual. Beauty is attributed to the Son because he is a perfectly adequate image of the Father that is absolutely equal to him. Equality in the Son is something specific to this person and is based on his ability to reflect, image, represent or express the Father adequately. It is easy to see that what is at work here is Bonaventure's principle of beauty no. 2: the image is 'beautiful' when it adequately represents its prototype. Although Augustine does not elaborate the following aspect, one can conjecture that the Son will be beautiful based on Bonaventure's principle of beauty no. 1 as well: insofar as he reflects the form of the Father,[19] who, according to Bonaventure, is principal beauty.

As some scholars point out,[20] Augustine's, and subsequently Franciscan, understanding of God is different from the henological,[21] apophatic and mystical tradition of some Christian Platonists such as pseudo-Dionysius or the later tradition of medieval mystics from the school of Albert the Great.[22] This tradition stems from Plotinus and Proclus and views God as a principle (the One) that is beyond being and therefore beyond beauty as a structured or relational principle, such as proportion. For Augustine and his medieval followers such as Bonaventure and Duns Scotus, God is not beyond being. Therefore God's beauty is not analogous or metaphorical: God is beauty. Furthermore, for Augustine God is essentially the Trinity, and Trinitarian relations, such as the proportion of equality, which is also the principle of beauty, are at the center of God's life. God

17   *CCSL* 50, 241.
18   *CCSL* 62, 38.
19   The Son is, traditionally, a "perfect image" of the Father; see further discussion below.
20   Cf. J.-M. Fontanier, *La beauté selon saint Augustin* (Rennes: Presses Universitaires de Rennes, 1998), 136ff.
21   Cf. J.A. Aertsen, "Ontology and Henology in Medieval Philosophy (Thomas Aquinas, Meister Eckhart and Berthold of Moosburg)," in *On Proclus and his Influence in Medieval Philosophy*, eds. E.P. Bos and P.A. Meijer (Leiden/New York/Köln: E.J. Brill, 1992), 120-40.
22   Although for such Procleans and Albertists as Thomas Aquinas and Meister Eckhart, God is the pure or mere act of being (*esse*), for all practical purposes this *esse* remains undetermined and unknown (cf. J. Owens, *Aquinas on Being and Thing* [New York: Niagara University Press, 1981]), i.e., for them God is not a being in the same sense (univocally) as creatures are beings.

possesses a conceivable relational nature, and it is this beautiful form that the Son reflects.

Bonaventure discusses Hilary's attribution of the notion 'form-beauty' to the Son in his Commentary on the *Sentences*, Bk. I, Dist. 31, p. 2, a. 1, q. 3. One of the obvious objections to such an attribution[23] is that the term *species* in its meaning 'form' cannot be specifically attributed to anything, and as 'beauty' it is more appropriate for the Father who is the source and prototype of all beauty. Bonaventure, however, defends the view that Hilary attributes 'beauty' to the Son as his personal property. Answering Objection no. 5, he states that there are two reasons for ascribing "perfect beauty" to the Son. First, the Son is beauty "because he is a perfect [that is, precise and excellent] and express likeness" and "therefore he is beautiful in relation to him whom he expresses," that is, the Father. In this case equality (in the sense of presenting an adequate or perfect likeness) can be seen as a personal property of the Son who "...in relation to the Father ... possessess the beauty of equality, because he expresses him perfectly, as a 'beautiful' [that is, excellent] image..." (loc.cit., q. 3, Ad 5). Again, this is the second principle of beauty in the image according to Bonaventure: the image is beautiful if it is extremely accurate. Although at this point Bonaventure does not refer to his principle no. 1 it is clear that it is also at work: the formal beauty of the Father as the prototype must rest on the Son as his perfect reflection.

The second reason for attributing beauty to the Son is that he is also "perfect beauty" insofar as he is the exemplar and principle of all, or is the *cause of beauty* in all. One must stress that the Son is beauty not as the 'cause of all,' which would rather be the Father or the Trinity as a whole, but precisely as the principle of imaging

and shaping, and therefore form and beauty, in all created things. In other words, he "has beauty in relation to all beauty modelled on the exemplar" (loc.cit., q. 3, Ad 5). Hilary's appropriation highlights the fundamental differences between the persons that come to light if one considers their relation to procession. Thus it is only the Son whose procession has a formal aspect that can be expressed by the terms *species* and likeness (cf. loc.cit., q. 2, Resp.; cf. q. 3, Ad 5). The initial objection that the principle 'form' as such is not limited to the Son is thus addressed: the Son is form and beauty quintessentially, as its first instance and exemplar.

Just how the Son can be viewed as such a formal exemplar for all things must be further clarified. According to Bonaventure, insofar as the Son is *species*, or the principle of form, likeness, and expression in things, he is also the principle of cognition, since cognition essentially happens through distinguishing and recognizing (copying or expressing) the form of things, be it their physical shape or concept: "by virtue of having the principle of perfect likeness he possesses the principle of cognition" (loc.cit., q. 3, Ad 5). This idea further reinforces the connection between the Son and creatures: in relation to them he serves as the principle of knowledge as well as of their form. The two aspects of species or beauty—that of "manifest likeness" and that of "cognition"—are interrelated. Since the Son "has in himself the principle of express or manifest likeness, therefore he also has the one of cognition, for express likeness is the principle of knowing" (loc.cit., q. 3, Ad 5). Thus according to Bonaventure the Son-species is, on the one hand, the quintessential exemplar or principle of form and beauty for everything, and on the other hand, "he contains the principle of knowing" all

23   Bonaventure's Objection No. 2.

by virtue of possessing the "blueprints" and schemata (formal layout) of things.[24]

The second person of the Trinity, then, Bonaventure summarizes, is unique in being connected, on the one hand to the Father through the principle of perfect likeness, and on the other hand to the created world through the principle of imaging, form, and expression. This double connection, which is specific to this person, Bonaventure contends, is most adequately expressed by the term 'beauty' which encompassess all the above meanings:

> [the Son] (1) in relation to the Father has the beauty of equality, because he expresses him in a perfect way, as a perfect image, and (2) in relation to things contains all their principles ... it is therefore clear that the principle of all beauty (*pulchritudo*) is rightly found [to be contained] in the Son. Thus insofar as the Son proceeds naturally, he possesses the principle of perfect and manifest likeness; [and] insofar as he possesses the principle of perfect likeness, he possesses the principle of cognition; and [finally] by virtue of both [likeness and cognition] he possesses the principle of beauty. For because the term *species* implies (1) likeness and implies (2) the principle of knowing, it also implies beauty... (loc.cit., q. 3, Ad 5).

The Son as the universal principle of form, likeness, and imaging thus plays the role of an "intermediary." This aspect of the second person of the Trinity makes it typologically akin to the modern notion of the aesthetic. As one may remember,

the revelatory role of the aesthetic in modern thought gives it a mediating role between the realms of the immanent and the transcendent.[25] Beauty-form (and therefore, one can imply, Christ precisely as beauty-form), is perfectly positioned to fulfil such a mediating role: in addition to its revelatory capacity, according to Bonaventure it has the capacity of preserving its formal characteristics virtually intact during its transition between the prototype and the image. Thus Christ as the second person of the Trinity contains the foundational principles of the possibility and validity of imaging and thus art. In fact, in Augustine and the subsequent theological tradition, including Bonaventure, the Son is frequently referred to as the "Father's art."

However, one might object, so far Christ has acted as a purely metaphysical principle that grounds the very possibility of artistic imaging and gives it validity. But is there any connection, in Franciscan thought, between this abstract principle and the actual physical reality of earthly beauty and form? In Chapter Two of the *Itinerarium* Bonaventure, detailing the process of our ascent to God, draws a close analogy between the mechanism of sense perception and the operation of Christ as the second person of the Trinity through the principles of "form-beauty" (*species*) and "likeness." The sensible world enters the human soul "through perception," and first of all exterior sensible qualities enter through the five senses. What is being transmitted here across the boundary between the object and the sense faculty almost intact is a certain formal aspect of a thing, or its *species*. The next stage in the process of the apprehension of the world is pleasure (*oblectatio*) which follows the perception of compatibility between the soul and the perceived *species* (2.5). If this apprehension is of a

---

[24] The Son "...in relation to the [created] things ... possesses all their 'reasons'..." (loc.cit., q. 3, Ad 5); see more on this, including other textual material from Bonaventure, in O. Bychkov, *Aesthetic Revelation*, 268ff.

[25] See O. Bychkov, *Aesthetic Revelation*, 15ff.

"compatible" thing, pleasure immediately follows, for "all pleasure is due to being proportioned [in relation to something]." 'Likeness' and 'form-beauty' (*species*) are the general principles of sense perception: the exterior sensible qualities enter the soul through "likenesses."

After sense perception and pleasure comes judgment (*diiudicatio*; 2.6). It determines the reason for taking pleasure in a thing, or the "cause of the beautiful, sweet and wholesome," which it finds to be the "proportion of equality." Judgment, Bonaventure concludes,

> is a process which allows the sensible shape (*species*), which has been received by the senses in a sensible way, to enter the thinking faculty through purification and abstraction. And it is in this manner that all this [visible] world has access to the human soul through the gates of the senses....

The important fact here is that 'form-beauty' or 'likeness' acts as a sort of an intermediary between the sensory and intellectual cognition: the latter can be further "purified" from the sensible components of the former without the loss of the formal composition of the object.

Having thus outlined the process of sense perception through species, Bonaventure comes to the key point of the *Itinerarium*: the analogy between this process and the nature and workings of Christ (2.7). It is the first stage of "perception" (*apprehensio*; cf. 2.4) that provides the closest parallel with Christ. It is important that the second person of the Trinity does not serve as the analog of the subsequent "upper" stages of the process of perception which Bonaventure rather compares to the impact of the "divine light," or God in general. This detail reinforces the unique role of

Christ as *species*, in that in this capacity he is analogous precisely to the sensible or aesthetic. *Itinerarium* 2.7 reads:

> For all these things are vestiges in which we can see our God. Indeed, the perceived shape (*species*) is a likeness [which has been] generated in the medium and subsequently impressed upon the organ, and through that impression it leads back to its origin, namely the object of cognition. This clearly shows, therefore, that the eternal light [i.e., God] generates out of itself a co-equal, consubstantial, and co-eternal likeness or splendor [i.e., the Son]. Now just as the object [of perception] generates its likeness throughout the whole medium, [and] just as [this] shape (*species*) [is united] to the corporeal organ, [in the same way] he who is the 'image of the invisible God,' and the 'splendor of his glory,' and the 'form of his substance' (Col. 1:15; *Hebr.* 1:3) ... is united through the grace of the union to the individual of rational nature [i.e., the human soul], in order that through that union he might lead us back to the Father, as to [our] original source and [final] object. Therefore if all knowable things have [the ability] to generate their own shape (*species*), they openly proclaim that the eternal generation of the Word, the Image, and the Son eternally proceeding from God the Father can be observed in them as in mirrors.

This text is important for two reasons. First, it contains an analogy between, on the one hand the function of 'form-beauty' or 'likeness' in sense perception, including aesthetic experience, and on the other hand the generation of Christ as the 'image,' 'likeness' and *species*. Bonaventure finds clear similarities between the functioning of these two mechanisms of mediation and presentation: on the one hand, sense perception, and on the other hand, mediation through Christ of a more spiritual kind. In both cases, at a certain point the human soul is led back by means of a *species* to the primary source of this *species* (the object of perception or the divine principle respectively), which in both cases is somehow manifested or presented. This parallel between *species Christi* and the operation of the sensible *species*—the closest analog to the aesthetic in modern terms—means that Christ's form-beauty works at least in the way that is analogous to the modern aesthetic. The analogy is strengthened by the use of identical phrasing: "through *species* as an intermediary," "through likeness as an intermediary," "through Christ as an intermediary."[26]

Second, the text suggests that the mechanism of sense perception (including the aesthetic range of it), which is analogous to the workings of Christ, can trigger in us a sudden insight into the nature of Christ. Thus, just as in modern thought analogies with aesthetic experience provide deeper insights into the nature of other phenomena, including the divine in general, in the case of Bonaventure such an analogy provides an insight of a specifically Christian kind: into the nature of the Trinity and the specific qualities of the Second Person of the Trinity. One could say, once again, using the terminology of modern theological aesthetics, that sense perception in Bonaventure, including the perception of the beauty of shape and sound, can be revelatory, albeit of specifically Christian principles.

———•———

To conclude, in medieval Franciscan speculative theology the formal structures of reality, including the divine reality, are consistently viewed as being transmitted across various levels of reality without the loss of their formal integrity. Coupled with the Scotistic notion of the univocity of being, this would mean that eternal formal or structural qualities of reality such as proportions would be fundamentally the same in both God and the created world. This is almost diametrically opposed, e.g., to the view of some Dominican mystics of the Albertist school who see God as being above being and form, as "holy darkness" and inscrutable mystery. For them God could be interpreted in aesthetic terms as "beauty" only in the sense of the Neoplatonic καλόν, that is, as a transcendent principle that only has revelatory capacity, not actual form or structure. Such a view seems to favor the art that is revelatory in nature, and the best type of art here would be the one that reveals the very impossibility of representation, such as Malevich's *Black Square*. No specific form in art has any significance as such, since no concrete artistic representation ultimately has any value. To the contrary, Franciscan speculative theology seems to encourage the arts that use concrete and specific forms that are both beautiful and relevant precisely in their formal specificity (Fig. 3; see M. Lavin, Fig. 1).

---

[26] *mediante specie; mediante similitudine; mediante Christo.*

THE TRANSUBSTANTIATION OF ST. FRANCIS OF ASSISI: SEARCHING FOR A PARADIGM

Xavier Seubert

his essay is an hypothesis concerning certain images in the Basilica of San Francesco in Assisi. In both the upper and lower churches of the basilica are depictions of standard and also curious parallels and juxtapositions between St. Francis of Assisi and Christ as Pantocrator and Redeemer. These images of Francis and Christ were produced between 1288 and 1319: a time of significant soul searching for the Franciscan Order in its relationship to Francis.[1] It was also a time of significant theological development with regard to the Order's understanding of Christ's presence in the sacrament of the eucharist.[2] Could these socio-political and intellectual developments have been part of the context in which the pictorial linkings between Christ and Francis were made? Could it be that these images not simply illustrate these developments, but perhaps articulate conclusions, which, for various reasons, were not expressed or could not be expressed? This essay will present some possible answers to these questions.

An important element in interpreting the images is the desire for absolute poverty which Francis enjoins on the friars. He describes this poverty in the two written rules in which he articulates the path of life for his followers: in chapter nine of the earlier rule and chapter six of the later rule. In the latter we hear:

> Let the brothers not make anything their own, neither house, nor place, nor anything at all. As pilgrims and strangers in this world, serving the Lord in poverty and humility, let them go seeking alms with confidence, and they should not be ashamed because, for our sakes, our Lord made Himself poor in this world. This is that sublime height of most exalted poverty which has made you, my most beloved brothers, heirs and kings of the Kingdom of Heaven, poor in temporal things but exalted in virtue. ... Giving yourselves totally to this, beloved brothers, never seek anything

---

[1]   See John Moorman, *A History of the Franciscan Order from its Origins to the Year 1517* (Oxford: Clarendon Press, 1968), 177-204; 307-49. See also Michael Robson, *The Franciscans in the Middle Ages* (Woodbridge, UK: The Boydell Press, 2006), 95-107; 119-140.

[2]   David Burr, *Eucharistic Presence and Conversion in Late Thirteenth-Century Franciscan Thought* (Philadelphia: The American Philosophical Society, 1984). See also Gary Macy, *Treasures from the Storeroom: Medieval Religion and the Eucharist* (Collegeville: Liturgical Press, 1999), 81-120.

else under heaven for the name of our Lord Jesus Christ. [3]

Francis's intuition is that, in order to receive the total self-gift of God in the Incarnation of the Son, the recipient must be correspondingly emptied of self. The divine kenosis, as described in Philippians 2:5-11, can only be authentically met by a kenosis of the human recipient. Absolute poverty for Francis was how the friars would open their lives to the inexhaustible gift of life. Inexhaustible gift was to be matched by the emptiness of receptivity.

In the previous century, Joachim of Fiore, a Cistercian monk from Calabria and one of the most important interpreters of the Book of Revelation in the history of Christianity, developed an apocalyptic interpretation of world history and God's effect within it.[4] In the Joachimite scheme of things, which was an important influence on the worldview of the Franciscans of the thirteenth century, poverty was a mark of the apostolic church and an indication of its authenticity. For the early Franciscans, Francis's embodiment of poverty was an important confirmation of his advanced life in the spirit, if not superiority to the hierarchical church. Poverty, however, entailed more than ascetic discipline. It was, before all else, a means of movement, both socially and spiritually. It was at the heart of the early internal struggles with regard to the Franciscan way of life.

In the 1270s, the controversy among Franciscans over poverty crystallized in questions raised by a young Franciscan scholar, Peter of John Olivi. In discussing evangelical perfection, Olivi concluded that the highest poverty was better than wealth and that *usus pauper,* which was the poor or limited use of goods, was an essential aspect of the Franciscan vow of poverty. Bonaventure and Pope Nicholas III had already indicated that Franciscan poverty consisted of owning nothing and using what was necessary. But Olivi's making the *usus pauper* an essential part of the vow of poverty caused difficulties because it severely circumscribed the meaning of using what was necessary.[5] This is only one limited aspect of the enormously complex discussions over poverty, but it gives an indication of the state of the controversy around the time when the pertinent images in the Basilica of San Francesco were produced.

Rather than sorting through this controversy, which would be well beyond the scope of this essay, I would like to suggest a metaphor for understanding both the issue itself and the images of Francis which were constructed within the context of the dispute. In a seminal essay on *communitas*[6] in which he developed an essential insight into the poverty of Francis, Victor Turner, the anthropologist of ritual movement and pilgrimage, described Francis as a perpetual liminar, or traveler over the threshold between radically different spheres of reality. Poverty for Francis was a means of movement; absolute poverty was a means of ceaseless movement. But movement into what? Turner's structures provide some clarification.

In all ritual, whether it be a Muslim pilgrimage, a Jewish seder, or a Catholic baptism or eucharist, there is movement from one point to another. Once one desires to move—once one is drawn to a certain experience, there are certain stages necessary for the movement to be effective. There is, first of all,

---

[3]   Regis Armstrong, Wayne Hellmann, William Short, eds., *Francis of Assisi: Early Documents, Vol. I* (St. Bonaventure, NY: Franciscan Institute Publications, 1999), 103.

[4]   Bernard McGinn, *The Calabrian Abbott: Joachim of Fiore in the History of Western Thought* (New York: Macmillan, 1985).

[5]   David Burr, "Spiritual Franciscan Controversy," in *The Origin, Development, and Refinement of Medieval Religious Mendicancies*, ed. Donald S. Prudlo (Leiden/Boston: Brill, 2011), 279-80.

[6]   Victor Turner, "*Communitas*: Model and Process," in *The Ritual Process: Structure and Anti-Structure* (New York: Walter de Gruyter, 1995), 131-165. See also Paul Garwood, "Rites of Passage," in *Oxford Handbook of the Archaeology of Ritual and Religion*, ed. Timothy Insoll (Oxford: Oxford University Press, 2011), 261-84.

a separation stage in which one steps beyond whatever structures would impede movement. In a pilgrimage, one leaves behind quotidian patterns of work and socialization and sets out toward the holy place. In a seder or eucharist, one enters a space and time that is removed from the structures and commerce of everyday: day-to-day structures no longer bind here. This is Turner's anti-structural stage.

One then comes to a margin or threshold beyond which one is moving into a definitively new reality. The releasing of oneself, together with others and beyond ordinary structures, into that towards which the movement aims, fosters an exhilaration and a transformation in the power of that which is aimed at. And this is experienced together with the others on the journey, for the journey itself forges the travelers into a unity which stands outside normal social boundaries. This is the experience of *communitas*, which is at the basis of all the subsequent forms of community that may result from the experience.

For Francis, *communitas* was movement into and union with the life of Christ; doing this together with his companions was the life of the brotherhood. Poverty was the relentless movement toward the threshold where one definitively, if ritually, left behind the world of power, wealth and hierarchy and entered the reality of Christ. Absolute poverty signaled that one was in a perpetual state of liminality. It was the unbroken cultivation of *communitas* and a relentless resistance to reaggregation back into the structures by which the world of power and wealth functions. To allow reaggregation would mean to relinquish or mitigate the power of *communitas*. This same reality is at the basis of St. Clare's refusal to accept a rule for herself that mitigated absolute poverty.[7] To say that one may not or cannot live absolute poverty, might be equivalent to saying that one is prohibited from moving over the threshold and into the reality of Christ, or that it is simply impossible to do so. Neither Francis nor Clare would admit that.

Turner's structures help illuminate the controversy over poverty in the Franciscan Order. It was not essentially a matter of ordering poverty among other goods (e.g., the need for books, the need for houses, the need for education, etc.) in sensible fashion and for practical reasons, such as work and ministry. To use Turner's phraseology again, poverty for Francis was movement. Absolute poverty was a never-ending movement into Christ in life with the brothers. It was a never-ending resistance to structures of normalcy in which, it might be thought, the union with Christ could be domesticated. There can certainly be union with Christ without absolute poverty, but it would not be the way of Francis and Clare.

From a theological point of view and as we saw above in Francis's paralleling of God's kenosis with the poverty of the friars, it was this level of reality which was at stake in the early Franciscan controversy over poverty. The papal decision contained in *Exiit qui seminat*[8] of Nicholas III in 1279 certainly reaffirmed the centrality of poverty for the Franciscan Order. But it recognized that some friars needed certain goods if they were to be productive in the mission of the Church and, certainly, if they were to be useful instruments of the papacy. *Exiit* declared that the friars own nothing. Everything they use is owned by the papacy. But

---

7   See Maria Pia Alberzoni, "Clare and the Papacy," in *Clare of Assisi and the Poor Sisters of the Thirteenth Century* (St. Bonaventure, NY: Franciscan Institute Publications, 2004), 29-97.

8   For the text see Armstrong et al., *Francis of Assisi,* Vol. III, 737-64, at 737: "This apostolic constitution, intended by Pope Nicholas III as a response to developments in both the Church and the Order over the past quarter of a century, is the most famous of the papal clarifications of the *Later Rule*.... it consists of a series of questions arising from passages in the *Rule* of 1223, to which the Pope gives a definitive interpretation. Many of these had been brought up in the two previous bulls, and although sometimes the Pope simply repeats the verdict of his predecessors, in most cases he gives a substantial elaboration of their position."

they have use of houses and education and material things necessary for their mission and to care for the sick, etc.

After the death of Bonaventure in 1274, anxieties about laxity in the Order became more vocal and disruptive. Bonaventure had successfully defended the Order and its way of life against attacks from the outside.[9] Now the internal dissatisfaction became more apparent. As mentioned above, the issue centered on Olivi's interpretation of *usus pauper*. Even though his works, for reasons that are not entirely clear, were condemned in 1283 and then posthumously by the Minister General John of Murrovalle in 1299, Olivi was a moderate who had developed a balanced understanding of poverty. But this was still unacceptable to a significant group within the Order.[10]

The understanding of *usus pauper* claimed that, when a Franciscan friar vowed poverty, he was also vowing *usus pauper*. In other words, even if you accepted the reality decreed in *Exiit qui seminat*, you were still obliged to live poorly and to use things in a manner which did not contradict a poor way of life. In fact, in his brilliant discussions on the centrality of the will in human perfection—discussions which highly influenced Duns Scotus's treatments on the subject—Olivi goes so far as to view *usus pauper* as the natural state of human being before the fall.[11]

In one of her studies of Olivi's influence on Scotus, Mary Beth Ingham states the following, which is reflective of Olivi's position:

The natural state of the will is that state of reflexive self-mastery, lost when innocence was lost. The vow of poverty offers the means by which the will can return to its original rectitude: full self-mastery and restrained use of goods of the world. The state of the highest poverty assists the will in the recovery of its excellence in all its dignity: its breadth, length and height…. The capacity for this type of heroic self-control or natural self-sacrifice reveals the native dignity of the human will.[12]

This very Scholastic discussion, in the best sense of the word, can also be viewed as an interpretation of a certain experience of St. Francis. It is first of all important to note that several Franciscan scholars have drawn attention to an interpolation of the *Rule* of 1223, the so-called *Regula Bullata*. Based on the scholarship of recent decades, it was commonly thought that the beginning of the *Rule* read: "This is the life of the Gospel of Jesus Christ that Brother Francis petitioned the Lord Pope to grant and confirm for him and his brothers." More contemporary research[13] considers another possibility: "This is the life that Brother Francis petitioned the Pope, etc." This is very important because it emphasizes that the life, which the brothers lived together, preceded the Gospel. The Gospel illuminated or clarified what was going on in "the life," but it was the lived life that was primary. "The

---

9   Both Bonaventure and Thomas Aquinas were principal defenders of the mendicants' right to poverty against the secular theologians at the University of Paris. See Andrew Traver, "The Forging of an Intellectual Defense of Mendicancy in the Medieval University," in *The Origin, Development and Refinement of Medieval Religious Mendicancies*, ed. Donald S. Prudlo (Leiden/Boston: Brill, 2011), 157-95.

10   David Burr, *The Spiritual Franciscans: From Protest to Persecution in the Century after Saint Francis* (University Park, PA: Pennsylvania State University Press, 2001), 50-65.

11   Johannes Schlageter, *Das Heil der Armen und das Verderben der Reichen* (Werl, Germany: Coelde Verlag, 1989), 126.

12   Mary Beth Ingham, "Self-mastery and Rational Freedom: Duns Scotus's Contribution to the *usus pauper* Debate," *Franciscan Studies* 66 (2008): 343-44.

13   David Flood, "Living as Franciscans," *Frate Francesco* 73 (2007): 131-57. Michael Blastic, *A Study of the Rule of 1223: History, Exegesis and Reflection* (St. Bonaventure, NY: Franciscan Institute Publications, 2008), 16-17. See also David Flood, "The Genealogy of the Franciscan Rule," *Frate Francesco* 76 (2010): 383-407.

life" was that which the Lord showed Francis to do. It was a direct experience. Poverty, the way of descent and denudation, was at the center of the experience of the life.

The Gospel subsequently clarifies why this is the case. God is poor and God descends because this is the only way that the reality of Love can effect its life-giving union with humanity and overcome the barriers caused by sin and the fall. The poverty of kenosis is how God moves into our reality and it is revealed to Francis that it is how he must move into God. To deny poverty would be to deny the direct communication of the Lord to Francis. This is where Turner's insight is very important. Poverty for Francis is not simply an ascetic tactic; it is the very choreography of Francis's union with Christ.

There are many statements of Francis which could exemplify all of this, but one from *A Letter to the Entire Order* eloquently underscores the point. Francis says:

> O wonderful loftiness and stupendous dignity! O sublime humility! O humble sublimity! The Lord of the universe, God and the Son of God, so humbles Himself that for our salvation He hides Himself under an ordinary piece of bread! Brothers, look at the humility of God, and pour out your hearts before Him! Humble yourselves that you may be exalted by Him! Hold back nothing of yourselves for yourselves, that He Who gives Himself totally to you may receive you totally![14]

As is clear in Francis's *Testament*, he believed that it was the Lord who revealed to him what he should do and what the life of the friars should be.

No matter where a friar stood with regard to the debate on the level of poverty the Order should espouse, the value of and the right to poverty would have been defended by all friars. In the papal bull, *Cum inter nonnullos* of 1323, John XXII declares the belief in the absolute poverty of Christ to be heretical: a belief variously held by both the spiritual and conventual parties of the Order.[15] This was the negative highpoint of papal commentary on and disposition of the *Rule*. Francis's understanding of the divine inspiration to him as the basis of the *Rule* created an unavoidable tension between the authority of Rome and the authority of Francis. One can hear echoing from the past the declaration of Peter of John Olivi in the eleventh of his *Questions on Evangelical Perfection*: If the Pope

> audaciously and pertinaciously wishes to introduce some profane novelty in opposition to the counsels and examples of Christ and the apostles; and in opposition to the testimonies most worthy of belief, the regular statutes, and the examples of the angelic man Francis…: and in subversion of the whole evangelical state; then in this case he would not act as the vicar of Christ but as a noonday devil, and he should by no means be obeyed but rather resisted with all one's powers as Lucifer and the noonday devil.[16]

Although Olivi's statement is extreme and the problem of *usus pauper* had reached a crisis point in the time of John XXII, the authority of Francis with regard to the life of the brothers and their poverty, no matter how one ultimately interpreted these

---

[14]   Regis Armstrong, et al., *Francis of Assisi*, Vol. I, 118.

[15]   C.H. Lawrence, *The Friars: The Impact of the Early Mendicant Movement on Western Society* (London/New York: Longman, 1994), 62-64.

[16]   Quoted in Burr, *The Spiritual Franciscans*, 64, footnote 62.

things, was foundational and always problematic.[17] The images with which we will be concerned in the Basilica of San Francesco might offer a solution, but they might also be a further exacerbation of the difficulties! At any rate this issue of poverty and of Francis's authority in the Order are one aspect of the context of these images.

Before addressing the images themselves, I would like to look at one other important element of the context in which the images would have been understood: the eucharist. In his *Eucharistic Presence and Conversion in Late Thirteenth-Century Franciscan Thought*, David Burr maps out the Franciscan concerns with regard to the doctrine of transubstantiation. The doctrine basically maintains that the eucharistic bread and wine are transformed by the power of God and at the words of the priest into the body and blood of Christ. The accidents of bread and wine remain. Otherwise there would be no physical, sacramental presence to the reality of Christ. Burr calls this the Thomist-Bonaventuran thesis:

> Eucharistic conversion is seen by both men as a necessary explanation of Eucharistic presence in the sense that it provides, not only a cogent explanation of such presence, but the only one conceivable. In each case, the ways in which Christ can be present are limited to two, one of which is deemed impossible.

From this perspective, consubstantiation and annihilation are ruled out, not only because they are contradicted by authority, but they rob one of that single remaining alternative.[18]

The solution of Bonaventure and Aquinas was not universally accepted. Although the Fourth Lateran Council (1215) uses the term, there was some discussion among the Franciscans from Olivi to Scotus as to its appropriateness and how it could be properly understood. Transubstantiation seemed to unduly limit the power of God. God, it was thought, was being confined to what human reason could figure out and this in only very complicated fashion. While not denying what was doctrinally intended, the discussion refined the understanding of the presence of the reality of Christ and how it could take place outside of the heavenly body of Christ.

This discussion centered on the eucharistic presence, but it necessarily broadened awareness of how Christ might be present outside the eucharist and especially in the lives of men and women. Scotus, expanding on distinctions developed by Olivi, advanced an understanding of the heavenly Christ acquiring another space without altering the form of Christ's body. The main point is that transubstantiation in its strictly eucharistic context, does not exhaust the ways in which Christ can be sacramentally, i.e., bodily present in the world.[19]

---

[17] In far more diplomatic fashion, Bonaventure, in addressing Francis in the thirteenth chapter of *The Major Legend*, says the following: "Carry the seal of Christ, the Supreme Pontiff, by which your words and deeds will be rightly accepted by all as authentic and beyond reproach." Armstrong, et al., *Francis of Assisi*, Vol II, 637. Christ, the Supreme Pontiff, i.e., superior to every authority on earth, has approved the life and words of Francis by sealing them with the "finger of the living God" in the very flesh of Francis.

[18] Burr, *Eucharistic Presence*, 15.

[19] Burr, *Eucharistic Presence*, 76-98. I would like to thank Oleg Bychkov for pointing out these two passages from Duns Scotus (in his translation) which he came across while working on the forthcoming edition-translation of Book Four of the *Parisian Lectures* (*Reportatio* IV-A), which confirm this point: *Rep.* IV-A, Dist. 10, q. 3, n. 72 (Civitas Vaticana, bibl. apost., cod. vat. lat. 883, f. 245rb), "As for his assertion that one cannot posit Christ's body anywhere except sacramentally, it is true that God de facto has not ordained for it to be anywhere except sacramentally. However, the question is about what is possible—and it seems to be possible for him to make his body dimensionally where the body of air of the same quantity and shape has been previously..."; ibid., n. 76 (ibid., f. 245va), "I reply to the question, by granting God's power everything that does not include a manifest contradiction, that it can make Christ's body, or any other body, exist simultaneously in two places dimensionally, locally, and in a quantitative manner, with all its accidents...."

Within this discussion a certain element is particularly important with regard to the images to be discussed: intentionality in the reception of the eucharist. One of the more detailed developments of intentionality in medieval theology is done by Scotus.[20] The main point of his distinctions is the necessity of the openness of faith to be able to authentically and really receive the presence of Christ. Where faith is absent, as in the case of a non-believer or a Christian who despises the eucharist, Christ is not present in that person's reception of the sacrament; he or she receives only the species. This dramatically points up the active relational character of the presence of Christ. This is not to say that the faith of the recipient determines the metaphysical reality of the sacrament. But it is to say that the sacrament cannot be ultimately effective in the life of this individual without faith.

These theological developments have important implications for artistic depictions of Francis of Assisi: he is a model of effective intentionality. His devotion to the eucharist is well documented in the early biographies. They celebrate his belief in eucharistic transubstantiation and his deep desire for unhindered union with Christ. His receiving the stigmata on La Verna is the culmination of this belief and desire. In the *Breviloquium*, where Bonaventure speaks of eucharistic transformation, he describes a reality which will take place preeminently in Francis. Notice in this passage that the food is not transformed into the one eating, but the one eating is transformed into the food.

> But the mind does not attain Christ except through understanding and love, through faith and charity, so that faith gives light to recognize him and charity gives ardor to love him. Therefore, if any are to approach this sacrament worthily, they must feed on Christ spiritually by chewing it by means of the recognition of faith and receiving it with the devotion of love. In this way they will not be transforming Christ into themselves, but instead will be taken up into the mystical body of Christ.[21]

The eucharistic parallels to Francis's transformation into Christ find artistic expression in the image of Christ as the Man of Sorrows. The association of Francis with this image develops fairly early among Franciscans.[22] It is an image which describes the fulfillment in Francis of what Bonaventure articulates in the above passage. In this image, of which there are many variations, Christ is depicted as crucified and dead and yet standing or rising out of a freestanding tomb. It depicts Christ rising within death and, as such, describes the truth of the Paschal Mystery. In the Franciscan versions of this image, such as the later Venetian by Michele Giambono (active 1420-1462),[23] a diminutive Francis is pictured near Christ. Red lines are drawn from the wounds of Christ to the stigmata of Francis. (Fig. 1)

Eucharistic overtones are evident in the sarcophagus, which is reminiscent of the eucharistic altar and, in the case of Giambono, in the elaborate altar cloth or humeral veil draped in front of the sarcophagus/altar. Christ the priest and victim is the source of the eucharistic reality. But there is no bread and wine in this image, only Francis. It is as if Christ the priest is consecrating Francis into his own reality. On La Verna Francis becomes the

---

[20]   Macy, *Treasures*, 47.
[21]   Dominic Monti, ed., *The Works of Bonaventure: Breviloquium,* Vol. IX (St. Bonaventure, NY: Franciscan Institute Publications, 2005), 244.
[22]   Anne Derbes and Amy Neff, "Italy, the Mendicant Orders, and the *Byzantine Sphere,*" in *Byzantium: Faith and Power (1261-1557)*, ed. Helen C. Evans (New York: The Metropolitan Museum of Art, 2004), 456-58.
[23]   Helen C. Evans, *Byzantium: Faith and Power* (1261-1557) (New York: The Metropolitan Museum of Art, 2004), 484-85.

Fig 1. "The Man of Sorrows"; Michele Giambono; Venice, ca. 1420-1430; tempera and gold on wood; The Metropolitan Museum of Art, New York City.

eucharist he loved so well. As I have tried to demonstrate elsewhere, this would be analogous to the transubstantiation of Francis into the reality of Christ by Christ himself.[24]

Transformation into Christ is the goal of Christian spirituality. This is accomplished gradually through hearing the Word, receiving the sacraments and leading a Christian life. Transformation takes place through various levels and stages of mediation. The stigmatization of Francis, on the other hand, is a transforming of Francis into Christ's image through the direct intervention of the Seraphic Christ. Christ communicates himself directly to Francis beyond any other mediation, strictly sacramental or otherwise.[25] Because of this Francis is called the *alter Christus*,[26] another Christ. This brings to mind another and similar phrase, *in persona Christi*, which was applied to the ordained priest, episcopal and papal offices. When compared, these two phrases raise the question, once again, of parallel authorities: that of Francis and that of the church hierarchy.

An ordained priest was said to act *in persona Christi*:[27] in the consecration of the species of bread and wine he was thought to act in the person of Christ. The priest, and included here are bishops and popes in the exercise of their respective offices, is an instrumental cause in the confecting of the eucharist and in the administration of the other sacraments. This means that the words and actions of the priest are the physical instruments or means by which the power of Christ is efficaciously present within a liturgical situation. The priest speaks the words of consecration for Christ and is thus instrumental in the reality of Christ being present on the altar, but it is Christ himself, and not the priest, who transforms the species into the sacred body and blood. The priest's words are the bodiliness for the speaking of Christ. It is Christ who transforms the bread and wine into his body and blood; the priest is the instrument through which Christ is able to say the words over the bread and wine. This instrumentality is why the priest is said to act *in persona Christi* in the middle ages. This same type of instrumentality is also foundational to the office of bishop and pope.

The spirituality of the priest, or his personal conformity to Christ, does and does not matter. It does matter in the sense that the more a priest is, through his personal spirituality, transformed into the reality of Christ, the more the sacramental signs he orchestrates will resonate with the essential meaning of the sacrament.[28] On the other hand, because it is Christ who is source and reality of the sacraments, the personal disposition of the priest does not effect the presence of Christ in the sacrament; it is Christ who does this. The minimum required of the priest is that he has the

---

[24] Xavier John Seubert, "Isaiah's Servant, Christianity's Man of Sorrows, and Saint Francis of Assisi," in *Passion in Venice: Crivelli to Tintoretto and Veronese*, ed. Catherine Puglesi and William Barcham (New York: Museum of Biblical Art, 2011), 28-32. In chapter thirteen of *The Major Legend of St. Francis*, Bonaventure refers to the stigmata as "the Lord's *sacrament*." Armstrong, et al., *Francis of Assisi*, Vol. II, 633.

[25] This brings to mind Aquinas' discussion on the ways in which God can operate: "But it must be observed that God did not bind his power to the sacraments, so as to be unable to bestow the sacramental effect without conferring the sacrament…"(ST IIIa, Q. 64, Art. 7). The union which the eucharist signifies is conferred on Francis outside of the eucharistic celebration. It is the freedom of God's power that was the concern of Olivi and Scotus in their discussion of transubstantiation.

[26] The *alter Christus* was intimately connected with the stigmata and its sealing of the life of Francis as an image of Christ. Julian Gardner provides an insightful development of Bonaventure's handling of this material in *Giotto and His Publics: Three Paradigms of Patronage* (Cambridge: Harvard University Press, 2011), 39-43. H.W. van Os, "Saint Francis of Assisi as a Second Christ in Early Italian Painting," *Simiolus* 7 (1974): 115-32. See also John V. Fleming, *From Bonaventure to Bellini: An Essay in Franciscan Exegesis* (Princeton: Princeton University Press, 1982), 139-40. See also Ann Astell, " 'Adorned with Wounds': Saint Bonaventure's *Legenda maior* and the Franciscan Art of Poverty," in *Eating Beauty: The Eucharist and the Spiritual Arts of the Middle Ages* (Ithaca: Cornell University Press, 2006), 125-27.

[27] See Dennis M. Ferrara, "Representation or Self-Effacement? The Axiom *In Persona* Christi in St. Thomas and the Magisterium," *Theological Studies* 55 (1994): 195-224; and idem., "*In Persona Christi*: Towards a Second Naiveté," *Theological Studies* 57 (1996): 65-88.

[28] See Karl Rahner, "Priest and Poet," in *Theological Investigations III* (Baltimore: Helicon Press, 1967), 294-317.

intention to do what the church does in the eucharistic celebration.[29]

The reality of Francis is something quite different. In the stigmatization, he himself is not an instrumental cause for some other effect. Rather, he is the effect itself: Christ's presence to him has transformed him into the image of Christ without any other mediation: Christ has transformed Francis into Christ's own life. Perhaps the only analogue for this is transubstantiation: Christ himself transforms the species of bread and wine into his own body and blood, but through the mediation of the priest. Francis is an *alter Christus* because Christ has directly transformed him into his own image without the normal sacramental mediation.[30] We will see how this is translated into some of the images in Basilica of San Francesco.

This brings us back to the discussion on intentionality as necessary for the valid reception of the eucharist.[31] The Franciscan Alexander of Hales developed this concept, in ways similar to his contemporaries, and it was advanced by both Franciscans and Dominicans. Alexander held that unless one had faith and the intention of receiving the sacrament, one did not receive the body and blood of Christ, but only the species. This reality was further heightened by the intensity of the love of the recipient for Christ. Behind all of these discussions of the eucharist was an implicit Franciscan understanding of what the sacrament was. It wasn't simply about the metaphysical and efficacious presence of Christ on the altar, although that was of utmost importance. It was about God's choosing to relate effectively to human beings and human beings responding effectively to God. In the case of Francis, this exchange results in the stigmata, or the

bearing of the marks of the crucified Jesus on his own body. This had tremendous implications for a world in which this holy commerce was not only thought possible, but was marvelously demonstrated on the body of Francis. Christ was in Francis and Francis was in Christ: a pinnacle of what the eucharist intended to effect.

It is clear that this is different from, although related to, the causality we have been considering. Instrumental causality means that a priest, bishop or pope are the instruments through whom Christ works an effect in and on God's people. They themselves do not need to be transformed into Christ. In fact, they can be quite sinful and still function as instruments. This is the anti-Donatist understanding, which I mentioned above. Francis's being effected into an image of Christ by Christ himself means that he, Francis, is the presence of Christ in an extraordinary and miraculous way. This further raises the question of the authority of Francis. Although he was obedient to the ecclesiastical authority to the end, the Lord told him what to do; the Lord gave him his rule of life; the Lord transformed him into an image of Christ himself. Is the immediacy of Christ to Francis a higher authority than the instrumentality of the ecclesiastical hierarchy? It is a question which is permanently enshrined in the images of the Basilica of San Francesco in Assisi.

What is the connection between all of this and our images? First of all, I am not saying that there is any direct connection between them, in the sense of a specific text being the inspiration of a specific image. What I have described is part of the intellectual atmosphere of the Order at this time, especially among intellectuals with

---

[29] This conclusion stems from the Donatist controversy of the fourth century. The Donatist held, among other things, that a priest who was a sinner could not administer the sacraments. This belief is combated by St. Augustine among others.
[30] Bonaventure expresses this poetically and repeatedly in the thirteenth chapter of *The Major Legend of Saint Francis*. See Armstrong, *Francis of Assisi*, Vol. II, 630-639. See also Hans Urs von Balthasar, "Bonaventure," in *Studies in Theological Styles: Clerical Styles*, vol. 1 of *The Glory of the Lord: A Theological Aesthetics*, trans. Andrew Louth et al., ed. John Riches (San Francisco: Ignatius Press, 1984), 270-76.
[31] Macy, *Treasures*, 36-58.

reservations about certain mainstream currents. Julian Gardner has established that the superiors of San Francesco during the time of the production of the images were from the Santa Croce friary in Florence and would have been in the conventual camp of the poverty controversy.[32] On the other hand, Napoleone Cardinal Orsini, the latest in a long line of Orsini patronage, was one of the main patrons of San Francesco at this time. Ubertino Casale, a protégé of Peter of John Olivi, was in the service of the Orsini cardinal in the early years of the fourteenth century. Hence, one cannot exclude a spiritual influence on the images of this period. Both groups would have had an interest in accentuating and making preeminent the spiritual authority of Francis. This preeminence is most clearly articulated in the Assisi images.

As Rosalind Brooke indicates, St. Bonaventure's understanding of Francis is the one which gets translated into depictions of Francis in the upper and lower churches of the Basilica of San Francesco. This is secured both in the ministers general, who were devoted to Bonaventure and were in office during the decoration of the basilica, and in the cardinals protector of the Order from the Orsini family, who were benefactors of the Basilica. Bonaventure was initially influential in having the Orsini appointed as protectors. These influences are solidified in the election of the Franciscan Jerome of Ascoli as Nicholas IV. He was successor to Bonaventure as minister general and was a protégé of the Orsini Pope Nicholas III who had raised Jerome to the office of cardinal.[33] The Bonaventuran identification of Francis with Christ as manifested in his *Legenda maior* and especially in chapter thirteen

on the stigmatization is the thread that runs through the decorations of the upper and lower churches of the San Francesco Basilica. Even if we often cannot always precisely pinpoint patron and artist, the influence of Bonaventure throughout is secure.

In the upper church of the Basilica of San Francesco in the Intercessor Vault,[34] (Fig. 2) which was done by the so-called Roman Masters between 1288 and 1290, the central image is of Christ the Pantocrator. (Fig. 3) This Christ is in a typical pose of blessing with his right hand, while in his left hand he holds a scroll indicating that he is the divine wisdom at the basis of all reality. The two middle segments of the vault, which flank Christ the Pantocrator, form a deësis consisting of Mary, the Mother of God, on Christ's right and John the Baptist, the Forerunner, on Christ's left. These two figures are positioned turning toward the Christ figure with their hands gesturing toward him in supplicatory fashion.

Up to this point the images are traditional. It is the image of Francis in the vault segment opposite Christ the Pantocrator which invites scrutiny. (Fig. 4) Francis, like Christ, looks outward, straight toward the viewer, unlike the figures of John and Mary, which are centered on Christ. Rather than gesturing supplicatingly toward Christ, he holds up his hands, palms outward, displaying the wounds in his hands while the wound in his side is conspicuous through an opening in his habit. It is as if he is the other side of the image of Christ. In the Pantocrator image, the Christ is the resurrected and glorious ruler of the cosmos. In the Francis image we see displayed the marks of the suffering which led to the glory of the resurrection. In the Christ

---

[32]   Gardner, *Giotto and His Publics*, 50, 61-2.

[33]   Rosalind B. Brooke, *The Image of St. Francis: Responses to Sainthood in the Thirteenth Century* (Cambridge: Cambridge University Press, 2006), 418-19.

[34]   Giorgio Bonsanti, ed., *The Basilica of St. Francis in Assisi: Upper Basilica* (Modena, Italy: Franco Cosimo Panini Editore Spa, 2002), 922-31, esp. at 923; Testi, 551-52.

Fig 2. "Vault of the Intercessors"; Roman Masters; Assisi, ca. 1288-90; fresco; Basilica of San Francesco, Assisi, Upper Basilica.

Fig 3. "Christ"; Roman Masters; Assisi, ca. 1288-90; fresco; Basilica of San Francesco, Assisi, Upper Basilica.

Fig 4. "St. Francis"; Roman Masters; Assisi, ca. 1288-90; fresco; Basilica of San Francesco, Assisi, Upper Basilica.

and Francis juxtaposition we see the two sides of the one reality: glory of the resurrection through the suffering of the cross. It is as if Francis, in his identification with Christ, becomes an extension of Christ himself.

The Pantocrator image of Christ relates to several details mentioned above. The image of Christ in the Intercessor Vault is orchestrated toward the main altar and, hence, is related to the eucharist which is celebrated there. One immediately thinks of this Christ as the source and goal of the eucharistic presence on the altar. The Pantocrator aspect of the image speaks of the omnipotence of God. The reference to the altar of the eucharist implies that through the omnipotence of God Christ can be present in heaven and also in the eucharistic meal. This omnipotence can also allow Christ to be present in an exclusive or preeminent way in Francis. This is especially true when you think of the eucharist, not as a static presence, but as a relational dynamic, which was so dear to Franciscans. The vault images, while confirming the sacramental reality of the liturgy of the Roman Church, also set limits, in the image of Francis, to the hierarchy's authority and governance in matters of ritual presence. The presence of Christ is effective in the life of Francis through the direct omnipotence of the dead, risen and glorified Christ. As I mentioned above, perhaps the only adequate analogy we have for this is transubstantiation.

I believe this interpretation is confirmed in another vault setting in the Magdalene Chapel in the lower church.[35] (Fig. 5) The arrangement of images, produced between 1307 and 1308, seems obviously to allude to the images in the Intercessor Vault of the upper church.[36] Christ the Redeemer

in a Pantocrator stance is flanked by Mary and Martha who are both turned towards him. (Fig. 6) Opposite the Christ figure is Lazarus, the brother of Martha and Mary, still draped in his funeral shroud, but luminous with light and stunned to be raised from the dead.[37] (Fig. 7) What is indicated here is that Jesus, in his omnipotence, has directly communicated his spirit to the very dead Lazarus and made him alive with his own life. The paralleled juxtapositions of the images of the two vaults imply the situation of Lazarus as a paradigm for the reality of Francis: the direct communication of life between Christ and his friend.

When one leaves the Magdalene Chapel and looks west toward the main altar one is struck by the image of Francis in glory which occupies the west segment in the vault of the presbytery.[38] (Fig. 8) The entire vault was decorated by the workshop of Giotto in the early fourteenth century. Francis is seated upon an imperial, Byzantine-like throne, the cloth of glory in the background protruding above to become a canopy over Francis's head. A brilliant gold nimbus surrounds his head while golden rays radiate from behind him. He holds a rod surmounted by a cross in one hand and a book in the other. The stigmata on his hands and side are visible. He is dressed in a magnificent habit/dalmatic with an underlying grey color and covered with medallions of gold. He is surrounded by angels, most of whom are looking away from him. The warning of God to Moses in Exodus 33:20 comes to mind: "You cannot see my face; for no one shall see me and live." Above Francis is a red standard on which is imaged a cross of triumph surrounded by seven stars, symbolizing either the seven churches in the Book of Revelation

[35] Giorgio Bonsanti, ed., *The Basilica of St. Francis in Assisi: Lower Basilica* (Modena, Italy: Franco Cosimo Panini Editore Spa, 2002), 390-405, esp. 398; *Testi*, 381-93.
[36] Brooke, *The Image of St. Francis*, 417.
[37] John 11:1-46.
[38] Bonsanti, *The Basilica of St. Francis in Assisi: Lower Basilica*, 406-45, esp. at 424-25; *Testi*, 393-99.

Fig 5. "Vault, Chapel of the Magdalene"; Maestro delle vele, Giotto, Workshop of Giotto; Assisi, 1307-1308; fresco; Basilica of San Francesco, Assisi, Lower Basilica.

Fig 6. "The Redeemer"; Workshop of Giotto; Assisi, 1307-1308; fresco; Basilica of San Francesco, Assisi, Lower Basilica.

Fig 7. "Lazarus"; Maestro delle vele; Assisi, 1307-1308; fresco; Basilica of San Francesco, Assisi, Lower Basilica.

Fig 8. "Presbytery Vault, St. Francis in Glory"; Maestro delle vele; Assisi, ca. 1315; fresco; Basilica of San Francesco, Assisi, Lower Basilica.

or the seven ages of the world of apocalyptic literature of the twelfth and thirteenth centuries . The standard is surmounted by what appears to be a seraph.

Julian Gardner has perspicaciously related this image of Francis to other images in Rome:

> His (Francis's) placement consciously imitated the enthroned Saviors of the great early Christian basilicas of Rome, such as Saint Peter's or San Paolo fuori le Mura, remade by Innocent III and Honorius III respectively.[39]

This placement, once again, has extraordinary implications. There is an implicit merging of the figures of Christ and Francis. Francis is also positioned above the eucharistic altar. His is the image which would be seen from the nave during any liturgical service. There is an intended confluence and identification among Christ, Francis and eucharist.

This is further confirmed in the image's probable interpretation of Francis as the Angel of the Sixth Seal from the Book of Revelation 6:12: "I saw another angel ascending from the rising of the sun, having the seal of the living God...." In the ribbing of the vault to the right of the Francis figure are a series of images from the Book of Revelation: the Lord of the Apocalypse, the Lamb, the Golden Altar, the Crystal Sea and the Cloud. This confirms the apocalyptic content of the vault decoration. Joachim of Fiore had identified Christ as the Angel of the Sixth Seal; Bonaventure and the Franciscans after him identify this figure with Francis. Francis becomes the one who is ultimately sealed by the living God and who seals others in gathering them into the Body of Christ. The Angel of the Sixth Seal

is the one who halts the destruction of humanity and the world until the allotted number of those to be saved are sealed with the sign, the Tau, which will save them from destruction. In a world of much violence and destruction, it was a most positive interpretation of history and Francis in his life and preaching was considered to be its inauguration. Francis here is not simply an instrument of God's plan for history; his person and preaching are themselves the inauguration of a new age and the realization of God's plan.[40] He is the fulfillment of the unity with Christ which is symbolized in the eucharist.

All of this is done through the direct communication of life between Christ and Francis, which culminates in the stigmata. This is what I mean by the transubstantiation of Francis into Christ. As theologically difficult as the analogy may be, it is perhaps the reason why Franciscans for centuries have articulated their union with the spirit of Francis in ways similar to their involvement in the very presence of Christ. The one is the other side of the other through the direct power of Christ in the life of Francis. The images I have discussed articulate this in ways that words are not yet able to express.

These images are only an indication of the same intuition of the union between Christ and Francis which is present in the fresco cycles of both the upper and lower churches of the San Francesco Basilica. As audacious as the suggestion of the direct transubstantiation of Francis through his immediate connection to Christ may seem, it is not unique in the history of Christianity. I would like to end with another paradigm which points up the very Catholic tradition in which a transubstantiation of Francis is involved: it is that of St. Ignatius of Antioch.

[39] Gardner, *Giotto and His Publics*, 91. H. W. van Os has identified a similar image in the fresco series done by Benozzo Gozzoli in the apse of the church of San Francesco in Montefalco in Umbria. The depiction of Francis as a "Second Redeemer" was produced in 1451-52. See van Os, "St. Francis of Assisi as a Second Christ," 130.
[40] Fleming, *From Bonaventure to Bellini*, 129-157.

Fig 9. "St. Francis in Glory"; Maestro delle vele; Assisi, ca. 1315; fresco; Basilica of San Francesco, Assisi, Lower Basilica.

St. Ignatius was the third bishop of Antioch, was born in Syria around 50 C.E. and was martyred in Rome between 98 and 117 A.D. Ignatius developed an understanding of his identification with Christ and Christ's suffering which resulted in a eucharistic reality for the community. Ignatius sees Christ's death as the threshold between earthly and heavenly realities. It is the point at which the one who is attached to us in his humanity becomes the source or conduit, if you will, of the heavenly reality into the lives of those connected to him.

This reality is described in terms of *agape*, the unifying and life giving love which comes from God, is symbolized in the eucharistic meal, and is the life of the community. *Agape* is very similar to the power of *communitas*, described by Turner. Ignatius is quite literal in describing his death in eucharistic terms. He sees his being killed by the circus lions and his subsequent cremation as the grinding of grains of wheat into flour and the baking of the bread. His death will release the power of *agape*, and this will affect and strengthen, not only his own community, but will also have a salvific affect on the crowd in the Coliseum. Through his moving over the threshold in imitation of Christ and into a death like his, the power of *agape*, which is ultimately the life of the Trinity,

is released in his body and into the lives of all those connected to him in love and also in the lives of all those witnessing the spectacle. Ignatius becomes the eucharistic meal for his community.[41]

In the same way, the life and body of Francis, which bear the very death marks of Jesus in the stigmata, stand perpetually at the threshold between the earthly and heavenly realities. This is the essence of absolute poverty. In Ignatian terms it expresses that Francis, as the traveler over the threshold, is a source and conduit of *agape*, of the Trinitarian heart of love which we call Christ, into the lives of all those who are connected to him. He himself becomes, in the most basic sense of the phrase, a eucharistic meal for his brothers and sisters.

This reality is declared in the images of the San Francesco Basilica, which are discussed above. They point up both the eucharistic reality of the poverty and life of Francis and the source and nature of his extraordinary authority, which was intuited as being outside of and perhaps beyond every other authority in church and world. This *alter Christus* appeared in the church of the thirteenth century as one "ascending from the rising of the sun and having the seal of the living God." (Fig. 9)

---

[41]   David C. Klawiter, "The Eucharistic and Sacramental Realism in the Thought of St. Ignatius of Antioch," *Studia Liturgica* 37 (2007): 129-63.

BONAVENTURE, BESSARION AND THE FRANCISCAN COAT OF ARMS

Irving Lavin

To Servus Gieben, O.F.M. Cap., in admiration and appreciation

n a brief appendix to an essay on Pisanello's portrait medal commemorating the visit to Florence of the Byzantine Emperor John VIII Paleologus, I recounted the story, reported in a sixteenth century biography of St. Bonaventure, of his having adopted an unorthodox coat of arms when he was made cardinal in 1273 by Gregory X, to serve as the pope's representative at the second Council of Lyon in 1272-74.[1] Bonaventure was a chief exponent of the purpose of the Council, to bring about the reconciliation and union of the Latin and Greek churches. Although it proved to be short-lived, the reunion was achieved, and it may be said to have been emblematized by the coat of arms Bonaventure adopted: not a gentilitial bearing, but an image of his personal mission in the form of two hands crossed and joined by the wound of a nail of the Cross (Fig. 1).[2] The biographer added that Bonaventure's escutcheon was the origin of the familiar blazon of the Franciscan order. Particularly interesting in this context is one of the early examples of the latter found in the friary church at San Francesco del Deserto, Venice, which clearly reflects Bonaventure's device—eminently appropriate because it was Bonaventure who in his *Legenda maior* recorded Francis's visit to the island to take refuge from a storm (Fig. 2).[3] The biographer's story has received confirmation in subsequent studies of the subject by Servus Gieben, but the problem remains as to how and when this institutional extrapolation took place.[4] There is no record of an official adoption of the seal, and no examples

---

[1] "Pisanello and the Invention of the Renaissance Medal," in Joachim Poeschke, ed., *Italienische Frührenaissance und nordeuropäisches Mittelalter. Kunst der frühen Neuzeit im europäischen Zusammenhang* (Munich: Hirmer, 1993), 67-84.

[2] The earliest depictions of St. Bonaventure with the motif appear in the late fifteenth century (Servus Gieben, *Lo stemma francescano. Origine e sviluppo* [Rome: Istituto Storico dei Cappuccini, 2009], 10, 14f). The motif is singularly like the crossed hands of the bust-length *Imago Pietatis* that were just then coming into vogue. The shift from the chest-length to the bust-length *Imago Pietatis* including crossed hands may be discerned in the comprehensive survey by Catherine Puglisi and William Barcham, "Gli esordi del Cristo passo nell'arte veneziana e la pala feriale di Paolo Veneziano," in Francesca Cavazzana Romane et al., eds., *"Cose nuove e cose antiche": Scritti per Monsignor Antonio Niero e Don Bruno Bertoli* (Venice: Biblioteca nazionale marciana, 2006), 403-30.

[3] St. Francis on the island is the main theme of Marilyn Aronberg Lavin's study in this volume, "The Joy of St. Francis: Bellini's Panel in the Frick Collection." The slab in which the device is carved, which includes an inscribed date 1499, is reproduced in Francesco Ferrari, O.F.M., *Il francescanesimo nel Veneto dalle origini ai reperti di S. Francesco nel Deserto: appunti per una storia della provincia veneta dei frati minori* (Bologna: Documentazione scientifica editrice, 1990), 398, pl. LXVI.

[4] S. Gieben, *Lo stemma francescano*, with earlier bibliography, especially idem, "S. Bonaventura e l'origine dello stemma francescano," *Doctor Seraphicus* 55 (2008): 67-80.

Fig 1. St. Bonaventure. Late Fifteenth Century. Museo Storico Francescano, Rome

Fig 2. Coat of Arms. San Francesco del Deserto, Venice

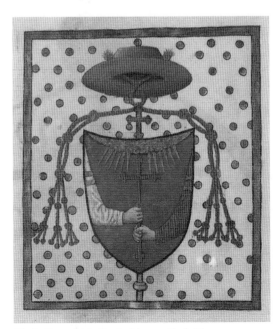

Fig 3. Bessarion's Coat of Arms. Cod. Marc. It. VII 2700 (=12998), fol. 2v. Biblioteca Marciana, Venice

Fig 4. Copy after Gentile Bellini, Bessarion holding his relic of the True Cross. Galleria dell'Accademia, Venice

of its use are known before the latter half of the fifteenth century.[5]

The purpose of this note is to suggest that the emblem of the order did not in fact arise until nearly two centuries after the Lyon conference, under virtually the same circumstances that had led St. Bonaventure to invent his personal device. I speak of course of the Ecumenical Council held at Florence, 1439-1445, under the auspices of Pope Eugenius IV. As an ecclesiastical leader passionately devoted to the reconciliation of the churches St. Bonaventure had an almost exact counterpart in Cardinal Bessarion (1403-72), who was no doubt intimately familiar with the history of the earlier council and, one can only assume, with the story of Bonaventure's coat of arms. When Eugenius named him cardinal in 1439 to represent the Catholic Church at the council, Bessarion also adopted a coat of arms markedly analogous to Bonaventure's, except that the two hands are now arms, conjoined by virtue of supporting the Cross (Fig. 3). The arms wear liturgical garb, one white, one red, each marked by two brocaded bands, again in reference to the Greek and Latin churches.[6] As a Greek, the two arms in Bessarion's escutcheon embrace the cross in a personal, as well as ecclesiastical way. These themes were surely reflected in the portrait of Bessarion by Gentile Bellini, preserved in an early copy, in which he is shown holding with both hands the famous relic of the True Cross which he bequeathed to the Scuola di Santa Maria della Carità in Venice, in 1472 (Fig. 4). Bessarion's device also ingeniously refers to an ancient tradition, primarily in his native Byzantium, but common also in the west, in which two lofty personages, Constantine and Helena, emperor and spouse, emperor and son, together display the cross, in reference to the Feast of the Exaltation of the Cross.[7] This motif was a major theme in Byzantine coinage, where pairs of rulers jointly sustain a cruciform staff (Fig. 5). Finally, in the scene of the Exaltation in his frescoed cycle of the story of the True Cross in Santa Croce, Agnolo Gaddi showed Heraclius holding the cross in his two veiled hands as he returns the relic to Jerusalem after recovering it in his victory over Chosroes (he actually returned only half the cross, the other he brought back to Constantinople) (Fig. 6). Bessarion must have known the cycle well from his time in Florence. Bessarion was named protector of the Franciscan order in 1458, and was thus in a unique position of personal and official authority to encourage and even influence the concept and design of a symbol of the order. The development was no doubt further encouraged by Sixtus IV's canonization of Bonaventure in 1482.

In its descent from Bonaventure, the emblem of the order, in which Christ's arm crosses with that of St. Francis, continued to reflect the major role the Order played in the history of efforts to reunite the main branches of Christianity, while also expressing the community's devotion to Francis's imitation of Christ and the indissoluble fraternal bond between the members of the order. Bessarion's reprise of the idea and basic scheme of Bonaventure's emblem helped to inspire the underlying theme of the device and inaugurate its ubiquitous adoption in the succeeding years: the spiritual consanguinity of all humans engendered by Christ's sacrifice on the Cross.

[5]   For a recent survey of the earliest, i.e., late fifteenth-century, examples, see Cesare Tinelli, "Überlegungen zum Franziskanischen Wappen," in *800 Jahre Franz von Assisi. Franziskanische Kunst und Kultur des Mittelalters*, exhib. cat. (Vienna: Amt der NÖ Landesmuseums, 1982), 376-81. None can be dated before Bessarion's cardinalcy.

[6]   See Raimondo Leonertz, in *Enciclopedia Cattolica*, 12 vols (Vatican City: Ente per l'Enciclopedia Cattolica e per il Libro Cattolico, 1949-54), II, cols. 1497-8.

[7]   On this gesture in relation to the liturgy, see Barbara Baert, *A Heritage of Holy Wood*: *The Legend of the True Cross in Text and Image* (Leiden: Brill, 2004), 124-32.

Fig 5. Michael VII Doukas and Maria of Alania, Phillip D. Whitting, Byzantine Coins. *(New York: Putnam, 1973), No. 457.*

Fig 6.

A BYZANTINE FRANCISCAN AND THE COINCIDENCE OF OPPOSITES*

Robert Lentz

he Franciscan tradition of art is as alive as the Franciscan movement. Some centuries have been more glorious than others. History—the judgment of those who follow you—will judge our work in this 21st century. I introduce myself to you as someone intensely interested in both Franciscan aesthetics and evangelization. As a Byzantine iconographer, I feel the need to introduce a greater expression of transcendence in our religious art, while, as one who is involved in evangelization, I do not want to lose our Franciscan charism of glorifying God in the "ordinary." For almost thirty years I have been an active agent in making iconographic symbolism more relevant to people of our time, and have noticed in the last ten years that my new images are being copied by other artists, both in the Americas and in Europe. In 2004, as I was walking towards the Basilica of San Francesco in Assisi, for example, just before I reached the main piazza, I glanced in the window of an ecclesiastical art store and saw an exact copy of my icon, *The Meeting of St. Francis and St. Clare*, (Fig. 1) painted by an Italian artist. Two years later, a different exact copy sat in the same window when I walked past. This iconographic type has now entered into the tradition. Back in the 90's, I depicted St. Clare with a cat. I now see cats with St. Clare, in other contemporary icons. In 1986, I placed bandages over Francis' stigmata when I painted his bust. Now bandaged Francises are popping up in the work of other artists. I have just finished a nine by seven foot panel icon of the Holy Trinity, based on the theology of St. Bonaventure, for a church in Houston, Texas. At its blessing, the archbishop referred to it as a new standard for images of the Trinity in our time. Through this image, Franciscan theology, with its exciting insights, is re-entering the life of the contemporary Church at large. As the maker of these images, which are influencing the art tradition you study, I offer you this paper, which is a reflection on my own life as an artist and a friar.

At the turn of the last century, just before the 1905 Revolution, my paternal grandparents left what was then the Russian Empire. Their coming to America was a traumatic event that left family roots both broken and tangled. After settling in Massachusetts, they moved to Buffalo. Anti-immigrant sentiment sent them across the continent to the Colorado Rockies, where their Model T Ford broke down and they could go no farther. To their dismay,

* "A Byzantine Franciscan and the Coincidence of Opposites" images provided by: Br. Robert Lentz, OFM, and Trinity Stores. www.trinity-stores.com, info@trinitystores.com, 800.699.4482

Fig 1.

they found that the Ku Klux Klan controlled the Colorado state government with the Grand Dragon sitting in the governor's chair and Klansmen in full regalia marching down Colfax Avenue, in Denver. They watched crosses burn in their neighborhood. I grew up with these stories.

I also listened to more magical stories as a child: stories of bands of wild Cossacks riding through villages in southwestern Russia, of endless fields of sunflowers, and of monastery churches full of icons. My grandmother's small house was full of images of saints, and I soon had the wall next to my bunk bed covered with paper holy cards. I learned to pray in the vast expanses of prairie that once opened to the horizon, east of Denver. My image of God was that of the transcendent Pantocrator, a face I had seen in my grandmother's icons, reinforced by my experience on the American steppes.

My favorite holy card was one of St. Francis of Assisi, with birds in his left hand and on his shoulders. I remember the gilt edges of the card and the bright colors of the print. It was no icon, but it became a window for me into heaven, nevertheless. From the time I was six years old, I knew I wanted to be like this saint. When I was eight, I made myself a habit out of gunnysacks and a rope. My father wasn't pleased at all. He had little use for priests and looked forward to having as many grandchildren as possible.

When I was 17 years old, I left for Detroit to become a friar in the Province of St. John the Baptist. I was drawn especially to the contemplative side of Franciscan life, which seemed to recede, like an ocean wave on a sandy beach, each year in the 60's. In theology, I longed for something more, too young to know that it was the mystical theology that lay behind my grandmother's icons. When the time came to make solemn vows, I left, instead, and

began a pilgrimage of almost 35 years, which has led me back into the Order, now as an old man.

This pilgrimage took me through Latin America to a Russian Orthodox orphanage in Santiago, Chile. I lived in several Russian and Greek monasteries, where I learned the tradition of hesychastic prayer and how to paint icons. I heard fascinating stories from exiled men and women who had fled the Bolsheviks in the 1920's. I listened to crazed Orthodox monks who expected the imminent arrival of the Antichrist and had found caves in nearby mountains where they intended to hide when he did appear. I entered fully into the ghetto of the Russian Church in Exile, exploring my family's roots and the theological world of the Byzantine East.

In 1982, I met a Catholic priest in San Francisco who worked with marginalized Catholics, not far from the Russian Cathedral on Geary Boulevard. When the flat above his became available, I rented it with another Russian artist. Throughout the week, Father Daniel O'Connor hosted support groups, evening retreats, and simple meals for all sorts of people pushed aside by the Church. For the first time in my life, I found myself surrounded by Communists of every hue, by feminists and gay folk, by atheists and artists. In the contemplative setting of his flat, I learned to listen to new stories and began to see God's face from different angles. In time, these new perspectives began to demand expression in the icons I was painting.

I cannot remember a time when I have not made images. As a tiny child, it was with crayons. I won a set of pastels in grade school and began to experiment with more sophisticated media. While my family fished in the high Rockies, I taught myself how to sculpt wood. I learned how to build walls with fieldstone and how to weave cloth. But it was the Byzantine icon that always fascinated me,

Fig 2.

trying as it did to express what happens when God touches a human life. My early attempts at making icons were earnest but comical. In the mid-70's I met an emigre from Leningrad who had studied iconography in a monastery in Pskov, but he was jealous of his knowledge and unwilling to help me learn. Finally, in 1978, I apprenticed myself to a master painter at Holy Transfiguration Monastery in Brookline, Massachusetts.

In the monastery workshop, we worked in silence, twelve hours a day, six days a week, and six hours on Sundays and holy days. My teacher had studied in Athens in the school of Photios Kontoglou, an Orthodox Greek from Asia Minor who had rediscovered Byzantine iconography while cleaning ancient icons on Mount Athos. In those days we used egg tempera on gesso composed of gypsum and animal skin glue. Each apprentice began with the humblest tasks and advanced to more difficult work when he had mastered simpler things. We worked in silence and followed the typicon of one of the sketes attached to St. Panteleimon's Monastery on the Holy Mountain. My fourth month I was finally allowed to paint faces, and the abbot began giving me old Russian icons to copy for his hermitage in Maine.

I learned iconographic canons as well as painting techniques. I was immersed in Patristic theology. When I left Boston to return to Colorado, I never anticipated leaving the protecting shell of Eastern Orthodoxy. Events in Chile and Colorado broke this shell wide open, but I realize now, from the perspective of so many years, that it was my love for St. Francis that really shattered the shell. In the 60's we weren't as deeply exposed to Franciscan spirituality as young friars are today. What we did receive in formation, however, changed my world forever. Francis opened my eyes to God's limitless love. After Francis, no

ghetto could ever hold me—not even a gilded ghetto topped with a cross.

I began with an icon of Dorothy Day, (Fig. 2) and then one of Oscar Romero. (Fig. 3) The third was of the Protestant holy man, Martin Luther King, and the fourth, the Hindu, Gandhi. Each step away from the ghetto cost me blood in the beginning. The Orthodox had filled my head with fear of the devil and the punishments awaiting anyone who betrayed the holy Tradition. Father Daniel O'-Connor's Irish humor blasted many of my Orthodox demons away, but it was my own experience of finding Christ in the alienated men and women who gathered at his house that eventually silenced the rest. Humor and these grace-filled encounters, held in contemplative prayer, brought the insights I needed to reclaim my life outside the ghetto.

I returned to the New Mexico desert, where I lived as an urban hermit in the barrios of Albuquerque, following the Third Order Rule for almost 20 years. I supported myself painting the icons for which I have become famous. My work has been controversial, especially among Byzantine Christians. I have never sought controversy, however, nor change for the sake of change. As a Byzantine Christian myself, I have a profound respect for Tradition. As I have ventured further and further from the customary, I have always tried to remain traditional, wrestling with the Tradition, trying to find ways to say new things. I have, in short, done theology in the margins, exploring Christological and ecclesiological questions with my brush.

Many theologians in various traditions have spoken at length about the role of the coincidence of opposites in the spiritual life. Any consideration of an encounter with the Divine must include the coincidence of opposites beginning with immanence and transcendence. I think, especially, of the great Muslim mystic from Spain, Ibn Arabi,

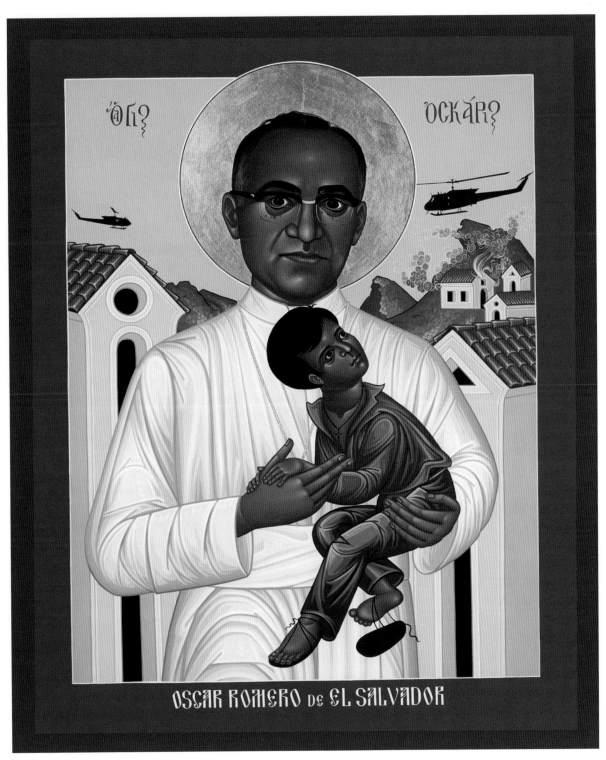

Fig 3.

whose writings often mirror the letters of Saint Clare to Saint Agnes of Prague. Saint Bonaventure's emphasis on Christ as the center rests upon Christ's role as the ultimate coincidence of opposites. I find in his teaching the key to my own life and my art.

At first glance, it would be hard to find spirituality closer to the core of the Latin Rite than Franciscan spirituality. Franciscan emphasis on the Incarnation of Christ, especially as expressed in popular devotions like the Christmas crèche and the Way of the Cross, have shaped what the Latin Rite has become in the twenty first century. As a young man in his early twenties who had grown up with a very different kind of spirituality, I often felt lost in the Latin Rite world of the Franciscan Order. I was too young to dig deeper, and, with the limited exposure to Franciscan spirituality I received, I didn't even know where to dig. After leaving the Order, I lived as a guest for a while in Sybertsville, Pennsylvania, where Franciscans from the Byzantine Rite Custody of Our Lady of the Angels had a friary, and even there felt more conflict than coincidence of opposites. It seemed the Pennsylvania friars had merely slipped a Byzantine veneer over Latin Franciscan life, a veneer that fit so poorly, their custody had nearly been destroyed several years before by a mass exodus of the friars in formation, who eventually became Orthodox.

As a Byzantine Christian, living once again in this seemingly very Latin Order, I am caught, once again, between opposites. The pull between the opposite poles is sometimes painful, but I am no longer a youngster. I often swim in Bonaventure's texts, as well as those of Ibn Arabi, plunging into depths I didn't know existed in my youth. The Christ I have discovered on my long pilgrimage is indeed the coincidence of all opposites. The symbolic center point of his cross, the point of coincidence, is also the center of my own heart. From that center I choose how to live my Franciscan life. Having once seen the shell of a ghetto crash around me, I am not interested any more in a veneer. As I have learned to plunge into the depths of both the Franciscan and the Byzantine traditions, so have I learned to search for what is of essence. When I search for the Franciscan "essence," I find ample room for my Byzantine soul.

I have traveled through Umbria four times in the past ten years. None of these times has been an official tour or pilgrimage. Each time I have searched out the various nooks and crannies of Francis's world, lingering where I have felt his presence, rather than where he was supposed to be. Aside from his tomb, Assisi has never held me. Gubbio and Perugia have been interesting because of their stories, but I weary of them after a few hours. It has been the rugged caves in the Rieti Valley, and the forests of La Verna that have caught and held my heart. I have spent days in St. Michael's cave at Poggio Bustone, so close to St. Francis that I almost felt I could touch his feet. Greccio, with its crowds, eludes me, but the springs at Fonte Colombo hold me fast. On La Verna I visit the basilica and the chapels and then flee to the mountainside, where I can, once again, spend days. The Francis I have come to know is a wild man burned by our transcendent God. He is brother to Gregory of Nyssa, Serafim of Sarov, Gregory Palamas, and all of Russia's holy fools. Francis, the greatest saint of the Latin Church, is universally loved because he has become a coincidence of opposites, like the Christ he so faithfully imitated. The Francis of the caves could create a crèche at Greccio, without losing his spiritual balance, precisely because he was so intimately acquainted with the God who is beyond all words.

Francis was born into a world with many Byzantine elements, but a world that was slowly

Fig 4.

slipping towards the Gothic and the Renaissance. The religious art all around him was closely related to the iconographic world of Byzantium. Umbria, especially, bore a Byzantine stamp because of the Syrian monks[1] who had fled there to escape violence in the East. The Crucifix he heard speak was a Byzantine icon painted, perhaps, by one of these exiled monks. This crucifix has become famous throughout the western world and is a central image in Franciscan life. That such a Byzantine image stands at the birth of this most seemingly Latin Order reveals a hidden coincidence of opposites that demands our attention.

On May 17, 2008, I delivered a paper at the University of Saskatchewan, in Saskatoon, Canada ("Christ In the Margins: Byzantine Iconography In the Twenty-first Century"). Bruce Russell, an art historian at the university, made an insightful reference to one of the frescos in the upper church of the Basilica of St. Francis in Assisi. In this fresco, which depicts the crèche Francis created in Greccio in 1223, Francis and others are behind the rood screen of a church much larger than anything in Greccio's cave. Above the door of this rood screen is a crucifix in the same shape as that of San Damiano. We see a plain brown panel, crisscrossed with braces and attached unceremoniously to a supporting tripod with a rope. It is the ugly back of an icon, not the luminous front. Bruce pointed out that the artist, one of those who began the tradition of Franciscan vernacular art, depicted Francis as having gone around the icon to its back side, rather than through it to glory.

The story we know of Francis and the San Damiano Crucifix, however, is that he somehow slipped *through* it to the reality of the Christ it de-

picted. What happened to Francis at San Damiano that day is what has happened for centuries to Byzantine Christians when they have prayed well before their icons: he discovered in the icon a window into heaven. The space between the experience of the holy founder and his followers decades later who sought to spread his teachings is a space that, in this case, eliminates the coincidence of opposites. In eliminating the coincidence of opposites, in emphasizing the immanent, rather than tying it to the transcendent, this artist in Assisi begins the process in Western religious art that eventually results in the sentimental, rather meaningless images we find in our church goods stores today. When Bruce spoke to me of this fresco, I immediately thought of the sense I have had for many years that the revolution initiated by the vernacular artists of the Franciscan movement has sometimes been catastrophic for the Western Church and its mystical tradition.

Though seldom understood by Western Christians, the Seventh Ecumenical Council[2] was the last of the great Christological councils of the Church. Far from being peripheral to Christian faith, icons, the council decreed, were an essential part of our belief, resting as they do, on the full humanity of the divine Christ. The ancient Church, both Western and Eastern, lived around the icon as a primary symbol of itself. The icon spoke of a sacred center around which human life revolved, a center that held all in its gravity—its focus of meaning—precisely *because* it was sacred. Ancient Christian art, art before the thirteenth century, emphasized transcendence, sometimes at the expense of immanence. With the rise of vernacular art, the sacred element in art was pushed to the

---

[1] Additional information about the presence and influence of these Syrian monks may be found in G. Penco, *Il monachesimo in Umbria dalle origini al secolo XII incluso* (Gubbio: Congress Centro Studi Alto Medioevo, 1962), 258-76.

[2] Footnote: J.D. Mansi, *Seventh Oecumenical Council, Acta*, in *Sacrorum conciliorum nova et amplissima collectio* (Florence, 1759-98), vol. 12, cols. 951-1154; vol. 13, cols. 1-485. Excerpts in English translation in *The Seven Ecumenical Councils*, ed. H.R. Percival, Select Library of Nicene and Post-Nicene Fathers, Second Series, vol. 14 (Oxford: James Parker and Company; New York: Christian Literature Company, 1900), 523-87.

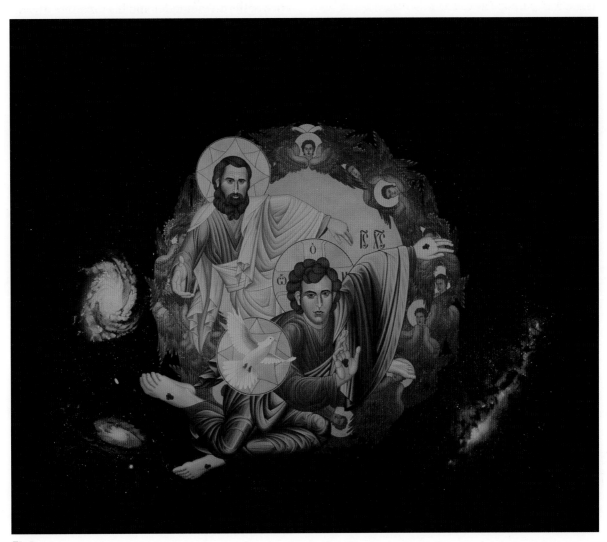

Fig 5.

side and became a veneer. Because of the powerful impact of art on the human psyche, an impact much more immediate and more powerful than words, the effect of this revolution, as it has led through the Renaissance to ever more humanistic styles, has perhaps even led us to the "death-of-God" theology of several decades ago. Christianity is a wisdom path, not merely a moralistic movement. Take away the coincidence of opposites and you have a path that leads nowhere.

Depicting sacred themes does not, by itself, make art sacred. In the sense in which I am using the term, neither does using such art in sacred ways. For art to be truly *sacred*, it must struggle to tie together both the immanent and the transcendent in its making. It will then be sacred, regardless of its use—just as a Byzantine icon, a Baule mask, or a Rothko painting is no less sacred when it ends up in an antique store. The sacred subject of a piece of art reveals itself as such, independently of external testimony. Art reveals the sacred solely through artistic devices. Art stands on its own.

In the thirteenth century, the new mendicant orders were faced with a Catholic laity who had been marginalized as much within their Church as they had in the rest of feudal society. Processes reaching back to the time of Theodosius and Justinian had brought about a situation in which all sacred power was concentrated in the hands of the clergy, with the laity going to the clergy in order to receive God. Holiness belonged in monasteries, not on muddy streets. The new vernacular art that spun out of the mendicant movement was an attempt to restore importance and dignity to ordinary secular life. As noble as this effort was, it eventually slipped away from the all-important coincidence of opposites, no longer dignifying secular life, but further degrading it as it ignored more and more the transcendent center which is the ultimate source of all dignity.

The more ancient Christian art, whether Byzantine or Romanesque, had as its primary goal communicating a sense of communion between the immanent and the transcendent. Figures in the ancient art seemed to emerge from their flat surfaces, to join congregations in an eschatological "communion of saints." Manipulation of perspective as well and the use of shadow and light contributed to this illusion. The bodies of the holy persons assumed poses that suggested this movement outward into the space before them. At the same time, even as the saints seemed to come forward to mingle with the faithful, there was no doubt about the holiness they had already achieved in their transcendent state. Light emanated from their faces and bodies. They had become part of God's "new creation."

In the new art that began to develop after the time of St. Francis, perspective is reversed and worshippers are invited to enter the images with their imaginations. Instead of heaven exploding eschatologically into worship space, ordinary, daily life enters the church building to tell a story. The stories the artists tell have emotional nuances that engage the imagination of their audience. Deep feeling takes the place of eschatological glory. Drama takes the place of communion.

While poorly executed Byzantine or Romanesque art might simply end up remote and austere, it always points towards an opposite transcendent pole. The new realistic art, however, dependent as it is on imagination and emotion, runs a more dangerous risk of becoming sentimental when it misses its mark. The transcendent pole, which draws salvation history forward, disappears in an emotional fog. Gone is the ancient sense of a transcendent center that dignifies ordinary human life.

Encountering this center in the years of his conversion is what enabled Saint Francis to embrace the leper, the wolf, and the Sultan of Egypt. (Fig. 4) The same Francis who desired to experience the humility of Christ's birth in the cave at Greccio, who brought farm animals and straw around the small altar in that cave, would write in a letter to the entire Order, just before he died, "Let everyone be struck with fear, let the whole world tremble, and let the heavens exult when Christ, the Son of the living God, is present on the altar in the hands of a priest! O wonderful loftiness and stupendous dignity! O sublime humility! O humble sublimity! The Lord of the universe, God and the Son of God, so humbles Himself that for our salvation He hides Himself under an ordinary piece of bread! Brothers, look at the humility of God, *and pour out your hearts before Him!*"[3] This mystical outburst is the cry of a saint who has seen the raging furnace that Bonaventure mentions near the end of Chapter Seven (Ch. 7.6) in his *Itinerarium Mentis in Deum.* It reflects the balance Francis found in his own spiritual life through Christ, the coincidence of opposites. While he longs to know Christ's poverty as a human, he has already seen the glory of his divinity—and all of this first in the icon crucifix painted by a Syrian monk.

Each time I have visited the Basilica of San Francesco in Assisi, I have tried to appreciate the bright frescos that line the nave of the upper church. It is purely a mental exercise for me, however, as my heart races toward the apse and the blackened, oxidized images of Cimabue. I have heard tour guides tell their groups how Cimabue was a step towards the more advanced art of the nave, the teacher Giotto and other new vernacular artists surpassed. And since my return to the First Order, as I have stood in the middle of the nave, I have wondered about my own icons and my iden-

tity as a friar, and how strange it sometimes seems to try to hold the two together.

These past two years, I have begun to see things in a different light as I have worked on a nine-foot icon of the Holy Trinity for All Saints Church in Houston, Texas. (Fig. 5) Preparation for painting the icon involved immersing myself in Bonaventure's teaching about the Trinity. The more I read and digested of his writings, the more similar he sounded to Eastern Orthodox theologians I already knew. Bonaventure knew the Eastern Fathers through Latin sources, and he embraced their theological insights because they harmonized so well with his own evolving Franciscan spirituality. The reading in the breviary from the *Itinerarium* on the feast of Bonaventure always brings tears to my eyes, as he challenges us to seek the spouse not the teacher, darkness not clarity, and to look not to the light but rather to the fire that enflames totally and that carries one into God.[4] In a sense, from his hermitage on La Verna, Bonaventure tells us to move past the bright frescos in the nave to something more transcendent if we would reach the goal of Christian life.

I have spoken of Christianity as a "wisdom path," and Bonaventure's short book is called an *itinerarium* or a "journey". Each of us is referring to a process of growth that challenges what we are and know and leads us towards something far beyond us. While the vernacular art that arose after the death of Saint Francis recognized the life of ordinary people and brought it into the churches, the stories it told led only a few feet down the *itinerarium mentis in Deum*, the path into God. With the passage of centuries, popular devotions like the crèche and the *via crucis* often devolved into sentimental exercises, far from the "sublime humility"

---

3   Francis of Assisi, "A Letter to the Entire Order," in *The Saint*, Vol. 1 of *Francis of Assisi: Early Documents*, eds. Regis J. Armstrong, J. A. Wayne Hellman and William J. Short (New York: New City Press, 1999), 118.

4   Cf. Bonaventure, *Itinerarium Mentis in Deum*, in Vol. II of *Works of St. Bonaventure*, trans. Zachary Hayes (Saint Bonaventure, New York: Franciscan Institute Publications, 2002), 139.

and the "humble sublimity" Saint Francis had praised. Separated from Francis' experience of divine darkness in the caves, these dangerous memories were tamed beyond recognition. As artists concentrated more and more on religious emotion, by the Victorian period Catholic churches and homes were filled with a surfeit of weak, insipid depictions of Christ and the saints. Having forgotten the coincidence of opposites, what began as a divine drama of opposites ended up as sacrine piety, worthy of the scorn it received after the Second Vatican Council.

Our Franciscan life itself can only collapse when it is not based on Christ, the coincidence of opposites Francis knew and lived so well. In recent documents, such as *Followers of Christ for a Fraternal World* (General Curia OFM, Rome, 2004), we are challenged to place prayer as the first priority in our life, ahead of fraternity, ahead of our work. Prayer is to our life what Francis's experience of God's transcendence was to the crèche he created at Greccio. Grounded in true knowledge of how sublime the Divine Mystery is, its corresponding humility becomes overwhelming. Our Order has been reformed so many times over the centuries, only to fall once again into mediocrity. I suggest that it has been a neglect of the coincidence of opposites, our only safe path, which has brought us so often to this state.

While I once wondered how to hold together my identity as a Franciscan with my Byzantine soul and the icons which are my work, I no longer feel this contradiction. Franciscan spirituality, at its best, is a coincidence of opposites: a meeting of the transcendent in the immanent, a joining of contemplative prayer with apostolic work, a school of theology where Greek and Latin Fathers meet and embrace. Bonaventure died during the Council of Lyons, a gathering of Orthodox and Catholic bish-

ops and theologians hoping to restore unity between the two Churches. He has been called the greatest synthesizer of the Middle Ages, this teacher of the coincidence of opposites. If we would remember Bonaventure's challenge to turn to the raging fire that carries the soul to God, if we can remember to hold a truly contemplative life together with our apostolic work, we would no longer seem so intensely Latin, but rather an Order open to all that is of Christ. Realizing this, I no longer worry about whether there is a place for a Byzantine friar painting icons in the Franciscan family.

Having said all this, I must admit that my icons differ quite a bit from those I was taught to paint at Holy Transfiguration Monastery in 1978. Long before my return to the First Order, I was choosing colors more varied and brilliant than those my teacher used, delighting in God's creation no less than Francis as he sang the Canticle of the Creatures. Long before I rediscovered Duns Scotus and his *haecceitas* or "thisness," I was rebelling against the Byzantine practice of depicting animals and birds in icons with less dignity than humans. My animals and birds await their fulfillment in Christ no less than the saints they accompany, and when I paint them I respect their God-given uniqueness. With Franciscan trust in the compassion of God, I found ways to express transcendence in the faces of my saints without the severity that one often finds in icons. Embracing life on the margins of the Church, four years after my apprenticeship in the Greek monastery, I have painted for the poor and marginalized ever since. My icons have included elements from their lives, no less than the vernacular frescos in Assisi, but I have not abandoned the element of transcendent presence that forms the essence of what an icon is. Whether it is a chipped coffee mug in the hand of Brother Matthias Barret, or a smelly

Billy goat rubbing against my Arab Good Shepherd, each of my icons expresses ordinariness with transcendence and is filled with little words that point to the one Word, Christ.

As I was looking at articles and papers I have written in the past, I was struck by the fact that I have never before stressed the need for transcendence in sacred art. In the past, I have defended Franciscan immanence in my icons, justifying the changes I have brought to Byzantine iconography, taking for granted that sacred art must depict transcendence. In both instances, however, it is an insistence that holiness must always contain this coincidence of opposites, since all holiness refers back to God, whose one and only Word is Christ. A challenge before Franciscan artists of the twenty first century is an enunciation of a uniquely Franciscan aesthetics. There was little room for a Franciscan artist in religious life forty years ago, but today we are carving out niches for ourselves as legitimate evangelizers in an evangelical order. At the heart of this aesthetics will be the coincidence of opposites, with all its ramifications. While I myself paint Byzantine icons, I will never insist that these are the only way the transcendent might be joined to the immanent. Rothko's abstract canvases and Rouault's haunting Christs often lead me to the "raging furnace" more quickly than an icon by Rublev. While I paint icons, I am Franciscan enough to search for Christ wherever he shows his lovely face. As a Byzantine Rite friar, however, I remind us all that his face will never be complete without the transcendent.

INDEX